HOBOMOK

and Other Writings on Indians

AMERICAN WOMEN WRITERS SERIES
Joanne Dobson, Judith Fetterley, and Elaine Showalter, series editors

ALTERNATIVE ALCOTT
Louisa May Alcott
Elaine Showalter, editor

MOODS
Louisa May Alcott
Sarah Elbert, editor

STORIES FROM THE COUNTRY OF
LOST BORDERS
Mary Austin
Marjorie Pryse, editor

CLOVERNOOK SKETCHES AND
OTHER STORIES
Alice Cary
Judith Fetterley, editor

HOBOMOK AND OTHER WRITINGS
ON INDIANS
Lydia Maria Child
Carolyn L. Karcher, editor

"HOW CELIA CHANGED HER MIND"
AND SELECTED STORIES
Rose Terry Cooke
Elizabeth Ammons, editor

THE LAMPLIGHTER
Maria Susanna Cummins
Nina Baym, editor

RUTH HALL AND OTHER
WRITINGS
Fanny Fern
Joyce Warren, editor

THE ESSENTIAL
MARGARET FULLER
Jeffrey Steele, editor

GAIL HAMILTON: SELECTED WRITINGS
Susan Coultrap-McQuin, editor

A NEW HOME, WHO'LL FOLLOW?
Caroline M. Kirkland
Sandra A. Zagarell, editor

QUICKSAND AND PASSING
Nella Larsen
Deborah E. McDowell, editor

HOPE LESLIE
Catharine Maria Sedgwick
Mary Kelley, editor

THE HIDDEN HAND
E.D.E.N. Southworth
Joanne Dobson, editor

"THE AMBER GODS" AND
OTHER STORIES
Harriet Prescott Spofford
Alfred Bendixen, editor

OLDTOWN FOLKS
Harriet Beecher Stowe
Dorothy Berkson, editor

WOMEN ARTISTS, WOMEN
EXILES: "MISS GRIEF"
AND OTHER STORIES
Constance Fenimore Woolson
Joan Myers Weimer, editor

AMERICAN WOMEN POETS
OF THE NINETEENTH CENTURY:
AN ANTHOLOGY
Cheryl Walker, editor

HOBOMOK
and Other Writings on Indians

LYDIA MARIA CHILD

Edited and with an Introduction by

CAROLYN L. KARCHER

RUTGERS UNIVERSITY PRESS

New Brunswick, New Jersey

FOR MY PARENTS
Selma Seidelman Lury and Robert M. Lury

Fifth paperback printing, 1995

Library of Congress Cataloging-in-Publication Data

Child, Lydia Maria Francis, 1802–1880.
Hobomok and other writings on Indians.

(American women writers series)
Bibliography: p.
1. Indians of North America—Literary collections.
2. Massachusetts—History—Colonial period, ca. 1600–
1775—Fiction.   I. Karcher, Carolyn L., 1945–
II. Child, Lydia Maria Francis, 1802–1880.   Hobomok,
a tale of eary times.   1986.   III. Title   IV. Series.
PS1293.A6   1986   813'.2   86-3683
ISBN 0-8135-1163-1
ISBN 0-8135-1164-x (pbk.)

CONTENTS

Contents

ACKNOWLEDGMENTS

In preparing this edition of Child's writings on Indians, I have incurred many debts. The greatest, as always, is to my husband Martin, who has read innumerable drafts of the introduction, offered helpful suggestions at every stage, and uncomplainingly sacrificed more pleasures and comforts than I dare to recall, under the pressure of deadlines. Credit for suggesting this project belongs to H. Bruce Franklin and Jane Franklin, who not only urged me to undertake the full-scale study of Child from which the introduction and headnotes are drawn, but stressed the importance of making Child's own writings accessible to the public. Milton Meltzer and Patricia G. Holland have shown a generosity rare in academic life by sending me their entire collection of xeroxed Child manuscripts, assembled while putting together their indispensable editions of Child's letters. Lucy Freibert took time out from her heavy schedule to translate the Latin quotations in *Hobomok*. Jane Tompkins has read several versions of the introduction, helped me to sharpen its focus, prodded me to meet her exacting standards, and shown faith in my work when I have most needed it. My assessment of Child's contribution to shaping early nineteenth-century American short fiction, as well as the historical novel, owes a great deal to Susan Koppelman, who has shared her ideas with me in long letters and stimulating conversations, and who also suggested the inclusion of "She Waits in the Spirit Land." Ormond Seavey initiated my research into Child's historical sources and brought Nathaniel Morton's *New En-*

Acknowledgments

gland Memorial to my attention as the main work through which Bradford's *Of Plymouth Plantation* was preserved until the rediscovery in 1856 of the lost Bradford manuscript. Sara Parrott introduced me to Elizabeth Stuart Phelps' reminiscences of Child in *Chapters from a Life*. Scott Guenther scrupulously checked all the quotations and bibliographical citations. Finally, I would like to acknowledge the generous support of the American Council of Learned Societies and the National Endowment for the Humanities, which made my work on Child possible through a research grant in the fall of 1982; and I would like to thank Joanne Dobson for her invaluable editorial guidance; Jane Dieckmann and Eileen Finan for their meticulous editing, which Eileen facilitated with astute decisions on editorial policy; and Leslie Mitchner for her role in initiating the American Woman Writers series, finalizing the selections for this volume, and supporting the project throughout with true appreciation of Child's writings.

INTRODUCTION

On an overcast day in the late 1870s, that indefatigable patron saint of nineteenth-century women authors, Annie Fields, wife of Boston's leading publisher, took one of her latest protégées, Elizabeth Stuart Phelps, on a literary pilgrimage. The object of their pilgrimage was a woman whose name had been a household word for fifty years, but who was shortly to be written out of history, along with the crusade against racial bigotry and discrimination to which she had devoted her life—the abolitionist Lydia Maria Child (1802–80). Child had played a formative role in developing the literary tradition of "Art for Truth's Sake" that heirs like Phelps were then carrying to new heights. Deeply moved by the encounter with her precursor, Phelps afterwards recalled, "She impressed me as a strong and lofty personality, so far above the usual social human being that her solitude and the sparseness of her environment seemed to partake of the character of luxuries which most of us were unfit to share" (182; ch. 12).

Child's strength, and the rebelliousness it sustained, had emerged at an early age. Before she was twelve years old, she had learned that a passion for books aroused pride when exhibited by a son and alarm when betrayed by a daughter. Although Child's father, Convers Francis, a baker by trade, viewed intellectual pursuits with scant enthusiasm, he had followed the advice of the family physician and sent his promising son to Harvard (*SL* 425–26). In contrast, he had tried to cure his daughter of her unfortunate predilection for reading by banishing her to the frontier town of Norridgewock, Maine, where her newly married sister could initiate her into domestic avocations befitting a woman. The experience of being denied the education lavished on her brother sowed the seeds of a feminist consciousness in the young Lydia Maria Francis, as it would in two women's rights leaders of the 1830s and 1840s who would acknowledge Child as a forerunner—Sarah Grimké and Elizabeth Cady Stanton.

Compounding the blow, for Child, was the recent death of her mother. Triply bereft—of her brother's intellectual companionship, of her mother's love and sympathy, and of the books she turned to for consolation—Child would express her "desperate resentment" toward her father in the novel she would write ten years later—*Hobomok, A Tale of Early Times* (1824). Her heroine, too, would find herself alone with an austere, unsympathetic father, and isolated in an atmosphere of "unreciprocated intellect," after being deprived one by one of a friend's "cheering influence," a role model's "firm support," and a mother's "mild, soothing spirit" (chs. 13, 16). Old enough to determine her own destiny, however, Mary Conant would spite her father by fleeing into the wilderness with an Indian—a parody of the exile from civilization that Roger Conant, like David Convers Francis, had chosen for his daughter.

Meanwhile in Norridgewock, Child defiantly continued to read, encouraged by her brother Convers, who introduced her to Homer, Johnson, Milton, and Scott. Soon she found herself rebelling against his authority as well. "Don't you think that Milton asserts the superiority of his own sex in rather too lordly a manner?" she challenged Convers in her earliest surviving letter, written at age fifteen (*Letters* 1). For proof, Child cited a passage that generations of feminists intent on exorcising "Milton's bogey" have singled out (Gilbert and Gubar 202 and 187–308):

> My author and disposer, what thou bid'st
> Unargu'd I obey; so God ordained.
> God is thy law, thou mine: to know no more
> Is woman's happiest knowledge, and her praise.
> (*PL* 4.635–38; as cited in *Letters* 1)

Although hastening to assure Convers that she "willingly acknowledge[d] the superiority of your talents and advantages, and . . . fully appreciate[d] your condescension and kindness," Child remained undaunted when he rejected her interpretation. "I perceive that I never shall convert you to my opinions concerning Milton's treatment to [sic] our sex" (2), she replied jauntily, confident that truth lay on her side, whatever Convers's claims to greater erudition.

The exchange was prophetic of the novel she would write in her brother's study in 1824—a novel conspicuously flouting patriarchal authority and revising patriarchal script. It was also prophetic of the opposing stands the two would take on abolition in 1833—his "prudent" and cool-headed, as behooved a Unitarian minister, hers principled and ardent, yet once again supported by an array of citations worthy of any scholar (*SL* 39; *Appeal in Favor of Africans*).

Despite his political timidity, Convers remained a mentor for his sister, at least until her marriage. In 1822, she moved into his household in Watertown, Massachusetts, a hub of Transcendentalist ferment, where such intellectuals as Ralph Waldo Emerson, Theodore Parker, and John Greenleaf Whittier congregated. Nearby in Cambridge lived young Margaret Fuller, with whom Child could share her new enthusiasm for Madame de Staël. Later Child attended Fuller's famous Conversations, and the two women renewed their friendship once again in the 1840s, when both were working as journalists in New York.

In 1828 Child began a new life with the idealistic reformer David Lee Child. That year, she and David joined in a crusade to save the Cherokee Indians, threatened with expulsion from their fertile and well-run farms in Georgia. David also started the process of winning Child over to radical abolitionism, which his own mentor, the militant William Lloyd Garrison, would complete some time in 1830 or 1831 (*SL* 474, 558).

By then, Child had launched a promising literary career, after sky-rocketing to fame with the publication of *Hobomok* in 1824. "We are not sure that any woman in our country would outrank Mrs. Child," judged the prestigious *North American Review* in 1833, adding, "Few female writers, if any, have done more or better things for our literature" (37: 139). The assessment was based on a vast output embracing—indeed pioneering—nearly every department in nineteenth-century American letters. Child's historical novels, *Hobomok* and *The Rebels; or, Boston before the Revolution* (1825), were among the earliest to domesticate the fashionable genre created by Sir Walter Scott, and to harness it to the purposes of American nationalism. The stories she published in all the leading annual gift books of the 1820s and 1830s helped define the conventions of short fiction, besides turning the genre into a vehicle for social protest (four of the stories Child wrote to promote sympathy for the Indians and to mobilize public opinion against their dispossession are reprinted in the present volume).

The children's magazine she founded in 1826 and edited for eight years, *The Juvenile Miscellany*, was the first to succeed in America and proved so popular that children used to sit on their doorsteps waiting for the mail carrier to deliver it. "No child who read the *Juvenile Miscellany* . . . will ever forget the excitement that the appearance of each number caused," reminisced a reader who had herself gone on to become a writer and editor of note, the abolitionist-feminist Caroline Healey Dall. "After the lapse of half a century, the mere names of some of the stories . . . bring vivid pictures of past delight before us" (525– 26).

Even more influential than the *Miscellany* were the domestic advice books Child produced, *The Frugal Housewife* (1829) and *The Mother's Book* (1831), the former running through a phenomenal thirty-three American and twenty-one European editions, the latter eight American and thirteen European editions. Memorializing Child in 1883, when *The Frugal Housewife* had long been superseded by Catharine Beecher's *Treatise on Domestic Economy* (1841), Dall still regretted its eclipse. "Modern cookery books invariably cater to the taste of those who live in luxury," she complained, whereas "Mrs. Child's book was meant for those who were poor" (525)— a major innovation. *The Mother's Book*, however, lived on in the children's fiction of Louisa May Alcott. Reared according to its precepts, the daughter of Child's girlhood friend Abba May Alcott applied them to her fictional progeny on inheriting Child's mantle as the premier children's writer of her day.

Like her domestic advice books, Child's five-volume *Ladies' Family Library* addressed new needs in an era when a changing economy was both enlarging and restricting women's opportunities. Its three volumes of biographies provided women with inspiring role models, whether as revolutionary thinkers and agitators like Madame de Staël and Madame Roland (the subjects of vol. 1, 1832), or as *Good Wives* (the title of vol. 3, 1833). More subversively, its two-volume *History of the Condition of Women, in Various Ages and Nations* (1835) amassed anthropological data showing that women's roles and occupations varied from culture to culture, contrary to nineteenth-century notions of "woman's sphere" (see the excerpt in the present collection). Without explicitly challenging current ideology, Child's *History of the Condition of Women* thus laid the groundwork for later feminist theory. "The first American storehouse of information upon the whole question," Matilda Joslyn Gage called it in the *History of Woman Suffrage* she coauthored with Elizabeth Cady Stanton and Susan B. Anthony (1: 38). Like Sarah Grimké in *Letters on the Equality of the Sexes and the Condition of Woman* (1838) and Margaret Fuller in *Woman in the Nineteenth Century* (1845), the three suffragists would mine it extensively.

Until 1833 Child succeeded in infiltrating radical ideas into her writings while apparently remaining within the bounds of accepted opinion. At the peak of her popularity, however, right after the *North American Review* had pronounced her "just the woman we want for the mothers and daughters of the present generation" (37: 139), Child forfeited her literary reputation by publishing *An Appeal in Favor of That Class of Americans Called Africans* (1833). The first book to advocate immediate emancipation, an end to all forms of racial discrimination, and the abrogation of laws prohibiting "marriages between persons of different color" (its most controversial feature), it surveyed slavery from a variety of angles—historical, political, economic, legal, and moral. It also marshaled facts supporting the conclusion that Africans were intellectually and morally equal to Europeans, and hence, that their emancipation and full integration into American society were practicable goals.

The elites who had been lionizing Child since the *succès de scandale* of *Hobomok* reacted swiftly with total ostracism. An immediate casualty was the *Juvenile Miscellany*, which folded as outraged parents withdrew their subscriptions. Readers likewise boycotted the best-selling manuals that furnished Child's principal source of income (her husband David being a notoriously incompetent breadwinner).

If Child lost her standing as America's favorite woman writer, she gained unprecedented political influence for a woman as one of the abolitionist movement's foremost propagandists. A roll call of the leaders who credited "Mrs. Child's Appeal" with recruiting them into abolitionist ranks offers a gauge of the book's persuasiveness: the fiery orator Wendell

Phillips, henceforth second only to Garrison in prominence; the venerated Unitarian clergyman William Ellery Channing, hitherto a fence straddler in the slavery controversy; the Massachusetts senator Charles Sumner, largely responsible for the legislative victories of Reconstruction; the militant Thomas Wentworth Higginson, commander of one of the first black regiments during the Civil War.

In this new phase of her career, Child pioneered yet another field—journalism. More than two years before Horace Greeley hired Margaret Fuller as a reviewer for his *New York Tribune*, Child assumed the editorship of the *National Anti-Slavery Standard* (1841–43). The column she began issuing in the *Standard*, "Letters from New-York," invented the genre of the journalistic sketch, which writers like Fanny Fern and Grace Greenwood were to cultivate in coming decades. Reprinted in two volumes, *Letters from New-York* ran into eleven editions, restoring Child to a measure of her former popularity (Letter 36, a refutation of racist theories serving to "prove" the inferiority of Indians and blacks, appears in the present selection). Even after leaving the *Standard*, Child continued to use newspaper articles as media for advocating abolition, black suffrage, woman suffrage, and Indian rights.

Also during the 1840s, Child developed the antislavery story into an instrument for arousing the sympathies of genteel readers hostile to abolitionism. Her story "The Quadroons" (1842) introduced into American literature the archetype of the "tragic quadroon," which Harriet Beecher Stowe's *Uncle Tom's Cabin* (1852) and William Wells Brown's *Clotel* (1853) would exploit.

In addition, Child published some thirteen antislavery works after the *Appeal*, two of which rivaled or surpassed it in impact. One was her passionate defense of John Brown in *Correspondence between Lydia Maria Child and Gov. Wise and Mrs. Mason, of Virginia* (1860), which reached a circulation of 300,000 and helped prepare the northern public to support a war against slavery. The other was her reader for ex-slaves, *The Freedmen's Book* (1865), distributed gratis at Child's own expense and designed with the threefold aim of teaching literacy, inculcating pride in the black heritage, and promoting black suffrage.

At no period of her life did Child confine herself to abolitionism, however. The problems of "fallen women" and urban poverty and crime

absorbed her in the 1840s, inspiring some of her best fiction and journalism. In the 1860s and 1870s, her uncanny ability to pinpoint and respond
to new needs prompted her to put together two collections of writings for
the elderly which would give them positive images of aging and help them
face death (*Looking toward Sunset*, 1865, and *Aspirations of the World*, 1878).
And throughout her career, she returned repeatedly to the issue that had
captured her imagination at the outset—the dispossession of the American Indian and the possibility of reconciling Indian and white through a
marriage of cultures. While exploring this issue, the oldest in American
history, Child founded both a female countertradition of American literature and an alternative vision of race and gender relations in one of our
earliest fictional genres, the American historical novel.

A genre created specifically to forge a nationalist consciousness and cultural identity in the newly independent United States, the American
historical novel inevitably exhibited the same central contradiction as
American history itself—the contradiction between an ideology based on
the premise that all men are created equal and a political structure based
on the assumption that people of color and white women do not fall under
the rubric "men."

    Like its prototype, the historical novel developed by Sir Walter Scott,
the American version of this genre celebrated the triumph of a tech-
nologically advanced civilization over a tribal society. Unlike Scott, however—identified by birth with one of the defeated ethnic groups whose
heroic struggle against Norman and British invaders he memorialized—
American writers belonged to the conquering race, which constituted
their sole audience. Their mission was not to reconcile the victor with the
vanquished, much less to offer a healing vision of the two groups' eventual
amalgamation under the victors' hegemony. Rather it was to justify the
complete obliteration of the vanquished race, and at the same time to
assert the victors' own cultural independence vis-à-vis the British they had
just overthrown.

    Ironically, as American writers were to find, the key to establishing a
distinctive cultural identity lay in exploiting the culture of the very race
their compatriots were so brutally extirpating. An early nineteenth-
century critic writing for the *North American Review*, the journal that was to

formulate the first major theory of American literature, put the case bluntly. The United States was "deficient in literature" because its colonial existence, inherently "opposed to literary originality," had deprived it of the basis for a true national literature. "The remotest germs of literature are the native peculiarities of the country in which it is to spring," he pointed out, and a "national literature seems to be . . . the legitimate product, of a national language" (W. Channing 1: 307–308, 312). Yet colonialism had saddled Americans with a literary tradition rooted in another continent, and with a language suited perhaps to describing the serenity of the Thames, but far too "tame" to convey the "majesty of the Mississippi" or the grandeur of Niagara (308–309). These handicaps notwithstanding, he opined, America did in fact have an indigenous literature that displayed "genuine originality," "haughty independence" of foreign influences, and poetic vigor equal to soaring with the eagle and thundering with the cataract: "the oral literature of its aborigines" (313–14). The inference was obvious, and critics in later numbers of the *North American Review* were quick to draw it: if American writers could mine the linguistic and mythological riches of this literature, they would develop the means of escaping their humiliating cultural subservience to England.

The reliance, for their prime claim to originality, on borrowings from a culture the nation was currently destroying—a culture whose destruction, indeed, the nascent "American" literature had the task of rationalizing—was not the only contradiction to beset the historical novels that appeared in response to such promptings. The mission of declaring the nation's cultural independence involved the further problem of defining its relationship to the colonial past. On the one hand Americans had rebelled against patriarchal authority by casting off the yoke of the king and rejecting the world view of their Puritan Founding Fathers as superstitious and bigoted. On the other hand they needed to legitimate the political system they had erected in the place of the old aristocratic and theocratic orders they repudiated.

The novelists who took up the challenge of creating an authentic national literature in the 1820s envisioned several different solutions to the problems of racial conflict and patriarchal authority. We are all familiar with the solution that prevailed historically and found consummate expression in the only novels of this period to survive in our literary canon—

those of James Fenimore Cooper. Cooper's scenario presupposed that on a national level, the encounter between "savage" and "civilized" races could take but one form—war—and could lead to but one outcome—the total defeat and extinction of the "savage" race. Though drenched in violence and replete with scenes of Indian tomahawking, scalping, and torture, Cooper's novels did not glorify the extermination of the Indians, as did those of his competitors, Robert Montgomery Bird and James Kirke Paulding. Instead, they mourned the "vanishing" of the red man as tragic but inevitable, and paid tribute to the noble qualities of those Indians who allied themselves with whites. Through Cooper's great mythic creation, the Indianized frontiersman Natty Bumppo, and through the friendship between Natty and the noble Indians Uncas and Chingachgook, the *Leatherstocking Novels* also sought to mediate the conflict between "savage" and "civilized" ways of life. Yet Cooper's scenario allowed no role in America's future, either for Uncas and Chingachgook or for Natty—all three are doomed to die without issue. In lieu of a reconciliation between Indians and whites, Cooper provided a reconciliation between Tory and Revolutionary. Obviously serving to reestablish patriarchal authority in the new order emerging from the routing of Indian savages and British tyrants, this solution left Anglo-American women on the sidelines— precisely the position they occupied in the political system.

Excluded as they were from the benefits that American democracy conferred on their male peers, middle- and upper-class white women often identified consciously or unconsciously with other excluded groups. In the 1830s an awareness of being "bound with" black slaves in almost every sense would propel large numbers of American women into the abolitionist movement. In the 1820s it led the women writers who helped shape the American historical novel to imagine alternatives to race war, genocide, and white male supremacy as modes of resolving the contradictions that riddled their society. Child's career illustrates how closely the two phenomena are connected.

When Child sat down to write *Hobomok* in 1824, she took her cue directly from one of the critics who had been calling on American writers to do for their native land what Scott had done for his, and to exploit the matchless resources that America's panoramic landscapes, heroic Puritan settlers, and exotic Indian folklore afforded the romancer. Leafing through an old volume of the *North American Review* in her brother's study, she had come across a long review of a narrative poem entitled *Yamoyden, A Tale of the Wars of King Philip: in Six Cantos*, by James Wallis Eastburn and Robert Sands (1820; 12: 466–88). *Yamoyden*, proclaimed its reviewer, John Gorham Palfrey (a man Child herself would subsequently inspire to join the antislavery movement [*SL* 286]), represented a landmark in American literature. "We are glad that somebody has at last found out the unequalled fitness of our early history for the purposes of a work of fiction," he pontificated (12: 480). That history, he went on, contained all the elements Scott had put to such effective use in his novels of border warfare—indeed the "stern, romantic enthusiasm" of America's Puritans; the "fierce," "primitive" character of her Indians, "with all the bold rough lines of nature yet uneffaced upon them"; and the vast scale of her picturesque scenery surpassed anything Scotland could boast. "Whoever in this country first attains the rank of a first rate writer of fiction," predicted Palfrey, "will lay his scene here. The wide field is ripe for the harvest, and scarce a sickle yet has touched it" (480, 483–85).

The prediction kindled the imagination of twenty-two-year-old Lydia Maria Francis. Had she not encountered Indians in the wilds of Maine, where she had spent eight years (*SL* 1)? And had she not read her Scott, as well as her annals of Puritan history? "I know not what impelled me," she later recalled; "I had never dreamed of such a thing as turning author; but I siezed [sic] a pen, and before the bell rang for afternoon meeting I had written the first chapter, exactly as it now stands. When I showed it to my brother, my young ambition was flattered by the exclamation, 'But Maria did you *really* write this? Do you *mean* what you say, that it is entirely your own?'" (*SL* 232).

Whether in fact *Hobomok* was entirely the fruit of Child's imagination, or owed more than she admitted to the epic poem that had occasioned Palfrey's momentous review, is an open question. The parallels between *Hobomok* and *Yamoyden* extend far beyond the titles that announce the two works' self-conscious use of native themes. Both describe their Indian title characters as "cast in nature's noblest mould"; both feature Anglo-American heroines who elope with Indian lovers in defiance of paternal wishes. And both model themselves after Shakespeare's *Othello* in having their dark-skinned heroes win the love of a white woman through eloquent recitals of their exploits and adventures (*Yamoyden* 124–28; *Hobomok* chs. 5, 13, 18). True, Palfrey's detailed summary of *Yamoyden* could have sufficed to provide Child with the germ of her plot, and the idea of drawing for inspiration on English literature's most memorable account of an interracial wooing was obvious enough to have occurred to her independently. In any case, if she did literally write the first chapter of *Hobomok* "exactly as it now stands" on the very afternoon that she read Palfrey's review, she had already conceived the embryo of a plot that differed substantially from *Yamoyden*'s, whatever hints she subsequently derived from directly consulting the poem cited so frequently in her epigraphs.

The differences illuminate the enormous gap that divided even the most progressive male writers of this period from their female counterparts, where their perceptions of the relationship between white supremacy and patriarchy were concerned. For Eastburn and Sands were unmistakably progressive. To the great annoyance of Palfrey, who chastised them for sentimentality, they presented the bloody uprising of 1675–76, led by the Wampanoag sachem Metacom ("King Philip"), from the Indians' point of view. Portraying the Puritans as "remorseless oppressors" and the Indians as "cruelly wronged" (Palfrey 486), they showed that the Indians were merely reacting against a long series of encroachments on their lands and rights, culminating in the incident directly responsible for the uprising—the Puritans' execution of three Wampanoag warriors. Nevertheless, Eastburn and Sands, like Cooper, centered their epic on race war and ended it with a reassertion of patriarchal authority. The love affair between the Nipnet Yamoyden and the Puritan Nora, which initially points toward an alternative future for the two warring races, and a larger role in determining her own destiny for the Anglo-American woman, culminates in tragedy. Nora is captured and delivered over to her father, who generously forgives her disobedience; Yamoyden sacrifices his life to save his hitherto estranged father-in-law from an Indian's tomahawk; and Nora dies in her husband's arms as her father promises to raise the couple's child. What becomes of this child the poem's epilogue does not specify, but the concluding lament over the tragic outcome of the marriage and of the Indian uprising intertwined with it does not portend for the child a hopeful resolution of the racial conflicts that have doomed the parents. No

doubt this reassuring negation of a threat to white supremacy and patriarchal authority saved Eastburn and Sands from the censure Child
would reap when she followed their lead in violating the taboo against
interracial marriage.

At the time she wrote *Hobomok*, Child evidently had a much lower
level of political consciousness on the Indian question than Eastburn and
Sands. She had not yet begun to contest the Puritan chroniclers' version of
the wars that decimated the Indians, as she would three or four years later
in a book aimed at arousing opposition to the United States government's
"crooked and narrow-minded policy" toward Indians: *The First Settlers of
New-England* (1828; iv). Nor had she come to view the Indians who defended their people's sovereign existence and territorial rights—rather
than those who sided with the whites—as the true heroes of an American
national epic: unlike Yamoyden, who joins King Philip's uprising despite
the pleadings of his English wife, Child's Hobomok betrays an Indian
conspiracy in order to save his white beloved and her family from
massacre.

What dictates the plot of *Hobomok* is not its author's awareness of
racial issues, but her rebellion against patriarchy. The result is a revolutionary insight into the connection between male dominance and white supremacy. This insight suggested to Child the central theme of *Hobomok* and
indeed of her entire life as a reformer and writer: interracial marriage,
symbolizing both the natural alliance between white women and people of
color, and the natural resolution of America's racial and sexual contradictions. Thus, if we are to understand *Hobomok* and the alternative vision of
race and gender relations it introduces into American literature, we must
take as our starting point the defiance of patriarchy which governs its
fictional strategies.

Even the most seemingly conventional strategies Child uses turn out
to be subversive. The book's main formal device, for example, the pretense
of relying on an "old, worn-out manuscript," allows Child to appropriate
the narrative authority of the Puritan chroniclers while rewriting the
hagiography they had bequeathed to posterity. It also allows her to evade
the sanctions against female authorship by speaking through a series of
male narrators. (Signed "By an American," *Hobomok* was published anony-
mously. Years afterward, in an article advocating woman suffrage, Child

indirectly explained why. During her girlhood, she recalled, the example of Hannah Adams, author of a "short History of the Jews," had been held up to drive home the lesson that a woman "unsexed herself" by exhibiting her learning in print [*Collected Correspondence* 71/1903].)

Under the cover of her principal male narrator, the purported "editor" of the old worn-out manuscript allegedly written by an ancestor who debarked at Naumkeak in 1629, Child announces at the outset that her source demands considerable revision. Its style is "antiquated and almost unintelligible," its content too familiar to readers brought up on John Winthrop's *Journal*, William Hubbard's *General History of New England*, and Nathaniel Morton's *New England's Memorial* to bear repetition: "Every one acquainted with our early history remembers the wretched state in which [newcomers] found the scanty remnant of their brethren" at Naumkeak, she asserts. Thus Child plans to substitute her own language and pass over her source's "dreary account of sickness and distress." The effect of these revisions, of course, is to undermine the authority of the original text and to deflate the myth that such "dreary" accounts served to consecrate— the myth of heroic martyrs battling God's enemies in the wilderness. The deflation is quite explicit in Child's description of the colony as it appeared to her ancestor, with "six miserable hovels" constituting the "whole settlement of Naumkeak" and a few "sickly and half starved" inhabitants presenting a "pitiful contrast to the vigorous and wondering savages who stood among them" (ch. 1).

A glance at Child's sources, which cite "half a score of houses" in lieu of "six miserable hovels" (Higginson qtd. in Morton 143n), reveals how consciously she went about writing an alternative history of the Puritan experiment—one that highlighted its underside and shifted the focus from the saints to the sinners, from the orthodox to the heterodox, from the white settlers to the Indians, from the venerated patriarchs to their unsung wives. To begin with, the historical prototypes of her principal male characters all occupied either marginal or deviant status in the Puritan community.

Roger Conant and John Oldham were disaffected members of the Plymouth colony. Oldham, in fact, had been expelled from Plymouth for fomenting dissension, along with John Lyford, to whose lechery Child alludes. Later, Oldham's murder by Indians, which Child's *First Settlers of*

New-England would blame on his hot temper, helped touch off the Pequot War. Ironically, in *Hobomok* Child transforms this humorless bigot into a "jocular" gadfly who blasphemes "the mysteries of godliness" and laughs at "his own disgraces with the most shameless effrontery" (ch. 1). As for Conant, credited by Hubbard "with courage and resolution to abide fixed in his purpose, notwithstanding all opposition and persuasion he met" (108), Child brings him to his knees by forcing him to accept his daughter's successive marriages to two men his religion brands as outcasts: the Indian Hobomok and the Episcopalian Charles Brown.

Mentioned only briefly in the chronicles, the Episcopalians Samuel and John Brown never reappeared in Naumkeak after their banishment by Endicott for "speeches and practices tending to mutiny and faction" (Morton 148). Fusing them into her hero Charles Brown, however, whom she pointedly names after the king the Puritans had fled, Child awards him the hand of her heroine and an honorable place in the colony that previously exiled him.

The Indian Hobomok, sometimes confused with the devil-god whose name he bore—a deity that a Puritan woman was hanged for allegedly taking as her husband in 1653 (Slotkin 142)—did earn this accolade from the chroniclers for furthering the colonists' "peace . . . with the natives":

> Hobamak, who came to live amongst the English, he being a proper lusty young man, and one that was in account amongst the Indians in those parts for his valour, continued faithful and constant to the English until his death. He, with the said Squanto, being sent amongst the Indians about business for the English, were surprised by an Indian Sachem named Corbitant, who was no friend to the English . . . and offered to stab Hobamak, who being a strong man, soon cleared himself of him; and with speed came and gave intelligence to the Governour of Plimouth. (Morton 70–71; cf. Winslow 521–24, 527–28, 541–42, 547–58, 567–74)

Yet Child goes her sources one better by elevating Hobomok to the rank of title character, marrying him to her Puritan heroine, and integrating the couple's son into white society—a daring inversion of her Puritan ancestors' "errand into the wilderness."

Repeatedly, Child revises patriarchal script by turning the peripheral into the central, the central into the peripheral. Nowhere is this more obvious than in the leading roles she accords the wives and daughters of the patriarchs, literally invisible in the chronicles. On the one hand Child emphasizes the heroism of women like Mrs. Oldham, careworn but uncomplaining, despite the vicissitudes her quarrelsome husband has brought on her, or Mrs. Conant and Lady Arabella Johnson, fated to wither and die under the blast of New England's harsh climate, "victims to what has always been the source of woman's greatest misery—love—deep and unwearied love" (chs. 3, 15). On the other hand Child holds up as role models the younger women who refuse to submit to patriarchy—the lively Sally Oldham, so adept at exposing the cant of the Puritan elders, and the heretical Mary Conant, whom Child will empower to transmute the errand of conquering or converting the Indian into an errand of embracing his ways.

Mary quickly wrests control of the plot from those twin personifica- tions of patriarchal authority, the tyrannical father intent on determining her fate and the male narrator intent on recording it. From the very first chapter—the chapter Child dashed off in response to Palfrey's review while her brother was preparing to deliver his Sunday sermon—it is apparent that Mary's rebellion against her father involves a rejection of his religious, racial, and sexual ideology, as well as an affirmation of her right to follow the inclinations of her heart. Neither Mary nor her mother shares Conant's religious convictions. Yet in the name of those convictions, Conant has uprooted them from their home in England, subjected them to the hardships of the bleak Puritan outpost he would have them regard as a "second Canaan," and forbidden Mary to wed the lover of her choice, the Episcopalian Charles Brown. With astonishing psychological acumen for a twenty-two-year-old woman living in a pre-Freudian age, Child hints that Conant has mistaken a grudge against his father-in-law for religious in- spiration, and that he is unconsciously inflicting on his wife and daughter the psychic wounds he himself once received as a victim of patriarchal tyranny, repudiated and consigned to poverty by his wife's highborn family (chs. 1, 16). Conant's case illustrates how patriarchal tyranny perpetuates itself by transforming scarred sons into obdurate fathers.

Conversely, the rebellion of his wife and daughter illustrates how the cycle of patriarchal tyranny can be arrested. Having learned a different lesson than her husband from "the remembrance of her own thwarted inclinations," Mrs. Conant adjures him on her deathbed to consent to Mary's and Charles's marriage (chs. 6, 15).

Mrs. Conant also dissents privately from her husband's narrow creed. In its stead, she articulates a religion of the heart which transcends the theological controversies of Puritan and Episcopalian. To her, such "matters of dispute" as doctrines, forms, and ceremonies represent the shadow of religion, not its substance. Even the Bible often strikes her as "a flaming cherubim, turning every way, and guarding the tree of life from the touch of man." The alternative to which she turns for religious inspiration is the book of nature: "in creation, one may read to their fill. It is God's library—the first Bible he ever wrote" (ch. 10).

Here, in embryo, a dozen odd years before Emerson proclaimed it, is the transcendentalist gospel. But more to the point, through Mrs. Conant Child is asserting her own right to the role of preacher/theologian that society had granted her brother Convers. It was a right she would exercise more openly in her future career, first as an abolitionist, then as the author of *The Progress of Religious Ideas through Successive Ages*, which scandalized nineteenth-century readers by putting Hinduism, Mohammedanism, and Buddhism on an equal footing with Christianity.

Child projected most of her iconoclasm not onto Mrs. Conant, but onto Mary, however. Noting that the evening star sheds the same light on the "cross-crowned turrets of the Catholic," the "proud spires of the Episcopalian," the "distant mosques and temples" of the East, "the sacrifice heap of the Indian, and the rude dwellings of the Calvinist," Mary discerns an analogy with the light of faith. "It cannot be," she concludes, that "as my father says . . . of all the multitude of people who view" these "cheering rays, so small a remnant only are pleasing in the sight of God" (ch. 6). So Child would conclude in *The Progress of Religious Ideas*, where she would write in the preface: "While my mind was yet in its youth, I was offended by the manner in which Christian writers usually describe other religions. . . . I recollect wishing, long ago, that I could become acquainted with some good, intelligent Bramin [sic], or Mohammedan, that I might learn, in some degree, how their religions appeared to *them*" (vii).

Introduction

The plot of *Hobomok* symbolically fulfills this fantasy, expressed repeatedly in Child's writings, and sometimes specifically formulated as the desire to be turned into an Indian for a while, "that I might experience the fashion of their thoughts and feelings" (see *Letters from New-York* #36 and "She Waits in the Spirit Land," both in the present volume). Through Mary Conant, Child succeeds in vicariously marrying and living the life of an Indian. Mary's odyssey also spells out the fantasy's underlying implication—that questioning the dogmas of a culture which relegates nonwhite, non-Christian peoples to inferior status necessarily entails joining with those peoples in throwing off the yoke of the Great White Father.

The scene that climaxes the novel's opening chapter dramatically reveals where Mary's repudiation of her father's bigotry will lead her. After an evening of "much holy and edifying discourse," punctuated by her father's harangues against Episcopalians, Mary steals out of the house by full moon and plunges into the woods. There, in a setting the Puritan fathers identified with the pre–Christian matriarchal world of nature and its tabooed sexuality—a world they peopled with witches, demons, and Indians cavorting in blasphemous orgiastic rites—Mary performs what can only be called a ritual of witchcraft. Its purpose is to ascertain whether Brown will become her husband despite her father's interdiction—that is, whether matriarchal nature will prevail over patriarchal culture, primitive sexuality over civilized repression, and female witchcraft over male Puritan ideology. Drawing a "large circle" on the ground, walking around it "three times," and retracing her steps backward, Mary chants:

> Whoever's to claim a husband's power,
> Come to me in the moonlight hour.
>
> . . . .
>
> Whoe'er my bridegroom is to be,
> Step in the circle after me.

Although Mary's witchcraft does not produce the result she expects, it foreshadows the course her rebellion against her father will take; for it succeeds in conjuring up, one on the heels of the other, the two men who will serve as her vehicles for defying her father's authority and challenging the values he represents. Hardly has she completed her incantation than, to her horror, the Indian Hobomok leaps into the circle in place of the lover she is awaiting. At first she takes him for a ghost. But he explains that he has come to perform a ritual of his own, which consists of throwing a bough on a heap of rocks, to "make the Manitto Asseinah green as the oak tree," and pronouncing "a short incantation." The coincidence symbolizes the historic affinity between ancient European and Indian fertility cults, as well as the unconscious bond between the female victims of male dominance and the nonwhite victims of European racism.

Hobomok's ritual too produces a result he does not expect, but one that foreshadows the course his relationship with Mary will take: just as he and Mary are leaving the woods, the Episcopalian Charles Brown suddenly appears. Described by Mr. Conant earlier in the evening as a "sprig from [the] tree of corruption" and a strange graft on the Puritan settlement's "pleasant plants," Brown indeed seems almost to have emerged from the Indian's boughs. He accounts for his arrival, however, by saying that he had dreamed Mary was in danger. As Brown and Mary walk off together, Hobomok brings his ritual to a close, muttering: "Three times much winnit Abbamocho said; three times me do." Once again, the parallel establishes Hobomok's ritual as an extension of Mary's.

What is the significance of the two lovers Mary's witchcraft has conjured up, and what is the relationship between them? It is tempting, at first, to speculate that the Episcopalian and the Indian embody opposite alternatives to the bigotry and asceticism of Roger Conant's Puritan world, from which Mary is so desperately seeking escape. If so, the Episcopalian would seem to personify the rich cultural heritage Mary has been forced to leave behind in England, and the Indian the tantalizing wilderness she has been forbidden to explore. Reduced to its simplest terms, this formulation would equate the Episcopalian with culture, the Indian with nature, and the combined appeal of the two men with the hunger Mary feels for the aesthetic and sensuous pleasures Puritan society bans—a hunger which the Puritans' New England descendants were to feel long after Puritanism itself was dead, and which Child herself would never be able to satisfy in her own life.

Child in fact provides much warrant for such an interpretation, in both her descriptions of the two lovers and in her accounts of how Mary's relationship with each has originated. For example, she traces Mary's acquaintance with Brown back to the ancestral mansion of Mary's maternal grandfather, where painting, sculpture, and poetry had left a deep impress "upon her young heart," and where she herself had been "the little idol of the brilliant circle" (chs. 6, 11). In this setting, Mary had greeted Charles as the very incarnation of the arts she had come to worship, the embodiment of all her aspirations. Child's evocation of the scene fuses the aesthetic, the sensual, and the spiritual. There Mary had "mingled with [Charles] in the graceful evolutions of the dance, while her young heart in vain strove to be proof against the intoxicating witchery of light and motion. And there, as she gazed on his lofty forehead, stamped with the proud, deep impress of intellect, and watched the changeful lustre of his dark, eloquent eyes, that alternately beamed with high or tender thoughts, she too became covetous of mental riches, and worshipped at the shrine of genius."

Summing up everything Charles represents for Mary are the gifts he and her grandfather send her after the Puritan elders have exiled Charles from Naumkeak for the crime of trying to reintroduce a religion they associate with the Whore of Babylon. A miniature of himself in a "glittering enclosure; and a splendid [Episcopal] prayer-book printed for the royal family," and bearing the arms of England and the portraits of King Charles and his "handsome . . . French queen" (ch. 14), they graphically highlight the magnificence of the aristocratic culture Charles personifies and the barrenness of the Puritan world that has banished him. The message is clear: all Mary needs to do to regain her rightful station in life is to take up this prayer book and follow her lover back to England, where she too can exercise the power of a queen.

On the face of it, the Indian lover whom Mary's witchcraft has conjured up ahead of Charles, and with whom she will elope after hearing that Charles has perished at sea, would seem to exert an entirely different appeal. "Unwarped by the artifices of civilized life," Hobomok displays a "tall, athletic form," a "healthy cheek," and "manly beauty": "This Indian was indeed cast in nature's noblest mould. He was one of the finest specimens of elastic, vigorous elegance of proportion, to be found among his tribe" (chs. 2, 5, 17). Though "rich . . . in native imagination," Hobomok's "uncultivated mind" is no match for Charles's, Child implies (ch. 19). Conversely, she shows, Charles is no match for Hobomok in the Indian's native element, the world of nature into which he melts at the end of the book.

If the dichotomy of nature versus culture differentiates the Indian from the Episcopalian, it also associates the Indian with women, traditionally consigned to the outskirts of culture. That may be why Child describes Hobomok's creed in almost the same terms as she does Mrs. Conant's and Mary's. Accordingly, Mary finds in Hobomok a kindred spirit sharing her "native fervor of imagination." Indeed the affinity between them lies deeper than Mary realizes. Just as Hobomok has looked upon Mary "with reverence, which almost amounted to adoration," ever since she nursed his sick mother back to life, so Mary will offer herself in marriage to Hobomok on her own mother's grave (chs. 4, 17). Once again, Child's symbolism hints at the factors that create a natural alliance between white women and people of color: roots in similar matriarchal traditions, and a common victimization under European patriarchy.

Ultimately to schematize the relationship between Mary's Indian and Episcopalian lovers as a dichotomy between nature and culture proves misleading, however, for the novel consistently links the two men to each other, as well as to its female rebels against patriarchy and Puritanism. To the Puritans both Episcopalians and Indians are minions of the devil, the "Black Man." Thus Roger Conant calls the Episcopalian a worshipper of Baal. Mary may think she loves Brown for his intellect, but her Puritan father knows better—he scents in the Episcopalian's allure the "flesh-pots of Egypt" (ch. 1).

Just as Brown, the standard bearer of culture, discloses affinities with nature, so Hobomok, that prince of nature, discloses affinities with culture. Like Othello, who wins Desdemona's love through spellbinding accounts of his adventures and of the exotic peoples he has encountered, Hobomok wins Mary's through "long stories, abounding . . . with metaphors" and fabulous "descriptions of the Indian nations," couched in "the brief, figurative language of nature" (chs. 12, 18). Breathing a natural poetry, his narratives are closer to the elegant literature Mary learned to value so highly in England than anything Puritan Naumkeak can boast.

Similarly, the native artistry he displays when he tells Mary how to arrange the shells of the wampum belt she is making for him reveals his kinship with the artists who produced the paintings in her grandfather's mansion. Such aesthetic impulses, Child underscores, have no place in Naumkeak, whose Puritan inhabitants are preoccupied by the "fierce contests of opinion" and blind to the "latent treasures of mind or the rich sympathies of taste," or even the spectacular pageantry of nature (ch. 13). It is because Hobomok feeds her craving for poetry and beauty that Mary prefers him to her fellow settlers, with whom she has nothing in common.

Like Brown, Hobomok also feeds Mary's craving for idolatry—the reverse of the continual diminishment she receives from her father and the Puritan elders who regard women as foolish and sinful temptresses. In both cases, the idolatry is at once quasi-religious and erotic, promoting Mary from the status of a "frail carcase" to that of a goddess, and offering her a spiritual role Puritanism denies her. For Brown Mary is the "little fairy" who has inspired him to plant the "Episcopal mitre in the forests of America"; for Hobomok, she is a "bright . . . emanation from the Good Spirit" (chs. 1, 6, 12). Like Brown's, Hobomok's idolatry excites Mary sexually. Even before Brown's reported death, Mary accompanies Hobomok on a hunt by torchlight which arouses in her the same mixture of aesthetic, sensual, and spiritual feelings she had experienced while dancing with Brown (ch. 12).

In short, the attraction Mary feels for her Episcopalian and Indian lovers is at bottom the same. Both represent a fusion of nature and culture. Both foster the aesthetic impulses Puritan society contemns. Both fulfill the spiritual aspirations thwarted in Mary by a religion that has ruled out the feminine principle. Both embody the sexuality Puritanism seeks to repress. And both, above all, provide a means of defying patriarchal authority, as vested not only in Mary's father but in the society for which he stands.

So closely does the plot intertwine the two lovers whom Mary's incantation summons to "Come to me in the moonlight hour" and "Step in the circle after me" that it irresistibly identifies them as doubles. Again and again in the book, the identities of Mary's Episcopalian and Indian lovers merge as her quest for the one leads her to the other. Again and again the object of that quest turns out to be what Charles and Hobomok alike offer

Introduction

Mary: the right to define her own fate, choose her own religion, reclaim her own sexuality, assert her own worth.

A few examples must suffice to illustrate this insistent pattern of doubling. The most striking occur in chapter 17, which opens and closes with scenes reenacting the episode in the forest. At the outset, Hobomok materializes out of Mary's thoughts while she is mourning Charles's death, the news of which the Indian has carried to Naumkeak. Like a projection of Mary's own unconscious desires, he arrives as if in answer to the question barely formed in her mind: "What now had life to offer?" Recognizing the parallel with the earlier episode, Mary immediately concludes that fate has decreed her marriage to Hobomok. Then she had defied her father's proscription of Charles by using witchcraft to ascertain her fate for herself. Now she spites him by invoking a parody of his Calvinist creed—"the utter fruitlessness of all human endeavour" to resist heaven's mandates—as a rationale for violating every principle he holds dear. Appropriately, Mr. Conant himself telescopes the two scenes when he attempts to throw Mary's Episcopal prayer book into the fire, thereby precipitating her elopement with Hobomok.

Climaxing the doubling in chapter 17 is the marriage ceremony with which the chapter ends. Not only does the ceremony correspond detail for detail with the rituals Mary and Hobomok have performed in the forest, complete with wand, circle, incantation, repetition in patterns of three, and retracing of steps backward, it actually culminates in the intrusion of Brown's ghostly presence. The pipe Hobomok produces for his guests to smoke, eliciting from Mary a "piercing shriek," proves to be the one Brown had sent him from England as a token of friendship, in the very package containing the miniature and the Episcopal prayer book destined for Mary. A phallic symbol, as well as a traditional Indian artifact used in rituals of bonding, and later adopted by Europeans, the pipe cements the unity of Mary's Indian and Episcopalian lovers. In effect, she has married them both. Therein, perhaps, lies the significance of the fantasies she has acted out in chapters 1 and 17.

Once we realize that Hobomok and Brown function as doubles rather than rivals in Child's plot, we can discern more than one meaning in the transformation Hobomok undergoes after three years of marriage: "he seems almost like an Englishman," notes Mary's friend Sally Oldham (ch. 19). We can also understand why Charles himself undergoes a reverse transformation in the interim—shipwrecked on an "East India" vessel, cast on the coast of Africa, and held prisoner for three years, he experiences the lot of the peoples the English have been colonizing. Much in the way dreams work, Child's plot repeatedly turns Charles into Hobomok, Hobomok into Charles.

The ending of the novel can best be read as the consummation of Mary's secret desire to enjoy both of the lovers her witchcraft has conjured up in defiance of her father's prohibitions. Charles materializes in the forest exactly as he did in the opening chapter, surprising Hobomok as the Indian is hunting game for Mary and their infant son. In the first scene Hobomok had appeared to be a ghost summoned by Mary's witchcraft. Now Charles, paralleling his mysterious arrival on the former occasion, when a dream that Mary was in danger had aroused him from sleep, appears to Hobomok to be a ghost. Previously Mary had yielded to fate in marrying Hobomok. Now Hobomok yields to fate by nobly ceding Mary to her first lover and vanishing into the wilderness.

In the very act of reclaiming his bride from the Indian she had married in his absence, however, Brown once again merges with his ostensible rival. The interview at which Brown asks Mary to be his wife, a few hours after the Indian has ceremonially divorced her, takes place in Hobomok's wigwam, and the words with which Charles greets Mary's son by Hobomok—"He is a brave boy"—are the "last words his father said to him" before leaving for the hunt that morning. Indeed the name Mary has given the child—Charles Hobomok Conant—identifies him metaphorically as her son by both lovers (in Indian custom, Mary explains, a child takes the surname of its mother rather than its father). Accordingly, Charles promises "He shall be my own boy" (ch. 20). Confirming the symbolic significance of this pledge, the dénouement supplies Charles and Mary with no other offspring; instead it follows "the little Hobomok" into maturity as a university education converts him into an Englishman.

Child's radical revision of patriarchal script thus culminates not in the reassertion of patriarchal authority, but in its overthrow, not in the death of a heroine who has dared to challenge the religious, racial, and sexual ideology on which patriarchy rests, but in her achievement of happiness and with it the triumph of the alternative values she has embraced. Mary returns to the Puritan community on her own terms, unscathed by her violation of its taboos against miscegenation and divorce. Far from paying any price for her transgressions, she finds herself rewarded by the unprecedented opportunity to remarry. And this time the Puritan elders who have previously banished her chosen lover for heresy fully countenance her marriage and the couple's reintegration into the community as religious dissidents. Even that personification of patriarchal authority, Mr. Conant, capitulates. Softened by the suffering he has undergone since Mary's elopement and blaming himself for having driven her to it, he joyfully agrees to hold the wedding under his roof. In return, Mary and Charles reserve a place for him at their fireside and tolerate his religious views—a bold reversal of roles.

The final element in the resolution of religious, racial, sexual, and generational conflicts with which the novel ends is the assimilation into Anglo-American society of the child embodying the marriage of America's white colonists and Indian aborigines—the alternative Child offers to white supremacy and race war. At the request of Mr. Conant, half of the family's legacy goes to educating Charles Hobomok Conant, who distinguishes himself at Harvard and finishes his studies in England, eventually losing all traces of his Indian identity and melting into his mother's people.

This resolution, however, conspicuously excludes Hobomok himself. In the last analysis, his function as Charles's double does not negate the sinister implications of his convenient decision to forego his rights and leave his English rival in possession of his patrimony. As several critics have pointed out, Child has succumbed here to the familiar white fantasy that the Indian will somehow disappear. Moreover, the happy ending she has provided represents a betrayal of the alliance with people of color which had allowed Mary to liberate herself from patriarchal oppression. It also belies the ideal of a mutually enriching cultural intermarriage, which Mary's attraction to Hobomok and the symbolic fusion of her two lovers' identities might suggest. Granted, Child does envisage assimilation in lieu of Indian genocide—and she is alone among early nineteenth-century novelists in doing so (though writers like William Byrd and Robert Beverley had advanced the idea in the eighteenth century). This said, her conception of assimilation amounts to cultural genocide. Only if Indians cease to be Indians, it implies, can they earn a place in the society that is dispossessing them. That is why Hobomok must go away, leaving to his half-English son the questionable honor of joining white society.

In short, despite its insights into the connections between male dominance and white supremacy, and despite its daring revisions of patriarchal script, Child's response to the call for an authentic national literature does not succeed in resolving the central contradictions of the American historical novel, nor those of American history itself: that white Americans win their political freedom at the expense of the Indians they exterminate and the Africans they enslave, and that they achieve their cultural independence by expropriating the cultures of the peoples they have systematically debased, devalorized, and deprived of an independent identity.

To her credit, Child began addressing these issues a few years after the publication of *Hobomok*. In her 1829 book, *The First Settlers of New-England*, she launched a career of campaigning against Indian dispossession, crowned forty years later by her eloquent *Appeal for the Indians* (1868). She also returned with greater political awareness to the theme of interracial marriage that she had instinctively recognized as both the crux of America's racial and sexual contradictions and the key to resolving them. Besides denouncing antimiscegenation laws in her 1833 *Appeal in Favor of That Class of Americans Called Africans*, Child dramatized their effects in her fiction. Short stories like "The Indian Wife" (1828), "The Quadroons" (1842), "Slavery's Pleasant Homes" (1843), and "The Falls of St. Anthony" (1846) trenchantly expose the hypocrisy of the double standard that prohibits interracial marriage, yet allows white men to treat women of color as fair game. And her last novel, *A Romance of the Republic* (1867), avowedly written "to undermine *prejudice*," features three interracial marriages. The novel's concluding tableau, in which the daughter of an interracial marriage embodies the Republic that has risen out of the ashes of Civil War, drives home the lesson that America's destiny lies in the amalgamation of its diverse racial strains.

True, Child would never fully transcend the limitations her first novel betrayed when it integrated Hobomok's son into American society at the price of erasing his Indian heritage. Even in *A Romance of the Republic*, where she pictures a reciprocal influence taking place between the quadroon heroines and their white benefactors, Child articulates an ideal of assimilation that remains profoundly ethnocentric. America's people of color, it posits, must melt into the predominant white culture, enriching that culture in the process, but losing their own distinctive identity. Our society continues to suffer from this failure of imagination in the progressive movement Child represented, which undertook the first stage of America's liberation from racism.

Nevertheless, in evaluating the contributions of a writer to whom we owe both a literary and a political alternative to the dominant racist tradition of American cultural history, we must recognize that however inadequate by our standards, her alternative was radical enough to warrant a counterattack aimed at expunging it from the historical record. That counterattack began with the first reviews of *Hobomok*, which clearly spelled out the guidelines American writers would have to follow.

While commending the anonymous author (whom they assumed to be a man) for "well conceived" characters, "acquaintance with the history and spirit of the times," skill at rendering "the strange mixture of good sense, piety, fanaticism, and intolerance, which distinguished our puritan ancestors," and success at capturing the "Indian character . . . and language," reviewers united in pronouncing the novel's plot "in very bad taste, to say the least" (*NAR* 19: 262; Sparks 21: 87, 90, 95). Their summaries (*NAR* 19: 262–63) were telling: "A high born and delicate female, on the supposed death of her lover, has, in a fit of insane despondency, offered herself as the wife of an Indian chief, and has become such, according to the customs of his nation. She lives with him three years, and an infant semisavage is the offspring of the union. At the end of that time, her white lover returns; her copper one with great magnanimity relinquishes her and departs, and she is married to the former." As this summary suggests, what reviewers found so "unnatural" and "revolting . . . to every feeling of delicacy in man or woman," was the sexual freedom Child had allowed a woman of their own social class—freedom to choose her mate without regard to race or class, freedom to take the initiative in proposing marriage, freedom to divorce and remarry, retaining custody of her child to boot—freedom, in sum, to flout every law of patriarchy without suffering the consequences. Hence the contrast between their reactions to the interracial love plots of Child's *Hobomok* and of Eastburn and Sands's *Yamoyden*, which had escaped censure by punishing its erring heroine with death.

Still, the men who ruled the early nineteenth-century literary establishment saw enough potential in *Hobomok*, as a historical novel serving nationalist aims, to encourage its author to persevere. Charitably imputing the faults they had criticized to "inexperience in this kind of writing," they expressed the hope "that the author may amend them and at the same time retain all the other qualifications for a good writer, which are here exhibited." The amendment they had in mind is chillingly obvious from one of the passages singled out for praise and quotation: the death bed scene of Mrs. Conant and Lady Arabella Johnson, both exemplary Puritan wives who have dutifully endured the hardships of exile for their husbands' sake. The message, of course, was that American writers had the responsibility of inculcating the values the white male governing elite deemed appropriate; and foremost among the values prescribed for women, as the martyrdom of Mrs. Conant and Arabella Johnson testified, were a submissiveness and self-sacrifice that could literally prove deadly.

The full significance of the attacks on *Hobomok* only becomes apparent, however, in the light of the three novels which Child's example would inspire to venture into the forbidden domain of miscegenation. Two years after the publication of *Hobomok*, James Fenimore Cooper would issue what may well have been his answer to its challenge: *The Last of the Mohicans* (1826). Shifting the focus back to race war as the correct prototype of relations between whites and Indians, Cooper raised the specter of a love affair between a white woman and an Indian only to dispel it, first by revealing that the woman was not white after all, then by killing off the would-be lovers and burying them in separate graves, so that even in death, their blood would not mingle.

But the ghost of *Hobomok* was not so easily laid. Before another year was out, a woman writer would seek to develop, rather than foreclose, the possibilities Child had opened up. Catharine Maria Sedgwick's *Hope Leslie* (1827) is in many ways a more progressive novel than *Hobomok*. For the first time in American literature, it embodies the noble Indian not in a warrior, but in a woman. A truly impressive literary creation, Sedgwick's

Magawisca is more than a match for Cooper's Uncas and Chingachgook. And unlike both Cooper's and Child's noble Indians, Magawisca remains loyal to her people. Granted, Sedgwick does not allow Magawisca the marriage with the white hero, Everell Fletcher, which the novel fleetingly appears to promise. Instead, modeling her work on Scott's *Ivanhoe*, she casts Magawisca in the role of Rebecca, and reserves the role of Rowena for her heroine, Hope Leslie. Even so, she does go further than Child in two other respects. First, she elaborates on the idea of an alliance between white women and Indians, turning it into a political—and feminist— gesture of solidarity when Hope Leslie helps Magawisca escape from prison. Second, she arranges the only lasting Indian-white marriage in the nineteenth-century frontier novel—the marriage between Hope's sister Faith, captured and adopted by Indians in her early childhood, and Magawisca's brother Oneco.

Despite these advances, Sedgwick avoids following Child's lead in presenting intermarriage and assimilation as viable alternatives to Indian genocide. Magawisca, like Cooper's Indians and their friend, Natty Bumppo, sees no possibility of reconciliation or integration with whites: "The Indian and the white man can no more mingle, and become one, than day and night," she tells Everell and Hope, when they urge her to remain with them (2. 260). As if to prove her point, Faith and Oneco remain childless. In contrast to Mary Conant, Faith Leslie can never be reintegrated into white society, even should she choose to be. By marrying an Indian and adopting his people's ways, she has irrevocably regressed to savagery.

The qualifications with which Sedgwick hedged herself when she hazarded entertaining the tabooed idea of racial intermarriage did not suffice to grant *Hope Leslie* a role any more significant than that of *Hobomok* in altering the form of the American historical novel—or the shape of the American literary canon. Notwithstanding the real merits of Sedgwick's novel, and the enormous popularity it enjoyed in its own day, *Hope Leslie*, like *Hobomok*, now lies forgotten. The last word on the subject of Indian-white relations, be they sexual or military, would be Cooper's. Once again, it seems to have come in response to a woman novelist's challenge.

In *The Wept of Wish-ton-Wish* (1829), Cooper authoritatively revised Sedgwick's plot, forcing it into the less subversive mold of Eastburn and

Sands's *Yamoyden*. Ruth Heathcote, like Faith Leslie (and like the historical Eunice Williams on whose story both Sedgwick and Cooper drew), is captured by Indians as a child, adopted by the tribe, and eventually married to an Indian chief. She, too, regresses to savagery, forgetting her mother tongue and the religion of her fathers and embracing Indian ways. And unlike Faith, but like Mary Conant, she actually bears her Indian husband a child. The end of the novel rights all wrongs and restores order, however. Paralleling the dénouement of *Yamoyden*, Ruth's husband Conanchet is killed by an Indian enemy (though at the behest of the Puritans), and she dies by his side, overcome with grief and shock. As if the abortive end of their marriage were not enough to counter the threat Sedgwick had introduced by permitting her Anglo-Indian couple to survive unharmed, Cooper puts into the mouth of Conanchet the moral that it is futile for people of different races to violate the ban of nature and the Great Spirit. In a final twist, he symbolically brings Ruth back into the fold. Just before her death, she suddenly loses all memory of her long sojourn among the Indians and mentally reverts to her state at the time of her capture—the state of a young child, virginal once more, and purged of her distasteful liaison. As for the child lying in her lap—a child whose mixed blood, according to her husband, makes it unfit to live among Indians—Cooper literally expunges it from the novel. Neither in his summary of the surviving characters' fates nor in his descriptions of the gravestones commemorating the dead does he account for the child. The dismissal of intermarriage from the history and literature of white America could hardly have been more definitive.

Cooper's vision of race and gender relations in the American historical novel triumphed over Sedgwick's and Child's not because it was intrinsically more realistic or better articulated, but because it coincided with the vision of America's ruling elites and met their need for a cultural mythology that could enlist broad support for their white supremacist policies. This upshot of the contest between patriarchal and feminist conceptions of America has had devastating consequences for our political and cultural life. Even critics who have unquestioningly accepted the validity of a literary canon occupied almost exclusively by middle- and upper-class white males have noticed the symptoms of impoverishment resulting from the purge of writers like Child and Sedgwick (and their

Introduction

black and Indian peers): the extremely narrow range of subjects and emotions explored in the "American novel" and the substitution of terror and violence for the novel's traditional themes of love and marriage. The impoverishment of our literature, in turn, has had the effect of inhibiting our very capacity to imagine, let alone create, alternatives to white supremacy, male dominance, and a perpetual state of war with other peoples that has left a trail of desolation stretching from the fire-gutted Pequot villages of Massachusetts to the napalmed peasants and defoliated rice paddies of Vietnam.

It is no accident that when the Vietnam War exposed the bankruptcy of an ideology first developed during the Puritans' campaigns against the Indians, it fueled a search not only for a better political order, but also for a worthier heritage from the past. Hence the outpouring of scholarship dedicated to rescuing from oblivion the writers and activists who once fought to create a truly free and egalitarian America. For the mission of constructing an alternative future goes hand in hand with the task of reconstructing an alternative past.

SELECTED BIBLIOGRAPHY

The following abbreviations have been used: *SL* for Child's *Selected Letters*, *NAR* for *North American Review*. Due to space limitations, most titles mentioned in headnotes and explanatory notes have been omitted here, as have widely known primary and secondary works.

WORKS BY LYDIA MARIA CHILD

An Appeal for the Indians. New York: William P. Tomlinson, 1868.

An Appeal in Favor of That Class of Americans Called Africans. Boston: Allen and Ticknor, 1833.

ed. *Aspirations of the World. A Chain of Opals*. Boston: Roberts, 1878.

The Biographies of Madame de Staël, and Madame Roland. Vol. 1 of *Ladies' Family Library*. Boston: Carter, Hendee, 1832.

The Collected Correspondence of Lydia Maria Child, 1817–1880. Ed. Patricia G. Holland, Milton Meltzer, and Francine Krasno. Millwood, NY: Kraus, 1980.

The Coronal. A Collection of Miscellaneous Pieces, Written at Various Times. Boston: Carter and Hendee, 1831.

Correspondence between Lydia Maria Child and Gov. Wise and Mrs. Mason, of Virginia. Boston: American Anti-Slavery Society, 1860.

Selected Bibliography

Fact and Fiction: A Collection of Stories. New York: C. S. Francis, 1846.

The First Settlers of New-England: or, Conquest of the Pequods, Narragansets and Pokanokets: as Related by a Mother to Her Children, and Designed for the Instruction of Youth. Boston: Munroe and Francis, 1829.

The Freedmen's Book. Boston: Ticknor and Fields, 1865.

The Frugal Housewife. Boston: Marsh & Capen, and Carter & Hendee, 1829.

Good Wives. Vol. 3 of *Ladies' Family Library*. Boston: Carter, Hendee, 1833.

The History of the Condition of Women, in Various Ages and Nations. Vols. 4 and 5 of *Ladies' Family Library*. Boston: John Allen, 1835.

Hobomok, A Tale of Early Times. Boston: Cummings, Hilliard, 1824. Review in *NAR* 19 (1824): 262–63.

Letters from New York, First Series. New York: Charles S. Francis, 1843.

Letters from New York, Second Series. New York: C. S. Francis, 1845.

Letters of Lydia Maria Child. Ed. John Greenleaf Whittier. Boston: Houghton, 1882.

ed. *Looking toward Sunset*. Boston: Ticknor and Fields, 1865.

Lydia Maria Child: Selected Letters, 1817–1880. Ed. Milton Meltzer, Patricia G. Holland, and Francine Krasno. Amherst: U of Massachusetts P, 1982.

The Mother's Book. Boston: Carter, Hendee and Babcock, 1831.

The Progress of Religious Ideas, through Successive Ages. 3 vols. New York: C. S. Francis, 1855.

"The Quadroons." 1842. *The Other Woman: Stories of Two Women and a Man*. Ed. Susan Koppelman. Old Westbury, NY: Feminist P, 1984. 1–12.

The Rebels; or, Boston before the Revolution. Boston: Cummings, Hilliard, 1825.

A Romance of the Republic. Boston: Ticknor and Fields, 1867.

"Slavery's Pleasant Homes. A Faithful Sketch." *The Liberty Bell* 4 (1843): 147–60.

SOURCES AND FURTHER READINGS

Andrews, Charles McLean. *The Settlements*. Vol. 1 of *The Colonial Period of American History*. 4 vols. New Haven: Yale UP, 1934.

Arch, Stephen Carl. "Romancing the Puritans: American Historical Fiction in the 1820s." *ESQ: A Journal of the American Renaissance* 39 (1993): 107–32.

Selected Bibliography

Baer, Helene G. *The Heart Is like Heaven: The Life of Lydia Maria Child*. Philadelphia: U of Pennsylvania P, 1964.

Barnett, Louise K. *The Ignoble Savage: American Literary Racism, 1790–1890*. Westport, CT: Greenwood, 1975.

Baym, Nina. *American Women Writers and the Work of History, 1790–1860*. New Brunswick: Rutgers UP, 1995.

————. *Feminism and American Literary History*. New Brunswick: Rutgers UP, 1992.

Bell, Michael Davitt. *Hawthorne and the Historical Romance of New England*. Princeton: Princeton UP, 1971.

"Biographical Memoir of Father Rasles." *Collections of the Massachusetts Historical Society*. 2nd ser. 8 (1819): 250–67.

Bradford, William. *Of Plymouth Plantation, 1620–1647*. 1856. Ed. Samuel Eliot Morison. New York: Random-Modern Library, 1952.

Brown, Dee. *Bury My Heart at Wounded Knee: An Indian History of the American West*. New York: Holt, 1970.

[Channing, E. T.]. "On Models in Literature." *NAR* 3 (1816): 202–09.

[Channing, W.]. "Essay on American Language and Literature." *NAR* 1 (1815): 307–14.

————. "Reflections on the Literary Delinquency of America." *NAR* 2 (1815): 33–43.

Chapin, Howard M. *Sachems of the Narragansetts*. Providence: Rhode Island Historical Society, 1931.

Clifford, Deborah Pickman. *Crusader for Freedom: A Life of Lydia Maria Child*. Boston: Beacon P, 1992.

Dall, Caroline Healey. "Lydia Maria Child and Mary Russell Mitford." *Unitarian Review* 19 (1883): 519–34.

Dekker, George. *The American Historical Romance*. Cambridge: Cambridge UP, 1987.

Dippie, Brian W. *The Vanishing American: White Attitudes and U.S. Indian Policy*. Middletown, CT: Wesleyan UP, 1982.

Drinnon, Richard. *Facing West: The Metaphysics of Indian-Hating and Empire-Building*. New York: NAL, 1980.

Eastburn, James Wallis, and Robert Sands. *Yamoyden, A Tale of the Wars of King Philip: in Six Cantos*. New York, 1820.

Eckstorm, Fannie Hardy. "The Attack on Norridgewock, 1724." *New England Quarterly* 7 (1934): 541–78.

Elbert, Sarah. *A Hunger for Home: Louisa May Alcott and* Little Women. Philadelphia: Temple UP, 1984.

————. *A Hunger for Home: Louisa May Alcott's Place in American Culture*, rev. ed. New Brunswick: Rutgers UP, 1987.

Evans, Sara M. *Born for Liberty: A History of Women in America*. New York: Free P, 1989.

Foster, Edward Halsey. *Catharine Maria Sedgwick*. New York: Twayne, 1974.

Francis, Convers. "Life of Sebastian Rale, Missionary to the Indians." *The Library of American Biography*. Ed. Jared Sparks. Vol. 17, *Lives of John Ribault, Sebastian Rale, and William Palfrey*. Boston: Little, Brown, 1845.

Fuller, Margaret. *Woman in the Nineteenth Century*. 1845. New York: Norton, 1971.

Gilbert, Sandra M., and Susan Gubar. *The Madwoman in the Attic: The Woman Writer and the Nineteenth-Century Literary Imagination*. New Haven: Yale UP, 1979.

Grimké, Sarah Moore. *Letters on the Equality of the Sexes*. Boston, 1838.

Hallowell, Anna D. "Lydia Maria Child." *Medford Historical Register* 3 (1900): 95–117.

Heckewelder, John Gottlieb Ernestus. *An Account of the History, Manners, and Customs of the Indian Nations*. 1819. Rev. ed. Philadelphia: Historical Society of Pennsylvania, 1876.

Hersh, Blanche Glassman. *The Slavery of Sex: Feminist-Abolitionists in America*. Urbana: U of Illinois P, 1978.

Herzog, Kristin. *Women, Ethnics, and Exotics: Images of Power in Mid-Nineteenth-Century American Fiction*. Knoxville: U of Tennessee P, 1983.

Holland, Patricia G. "Lydia Maria Child As a Nineteenth-Century Professional Author." *Studies in the American Renaissance* 1981: 157–67.

Hubbard, William. *A General History of New England*. 1815. New York: Arno, 1972.

Karcher, Carolyn L. "Censorship American Style: The Case of Lydia Maria Child." *Studies in the American Renaissance* 1986: 283–303.

————. *The First Woman in the Republic: A Cultural Biography of Lydia Maria Child*. Durham: Duke UP, 1994.

————. "From Pacifism to Armed Struggle: Lydia Maria Child's 'The Kansas Emigrants' and Antislavery Ideology in the 1850s." *ESQ: A Journal of the American Renaissance* 34 (1988): 141–58.

————. "Lydia Maria Child's *A Romance of the Republic*: An Abolitionist Vision of America's Racial Destiny." *Slavery and the Literary Imagination: Selected Papers from the English Institute, 1987*. Ed. Arnold Rampersad and Deborah E. McDowell. Baltimore: Johns Hopkins UP, 1989. 81–103.

————. "Patriarchal Society and Matriarchal Family in Irving's 'Rip Van Winkle' and Child's 'Hilda Silfverling.'" *Legacy* 2 (1985): 31–44.

————. "Rape, Murder, and Revenge in 'Slavery's Pleasant Homes': Lydia Maria Child's Antislavery Fiction and the Limits of Genre." Revised and expanded for *The Culture of Sentiment: Race, Gender, and Sentimentality in Nineteenth-Century America*. Ed. Shirley Samuels. New York: Oxford UP, 1992. 58–72, 289–94.

Kerber, Linda K. "The Abolitionist Perception of the Indian." *Journal of American History* 62 (1975): 271–95.

[Knapp, J.]. "National Poetry." *NAR* 8 (1818): 169–76.

Kolodny, Annette. *The Land before Her: Fantasy and Experience of the American Frontiers, 1630–1860*. Chapel Hill: U of North Carolina P, 1984.

Lerner, Gerda. *The Grimké Sisters from South Carolina: Rebels against Slavery*. Boston: Houghton, 1967.

Maddox, Lucy. *Removals: Nineteenth-Century American Literature and the Politics of Indian Affairs*. New York: Oxford UP, 1991.

Mardock, Robert Winston. *The Reformers and the American Indian*. Columbia: U of Missouri P, 1971.

Marshall, Ian. "Heteroglossia in Lydia Maria Child's *Hobomok*." *Legacy* 10 (1993): 1–16.

Mayo, Lawrence Shaw. "The History of the Legend of Chocorua." *New England Quarterly* 19 (1946): 302–14.

[Mellen, G.]. "Works of Mrs. Child." *NAR* 37 (1833): 138–64.

Meltzer, Milton. *Tongue of Flame: The Life of Lydia Maria Child*. New York: Crowell, 1965.

Selected Bibliography

Mills, Bruce. *Cultural Reformations: Lydia Maria Child and the Literature of Reform*. Athens: U of Georgia P, 1994.

Morton, Nathaniel. *New England's Memorial*. 1669. 5th ed. Boston, 1826.

Nelson, Dana D. *The Word in Black and White: Reading "Race" in American Literature. 1638–1867*. New York: Oxford UP, 1992.

North American Review (NAR). See Channing, E. T., Channing, W., Knapp, J., Mellen, G., Palfrey, John Gorham, and Sparks, Jared.

Ortner, Sherry B. "Is Male to Female as Nature Is to Culture?" *Woman, Culture, and Society*. Ed. Michelle Zimbalist Rosaldo and Louise Lamphere. Stanford: Stanford UP, 1974. 67–87.

Osborne, William S. *Lydia Maria Child*. Boston: Hall-Twayne, 1980.

[Palfrey, John Gorham]. Review of *Yamoyden*. *NAR* 12 (1821): 466–88.

Peace Commission Report. See United States.

Pearce, Roy Harvey. *The Savages of America: A Study of the Indian and the Idea of Civilization*. Rev. ed. Baltimore: Johns Hopkins UP, 1965.

Person, Leland S., Jr. "The American Eve: Miscegenation and a Feminist Frontier Fiction." *American Quarterly* 37 (1985): 668–85.

Phelps [Ward], Elizabeth Stuart. *Chapters from a Life*. 1896. New York: Arno, 1980.

Samuels, Shirley, ed. *The Culture of Sentiment: Race, Gender, and Sentimentality in Nineteenth-Century America*. New York: Oxford UP, 1992.

Sanchez-Eppler, Karen. *Touching Liberty: Abolition, Feminism and the Politics of the Body*. Berkeley: U of California P, 1993.

Sedgwick, Catharine Maria. *Hope Leslie*. Ed. Mary Kelley. New Brunswick: Rutgers UP, 1987.

Slotkin, Richard. *The Fatal Environment: The Myth of the Frontier in the Age of Industrialization, 1800–1890*. Middletown, CT: Wesleyan UP, 1986.

————. *Regeneration through Violence: The Mythology of the American Frontier, 1600–1860*. Middletown, CT: Wesleyan UP, 1973.

[Sparks, Jared]. "Recent American Novels." *NAR* 21 (1825): 78–104.

Stanton, Elizabeth Cady. *Eighty Years and More: Reminiscences 1815–1897*. 1898. New York: Shocken, 1971.

Stanton, Elizabeth Cady, Susan B. Anthony, and Matilda Joslyn Gage, eds. *History of Woman Suffrage*. 5 vols. 1882–1922. New York: Arno, 1969. Vol. 1.

Selected Bibliography

Tompkins, Jane. *Sensational Designs: The Cultural Work of American Fiction, 1790–1860*. New York: Oxford UP, 1985.

United States. Cong. House. *Annual Report of the Commissioner on Indian Affairs*. 40th Cong., 3rd sess. 1868. House Executive Document 1: 486–510.

Wald, Priscilla. *Constituting Americans: Cultural Anxiety and Narrative Form*. Durham: Duke UP, 1995.

Winslow, Edward. *Good News from New England*. 1624. *The Story of the Pilgrim Fathers*. Ed. Edward Arber. Boston, 1897. 509–98.

Winthrop, John. *The History of New England from 1630–1649*. Ed. James Savage. 2 vols. Rev. ed. Boston, 1853.

Yellin, Jean Fagan. *Women and Sisters: The Antislavery Feminists in American Culture*. New Haven: Yale UP, 1989.

A NOTE ON THE TEXT

The text of *Hobomok* has been reset from the 1824 edition. To preserve the flavor of the original, I have not tampered with spelling or punctuation, except for the sake of clarity. A handful of misprints have been silently corrected, and in a single case a word in brackets has been inserted where a sentence failed to make sense without it. Otherwise old-fashioned spellings and hyphenations have been retained (*ancle, to-day*), including the inconsistencies common in nineteenth-century texts. Such typographical features as the use of periods after titles have not been reproduced, however. The same procedures apply to the other selections.

The texts of "The Lone Indian" and "Chocorua's Curse" are those of *The Coronal* (1832). The extract from *History of Women* is taken from the 1835 edition, and "She Waits in the Spirit Land" and "A Legend of the Falls of St. Anthony" from the 1847 edition of *Fact and Fiction*. The text of Letter 36 comes from the 1852 edition of *Letters from New-York*, First Series. In cases where more readily available editions have been used instead of first editions, they have been checked against first editions. The text of *An Appeal for the Indians* is the 1868 Tomlinson edition. I am grateful to the Historical Society of Pennsylvania for supplying a xerox copy of it. The texts of "The Church in the Wilderness," "Willie Wharton," and "The Indians" are taken, respectively, from Nathaniel Willis's gift book, *The Legendary* (1828); the *Atlantic Monthly* 11 (March 1863): 324–45; and *The Standard* 1 (May 1870): 1–6.

HOBOMOK

A Tale of Early Times

By an American

Then all this youthful paradise around,
And all the broad and boundless mainland, lay
Cooled by the interminable wood, that frowned
O'er mount and vale.
        —*Bryant*

PREFACE

IN THE SUMMER of 1823, my friend ——— entered my study with an air which indicated he had something to communicate.

"Frederic," says he, "do you know I have been thinking of a new plan lately?"

"A wise one, no doubt," replied I; "but, prithee, what is it?"

"Why, to confess the truth, your friend P———'s remarks concerning our early history, have half tempted me to write a New England novel."

"A novel!" quoth I—"when Waverly is galloping over hill and dale, faster and more successful than Alexander's conquering sword? Even American ground is occupied. 'The Spy' is lurking in every closet,—the mind is every where supplied with 'Pioneers' on the land, and is soon likely to be with 'Pilots' on the deep."

"I know that," replied he; "Scott wanders over every land with the same proud, elastic tread—free as the mountain breeze, and majestic as the bird that bathes in the sunbeams. He must always stand alone—a high and solitary shrine, before which minds of humbler mould are compelled to bow down and worship. I did not mean," added he, smiling, "that my wildest hopes, hardly my wildest wishes, had placed me even within sight of the proud summit which has been gained either by Sir Walter Scott, or Mr. Cooper. I am aware that the subject which called forth your friend's animated observations, owed its romantic coloring almost wholly to his own rich imagination. Still, barren and uninteresting as New England

3

history is, I feel there is enough connected with it, to rouse the dormant energies of my soul; and I would fain deserve some other epitaph than that 'he lived and died.'"

I knew that my friend, under an awkward and unprepossessing appearance, concealed more talents than the world was aware of. I likewise knew that when he once started in the race, "the de'il take the hindmost" was his favorite motto. So I e'en resolved to favor the project, and to procure for him as many old, historical pamphlets as possible.

A few weeks after, my friend again entered my apartment, and gave me a package, as he said, "Here are my MSS., and it rests entirely with you, whether or not to give them to the public. You, and every one acquainted with our earliest history, will perceive that I owe many a quaint expression, and pithy sentence, to the old and forgotten manuscripts of those times.

"The ardour with which I commenced this task, has almost wholly abated.

"Seriously, Frederic, what chance is there that I, who so seldom peep out from 'the loop-holes of retreat,' upon a gay and busy world, can have written any thing which will meet their approbation? Besides, the work is full of faults, which I have talents enough to see, but not to correct. It has indeed fallen far short of the standard which I had raised in my own mind. You well know that state of feeling, when the soul fixes her keen vision on distant brightness, but in vain stretches her feeble and spell-bound wing, for a flight so lofty. The world would smile," continued he, "to hear me talk thus, concerning a production, which will probably never rise to the surface with other ephemeral trifles of the day;—but painful, anxious timidity must unavoidably be felt by a young author in his first attempt. However, I will talk no more about it, 'What is writ, is writ—would it were worthier.'

"If I succeed, the voice of praise will cheer me in my solitude. If I fail, thank Heaven, there is no one, but yourself, can insult me with their pity."

Perhaps the public may think me swayed by undue partiality,—but after I had read my friend's MS. I wrote upon the outside, "Send it to the Printer."

CHAPTER I

How daur ye try sic sportin,
As seek the foul thief ony place,
For him to spae your fortune?
Nae doubt but ye may get a *sight*!
Great cause ye hae to fear it;
For mony a ane has gotten a fright,
An' liv'd and died deleeret.
            —*Burns*

I NEVER VIEW the thriving villages of New England, which speak so
forcibly to the heart, of happiness and prosperity, without feeling a glow of
national pride, as I say, "this is my own, my native land." A long train of
associations are connected with her picturesque rivers, as they repose in
their peaceful loveliness, the broad and sparkling mirror of the heavens,—
and with the cultivated environs of her busy cities, which seem every
where blushing into a perfect Eden of fruit and flowers. The remembrance
of what we have been, comes rushing on the heart in powerful and happy
contrast. In most nations the path of antiquity is shrouded in darkness,
rendered more visible by the wild, fantastic light of fable; but with us, the
vista of time is luminous to its remotest point. Each succeeding year has
left its footsteps distinct upon the soil, and the cold dew of our chilling
dawn is still visible beneath the mid-day sun. Two centuries only have
elapsed, since our most beautiful villages reposed in the undisturbed
grandeur of nature;—when the scenes now rendered classic by literary
associations, or resounding with the din of commerce, echoed nought but
the song of the hunter, or the fleet tread of the wild deer. God was here in
his holy temple, and the whole earth kept silence before him! But the voice
of prayer was soon to be heard in the desert. The sun, which for ages
beyond the memory of man had gazed on the strange, fearful worship of
the Great Spirit of the wilderness, was soon to shed its splendor upon the

altars of the living God. That light, which had arisen amid the darkness of Europe, stretched its long, luminous track across the Atlantic, till the summits of the western world became tinged with its brightness. During many long, long ages of gloom and corruption, it seemed as if the pure flame of religion was every where quenched in blood;—but the watchful vestal had kept the sacred flame still burning deeply and fervently. Men, stern and unyielding, brought it hither in their own bosom, and amid desolation and poverty they kindled it on the shrine of Jevovah. In this enlightened and liberal age, it is perhaps too fashionable to look back upon those early sufferers in the cause of the Reformation, as a band of dark, discontented bigots. Without doubt, there were many broad, deep shadows in their characters, but there was likewise bold and powerful light. The peculiarities of their situation occasioned most of their faults, and atoned for them. They were struck off from a learned, opulent, and powerful nation, under circumstances which goaded and lacerated them almost to ferocity;—and it is no wonder that men who fled from oppression in their own country, to all the hardships of a remote and dreary province, should have exhibited a deep mixture of exclusive, bitter, and morose passions. To us indeed, most of the points for which they so strenuously contended, must appear exceedingly absurd and trifling; and we cannot forbear a smile that vigorous and cultivated minds should have looked upon the signing of the cross with so much horror and detestation. But the heart pays involuntary tribute to conscientious, persevering fortitude, in what cause soever it may be displayed. At this impartial period we view the sound policy and unwearied zeal with which the Jesuits endeavored to rebuild their decaying church, with almost as much admiration as we do the noble spirit of reaction which it produced. Whatever merit may be attached to the cause of our forefathers, the mighty effort which they made for its support is truly wonderful; and whatever might have been their defects, they certainly possessed excellencies, which peculiarly fitted them for a van-guard in the proud and rapid march of freedom. The bold outlines of their character alone remain to us. The varying tints of domestic detail are already concealed by the ivy which clusters around the tablets of our recent history. Some of these have lately been unfolded in an old, worn-out manuscript, which accidentally came in my way. It was written by one of my ancestors who fled with the persecuted nonconformists from the Isle of Wight, and about the middle of June, 1629, arrived at Naumkeak on the eastern shore of Massachusetts. Every one acquainted with our early history remembers the wretched state in which they found the scanty remnant of their brethren at that place. I shall, therefore, pass over the young man's dreary account of sickness and distress, and shall likewise take the liberty of substituting my own expressions for his anti-quated and almost unintelligible style.

"After a long and wearisome voyage," says he, "we gladly welcomed the peninsula of Shawmut, which, as it lay stretched out in the distance, proclaimed the vicinity of Naumkeak. But the winds seemed resolved to show the full extent of their tantalizing power. All the livelong day we watched the sails as they fluttered loosely round the mast, and listened to the hoarse creaking of the shrouds. Evening at length came on in her softened beauty; and I shall never forget the crowd of sensations which it brought upon my mind. I was in a new world, whose almost unlimited extent lay in the darkness of ignorance and desolation. Earth, sea, and air, seemed in a profound slumber,—and not even the dash of the oar broke in upon their silence. A confusion of thoughts came over my mind, till I was lost and bewildered in their immensity. The scene around me owed nothing of its unadorned beauty to the power of man. He had rarely been upon these waves, and the records of his boasted art were not found in these deserts. I viewed myself as a drop in the vast ocean of existence, and shrunk from the contemplation of human nothingness. Thoughts like these flitted through my mind, till they were lost in dreaming indis-tinctness. The glittering forehead of the sun was just visible above the waves when I awoke. The wind being fair, the sails were soon spread, and our vessel passed through the waters with a rapid and exhilarating motion. Various accounts had reached us with regard to the New England planta-tions. The friends of the London company had represented it as a second Canaan; while Mr. Lyford, and other discontented members of the Plymouth church, spoke of it as bleak and sterile,—the scene of tu-multuous faction, and domineering zeal. During our voyage I had endeav-ored to balance these contradictory reports, and to prepare my mind for whatever the result might be; but my philosophy nearly forsook me when I saw our captain point to six miserable hovels, and proclaim that they constituted the whole settlement of Naumkeak. The scene altogether was

7

far worse than my imagination had ever conceived. Among those who came down to the shore to meet us, there were but one or two who seemed like Englishmen. The remainder, sickly and half starved, presented a pitiful contrast to the vigorous and wondering savages who stood among them. I dashed a tear from my eye as the remembrance of England came before me, and jumping upon the beach, I eagerly sought out my old acquaintance, Mr. Conant. He gave me a cordial welcome; but after the numerous greetings had passed, as I slowly walked by his side, I thought his once cheerful countenance had assumed an unusual expression of harshness. He had indeed met with much to depress his native buoyancy of heart. In his younger days he had aspired to the hand of a wealthy and noble lady. Young, volatile, and beautiful, at an age when life seemed all cloudless before her, she left the magnificent halls of her father, and incurred his lasting displeasure by uniting her fortunes with her humble lover. Years rolled on, and misfortune and poverty became their lot. Frustrated in his plans, thwarted by his rivals, misanthropy and gloom sunk deep down into the soul of the disappointed man. It was then the spirit of God moved on the dark, troubled waters of his mind.[1] The stream of life gushed from the fountain within him; but it received the tinge of the dark, turbid soil, through which it passed; and its clear, silent course became noisy amid the eddies of human pride. One by one all the associations connected with the religion of his fathers, were rent away, till kneeling became an abomination, and the prayers of his church a loathing. The arm of royal authority then held a firm grasp on the consciences of men, and England was no place for him who spoke against the religion of his king. So their children were called together, and the gay young beauty who had sparkled awhile in the court of king James, slept in a rude shelter on a foreign soil. Two boys, the pride of their father's heart, had fallen victims to sickness and famine; and their youngest little blooming fairy had been lately recalled from the home which her grandfather's pity had offered, to watch the declining health of her mother. But the love of woman endured through many a scene of privation and hardship, even after the character of its object was totally changed; and the rigid Calvinist, in that lone place, surrounded by his lovely family, seemed like some proud magnolia of the south, scathed and bared of its leaves, adorned with the golden flowers of the twining jessamine.

"Breakfast was on the board when I first entered, and after the usual salutations had passed, I with several of my companions, sat down to partake of it. It consisted only of roasted pumpkin, a plentiful supply of clams, and coarse cakes made of pounded maize. But unpalatable as it proved, even to me, it was cheerfully partaken by the noble inmates of that miserable hut. As for Mary, her eye sparkled as brightly, and the rich tones of her voice were as merry, as they could have been when her little aerial foot danced along the marble saloon of her grandfather. My eye rested on her, with a painful mixture of sadness and admiration, as in rapid succession she inquired about the scenes of her youth. Even the rough sailors, who were with me, softened their rude tones of voice, and paid to gentleness and beauty the involuntary tribute of respect. Whether the father felt any uneasiness as to the effect of this silent flattery on the young heart of his daughter, or whether habitual asperity had triumphed over natural affection I know not; but he replied in an angry tone, "Wherefore, Mary, do you ask about those, who bow the knee to Baal, and utter the mummery of common prayer? Methinks it is enough that the hawk has already brought hither a sprig from their tree of corruption, wherewithal to beguile your silly heart."

A blush, which seemed to partake of something more unpleasant than mere embarrassment, passed over the face of the maiden as she answered, "It surely is not strange that I should think often of places where I have enjoyed so much, and should now be tempted to ask questions concerning them, of those who have knowledge thereof."

"Aye, aye," replied the stern old man, "encamped as you are in Elim, beside palm-trees and fountains, you are no doubt looking back for the flesh-pots of Egypt.[2] You'd be willing enough to leave the little heritage which God has planted here, in order to vamp up your frail carcase in French frippery. But I would have you beware, young damsel. Wot ye not that the idle follower of Morton,[3] who was drowned in yonder bay, was inwardly given to the vain forms of the church of England?—and know ye not, that was the reason his God left him, and Satan became his convoy?"

His voice grew louder towards the close, and I saw Mrs. Conant lay her hand upon his, with a beseeching look. Her husband understood the meaning, for he smiled half reluctantly, and rejoined in a subdued tone, "You know it is enough to provoke any body who has a conscience." I was

9

at the time surprised at his sudden change of manner; but during the whole of my intercourse with him afterwards, I noticed that a spirit of tenderness toward his sick wife had survived the wreck of all his kindest feelings. It was indeed but oil upon the surface. The stream pursued its own course, and a moment after it would boil and fret at every obstruction. Willing to change the current of his thoughts, I asked whether he had tobacco.

"No," replied he; "but I believe neighbour Oldham hath some; and I will straightway send to him. But by the way, I have been thinking you'd bring us a stock. To my mind, among all king James' blunders with regard to his colonies, (and they were many, God rest his soul,) he never committed a greater, than that of discountenancing the culture of the 'base weed tobacco.'"

"We have a little on board," answered I, "but we have especial orders to see that none be planted in the colony, unless it be some small quantity for mere necessity, and for physic to preserve health, and that is to be partaken by ancient men, and none other."

My friend looked as if he disliked such tokens of restraint. He even went so far as to whisper in my ear, that the "colonies would never do well as long as their prosperity could be hindered by their papistical step-mother from the court of France; and that to be uxorious was a very virtuous vice among common folks, but a very vicious and impolitic virtue in a king."[4]

There were several sailors present who were soon to return to the mother country, and there was little safety in speaking aloud of the king's blind and foolish passion for his Romish queen. So I was fain to speak of the good wishes of my sovereign, and to lament their decrease of numbers, and their late dissatisfaction with the Plymouth elders.

"I have little to say about our troubles," replied Mr. Conant; "but as for numbers, the besom[5] of disease and famine hath been among us, and we are now as an olive tree 'with two or three berries in the top of the uppermost bough, four or five in the outmost fruitful branches thereof.' The Lord's will be done. He hath begun his work, and he will finish it. But it grieveth me to see the strange slips which are set upon our pleasant plants; and when I think thereof, I marvel not that they wither."[6]

"I have heard that Mr. Brown and his brother have been among you some weeks," said I,—"forasmuch as they are staunch Episcopalians, you may refer to them."

"Whom should I mean," rejoined he, "but the two men who like Nabab and Abihu have offered strange incense to the Lord, which he commanded them not? Verily, in due time he will send forth his fire and destroy them from the face of the earth." [7]

As I saw the tears start in Mary's eyes, I felt a vague suspicion that the conversation was, in some way or other, painful to her; and I perceived that the entrance of Mr. Oldham with his tobacco was a relief to her.

"Ah," said the jocular old man, "it's a discrepant way of doing business, to put a neighbour's paw into the fire, instead of helping one's self. Here's Good-man Conant would fain have a fair name on 'tother side the water; but after all, he hath much likeness to Rachel of old, only he keepeth the images in another's tent. But come, let's fill a pipe and talk of bye-past times."

All that I could relate concerning our godly brethren in Europe, was amply repaid by Mr. Oldham's humorous description of his own wanderings, mistakes, and sufferings. I had heard that he would speak of his own disgraces with the most shameless effrontery, and laugh at them more loudly than any other man; and I knew that many pious men had doubted the vitality of his religion, and had felt themselves darkened by intercourse with him;—but although I was shocked at the blasphemous lightness of his speech, I could hardly refrain from countenancing his ludicrous expressions and gestures by a smile.

"I can give you no idea of that gauntlet at Plymouth," said he, "when I passed through a band as long as the laws of the Levites, and every man gave me a tug with the butt of his musket. But after all you may think, it was a season of comfortable outpouring. Two passages of Scripture came to my mind, and I was gifted with great light thereupon. David hath it, 'By thee have I passed through a troop;' [8]—and Amos speaketh at a time when, 'If a man fled from a lion, a bear met him; and if he laid his hand upon the wall, a serpent bit him.' [9] Well, it was much the same with me: but as I told you, it was a time of great light, though it was nothing like the first dawning. I'll tell you how that was. I was sitting thus, with my mug of flip [10] before me, and one hand upon each knee, looking straight into the fire, when suddenly I bethought that I was like that smoking brand, with none to pluck it from the burning. So I took a draught of the good stuff, and all at once a light streamed around me, ten times brighter than the earl of Warwick's big lamp."

"Hush," said Mr. Conant. "I cannot have you profane the mysteries of godliness after this fashion. You may mean well,—God grant that you say it not in a spirit of devilish mirth, but forasmuch as you are in my house, I would beg of you to forbear such discourse."

I willingly omit the altercation which followed, which is given at full length in the manuscript; and I likewise pass over the detailed business of the day, such as the unlading of vessels, the delivery of letters, &c. &c., and lastly the theological discussions of the evening.

After much holy and edifying discourse, continues the narration, the family had all retired to rest. But notwithstanding the fatigues of the day, my conflicting feelings would not suffer me to sleep. At length, wearied with the effort, I arose from the bed of straw, and cautiously lifting the wooden latch, I stepped into the open air. As I stood gazing on the reflection of the moon, which reposed in broken radiance on the bay beyond, I tried to think soberly of the difficulties to which I and my oppressed brethren were exposed, and to decide how far I could conscientiously purchase peace and prosperity by conforming to mummeries which my soul detested. Human weakness prompted me to return, and again, when I had most decidedly concluded to stay in New England, the childish witchery of Mary Conant would pass before me, and I felt that the balance was weighed down by earthly motives. I looked out upon the surrounding scenery, and its purity and stillness were a reproach upon my inward warfare. The little cleared spot upon which I was placed, was every where surrounded by dark forests, through which the distant water was here and there gleaming, like the fitful flashes of reason in a disordered mind; and the trees stood forth in all the beauty of that month which the Indians call the "moon of flowers." By degrees the tranquil beauty of the scene, and the mysterious effect of the heavenly host performing their silent march in the far-off wilderness of light, called up the spirit of devotion within me;—and at that moment, forgetful of forms, I knelt to pray that my heart might be kept from the snares of the world.

A shadow was one moment cast across the bright moonlight; and a slender figure flitted by the corner of the house. All that I had heard of visitants from other worlds fell coldly on my heart. For a while, I was afraid to ascertain the cause of my fear; but after the person had proceeded a few hesitating steps, she paused and looked back, as if apprehensive of danger. The rays of the full moon rested on her face, and I at once perceived that it was Mary Conant. Had my first fears been realized, I know not that I should have felt more surprise. Among all my conjectures, I could not possibly imagine for what purpose she could be making an excursion at that lonely hour of the night. I remembered the hint, which her father had given, concerning the beguilement of her silly heart, and I could not but suspect that this walk was, in some way or other, connected with the young Episcopalian. Whatever was her project, she seemed half fearful of performing it; for she cast a keen, searching glance behind, and a long, fearful look, at the woods beneath, before she plunged into the thicket. After a moment's consideration, I resolved to follow her, and stepping from behind the tree which had afforded me concealment, I cautiously proceeded along the path which she had taken. She had stopped near a small brook, and when I first discovered her, she had stooped beside it, and taking a knife from her pocket, she opened a vein in her little arm, and dipping a feather in the blood, wrote something on a piece of white cloth, which was spread before her. She rose with a face pale as marble, and looking round timidly, she muttered a few words too low to meet my ear; then taking a stick and marking out a large circle on the margin of the stream, she stept into the magic ring, walked round three times with measured tread, then carefully retraced her steps backward, speaking all the while in a distinct but trembling voice. The following were the only words I could hear,

> Whoever's to claim a husband's power,
> Come to me in the moonlight hour.

And again,—

> Whoe'er my bridegroom is to be,
> Step in the circle after me.

She looked round anxiously as she completed the ceremony; and I almost echoed her involuntary shriek of terror, when I saw a young Indian spring forward into the centre.

"What for makes you afraid of Hobomok," said the savage, who seemed scarcely less surprised than herself.

"Wherefore did you come hither," replied the maiden, after the tones of his voice had convinced her that he was real flesh and blood.

"Hobomok much late has been out to watch the deer tracks," answered the Indian; "and he came through the hollow, that he might make the Manitto Asseinah* green as the oak tree."

As he spoke this he threw a large bough upon the heap of rocks to which he had pointed, and looking up to the moon, he uttered something in the Indian tongue, which seemed like a short incantation or prayer. Just as he turned to follow Mary, who was retreating from the woods, a third person made his appearance, in whom I thought I recognized young Brown, specified by Mr. Conant as the strange slip on their pleasant plants. Mary eagerly caught his arm, and seemed glad amid her terror and agitation, to seek the shelter of his offered protection. A few friendly words of recognition passed between him and the savage, and the young couple proceeded homewards. A mixed feeling of diffidence and delicacy, had induced me to remain concealed from Mary while I watched over her safety; and the same feeling prompted me to continue where I was until she and her favoured lover were far out of sight and hearing. Hobomok looked after them with a mournful expression of countenance, as he said, "Wonder what for be here alone when the moon gone far away toward the Iroquois. What for squaw no love like white woman." He stood silent for a short time, and then, taking a large knife from his belt, he cut down two young boughs from the adjoining trees, and threw them, one after another, on the sacrifice heap of his God, as he muttered, "Three times much winnit Abbamocho† said; three times me do."

It seemed but an instant after, that the sound of his heavy tread was lost in the distance.

*Signifying Spirit Rocks. It was considered an act of devotion among the Indians to throw a stick or stone upon them as they passed. [Child's note, as are subsequent footnotes throughout *Hobomok*.]

† Meaning "very good devil," a term they generally applied to those prophets or priests who had effected any great cures.

CHAPTER II

In court or hamlet, hut or grove,
Where woman is, there still is love.
Whate'er their nation, form, or feature,
Woman's the same provoking creature.
—M. S.

A LETTER from Governor Craddock to Governor Endicott, which had reached them the April before, had given them timely notice of the intended recruits; in which were the following orders. "The desire of the London Company is that you doe endeavour to gett convenient houseings for the cattell against they doe come; and withal we doe desire whatever bever or fishe can be gotten readie. There hath nott bine a tyme for sale of tymber, these twoe seven years, like unto the present; therefore pittie the shipps should come backe emptye. I wish alsoe that there bee some sassafras and sassaparilla sent us, alsoe goode store of shoemacke, silke grasse, and aught else that may bee useful for dyinge or physicke."

To comply with these various orders, necessarily produced a good deal of hurry and bustle in the infant settlement; and for a long while the sound of the axe was busy and strong among them. And when at length the expected vessels did arrive, and their fine flock of horses, cows, sheep, and goats were well provided for, there was still enough to employ the kind-hearted and healthy, in administering comfort and support to those who had landed among them, weary and sick unto death. My ancestor had already witnessed many of his companions depart this life, exulting that though they were absent from kindred and friends, they were going far beyond the power and cruelty of prelates. Wearied with the wretchedness of the scene, on the 28th of June he departed from Naumkeak, which had now taken the name of Salem, in memory of the peaceful asylum which it

15

afforded the fugitives. Whether the suspicion of Mary's attachment had any thing to do with the old bachelor's final arrangements, he saith not; but when he again visited America, although he brought a young wife with him, I find he has not failed to speak of her wayward fate with frequent and deep-toned interest.

These brief and scattered hints have now become almost illegible from their age and uncouth spelling, and it was with difficulty I extracted from them materials for the following story.———In a situation so remote, and circumscribed, it may well be supposed that the arrival or departure of a vessel was considered as an affair of great importance, and felt through every fibre of the community. On the occasion I have just referred to, most of the white people from the neighbouring settlements had collected on the beach, together with an almost equal number of the dark children of the forest. Mary had sprung upon a jutting rock, and her sylph-like figure afforded a fine contrast to the decaying elegance of her mother, who was leaning on her arm, the cheerful countenance of Mr. Oldham's buxom daughter, and the tall, athletic form of Hobomok, who stood by her side, resting his healthy cheek upon the hand which supported his bow. By them, and all the motley group around them, the departure of the English vessel was viewed with keen, though varied emotion. The uniform gloom of Mr. Conant's countenance received for one moment a deeper tinge. It was but a passing shadow of human weakness, quickly succeeded by a flush of conscious exultation. His wife, who had left a path all blooming with roses and verdure, and cheerfully followed his rugged and solitary track, pressed back the ready tears, as the remembrance of England came hurrying on her heart. Mary's eyes overflowed with the intense, unrestrained gush of youthful feeling. But amid all the painful associations of that moment, the deep interest displayed by my ancestor did not pass unnoticed; and surely the vanity which prompted a lingering look of kindness, might be forgiven, in one growing up in almost unheeded loveliness. "Farewell," said she, as she placed a letter in his hand. "Give this to my grandfather; and many, many kind wishes to good old England."

"Yes," interrupted her father, "many kind wishes to the godly remnant who are among them. And since Naumkeak has become old enough to receive a christian name, say ye to them that 'in Salem is his tabernacle, and his dwelling-place in Zion. Here he will break the arrows of the bow, the shield, the sword, and the battle.'¹ But to them who are yet given to the pride of prelacy, and the abomination of common prayer, and likewise to them who are weather-waft up and down with every eddying wind of every new doctrine, say ye to them, that their damnation sleepeth not, and the mist of darkness is reserved for them forever, being of old ordained to condemnation."²

This speech was fiercely answered by a dark, lowering looking savage, who stood among the crowd.

"That is Corbitant," said Mary,—"What is it that he says?"

"Your father say Indian arrow be broken at Naumkeak," replied Hobomok,—"Corbitant say the feather be first red with white man's blood."

He would have added more, but the vessels were now sweeping past the rock on which they stood, and every eye was fixed on their motion. Many a hearty salutation, and blunt compliment were paid to Sally Oldham, and many a hat was waved in respectful adieu to Mrs. Conant and her daughter. The loud response which the sailors gave to the kind farewells of their friends on shore, was soon lost in the distance, and one by one the people slowly dispersed. Mrs. Conant took the arm of her husband, and Mary lingered far behind, in hopes of obtaining a conference with Sally Oldham. But one Mr. Thomas Graves seemed to have been deeply smitten with the comely countenance of the latter damsel; and never for a moment doubting that the fascination was reciprocal, he became somewhat obtrusively officious. It was singular to observe the difference of deportment between him and the Indian. Whenever Hobomok gazed upon Mary, it was with an expression in which reverence was strikingly predominant. And now, with more than his usual taciturnity, he walked at a short distance before them, and eagerly pointed with his bow, when it was necessary to obviate any little difficulties in their path. But he from the Isle of Wight, seemed resolved that one of the young ladies should be aware of the presence of a noisy admirer, and with abundance of stammering awkwardness, he began, "You are Mr. Oldham's daughter, I think?"

"I have been told so, sir," replied the mischievous girl.

"The world is dark and dismal enough in any place," continued the man of a wo-begone countenance,—"more especially when we think of the regiments of sin which are marching up and down in its borders; but I should think it would be ten times darker to a well-favored young woman, here in this wilderness."

"If you mean me," answered the maiden, "I pass my time merry enough, in the long run; but there is no danger of our forgetting the dolors while we have your visage amongst us."

"I sha'nt be called to give an account of my looks," replied the offended suitor, "inasmuch as God made them in such form and likeness as pleased him. But I perceive you have no savor of godliness about you, and are clean carried away by the crackling thorns of worldly mirth."[3]

"My friend is like Rachel of old," interrupted her smiling companion. "She feedeth her cattle and draweth them water, and waiteth for some Jacob to journey hither."

"And what would you say, damsel, if he were at your very door," rejoined Mr. Graves, with an uncouth distension of his jaws, which was doubtless meant for one of love's gentle, insinuating smiles. "And when Jacob knew Rachel he kissed her," continued he, as he courageously put his arm round her neck, to suit his action to the words.

"I have had enough of that from the sanctified Mr. Lyford," said the resolute maiden, as she gave him a blow, which occasioned a sudden and involuntary retreat.

"Well done, Sally," said the hoarse voice of her father, who just then stept from among the trees, half choked with laughter, and for a moment forgetful of the decorum which he usually maintained in her presence. "Why, fellow, thou'rt smitten indeed; but it ill beseemeth thee to put on a rueful face at this disaster. The damsel is not worth the tears, which an onion draweth forth."

Sally gladly left her discomfited lover to recover himself as he could, and bidding a hasty good-morning to Hobomok, as he stood laughing and muttering to himself, she followed Mary, who with an air of girlish confidence had beckoned her into a narrow footpath which led through the woods. For a few moments the girls united in almost convulsive fits of laughter.

"Did you ever see such a fellow?" said Sally. "Every day since they landed, he has been at my elbow, trying to make love by stammering and stuttering about the crackling thorns of worldly mirth; and I verily think he believes that I have been greatly delighted therewith. A plague on all

such sanctified looking folks. There was Mr. Lyford, (I don't care if he was
a minister) he was always talking about faith and righteousness, and the
falling-off of the Plymouth elders, and yet many a sly look and word he'd
give me, when his good-woman was out of the way. I marvel that fools can
always find utterance, inasmuch as some men of sense are so dumb."

"Men of sense will speak all in good time, if you will wait patiently,"
answered Mary. "But you don't know how glad I am that it happened to be
your father, instead of mine, who saw you strike Mr. Graves."

"So am I," replied her companion. "Though he is your father, to my
thinking he is over fond of keeping folks in a straight jacket; and I'm sure
our belt is likely to be buckled tight enough by the great folks there in
London. In my poor judgment it is bad enough that we've come over into
this wilderness to find elbow room for our consciences, without being told
how long a time we may have to stop and breathe in. Every bout I knit in
my stocking is to be set down in black and white, and sent over to the
London Company[4] forsooth. I suppose by and by the drops we drink and
the mouthfuls we eat must be counted, and their number sent thither."

"I am sure," replied Mary, "when you remember how many Indians
we have lately met, whom Morton's unthinking wickedness has armed
with powder and firelocks, you will be glad that we have three hundred
more defenders around us, whatever price we may pay therefor. Indeed
Sally, I'm weary of this wilderness life. My heart yearns for England, and
had it not been for my good mother, I would gladly have left Naumkeak
to-day."

"I can't but admire ye've been content so long, Miss Mary, considering what ye left behind you. If you'd staid there, who knows but you might
have been Lady Lincoln? But as for this purlieu of creation, I know of no
chance a body has for a husband, without they pick up some stray Narraganset, or wandering Tarateen."

"O, don't name such a thing," said Mary, shuddering.

"Why, what makes you take me in earnest?" answered Sally. "But
perhaps since there are so many young folks to pick and choose among,
you'll be weary of my crackling mirth, as that stupid Graves calls it."

"No, Sally, these new comers won't make me forget how kind you
have always been in sickness and health; but, to tell you the truth, there is
something troubles me—and if you'll promise not to tell of it, I'll tell you."

"O, I'll promise that, and keep it too. If I was disposed to tell your secrets, I don't know any body but owls and bats I should tell them to."

"Well then, you must know, the other night I did a wicked thing. It frightens me to think thereof. You know the trick I told you about? Well, a few weeks ago, I tried it; and just as I was saying over the verses the third time, Hobomok, the Indian, jumped into the circle."

"Hobomok, the Indian!"

"Yes;—and I screamed when I saw him."

"I believe so indeed. But was it he, real flesh and blood?"

"It was he himself; though I thought at first, it must be his ghost?"

"But how came he there, at that time of night?"

"That's more than I can tell. He said he came to throw a bow on the sacrifice heap, down in Endicott's hollow; but I don't know what should put it into his head just at that time. What do you suppose did?"

"I'm sure I don't know, Mary. I think it is an awful wicked thing to try these tricks. There's no telling what may come of asking the devil's assistance. He is an acquaintance not so easily shook off when you've once spoke with him, to my certain knowledge. My father says he's no doubt the Lord has given Beelzebub power to choose many a damsel's husband, to recompense her for such like wickedness. I'm sure I have been curious enough to know, but I never dared to speak to Satan about the matter."

"I believe it is a sin to be repented of; but what could I do? Father won't suffer me to see Charles any where, if he can help it; and if I dared to be disobedient to him, I wouldn't do it while my poor mother was alive, for I know it would break her heart. But there are two things more about this affair which puzzle me. Just as I came out of the hollow, I met Charles. He said he dreamed I was in danger there, and he could not help coming to see whether I was there or not. So I told him how foolish I had been, and he laughed, and said he should be my husband after all. But the strangest thing of all, is, that Englishman you saw me give a letter to, to-day, whispered in my ear never to try a trick again, for fear worse should come of it. I wonder how he knew any thing concerning it?"

"Likely as not, he followed you. Or may be Hobomok told him. But I am glad Mr. Brown dreamed about it. After all, I guess he is to be the one; and Hobomok only came that way after some stray fox or squirrel he caught sight of."

"I don't know how it was," replied Mary, with a deep sigh. "I suppose I must submit to whatever is fore-ordained for me. Folks who have the least to do with love are the best off. The longer you keep as free from it as you are now, the happier you'll be."

"May be you don't know how free that is," rejoined Sally. "If you had half an eye for other folks' affairs, you would remember something about a young man in Plymouth who used to help me milk my cows, inasmuch as you have often heard me speak of him. Do you know I spoke to him on the beach this morning? I should have had a good opportunity to have seen him again, if it had not been for that everlasting fellow, talking about 'crackling thorns;' I would not care an' he had one of them in his tongue. How-somever, if I guess right concerning Mr. Collier, he did'nt come up to see the cattle. But I can't stop to say any more, for the cows an't milked yet; and now these new orders have come from London, and there are so many sick folks from the vessels, we shall have enough to do. So, good bye," said the roguish damsel, as she sprung over the log inclosure, into her father's farm-yard.

CHAPTER III

I would not wish
Any companion in the world but you;
Nor can imagination form a shape,
Beside yourself, to like of.

— *Tempest*

NOTWITHSTANDING her increase of avocations, and the many wearisome nights she had spent in tending the sick who had come among them, there was no one more heartily rejoiced at the new order of things than Sally Oldham, whom I find mentioned in the manuscript as "a promp and jolly damsell, much given to lightnesse of speeche, but withal virtuous." The merry maiden, amid all the labours and privations necessarily attendant upon their lonely situation at Plymouth, had found means to put on the airs of rustic coquetry with considerable success; and therefore she had felt no little regret when her father's passionate and unjustifiable conduct toward the ruling elders, had subjected him to the shameful punishment referred to in the first chapter, and driven his family from their comparatively comfortable home. Her only consolation during this period was in recounting to Mary the numerous acts of gallantry she had received from her Plymouth lovers. The young man whom she had seen upon the beach, on the morning of the 28th, had a kinder remembrance than all his competitors; and when she heard that he had walked from Plymouth, with Hobomok for his guide, in the true spirit of female vanity, she judged that nothing but her own pretty face was the object of his journey. Still it seemed she had some fears about his diffidence, for when she had taken her milking-pail and quietly seated herself beside the miserable pile of logs and boughs, which she dignified with the name of a cowhouse, she muttered to herself, "I wish Collier was a little easier to take a hint." Her cogitations

22

were interrupted by a well known voice, which had become associated in Sally's mind with nought but "the crackling of thorns." "What brought you hither, Mr. Graves?" inquired the maiden.

"I thought," replied he, as he stood scratching his head with one hand, and holding out the other in token of amity, "I thought, may be, you'd repent your rashness this morning, inasmuch as husbands don't grow on every tree in these deserts."

Nothwithstanding this cogent argument, well backed with humble gestures, the offered peace was rejected; and his clammy hand remained awkwardly upraised in the air, like the quivering claw of a dying lobster.

"I tell you sir," rejoined the angry damsel, "that I am weary of your unsavory discourse; and if husbands like you, grew by hundreds on the lowest boughs of the trees, they might stay there till doomsday before I'd stop to pluck 'em therefrom."

"But you'll let me take the milk across for you," continued the persevering suitor, as she stept upon a narrow board that was laid across a deep ditch. Sally, in the wickedness of her heart, held out the pail to him; but just as he was in the act of taking it, she managed by a gentle motion, to place him ancle-deep in the mud below; then turning round for an instant, with a loud and provoking laugh, she soon disappeared.

As Mr. Graves rose, and struck off the mud from his clothes, he murmured, "It is plain she is given over to a reprobate mind;" and it was noticed he never afterwards darkened Mr. Oldham's dwelling.

To Sally the day seemed to pass tardily away, for she had predicted, that the evening would bring a visit from Mr. Collier; and accordingly the manuscript states, that "the curtains of nighte were but halfe shut, when he seated himselfe beside Mr. Oldham, who was turning down many a dropp of the bottell, and burning tobacco with all the ease he could, discoursing between whiles of the dolorous beginning of the settlement, when their cups of beer ran as small as water in a sandie landie, and they were forced to lengthene out their own foode with acorns; and anon talking of the greate progress they would make with their fellowe labourers, now the summer sun had changed the earth's white-furred gowne into a green mantell."

"I must say," observed the young man, "that it is a bosom-breaking thing to me, when I think the gulf atween us and old England is too wide to leap over with a lope-staff.[1] I am the last who would put my hand to the plough, and then look back; but I must say, could I have cast up, in the beginning, what this wilderness work would have cost us, I should have been staggered much, and very hardly have set sail."

"Why, to my thinking, Mr. Collier," replied Oldham, "England is no place now-a-days for christian folks to live within. They talk about their reformed church, but I tell you their bishops, their deans, and their deacons, are all whelps from the Roman litter; and tame 'em as you can, the nature of the beast will shew itself. It is a sad pity that king Charles (I mean no disrespect to his majesty) should suffer those black coats from the ninneversities to get upon his royal back—I trow they'll ride him to destruction. But, as I was saying, England is full of malignant enemies to the true faith; and after all, a body can as pithily practise the two great precepts of the gospel in this, as well as in any other place; which precepts I take to be mortification and sanctification."

"Nobody can doubt there is room enough to practise the first, father," interrupted Sally, who had all along been quietly knitting in the corner, and who had begun to be weary of such sober discourse.

"You talk like a prating idiot, as you are," replied her father, furiously. "What with your own hankering after French gew-gaws, and the grand stories of your Moabitish companion,[2] you have your head clean turned from sound sense and sober godliness."

"You know, Goodman," rejoined his wife, "that howsomever gracious and obedient our children may be, there have been no small hardships during our sojourning here, both for their young hearts and limbs too. Besides, Sally is included in the covenant with her parents,[3] and to my mind, no member of Christ's body should be wrested from his church by harsh words."

"You utter the sayings of a foolish woman," answered her angry spouse. "I'm far from being clear whether the covenant we entered into is binding. Them ruling elders there at Plymouth, brought an abundance of pragmatical zeal, and rigid separation from the Netherlands. They've clapped a vizor on their own traditions, and placed them cheek-by-jowl with revealed truth; and many an honest man will be puzzled to distinguish 'em therefrom. And still more am I in the dark whether this stray imp, laughing with every idle fellow she meets, (the better for her that she meets few of them)"—Just at that moment, recollecting the discomfiture of Mr. Graves, his natural propensity to fun overcame his resentment, and he placed both his hands upon his sides, and burst into a broad laugh. The look of surprise which his wife and Mr. Collier glanced towards him, and the drollery which was peeping out of the corners of Sally's mouth, recalled him to decorum; and looking towards his daughter with an expression that seemed to say, "You'd no right to understand me," he passed his hand over his face and resumed, "I say, I am much in the dark whether she be implied in the covenant with us. It is not every child of a righteous man who is among the elect; nor is the offspring of the wicked always fore-ordained to damnation. If there be a good child in Jeroboam's family, he is specified; and if there be a cursed Ham among the children of Noah, he hath his brand."[4]

"Well, Goodman Oldham," interrupted his guest, "it is not for us to tell who is among the elect, and who not, forasmuch as we cannot enter into the counsels of the Most High. And surely when the hearts of stout men grow faint in this enterprise, we need not marvel that women, and young women too, should betimes think of their hardships, and complain thereof. Jacob was regardful of the weakness of the women and little ones of his land."

"I'm sure I never murmured when worst came to worst," said Sally, as she glanced an eye of moist gratitude on her kind advocate.

"I tell you," said Mr. Oldham, without noticing her interruption, "you don't know as much about these weaker vessels as I do; and mayhap you feel concerning them as I used to in by-gone times. But I tell you they are the source of every evil that ever came into the world. I don't refer in special manner to that great tree of sin planted by Eve; but I say they are the individual cause of every branch and bud from that day downwards. I charge you enter not into their path, for destruction láyeth wait therein."

"You are one of the last men who should say so," answered his companion, as he looked towards his care-worn and uncomplaining wife.

"She is as good as any of her kind, to be sure," said the rigid old man, as he took his tobacco from his mouth, and drank a hearty draught of cider from the stone mug; then replacing his tobacco, and drawing his sleeve across his mouth, he passed the beverage to Mr. Collier, as he said, "It is a long time since I have tasted the like of this. It's as good as was ever tipped over the tongue of king Charles, God help him, and Satan leave off helping the queen and his bishops. I'd fain stay and argue with you a bit, Mr. Collier, inasmuch as I've been told you are falling into some Antinomian notions; but I must go up to Governor Endicott's awhile, to see how the cattle are to be divided atween us; and I must stop to see a few of the poor sick souls about us. So if you want, you can draw more upon the cider, and may be my good woman will give you a bit of bread and cheese. We have plenty of provisions since the ships were sent hither, the Lord be thanked." So saying, the old man took down his hat from the wooden peg on which it always hung, and closed the door after him.

"Mr. Oldham is a strange talking man," observed his wife; "but he barks worse than he bites."

"I know his ways," answered Mr. Collier. "It is a pity he strikes fire so quick; but it proveth there is good metal in him. And now, Sally, I have a present for you," continued he, as he placed a letter in her hand, which she received with blushing curiosity, and read as follows:

"Deere Maidene,

"This comes to reminde you of one you sometime knew at Plimouth. One to whome the remembrance of your comely face and gratious behaviour, hath proved a very sweete savour. Many times I have thought to write to you, and straightnesse of time only hath prevented. There is much to doe at this seasone, and wee have reason to rejoyce, though with fier and trembling, that we have wherewithal to worke.

"Forasmuch as it is harde to saye unto a damsell, wilt thou bee my wife? I have chosene the rather to place it upon pure white paper, the embleme of your hearte. Which if you will pleese soe to answer, you will much oblige your dutyfull servante. For as Jacob loved Rachelle, and toyled many yeers for her, so loveth
        Your trew freynde,

JAMES HOPKINS."

Mrs. Oldham, with a slight tincture of the modern policy of mothers, had gone out to "neighbour Conant's," when Sally first began to read the foregoing; and luckily she was not there to witness the vexed and disappointed looks of her daughter.

"I suppose I know the writer," said Mr. Collier, smiling as she laid down the paper, "What answer shall I carry thereto?"

"It is from that screech-owl of a Hopkins, who used to be forever bawling Old Hundred in my ears," replied the maiden; "and you may say to him that I have much more kindness for his sheep than for him."

"Peradventure you are in sport," said her astonished visitor. "You'll find few men in this wilderness of more respectability than my good friend Hopkins."

"Well, if he can find a Rachel, assuredly I have no objection to his toiling for her; but if I should be very near her, I should verily whisper in her ear to give him twice a fourteen years' tug." [5]

"So you are really going to break poor James' heart?" inquired her friend, after a moment's pause.

"If so be there is such a thing as a heart in his big carcase of clay," rejoined the maiden, "I'm willing it should be shattered a bit."

"Poor fellow, what will he think of all this?" inquired the young man, thoughtfully.

"There's divers things he might think," answered the damsel, who began to be out of patience with his stupid modesty. "He might think, if he wanted a wife again, that she was worth the trouble of coming after; or peradventure he can send to king James' plantation and buy one, for a hundred pounds of tobacco. Think you that Isaac would have had good speed with the daughter of Bethuel, with all his jewels of silver and gold, if he had sent by so clever a messenger as yourself, John?" [6]

If one might judge from the expression of the young man's face, he did at length begin to have a faint perception of the truth. An awkward silence followed, till Sally, struck with the ludicrous situation of them both, burst into her usual laugh. "I tell you what, Mr. Collier," said she, "to my thinking, you are the stupidest fellow I ever looked upon; and when you set out upon other men's business, I advise you to do it faithfully, but nevertheless to keep an eye upon your own."

The young man rested one hand upon his knee, turned his bright blue eyes and sun-burnt face towards her, and seemed lost in utter bewilderment.

"But,—hem—but what can I do?" said he.

"I know what you *can* do; but what you *will* do, is of your own choosing. I have heretofore told you what to say to Hopkins; and I now tell you, John Collier, if you had sent by him, instead of he by you, and my father had said to me, 'wilt thou go unto this man?' I should verily have said, 'I will go.'"[7]

"And I," rejoined the Plymouth messenger, smiling as he rose and laid his hand upon her shoulder, "I would assuredly have come out to meet thee, and bring thee into my tent. But what perplexes me most is, how I am to account for this to my friend Hopkins and the church."

"You may tell James," replied she, "that you was blind, till I would put eyes into your head; and as for the church, it is enough for them to square and clip our consciences without putting a wedge atwixt folk's hearts."

"It is not well to give away to lightness of speech in speaking of the dignities of the church," observed her lover, "though I know well you mean no harm."

• What farther passed between the young people, before the return of the family, is not specified in the manuscript; but an asterisk points to the bottom of the page, where it saith that "the matteer was made knowne to her parents, wherewithall they were welle pleased; more especially as they founde he was nott given to the dreadfull herese of the Antinomians."

~ Mr. and Mrs. Oldham returned shortly, at least it seemed so to those they had left behind. The old man replaced his hat upon its accustomed peg, drew to the fire his large oaken chair, the pride and ornament of his house, and, after a few discontented remarks about the intended division of the cattle, he took down the big Bible from the shelf, which had been nailed up on purpose for its reception, and read in a loud monotonous tone the 9th chapter of Romans. The prayer which followed was in somewhat too harsh and austere a tone for the voice [of] christian entreaty, but in that rude place it was impressive in its solemn simplicity. The family devotions were concluded with the favourite tune of the great Reformer, in which the clear, rich, native melody of the daughter, contrasted finely with the deep, heavy bass of the father. Soon after, Sally and her mother closed the door which separated their humble little apartment from the outer room, leaving Mr. Oldham and his visitor to discourse about the Antinomians, Anabaptists, and sundry other sects, which even at that early period began to trouble the Seceding Church.

CHAPTER IV

Know ye the famous Indian race?
How their light form springs, in strength and grace,
Like the pine on their native mountain side,
That will not bow in its deathless pride;
Whose rugged limbs of stubborn tone,
No plexuous power of art will own,
But bend to Heaven's red bolt alone!
　　—*Yamoyden*

JACOB'S HEART could not have swelled with more exultation, when he journeyed from Padan-aram with his two bands,[1] than was evinced by our forefathers, when they exhibited their newly arrived riches to the wondering natives. As for the poor, unlettered Indians, it exceeded their comprehension how buffaloes, as they termed them, could be led about by the horns, and be compelled to stand or move at the command of men; and they could arrive at no other conclusion than that the English were the favorite children of the Great Spirit, and that he had taught them words to speak to them. To these, and similar impressions, may be ascribed the astonishing influence of the whites over these untutored people. That the various tribes did not rise in their savage majesty, and crush the daring few who had intruded upon their possessions, is indeed a wonderful exemplification of the superiority of intellect over mere brutal force. At the period of which we speak, the thoughtless and dissipated Morton, whom we find mentioned so frequently in our early history, had done much to diminish their reverence for the English. Partly from avarice, and partly from revenge of Governor Endicott's spirited proceedings against his company at Merry Mount, he had sold them rifles, and taught them to take a steady and quick-sighted aim; so that they now boasted they could speak thunder and spit fire as well as the white man. Of late, too, their councils became dark and contentious, for their princes began to fear encroachments upon their dominions, and their prophets were troubled with rumors of a strange God. The Pequods looked with hatred upon the English, as an obstacle to their plan of universal dominion; the Narragansets stood trembling between the increasing power of their new neighbours, and the haughty threats of their enemies; some of the discontented sachems of Mount Haup had broken out in open rebellion; and even the firm faith of Massasoit himself had, at times, been doubted. In such a state of things, embassies and presents were frequently necessary to support the staggering friendship of the well disposed tribes. Accordingly, the second day after his arrival from Plymouth, Hobomok proceeded to Saugus, carrying presents from the English, and a message from Massasoit to Sagamore John. At this wigwam he met Corbitant,[2] a stubborn enemy to the Europeans, and all who favored them. He had been among the Pequods of late, and was exasperated beyond measure that he had in vain offered their war-belt (in token of alliance against the English) to Miantonimo,[3] the great sachem of the Narragansets. Possessed of a mind more penetrating, and a temper even more implacable than most of his brethren, his prophetic eye foresaw the destruction of his countrymen, and from his inmost soul he hated the usurpers. Besides, there was a personal hostility between him and Hobomok concerning an affair of love, in which Corbitant thought one of his kindred had been wronged and insulted; and more than once they had sought each other's life. At the moment Hobomok entered, he was engaged in eager conversation with Sagamore John, concerning his connexion with the English, and scarcely was seated, ere he exclaimed,

"Shame on you, Hobomok! The wolf devours not its own; but Hobomok wears the war-belt of Owanux,* and counts his beaver for the white man's squaw. Oh cursed Owanux! The buffalo will die of the bite of a wasp, and no warrior will pluck out his sting. Oh cursed Owanux! And yet Miantonimo buckles on their war belt, and Massasoit says, their pipe smokes well. Look to the east, where the sun rises among the Taratines;[4] to the west, where he sets among the valiant Pequods: then look to the south, among the cowardly Narragansets, and the tribes of Massasoit, thick as the trees of his forests; then look far to the north, where the Great Spirit lifts

* Englishmen.

his hatchet* high above the head of the Nipnet![5] And say, are not the red men like the stars in the sky, or the pebbles in the ocean? But a few sleeps more, let Owanux suck the blood of the Indian, where be the red man then? Look for yesterday's tide, for last year's blossoms, and the rainbow that has hid itself in the clouds! Look for the flame that has died away, for the ice that's melted, and for the snow that lights on the waterfall! Among them you will find the children of the Great Spirit. Yes, they will soon be as an arrow that is lost in its flight, and as the song of a bird flown by."

This was uttered with a smile of bitter irony, and in a tone so loud and fierce, that every eye was fixed on the speaker. Sagamore John laid down his pipe to listen; his squaw shook her head mournfully as he uttered his predictions; and his sons stood gazing upon Corbitant, till the fire flashed from their young eyes, and their knives were half drawn from the belt. Even Hobomok, whose loves and hates had become identified with the English, admired the eloquence of his enemy, and made a melancholy pause ere he answered, "Corbitant knows well that the arm of Hobomok is not weak, nor his cheek pale in time of battle; but if the quiver of the Narragansets be filled against the Yengees,† know you not, that they themselves will be trodden down, like snow, in the warpath of the Pequods?"

"That's the song of the lame bird, to lead from its nest," replied Corbitant, sarcastically. "Would Hobomok weep, if the Pequod should lift his head to the clouds, and plant one foot among the Taratines, and the other far, far away among the Caddoques? Would he utter one groan, if the hatchet of Sassacus were buried deep in the brains of Pokanecket's child?[6] No! and yet Hobomok asked that the child of Pokanecket might be his squaw; but his beaver skins were not brought, and she cooked the deer for Ninigret's son.‡[7] Hobomok saves his tears for the white-faced daughter of Conant, and his blood for the arrow of Corbitant, that his kinswoman may be avenged."

Hobomok lifted his tomahawk in wrath, as his adversary uttered

---

*The constellation of the northern bear.

†The Indian term for English, from which Yankee is probably derived.

‡In an Indian courtship the young man makes a present of beaver skins, and the intended bride returns venison of her own cooking.

these insulting words. "Who dares speak of groans and tears," said he, "to him whose heart has been calm in the fight, and whose eye winked not at the glancing of arrows?"

Corbitant answered by a scornful laugh, and the hatchet would have descended on his head, had not Sagamore John stept between them, as he said, "Listen to the words of an ancient chief. The Great Spirit loves not the sacrifice of young blood, when it is shed in quarrel. Smoke the pipe of peace, my children; and I will tell you of days that are gone by, when the war-whoop of John was heard the loudest among his tribe, and his arrow brought down the deer at her swiftest speed."

To have refused to listen to the stories of an old man would have been contrary to all rules of Indian decorum; but before the fierce, young spirits composed themselves to respectful silence, a challenge of proud looks was exchanged, as Corbitant muttered, "When the big sea-bird up yonder, go back to their great land-chief, king Charles, the white squaw's father, say Indian arrow be broken at Naumkeak. Let him look to't that the wolf be not near his wigwam."

Hours passed away while the young sons sat devouring the words of their father, and even his guests seemed to have forgotten their own hatred, in the eager reverence with which they listened to him. His squaw, in the mean time, had taken her coarse, roasted cakes from the fire, and placed some cold venison before her visitors, and pointed to it with a look of pride, as she said, "The arm of my sanup[8] is old, but you see his arrow is yet swifter than the foot of the deer. May his sons bring him food in his old age."

The hospitable meal was gratefully partaken, and all John's exploits in war and hunting being told, Hobomok, having found means to transact the business for which he came, arose to depart. Corbitant, too, threw his quiver over his shoulder, and tightened his belt, as if preparing for a journey. Sagamore John, laying his hand upon his arm, whispered something in his ear, and he reluctantly resumed his seat. In the height of gratitude for some recent favor, he had promised to obey the old chief in his first request, provided it had no connexion with the English; and now that twenty minutes of his time were asked, he would gladly have given all the animals he ever caught, to be released from his promise. However, his word was unbroken; and Hobomok went forth alone. For a few moments he hesitated whether or not to go back and seek satisfaction for the insults he had received from the kinsman of his once betrothed bride. But he remembered what Corbitant had said about the Indian arrows being broken at Naumkeak, and though he did not exactly understand the import of his words, he well knew that an Indian never spoke thus, without some deep laid plan of vengeance. An undefined apprehension of danger to Mr. Conant's family passed over his heart, and after a few reluctant steps backward, he turned round hastily and walked forward, as he said, "It isn't the love of life,—but if I should be killed in these woods, who will be left to tell *her* of her danger? 'Twould be pity so young a bird should be brought down in its flight."

As he walked on in a hurried, irregular pace, love, resentment, and wounded pride, were all busy at his heart-strings. He had left Pokanecket's daughter, because he loathed the idea of marriage with her; but he never had thought, and till now he never had been told, that Mary Conant was the cause. Soon after her arrival at Plymouth, Mary had administered cordials to his sick mother, which restored her to life after the most skilful of their priests had pronounced her hopeless; and ever since that time, he had looked upon her with reverence, which almost amounted to adoration. If any dregs of human feeling were mingled with these sentiments, he at least, was not aware of it; and now that the idea was forced upon him, he rejected it, as a kind of blasphemy. With these thoughts were mixed a melancholy presentiment of the destruction of his race, and stern, deep, settled hatred of Corbitant.

As he came in sight of the seacoast, the sun was just setting behind the ledge of rocks which stretched along to his right; and the broad blue harbour of Salem lay full in his view, as tranquil as the slumbers of a young heart devoid of crime. The spring birds were warbling among the trees, or floating along so lightly, that they scarcely dipped their wing in the still surface of the water. There was something in the unruffled aspect of things, which tended to soothe the turbulence of human passion. By degrees the insults of Corbitant, the remembrance of Pokanecket's child, the clouds which imagination had seen lowering over the fate of his nation, and even the danger of his English friends, became more dim and fleeting; till at length, the spirit of devotion sat brooding over the soul of the savage. The star, which had arisen in Bethlehem, had never gleamed along his path; and the dark valley of the shadow of death had never been illuminated with the brightness of revealed truth. But though the intellect be darkened, there are rays from God's own throne, which enter into the peacefulness and purity of the affections, shedding their mild lustre on the ignorance of man.

Philosophy had never held up her shield against the sun, and then placed her dim taper in his hand, while she pointed to the "mundane soul," in which all human beings lost their identity; nor had he ever read of that city "whose streets were of gold, and her gates of pearl, in the light of which walked the nations of them which were saved;"[9] but there was within him a voice loud and distinct, which spoke to him of another world, where he should think, feel, love, even as he did now. He had never read of God, but he had heard his chariot wheels in the distant thunder, and seen his drapery in the clouds. In moods like these, thoughts which he could not grasp, would pass before him, and he would pause to wonder what they were, and whence they came. It was with such feelings that he stopped, and resting his head against a large hemlock, which lifted its proud branches high above the neighboring pines, he gazed on the stars, just visible above the horizon. He stood thus some moments, when a rustling sound broke in upon the stillness, and an arrow whizzed past him, and caught in the corner of his blanket. He turned round suddenly, and saw Corbitant advancing towards him with an uplifted hatchet.

"Ha!" said he, with his accustomed laugh of scorn, "I thought Hobomok winked not at the glancing of arrows. When did Corbitant flee to the woods, to save life, when he had been dared to the fight?"

Few words passed between them, and desperate was the struggle which ensued. For awhile it seemed doubtful who would get the victory, amid the fierceness of their savage warfare; till at length a violent blow on the temple laid Corbitant senseless on the ground.

"Love your enemy," was a maxim Hobomok had never learned, and the tomahawk was already raised above the head of his stupified victim, when the sound of voices was heard in the thicket, and springing into his former path, he pursued his way homeward, as fleetly as some wild animal of the forest. A few moments brought in view the settlement of Salem; and amid the lights, which here and there twinkled indistinctly through the trees, he quickly distinguished the dwelling of Mary Conant.

CHAPTER V

The light within enthusiasts, who let fly
Against our pen-and-ink divinity;
Who boldly do pretend, (but who'll believe it?)
If Genesis were lost they could retrieve it.
   —*Nicholas Noyles*

DURING their solitary stay at Naumkeak, wasted as the young colony had been with sickness, famine, and fearful apprehension, the buoyant spirits and kind heart of Sally Oldham, had proved an almost solitary source of enjoyment to Mary Conant. True, there were few points of congeniality either in native character, or habitual tendency of mind. The nobler principles of the soul may long remain latent amid the depressing atmosphere of circumstance and situation; but the rich-toned instrument needs but a skillful hand to produce the finest combinations of harmony, and even to the rude touch of the winds, it will occasionally yield its sweet response of wayward melody. Indeed it seemed as if the chilling storms, which had lowered over the young life of Mary Conant, had not only served to call forth the fervid hues of feeling in their full perfection, but had likewise strengthened her native elegance of mind. The intellectual, like the natural sun, sheds its own bright and beautiful lustre on the surrounding gloom, till every object on which it shines seems glowing into life; and amid all the dreariness of poverty, and the weight of affliction (the heavier, that it was borne far from the knowledge and sympathy of the world), Mary found much to excite her native fervor of imagination. The stars were there, in their silent, sparkling beauty, and the fair-browed moon smiled on the hushed, still loveliness of nature. The monarch of day paused ere he gathered around him his brilliant drapery of clouds, and gazed on these wild dominions with as much pride as upon fairer and warmer climes. But all associations of this nature formed a "sanctum sanctorum" in the recesses of Mary's heart, and Sally Oldham was one of the last to penetrate it. She thought nothing of the stars but of their lucky or unlucky influences, viewed the moon as a well-favored planet, that had much to do with the weather, and saw nothing in the setting sun but a hint to do her out-door work. But whether the understanding finds reciprocation or not, the heart must have sympathy; and amid the depression of spirits, naturally induced by the declining health of her mother, and the disheartening influence of the stern, dark circle in which she moved, Mary found a welcome relief in unlocking all her hopes, fears, and disappointments to her untutored friend. Her usual placid state of feeling had been restored by the ample confession she had made concerning an action, which she more than half feared would call down the vengeance of Heaven upon her; and when Hobomok entered the room, after the excursion mentioned in the last chapter, she was quietly seated amid the circle, which had assembled at her father's house. It was indeed a scene of varied character. The mother and daughter, as we have already observed, possessed that indefinable outline of elegance, which is seldom entirely effaced from those of high birth and delicate education. In immediate contrast were the stern, hard features of Mr. Conant, and the singular countenance of Mr. Oldham, which reminded one of gleams of light through a grated window, for the deep furrows of passion, and the shadows of worldly disappointment, were in vain cast over its natural drollery of expression. Then there was the fine, bold expression of Governor Endicott, and the dolorous visage of Mr. Graves, which seemed constantly to say, "the earth is a tomb and man a fleeting vapour;" and lastly the manly beauty of Hobomok, as he sat before the fire, the flickering and uncertain light of a few decaying embers falling full upon his face. This Indian was indeed cast in nature's noblest mould. He was one of the finest specimens of elastic, vigorous elegance of proportion, to be found among his tribe. His long residence with the white inhabitants of Plymouth had changed his natural fierceness of manner into haughty, dignified reserve; and even that seemed softened as his dark, expressive eye rested on Conant's daughter.

"We have heard somewhat of an alliance betwen the Pequods and Narragansets," said Governor Endicott, as Hobomok seated himself. "What says Sagamore John concerning this matter?"

"He said it was a cloud gone by," was the laconic answer.

"And do you think the Pequods will ever prevail on them to join against us, Hobomok?"

"The quiver of the Pequod is full of arrows," replied the Indian; "his belt is the skin of a snake, and he suffers no grass to grow upon his war-path. He needs not the sinew of the Narraganset to draw the arrow to the head."

"When you were among the Narragansets what was their speech thereupon?" inquired the chief magistrate.

"Miantonimo called king Charles his good English father," answered Hobomok. "He wore not the belt of the Pequod, and his sachems smoked not the pipe of Sassacus. But that was a few sleeps ago. A man may tell the changes of the moon, but it is not so with the word of a Narraganset."

He rose as he said this, and stood for some moments at the aperture which admitted the light, gazing intently on the surrounding woods; but if there was any thing like anxiety in his mind, it was cautiously concealed from the view of others.

"Well," said Mr. Conant, interrupting the silence, "even if Massasoit joins himself unto them, we are strong in numbers and doubly strong in the Lord of Hosts."

"The sachem of Mount Haup is true as the course of the sun," rejoined the Indian, somewhat indignant that his friendship should be doubted.[1] "If an arrow comes among us, it comes from Corbitant's quiver. But though the rattlesnake's death be on its feather, the wise man must aim it, and the Good Spirit must wing it to the mark. When you pray to the Englishman's God, he sends your corn drink, and you say he make the waters in two tribes, for the white man to pass through. Is he not big-ger than the Pequods and the Mohegans, the Narragansetts and the Tarateens?"

Without waiting for an answer, he took up the cap which lay on the floor beside him, and left the house.

"It is a shame on us that an Indian must teach us who is 'our shield and our buckler,'" observed Mr. Conant. "To my mind there is more danger of Satan's killing us with the rat's-bane of toleration, than the Lord's taking us off with the Indian arrows. It behoveth the watchmen of Israel to be on their guard, for false prophets and false Christs are abroad in the land. 'One saith he is in the desert, and another saith he is in the secret chambers;'[2] and much reason have the elect to laud the God of Israel, that his right hand upholdeth them in slippery places."

"I am much in the dark whether you can clearly prove, from Scripture, that the elect are always upheld in slippery places," said Mr. Oldham. "What do you make of the falling off of Judas Iscariot?"

"What do I make of it, man? Why that he never was among the elect. Christ saith, 'none of them have I lost but the son of perdition, that the Scriptures might be fulfilled.'"

"Why, Paul himself seems not to have been clear upon the subject," continued Mr. Oldham; "for he says, 'lest when I have preached unto others, I should myself prove a cast-away.' And know you not that God's chosen people staid so long in Egypt that they forgot the name of Jehovah? And what with the brick bondage of spiritual Egypt on the one hand, and the flesh-pots on the other, I think there is much danger that the elect may so lose the sound of his voice, that they will not know it, when it calls them from the four winds of heaven."

"I have found by experience," said Governor Endicott, "that the more doubts we let in at the floodgate, the faster gripe Satan hath upon our souls. St. Augustine hath it, 'Nullum malum pejus libertate errandi;' and I believe he is in the right."

"I don't know any thing about your outlandish tongue," replied Mr. Oldham; "and, I mean no disrespect to your Honor, but I think it savors of Babylon to be calling on the name of this saint and that saint. I marvel when christians have turned the pope out of doors, they don't send his rags out of the window. To my thinking, the devil will send him back again after his duds, forasmuch as they are suffered to remain in the church."

"Augustine was a holy man," rejoined Governor Endicott; "though in many things, the Lord suffered him to remain in darkness. He it was, who left a burning coal upon the altar, wherewithal Calvin and Luther lighted up the great fire of the Reformation; a fire which burneth yet, and which will burn, until Babylon be consumed, with her robes and her mitres, her cross and her staff, her bishops and he prelates, her masses and her mummeries. Yea, let the disciples of the hell-born Loyola strive against it as they will. But as for St. Augustine, my friend, you'll acknowledge the spirit of the matter to be good, though it is clothed in outlandish dress, when

I tell you that it meaneth, 'there is no evil worse than the liberty of wandering.'"

"There is much truth in that, no doubt," replied Mr. Graves; "but I maintain it is contrary to the declarations of Scripture, unless you can prove that it appertains to the unpardonable sin."

"St. Augustine probably wrote it without any especial reference to that passage," said the Governor.

"And I maintain that it's popish blasphemy to write any thing without an especial reference to the declarations of Scripture," replied his antagonist, who seemed to stand on the battle ground of controversy, calling out, like Goliah, 'Choose you a man for you, and let him come down to me that I may fight him.'[3] "And as for you, Mr. Oldham, if you have such doubts as you've been speaking of, it is because you have sinned yourself into them; and I marvel if it be not by the leaven of idle words, and levity of speech."

"God gave us laughter as well as reason, to my apprehension," rejoined Mr. Oldham, "Solomon saith, 'there is a time for all things;' and the commentary that I put upon the text is, that there is a time to smoke a pipe and crack a joke, as well as to preach and pray."[4]

"You know not what you say, nor whereof you affirm," answered Mr. Conant. "Recreation is no doubt good to oil the wheels as we travel along a rugged road; but a wise man will do as Jonathan, who only tasted a little honey on the end of his rod.[5] As for that text of Solomon, it is a sort of flaming cherubim that turneth every way, and many a man hath it slain."[6]

"I'm thinking at any rate," retorted Oldham, "that a scythe cuts the better, if a man stops to whet it atween whiles."

"That's true enough," replied he from the Isle of Wight, "but what would you say to see a man whetting his scythe the whole day instead of mowing? I tell you, Mr. Oldham, he that gives up, even for an hour, the blessed comforts of the gospel and the inward outpouring of prayer, for the mere crackling thorns of worldly mirth, does but exchange his pearls for old iron."

"I think," interrupted Governor Endicott, "that there is much appertaining to error implied in the doctrine of inward outpouring.[7] That egg was laid in the Netherlands, and if it be kept warm, I've a suspicion that the viper will hereafter spring out of its shell, and aim at the vitals of the church. It is a wandering meteor of human pride, and doth but serve to lead from the true light of revelation."

"Ah, it is a sad thing," observed Mr. Conant, "that before we have got the church of Christ well balanced, Satan, seeing the dominion of the beast going down in one quarter, straightway sendeth forth his ministers to and fro in the earth, and teacheth them to cry down Antichrist as much as the boldest of us, at the same time that they lead poor souls into more horrid blasphemies than the papist. These gross errors, broached in the dark, are sliding like the plague into the veins of the church; but in none of them the devil so plainly sheweth his horns, as in this doctrine of inward light."

"According to my notions," said Mr. Graves, "scripture would be but a dead letter without inward light. I'm thinking a clock would be but a sorry thing, with its clever-figured face, if there was no wheel-work to set it agoing."

"Your comparison hath no savor of similitude," replied the Governor. "I grant there is a concealed life and spirit in the letter of the Bible; but God hath hidden it, and it is not for man to penetrate into the mysteries of godliness. The index of the clock sufficeth to do our daily work by, and is of no further use to him that knows the wheels which move it, than to him who never thought thereupon."

This probably would have paved the way for fresh controversy, had not the entrance of Hobomok interrupted the conversation. His appearance betrayed no marks of agitation, nor was any surprise excited when he stooped and spoke to the Governor, who immediately followed him out of the room. As soon as they were out of hearing, Hobomok told him his suspicions of Corbitant, and added that he was certain there were a number of Indians in ambush in the woods below. The chief magistrate determined at once that a company should be collected silently and speedily. Hobomok was deputed to give orders to several individuals to proceed to his house with as little appearance of alarm as possible; and the Indian set forth upon the expedition; first requesting the Governor not to lose sight of Mr. Conant's house. When Governor Endicott returned to the company he had left, he stated the fears of their Indian friend as gently as possible; but cautiously as they were told, it proved too much for the weak nerves of Mrs. Conant. Since her residence in the wilderness, alarms of this kind had been frequent, and she had borne them with fortitude; but now the body weighed down the firmness of the soul; and her husband was obliged to leave his fainting wife to the care of her daughter, with an assurance that their safety should be cared for. They were indeed well protected; for Hobomok, the moment his errands were hastily delivered, had returned to guard them with the quick eye of love, and the ready arm of hatred.

The company so suddenly collected, pursued a circuitous rout, and came at once upon the unguarded enemy. The band which they discovered consisted of twenty Indians, most of whom were petty sachems of Massasoit, who had been wrought upon by the eloquence of Corbitant, for the purpose of setting fire to Mr. Conant's house, and murdering the inhabitants, if possible.

From his own account, it seemed that Mr. Conant's quotation with regard to the arrows being broken at Salem, had been construed by Corbitant into a defiance of the neighboring tribes; and that he had taken this step to revenge the insult; however, it is probable that the blow was aimed, through them, at the heart of Hobomok. Ambush and stratagem are the pride of Indian warfare, and now that their designs were so completely traversed, they attempted no resistance. The captives were placed in an enclosed piece of public land, and a guard of thirty men set over them. Mr. Conant returned to his family, and Mary, inured to such occurrences, slept peacefully within their humble dwelling, unconscious that Hobomok watched it the livelong night, with eyes that knew no slumber. Every man saw that his gun was loaded and his pistols within reach; and at midnight nothing was seen in motion but the sentinels, as they passed backward and forward, their arms gleaming in the moon.

CHAPTER VI

If heaven a draught of heavenly pleasure spare,
One cordial in this melancholy vale,
'Tis when a youthful, loving, modest pair,
In other's arms breathe out the tender tale,
Beneath the milk-white thorn that scents the evening gale.
  —*Burns*

THE DAWN presented a scene unusual to the inhabitants of Salem. The prisoners, some standing erect, some seated on the ground, and others leaning upon their bows, wore one uniform expression of defiance and rage. The Englishmen who stood around them, resting on their loaded guns, had that look of peculiar ghastliness which the light of morning gives to men who have passed a sleepless and anxious night. However, the sun had hardly placed his golden circlet on the summit of the highest eastern hills, before the deep rolling of the drum was heard along the street, and fresh recruits passed on, to take the place of their companions. In the mean time a council was called at the chief magistrate's, to determine what should be done with the prisoners.

"My countrymen," said Governor Endicott, "you all know for what purpose you are now called hither. Well it is for us that our brethren from the Isle of Wight have arrived among us; inasmuch as the wickedness of Morton hath made these savages very daring of late. But, as I was about to say, while we were sitting in the house of Mr. Conant, talking of God, and the things appertaining to salvation, Hobomok came among us and gave warning of a party of Indians in the hollow; forasmuch as he, whom we all know the Lord hath gifted with great quickness of ear, heard a low whoop therefrom. You know how the thing hath proved, and how wonderfully we have been saved from the malice and strategems of our enemies; and now I

42

would fain ask your judgment concerning what is best to be done in this matter."

After some discussion it was determined that Mr. Conant should take with him a strong guard, and convey the captives to their head sachem, Massasoit. Upon which, their godly minister, Mr. Higginson, arose and desired them to join with him in a petition to the throne of grace. Every hat was reverently laid aside, and a short, impressive prayer was made with the involuntary eloquence of recent gratitude. A strong guard was equipped, and as they passed in review before the Governor, the ensign stepped out and delivered the colors of the red cross, which had been unfurled the night before.

"It is marvellous in my eyes that the Lord fighteth on our side, while we march under such a badge of Antichrist," said Governor Endicott. "It as much beseemeth a christian to carry the half-moon of Mahomet, as such an emblem of popish victory. However, the pleasure of the king be obeyed."

Hobomok, who had been waiting for "the council fire to be extinguished," fell into the rear of the company, and re-conducted Mr. Collier to Plymouth.

During several hours the settlement continued in that state of excitement which might naturally be supposed to follow an alarm so unexpected. All the people that were near, called at Mr. Conant's, one after another, to hear the extent of the danger to which they had been exposed, till Mary and her mother were weary of repeating the story.

"I have come hither to find out the root of the matter, Madam Conant," said a neighbouring widow. "I heard last night that there was three hundred Indians found in Endicott's Hollow; and there I sat trembling afraid to venture out, till Jacob came home and told me something about the business."

"And I," observed another, "heard that Corbitant shot Governor Endicott in the mouth. Oh, it was a woful night to us women folks who have just come among you. We never hear of such like proceedings in our island."

"The matter hath no doubt been much magnified," replied Mrs. Conant. "We have reason to be thankful the Indians were few and easily surprised. But here is neighbour Oldham, who was one of the company. He can tell you every thing connected therewith."

"There was but one arrow fired," said Mr. Oldham; "and, as the Lord would have it, that stuck fast in a bit of cheese rind in my jacket pocket. Which, I think, proveth good the old saying, that 'a little armour serveth a man if he knoweth where to put it.' But, after all our affrightment, this hath proved a small matter. The Lord hath merely given us a jog on the elbow at this time; that we may remember the dangers wherewithal we are surrounded, and wake up our sluggish souls, that have become somewhat perfunctory in his service."

"That's what my good man said, when he was dying," rejoined the widow. "Poor soul, the Indian shot him through and through, when he was digging for clams in the sands down there at Plymouth; and when I pulled out the arrow and bound up his wounds, he told me, it was all a chastisement of the Lord, in that we had fallen into rebellious ways."

"And I remember as well as if it was but yesterday," said another, "how my poor Joseph looked in them dreadful times. A bright and handsome boy he was once, but he overworked himself; and then he grew poor, and pale as a ghost, and what was worst of all, I hadn't food wherewithal to keep life in his body."

"Ah there is nobody knows the troubles and distresses of a new settlement, but those who have tasted thereof," observed Mrs. Conant; and she paused and sighed deeply, as the painful remembrance of her own lost sons passed before her. "But one must not talk of their own griefs at such a time," continued she. "There is great commotion throughout the world; and it is plain to perceive that Jehovah is shaking the heavens above our head, and the earth beneath our feet."

"Ay, ay," answered Oldham, "these are fearsome times in church and state, when the domineering bishop of London, whom no godly man ever yet knew without giving *laud* to the devil by reason of the acquaintance.[1] I say it is fearful times when such like men have power to drive God's heritage into the wilderness, where they must toil hard for a scanty bread, and that too with daily jeopardy of life and limb."

"And they tell me likewise," rejoined Mrs. Conant, "that Sir Ferdinando Gorges[2] is likely to make difficulty about the Massachusetts patent; and that the Lord, for further trial of our faith, hath suffered more enemies to be stirred up against us in England, who are ready, like Amalek of old, to smite Israel while they are weak and unable for defence."

"Oh yes," replied Mr. Oldham; "and the Earl of Warwick, and divers other great folks who hold possessions here, 'sit under their vine and their fig-tree, with none to molest or make them afraid,' and little know they concerning our troubles, and never a hand of theirs would ward off a blow, unless where the matter of filthy lucre was concerned."

"Nevertheless," said Mrs. Conant, "the work will prosper. Though there appeareth now but a little cloud, about the bigness of a man's hand;[3] yet the Lord Christ is in it, and out of it shall shine the perfection of beauty."

"I could listen to your edifying discourse all the day long, but there is no time for folding of hands now-a-days," interrupted the widow, as she threw her cloak over her shoulders. "My red cardinal is over warm for the season to be sure, but then I think it is but decent to have something over a body's head."

"I marvel that you should think it decent to call a christian garment by a name that appertains to the scarlet woman of Babylon," said Mr. Oldham.

"It's no name of my making, Goodman; nor did I know that evil was signified thereby," answered the widow. "But I must be stirring homewards. The Lord bless you all."

The other visitors gradually followed her example, and quietness and order were soon restored to the household.

"Mother," said Mary, after their guests had all departed, "you know father has gone to Plymouth for two or three days?"

"To be sure I do, my child," replied Mrs. Conant, smiling. "And what then?" Mary hesitated a few moments ere she added, "I have seen Charles Brown this morning; and he is coming here this evening, that is, if you have no objection thereto."

"You well know my heart, my dear Mary," replied her mother, "but I ought not to do wrong because your father is absent."

"You don't think it is wrong—in your conscience you can't think it's wrong," said Mary, as she kissed her forehead, and looked up archly in her face. "So do say he may come."

"You have sacrificed much for me, my child." answered the indulgent parent. And, pausing a moment, she continued, "Perhaps I do wrong thus to violate the injunctions of my husband, but I know you are prudent, and you may e'en follow your own dictates concerning this matter."

The young man to whom we have so often referred, was a graduate at Oxford, and of no ordinary note in his native kingdom. He had known Mary before she left the mansion of her noble grandfather; and the remembrance of the little fairy just blushing into womanhood had proved powerful enough to draw the ambitious young lawyer from the fair hopes of distinction in England, to the wild and romantic scheme of establishing the Episcopal mitre in the forests of America. The state in which he found things on his arrival, induced him to abandon his favorite project; and prudence for awhile enabled him to conceal his high church principles. But the crown and the mitre were interwoven with every association of his heart, and in that hot-bed of argument he found the attempt at neutrality was in vain. Notwithstanding the first settlers at Naumkeak had taken the liberty of nonconforming to the rules of their mother church, and to the established regulations of the Plymouth elders, Mr. Brown soon found that they complained loudly of the spirit of the times. Mr. Conant in particular, stated that New England was likely to become "a cage for every unclean bird. A free stable-room and litter for all kinds of consciences."[4] Such expressions extorted from Brown an involuntary reproach upon those false guides who had first taught men to wander from the true church. This was, of course, the watch-word of animosity; and from that time the young man was considered as Ishmael in the house of Abraham. However, long after the old man discovered the abomination of his sentiments, he continued a daily visitor at Mr. Conant's, who "felt it his duty to controvert the matter with him, inasmuch as the Lord might please to make him the instrument of his redemption." But it could not long remain concealed that metal more attractive than the iron glove of controversy, had drawn him to their fire-side; and, with more anger than Mrs. Conant had ever before seen him manifest, he forbade him the house forever.

With all Mary's habitual sweetness of disposition, this course of conduct did serve to diminish her filial respect and affection. She had no sympathy with her father's religious scruples, for her heart very naturally bowed down before the same altar with the man she loved. None could form an idea of the depth and fervor of her affection, who had not, like her, left a bright and sunny path, to wander in the train of misery, gloom, and famine. During her stay at her grandfather's, she had become familiar with much that was beautiful in painting, and lovely in sculpture, as well as all that was elegant in the poetry of that early period; and their rich outline was deeply impressed upon her young heart. For her mother's sake, she endured the mean and laborious offices which she was obliged to perform, but she lived only in the remembrance of that fairy spot in her existence. Alone as she was, without one spirit that came in contact with her own, she breathed only in the regions of fancy; and many an ideal object had she invested with its rainbow robe. When at length she found a being who understood her feelings, and who loved, as she had imagined love, her whole soul was rivetted. The harshness of her father tended to increase this, by rendering the stream of affection more undivided in its source. In such a state of things, their interviews must of course be transient and unfrequent; but when they did occur, the cup of joy, so seldom tasted, sparkled to the brim. Let the philosopher say what he will about these humbler blossoms of the heart, earth has nothing like them, for loveliness and fragrance. And he, who through the dim lapse of years, remembers the time when two full, gushing tides of young affection, were mingled in one common stream, will hardly be willing to acknowledge that the world is altogether "vanity and vexation of spirit."

The remembrance of her own thwarted inclinations wrought power-fully on the mind of Mary's gentle and affectionate mother, and she at length gave their meeting her unqualified consent. The bowl of chocolate was prepared that night with even more careful fondness than usual; and as Mrs. Conant at an early hour laid her head upon the pillow, she was just preparing to say, "I fear I do wrong, my child," but Mary kissed away the sentence.

The absence of so many of the inhabitants, and the fear of some fresh alarm, made it expedient that the outskirts of the settlement should be guarded, and Mary well knew that Brown was on that duty. In expectation of his arrival, she stationed herself at the door, and looked out upon the still brightness around. The lonely spot was fair and tranquil, and earth, sea, and sky, beneath the unvaried radiance of the moon, "seemed just waking from some heavenly dream." The evening star was sailing along its peaceful course, and seemed, amid the stainless sanctity of the heavens, like a bright diadem on the brow of some celestial spirit. "Fair planet," thought Mary, "how various are the scenes thou passest over in thy shining course. The solitary nun, in the recesses of her cloister, looks on thee as I do now; mayhap too, the courtly circle of king Charles are watching the motion of thy silver chariot. The standard of war is fluttering in thy beams, and the busy merchantman breaks thy radiance on the ocean. Thou hast kissed the cross-crowned turrets of the Catholic, and the proud spires of the Episcopalian. Thou hast smiled on distant mosques and temples, and now thou art shedding the same light on the sacrifice heap of the Indian, and the rude dwellings of the Calvinist. And can it be, as my father says, that of all the multitude of people who view thy cheering rays, so small a remnant only are pleasing in the sight of God? Oh, no. It cannot be thus. Would that my vision, like thine, could extend through the universe, that I might look down unmoved on the birth and decay of human passions, hopes, and prejudices."

These thoughts were interrupted by the appearance of Brown, as he came whistling along the footpath, the light of evening resting full upon his handsome features.

"The moon has seemed to rise slowly and wearily since I have been looking out for you," said the maiden, as her lover gaily imprinted a kiss upon her hand.

"I could wish she would stop her shining course awhile," replied he; "for, setting aside the expectation of meeting you, it is one of the brightest nights I ever looked upon."

"I have been watching it," answered Mary, "till it hath almost made me sad. At this moment she is shining on the lordly palaces and blooming gardens of good old England, is she not?"

"Ah yes; and such thoughts make even my heart sicken within me. But it is not so when I think of you. Love 'maketh the desert to blossom as the rose.' Besides, my dear Mary, I trust we shall both live in England again."

"Never while my mother lives, Charles. I would not leave her even for you. But she will soon go from us to be no more. I picked a little shivering violet the other day, and it seemed the sweeter for the cold dew that was on it. And I thought it was so like to my mother; for the sicker she is, the more she seemeth like an angel."

I know not why it is, but, in minds of a certain tone, the richest melody of love is always mingled with notes of sadness; and, in the full communion of unreserved tenderness, the maiden leaned her head upon the shoulder of the young man, and wept in silence.

"My dear Mary," said Brown, "it is not well to be melancholy. We both ought to recollect that there is One above who will defend us, though every earthly friend be taken. As for your father, he may be conscientious in this matter; but I more than half suspect that he cares more about having his own way, than he does for all the prayers and churches in christendom. If so, I know your kind mother will use all her influence to overcome his obstinacy."

"I know it too," replied Mary; "but her counsels have little weight with him when he has determined upon a course. However, he loves her; and I believe she loves him as well as she ever could in her earliest days."

"Do you think you could endure so much for me, Mary?" asked her lover, while his bright dark eye rested with more than usual admiration on the passive beauty of her countenance.

"A cold heart may make promises and protestations," she replied; "and when we dream of love we are always too apt to think of the paradise, rather than the thorny hedge which the sin of Adam has placed around it; but let the storm come upon you, Charles, and see if my head shrink from the tempest."

"I know by experience how hard it is to escape from the entanglements of the heart," answered Brown. "My life was full of enjoyment before I met you in Lincolnshire; and now, when I try to think of any source of happiness in which you have no share, I am forced to acknowledge that you are, in some way or other, connected therewith. You remember that those who entered Spencer's shady grove,

> Whose loftie trees yclad with sommer's pride,
> Did spred so broad, that heaven's light did hide,
> Not perceable with power of any starr;
> When weening to returne whence they did straye,
> They cannot finde that path which once was showne,
> But wander to and fro in waies unknowne.[5]

And isn't it so with the path of love, my Mary?"

A smiling glance from the bright eye of the maiden gave an answer of silent eloquence. The interview was prolonged to a late hour; and the conversation of the lovers became gradually more and more marked by that tenderness of expression, which, "like the rich wines of the south, is so delicious in its native soil; so tasteless in the transportation."

CHAPTER VII

"The church was umpire then."

AMONG ALL the varieties of human character, from the refined enthusiast in classic literature, down to the ignoramus who signs a cross in behoof of his name, there are very few who have strength enough to resist the flattering suffrage of exclusive preference. Gratified vanity proves a powerful pleader in most hearts upon such occasions; and if love itself be not induced, the resemblance passes for awhile as current coin. I say for awhile, for most of the unhappy marriages which have come under my own observation, have originated in this mistake. However, I shall not stop to moralize upon the subject. Suffice it to say, that Collier, under the dominion of such feelings, returned to Plymouth with a lightsome and happy heart; nothing disturbed, save by his anticipated eclaircissement with Hopkins. Much as he dreaded the interview, he found his friend even more unwilling to relinquish his claims, than he had expected.

The low, flat-roofed fort of Plymouth, and the adjacent wigwam of Hobomok, were just rising on the sight, when the anxious young man came out to meet them.

"What's the news, John?" inquired he.

"That twenty Indians have been surprised in a plan of setting fire to the house of that wise and godly man, Mr. Roger Conant," rejoined the traveller. "They are this day sent, under guard, to the sachem of Mount Haup; and with them we came some ways in company."

"Ah, indeed," replied Hopkins. "I thought the Indians were quiet enough of late; but it is plain there will be no peace in the land while Corbitant is therein. That sachem is a hot-headed fellow, and implacable withal. Albeit," continued he, as they entered the house, "I will hear your Indian stories at a more convenient season. What did Sally say, when she found she had been thought of these three years, and she all the while knew nothing about the matter?"

"Why, to speak the truth, James, I have no very pleasant duty to perform in this business; for the damsel hath expressly declared, she doth not look upon you with as favorable eyes as upon some others."

"That's what they always say," answered the confident lover. "Peradventure she thinks that dear bought goods are most valued. I tell you, man, she hath expressed her liking for me a hundred times, and would now, if you had been bold in the business."

"Hath she?" inquired his messenger. "Bethink you, Hopkins; hath she ever told you she loved you before others?"

"A hundred times," replied he. "That is, I mean—you know I don't mean,—I would'nt say it if I did—that she hath done so unbecoming a thing as to tell me she would marry me, before she knew whether I would or no; but, nevertheless, I repeat she hath said it a hundred times over, by her looks and actions. And I should like to know, forsooth, whom she may prefer to me, in this wilderness? Haven't I loved her these three years? And didn't I do all I could for 'em when the elders saw fit to dismiss her father? And haven't I put up the best house in Plymouth, wherewithal to please her?"

"I know all that," rejoined his friend; "and assuredly I thought your suit would be favorably received. I marvel that it was not; but I had as good tell it at once, as not.—The maiden hath declared she loveth another man better."

"And I should like to know who it might be?" said the indignant lover.

The young man judged by his countenance, that he was "nursing his wrath to keep it warm," and he felt more and more the awkwardness of his ungracious mission. He blushed, stammered, hesitated, and finally answered, "The maiden told me in express words, that if you and I had changed places, the messenger would have returned with 'yea' in his mouth."

Mr. Hopkins turned his face toward the window, and bit his thumb some time, without speaking a word.

"I suppose you will take it unkind," observed Collier, interrupting the silence. "But what could be done in such a case?"

"Talk to me no more about it," replied the disappointed suitor. "I am not the man to break my heart about a foolish damsel. If she pleases to shape her course in this way, I can assure her there is no love lost between us. But after all, Collier, this is a confounded unfriendly job, on your part; and I shall state as much to the church."

"I beg of you not to make the affair public," said his friend; "if you will hear to reason, you will see I could not have done otherwise than I have."

"I don't want to hear any reasons about it," retorted his offended companion. "I tell you once more, I don't care a pin concerning the matter; but when I see wolves walking about in sheep's clothing, I'll e'en strip off their fleece." And without waiting for an answer, he took up his hat and walked out of the house. He had said and thought that he cared nothing about his disappointment; but when he was alone, and all restraint of manly pride was removed, he found that the thread, so unexpectedly broken, was interwoven with the whole web of his existence; and spite of himself, a few reluctant tears rolled down his weather-beaten face. However, resentment was uppermost; and the following day his rival was summoned to appear before the church, to answer certain charges brought against him by James Hopkins. Collier would gladly have avoided a public conference on such a subject, but under existing circumstances, there was but one alternative. He must either suffer under a suspicion of his good faith, or he must candidly state events as they happened. In these degenerate times, when even plighted love is broken with such frequent impunity, it would excite a smile to have seen the elderly men assembled at Mr. Brewster's, and with serious aspects discussing so important an affair. But in those days, the church kept careful watch upon the out-goings and in-comings of her children, and suffered not the pollution of a butterfly's feather to rest upon her garments.

After the disputants were seated, the worthy clergyman began;

"It is with much grief we notice the falling out of two godly young men, sons of right worthy gentlemen among us. Especially as one is accused of having dealt treacherously with the other, and spoken deceitful words unto him."

Then Mr. Collier answered; "I feel it is an unpleasant duty to vindicate myself from this aspersion, inasmuch as Mr. Hopkins is my valued friend, and hath been somewhat too hasty in this matter, refusing to hear explanations which I have sought to give unto him. I likewise think that the things appertaining to love are of too light a nature to be brought before the church, that they should discuss thereupon. But that you may know that in nothing have I dealt treacherously with my friend, you shall hear the conclusion of the whole matter. Hearing that the vessels were soon to leave Naumkeak, and having business wherewithal they were connected, I had a mind to take Hobomok for my guide, and journey thither. Whereupon Mr. Hopkins gave me a letter for Mr. Oldham's daughter (whom you all know is a comely damsel, and, withal of a cheerful behaviour); which letter I delivered to the same, and asked an answer thereto. Then she said to me, that had I sent by Mr. Hopkins, instead of he by me, she should verily have said, 'I will go.' I spoke much to her concerning my friend's merits, but finding her mind was determined in this matter, I e'en told her I would have come out to meet her, as Isaac of old, when he brought the daughter of Bethuel into his tent. The maiden, you know, is well to look upon, and altogether such an one as no man need be averse to, as an helpmeet. Now whether or not guile be found in me, I leave to your judgments; and if you so decide, I'm willing to be lopped off, as an unworthy member, from the church of Christ gathered in this place."

"Hear him," interrupted Hopkins. "He saith not a word about relinquishing the damsel. It seems he had even rather be cast out as 'an heathen and a publican.' His love must have grown up wondrous sudden; for he denieth that he bewitched her with love potions, and implieth that when he went to Naumkeak he had no thoughts save of procuring her for my wife."

"I not only imply it," answered Collier, "but I expressly declare that I then had no thought respecting her wherewithal you were not connected. And now I do truly say, that I had rather be sent out from among my brethren, although it would be very grievous unto me, than to dismiss the maiden, whom of a surety, I do regard with much complacency since she hath so declared her sentiments."

"Of a truth, I see nothing wherein you have erred, according to your own account," observed elder Brewster; "but there is a gentleman soon going to Naumkeak, to convey a letter from our honorable chief magistrate to the reverend Mr. Higginson, respecting the baptism of his son, and, for the further satisfaction of Mr. Hopkins, it may be well that he return with a written statement of facts. Till which time, we do defer our decision."

Poor Sally was in great consternation when the Plymouth messenger arrived, and informed her of the serious aspect which the business had assumed.

"Oh, Mary," said she, "what shall I do? You know that Mr. Hopkins who bawled himself into love with me, and had'nt courage to sing the last note after all? Well, he has made a great fuss between Mr. Collier and the church, and they have sent to me to write all that I said concerning him."

"I always wondered how you could have spoken to Mr. Collier after such a fashion," replied Mary. "I see nothing you can do but to write the whole truth."

"Will you write it for me?"

"Oh, yes, if you'll provide words to the purpose."

So the pen and ink was brought forward, and Mary wrote a letter which she indited as follows:

"Reverende Sirs,

"Whereas Mr. Collier hathe beene supposed to blame concerning some businesse he hath of late endeavoured to transacte for Mr. Hopkins, this cometh to certifie that he did faithfully performe his dutie, and moreover that his great modestie did prevente his understanding many hints, until I spoke even as he hath represented. Wherefore, if there be oughte unseemly in this, it lieth on my shoulders.

"With all dutie and respecte,

"Her

Sally ✕ Oldham

marke."

N. B. "Sence my Dawter hathe shewed mee this Yepistall I dwoe furthere righte with my owne Hande a feu words of Add vice untwoe you att Plimouth, respecting Churche Govermente. Twoe my thinking you runn ewer Horses over harde, draweinge the Ranes soe tite, thatt maybee thale rair upp and caste thare rideers intwoe the mudd. U may rubb folkse Nose on the Grinnstone thinking to ware them twoe the Gristell, and in the eende you maye make them twoe Sharppe for ewer owne cumfurt. Dwoe nott construw this intwoe Dishrespecte from hymm whoe hathe mutch Occashun to remember thatt you awl gave hymm a helping Hande in *the Race he runn among you*. U sea by this thatt I am noe Skribe and you new heretoefore thatt I was noe Farisee.

"iohn Oldham."

Upon the receipt of this document, the elders thought fit to take no notice of Mr. Oldham's advice, though all thought it contained too much of his accustomed impudence. Sally's testimony was so simple and decisive, that Mr. Brewster at once gave a concluding answer.

"Although we deem it unseemly for young women to pursue such like courses (indeed were she within our jurisdiction, we should give her public reproof therefor), and though we do fear that the daughter hath much of the corrupt leaven of the father, yet we do not see that we have a right to constrain the consciences of men in these particulars, especially as the apostle saith 'the believing husband may sanctify the unbelieving wife.' Therefore, we do leave Mr. Collier to pursue whatsoever course he deemeth expedient, trusting that, whatever he doth, he will do it in the name of the Lord. Moreover, we do think it proper that Mr. Hopkins make an apology to him, inasmuch as he hath not been slow to anger, nor charitable concerning his brother in the church."

The penance was performed with as good a grace as could be expected, and the young men returned to their respective employments.

꘎꘎꘎꘎꘎꘎

CHAPTER VIII

Take her, she's thy wife.[1]
—*Shakspeare*

IT MAY EASILY be imagined how things continued at Salem for several succeeding weeks. Mr. Collier was as frequent a visitor as distance and difficulty of travelling would permit; Hobomok divided his time almost equally between his mother's wigwam, and the dwelling of Mr. Conant; and Mary obtained a "paradisaical interview" with Brown, as often as possible; Mrs. Conant, sinking in a slow, but certain decline, seemed

> "Like a spirit who longs for a purer day,
> And is ready to wing her flight away;"

her husband, prudent, moderate, and persevering in public affairs,—at home, sometimes passionate, and always unyielding; and Mr. Oldham, the same as ever, an odd mixture of devotion and drollery.

The manuscript mentions numerous controversies between Mr. Higginson, Mr. Conant, Mr. Oldham, and Mr. Graves; but their character is so similar to those I have already quoted, that I forbear to repeat them. One maintained justification by faith, and another by works; and the light-within-enthusiast, from the Isle of Wight, continued to defend his doctrine of the inward outpouring of prayer, and eventually became one of the most celebrated among the Familists.[2]

Sally listened to all their arguments with heedless gaiety; Mary heard their wild war of words, with increased weariness; and as her noble mother approached the confines of another world, and received its calm, heavenly influence, she looked with compassion on the wild and ever-varying light of human doctrines.

But while things remained unaltered in these two families, the spirit of improvement was rapidly extending in the village, and the young English lawyer had commenced his efforts for the establishment of the Episcopal church. He met with a hearty co-operation from his brother Samuel, who had been a merchant of high respectability in his native land, and from Mr. Blackstone, the solitary hermit at Tri-Mountain, who originally came to America with the same design.[3] These movements, of course, called forth all the energy of the non-conformists, and consequently the number of Brown's adherents increased; for the love of excitement is a fundamental principle in the human mind, and men will seek it wherever it is to be found;—whether in the contests of gladiators, the clashing of arms, the painful power of tragic representation, or the tumultuous zeal of jarring sectaries.

Things were in this state, when it was announced in three successive meetings,

"Be it known unto all, that John Collier of Plymouth, and Sally Oldham of Salem, are about to enter into the holy state of wedlock. If any man hath objection, let him proclaim it publicly."

No man, excepting Mr. Thomas Graves, had any objection, and on the 5th of August a small company collected at Mr. Oldham's, to witness the bridal. Mrs. Conant claimed the privilege of giving the wedding gown, a beautiful chintz, adorned with flowers even larger than life, which had been a favorite morning dress with the Lady Mary before her marriage. Governor Endicott, likewise, "though he approved not of the drinking of wine, and had abolished it at his own table, yet he could not forbear sending a little on this occasion, inasmuch as it was the first wedding they had had among them." The manuscript mentions the chief magistrate as "bolde and undaunted, yet sociable, and of a cheerful spirite, loving or austere, as occasion served." On the day of the wedding he unbent his stateliness more than usual, and held much courteous discourse with Mr. Conant's and Mr. Oldham's families, while the young couple sat beside each other, silently and timidly waiting for the arrival of Mr. Higginson. Mary sat on the left hand of the bride, and their countenances, both interesting, presented a striking contrast of beauty. Sally's clear, rosy complexion was becomingly heightened by the excitement of her wedding day; her bright, roguish blue eyes sparkled; and her round, Hebe form appeared to the utmost advantage in her handsome dress. In short she seemed the living, laughing representation of health. But Mary's slender figure, her large, dark eyes, with their deep, melancholy fringe, and the graceful carriage of her neck and shoulders, brought before the mind a Parian statue, or one of those fair visions which fancy gives to slumber. The old men gazed on them in their loveliness, and turned away with that deep and painful sigh, which the gladness of childhood, and the transient beauty of youth, are so apt to awaken in the bosom of the aged. "Alas, that things so fair should be so fleeting," has been repeated thousands of times; and yet how keenly it still enters into the soul, when early fascinations have faded away, and imagination has scattered her garland to the winds. Who has looked on young, sunny smiles, and listened to loud, merry tones, without a feeling almost amounting to anguish, when he has thought of the temptations which would infest their path, and the disappointments which would inevitably crush their budding hopes? Perhaps these ideas, under various modifications, might be the reason of the general silence, for every one seemed fearful of hearing his own voice. Even Sally's giddy temper seemed to be wholly subdued by the solemnity of the vow she was about to take. She sat reserved and diffident, and a crowd of thoughts pressed upon her mind, till she hardly knew whether they were pleasant or painful. At length, however, she ventured to raise her hand to her mouth, and whisper to Mary, "I asked Brown to come to-day; and then I told him not to come; because it would make trouble for you." The ice once broken, whispers were soon heard around the room, and presently Mr. Conant rose and took two or three turns through the apartment, and looked out of the window, as he said, "We shall have a favorable day for our ordination to-morrow, God willing. But they tell me we are to be pestered with the presence of the papistical Mr. Blackstone."

"Well, if he cometh hither, I'll give him the plague, if I can catch it for him," said Mr. Oldham. "They tell me he giveth much countenance to Brown's untoward company."

"It was said in Lincolnshire," observed Mary, who was anxious to change the conversation, "that love was the occasion of his coming hither; and that if a young lady in Huntingdonshire had smiled upon him, he had not been thus wedded to his canonical robe."

"I never heard of a man's being crazy, or in any wise straying from the common path," replied Mr. Oldham, "but that some pretty piece of Eve's flesh, with a head as empty as a New England purse (and it cannot well be emptier), hath straightway supposed herself the cause thereof. Their vanity is as long as the polar nights, and as broad as a Puritan's shoulders need to be. Here is Sally now, who for a wonder is as demure as you please, has thought her carcass such a valuable cargo that every body she sees must needs want the freight. And her head, no doubt is somewhat higher with her Egyptian garments."

"Say nothing about the dress, my friend," interrupted the Governor. "A goodly book should have a comely covering; and as for these women, it is as well to let them alone. It is meet they should stand by themselves, like Quæ Genus in the Grammar;[4] being deficients or redundants, not to be brought under any rule whatsoever."

"Yes, there is many a queer genius among 'em," answered Mr. Oldham; "and deficient enough in all conscience. But as to the subject that we were speaking of, I am wearied with these Episcopalians, who have come hither to make God's temple a dancing school for the devil."

"No doubt they will work their own destruction, and be caught in their own snare," said the Governor.

"Oh yes;" replied Oldham, "the devil will get out of breath with them in good time. I trow, he is broken-winded already with their pre-latical galloping. I wish somebody would give them such a helping hand as I had during my race at Plymouth. I believe I have told you, Governor Endicott, concerning the comforting passages of scripture which the butt end of their muskets brought to my mind. It isn't every man who finds such a boost to his heavy heels. I mean no offence to you, Mr. Collier, but I am thinking if they buckle the girth much tighter, the horse will grow kickish. Come, laugh and be jolly, man—It is your wedding day—and such a day does not often come in a body's pilgrimage. But here cometh Mr. Higginson at last."

The reverend clergyman apologized for his delay, and entered into a conversation concerning the necessary preparations for the anticipated ordination. Mr. Oldham was evidently disposed for a merry-making; but a glance from his matronly dame, and the solemn tones of Mr. Higginson's voice, served to counteract the propensity.

He threw one knee over the other, drew in his lips, and passed his hand over his face, to cover it with the coat of sobriety. But the attempt was in vain, for in his most serious moods his mouth looked as if it contained an imprisoned laugh, which was struggling hard to make its escape from his small, black, piercing eyes.

The bride and bridegroom were soon requested to "stand before the holy man," and pronounce the vow which was to fix the coloring of their future lives. Sally went through the ceremony with modest propriety, and when they were pronounced "man and wife," many a one said, "They're a comely couple; and no doubt the Lord will bless them." Mr. Higginson sat in front of the young couple, and gave them much fatherly advice; which by the way is never less attended to, than at such a period. The bride sat picking the corner of her handkerchief, and seemed to listen with becoming reverence, though in fact she thought not a word about the discourse excepting to wish in mercy that it was concluded. At length, however, the friendly admonitions of the good man were exhausted, and wine, which had never before been drunk in that cottage, was handed to the guests. The older part of the company soon retired, and the young visitors gave themselves up to something like merriment.

CHAPTER IX

I seek divine simplicity in him,
Who handles things divine.
—*Cowper*

SUCH A SETTLEMENT as Salem during the summer of 1629, would seem insignificant enough to modern eyes; but compared with what it had been, it seemed rich and populous. Instead of the six miserable hovels, which it presented in June, there were now to be seen a number of comfortable dwellings, and a respectable edifice which served for various public uses. To Mr. Conant and his three solitary associates, were now added a large number of robust men, with their sober matrons and blooming daughters. And the place which a few months before had only echoed the occasional sound of the axe, or the shrill whoop of the hunter, was now busy with the hum of industry, and the clear, loud laughter of youth. With a decorum which characterized all the New England villages, they early began to arrange matters for the regular organization of a church. Two silenced non-conformists, Mr. Francis Higginson and Mr. Skelton, had arrived in the same vessel with my ancestor.[1] Since that period they had been engaged in a controversial discussion with the Plymouth elders respecting church discipline, and at length, their jarring opinions being carefully balanced, on the 6th of August one was ordained teacher, and the other pastor of the church in Salem. Numerous were the preparations, both important and minute, for the solemnities of that day. Governor Bradford and his assistants, together with the clergy, were invited from Plymouth. Birds were brought down from their flight, and beasts slain for the occasion. The loaded fire-places sent forth a savory incense; and despite of the admonitions of their parents, there was as much "outward adorning, plaiting of the hair," &c. as the slender wardrobe of the maidens would permit. The day was rich in cloudless, autumnal beauty. It seemed as if radiant spirits were gazing from the battlements of heaven upon a bright and happy world. It is astonishing with what facility we accommodate all the scenes of nature to our own state of feeling; so that beauty seems almost like an ideal outline, changing beneath the capricious hand of association,—meeting the eye, but to take its coloring from the heart. The feelings of the young bride involuntarily danced in sympathetic buoyancy with the season, though she saw nothing in it save promised abundance. To Mary, its full maturity seemed but the shadow of coming decay; and her dark eye rested upon Brown, as he walked before her in manly elegance, with a chastened tenderness that partook of sadness. Many a stolen glance was exchanged between the young men and maidens on their way to church, and with many a low courtesy and reverential bow, were the gentlemen in black saluted as they passed along. The assembly were at length collected, and with serious, staid deportment, awaited the commencement of the services. The Plymouth elders, detained by contrary winds, had not yet arrived, and there was a long pause of expectation, during which nothing was heard except the occasional movements of the sentinel, as he stood at the open door of the building. It was, indeed, a strange sight to see men in the house of God with pistols in their sword belts; but alarms from the Indians were then so much to be dreaded, that the protection of the Bible needed the aid of dagger and firelock. However, the expected brethren arrived not, and wearied with the delay, Mr. Higginson arose and made a solemn and impressive prayer. A psalm was then read by Mr. Skelton; and though in the music which followed there was no deep-toned organ to dive down into the recesses of the soul, and carry from thence man's warmest aspirations after heaven, yet there were some fine tones, which struck upon the ear in their bold harmony. And now every one was preparing to give earnest and devout attention to the reverend speaker, who was about to name his text; for in those days a sermon was an exhilarating draught, though converted by the impious chemistry of modern times into a soporific drug. Notwithstanding it was loaded with some dozens of *doctrines*, and more *uses* than twenty sermons of these days will ever arrive at, and an *improvement* at the close, and a *finally* at the end of that, yet the manuscript asserts, that "the eies of men slumbered nott, neither were they wearie with hearing." Indeed the appearance of the learned and pious minister predisposed the mind to attention. His manner was dignified and simple; and as he rose to speak, he seemed bowed down with a humble and conscientious sense of his own unworthiness. Encumbered as I have mentioned, it cannot be supposed that the whole sermon would be interesting even to the antiquarian; but as a specimen of the eloquence of those times, I cannot forbear a few extracts.

"My text," said he, "is in the 105th Psalm, 43d verse. 'He brought forth his people with joy, and his chosen with gladness.' And who, my hearers, hath more need than ourselves to bring to remembrance this passage? Surely he hath brought *us* out 'with a mighty hand and a stretched-out arm.' And shall we not find the wilderness sweet, fed as we are with the manna of his grace? And is there not abundant cause to fill the vessels of our affections daily therewith? Yea, though God hath brought us out from among the horsemen and chariots of Pharaoh, though he hath sweetened the waters of Marah, and given us Elim wherein to encamp, yet may not the name of Jehovah be forgotten in the desert, as well as in Egypt? Yes, even in these days when heaven and earth are trembling at the voice of Almighty wrath, I fear there are many drowsy souls among us. Oh, awaken, I pray you; lest Satan have a commission from God to rock you, and you be lost forever! It is fearful to think how you may fall asleep on the brink of a precipice, and dream that you are created a king, and guarded with a goodly train of ancient nobles, and stately palaces, and enriched with the revenues, majesty, and magnificence of a mighty kingdom,—and after all, the thunder of divine vengeance may sound in your ears, and starting up at the terrible noise thereof, you may fall into the raging sea of fire which burneth forever. There must be no halt, between christians among us. We must be zealous. But look unto thine heart, set a watch over thy tongue, beware of wildfire in thy zeal. There is much need of this caution in these days, when tongue is sharpened against tongue, and pen poisoned against pen, and pamphlets come out with more teeth to bite, than arguments to convince. This is but to betray the truth, and do the devil's service under God's colors. There are some among us, (and he looked full upon Brown, as he spoke,) who are violent and impatient in matters of religion,—given to vain forms, and traditions of men; adhering with a blind, pertinacious zeal to the customs of their progenitors. Of such I would have you beware. Nor would I have you roaming about, giving your ear to every new doctrine. Liberty of conscience is the gilded bait whereby Satan has caught many souls. The threshold of hell is paved with toleration. Leave hidden matters with God, and difficult texts of scripture with the elders of the church. I cannot, if I would, tell you the value of a godly, exemplary ministry among you. May we prove to you 'a savour of life unto life, and not of death unto death.' God, in his mercy, hath brought us out of England, which I fear is becoming sadly degenerate, and planted us among his heritage here; and the first use I would make of the office wherewithal I am honored, is to say to you, talk little about religion, and feel much of its power. Follow the light which is given you. 'Commune with your own heart, and be still.' Be constantly preparing something for others to copy. 'Nulla dies sine lineâ.'[2] The more of heaven there is seen in your daily deportment, the more is God glorified. Carry yourselves as if your business was with eternity, your trade and traffic there; like the citizens of the New Jerusalem, 'having your conversation in heaven, looking for the coming of the Lord Jesus Christ.'[3] But what shall I say to you who have lusts too strong for your light, and corruption too strong for your convictions,—who go to hell just by heaven? I do humbly hope that I may so discharge the duties of mine office, that my hands may be washed of your damnation. But I beseech you to think in time. Consider if all your idle talk and wicked thoughts were written, what volumes of vanity and blasphemy it would make. However, angels take note, and conscience books them all. As for you who are careless and profane among us, who had rather dance round the May-pole of Morton, bedecked with ribbons and lascivious verses, than be hearing the wholesome and lion-like truths of the gospel,—you might laugh at me, were I to charge you not to meet me out of Christ; but I do charge you not to do it, and let him laugh who wins."

As Mr. Higginson drew toward the close of his discourse, shadows were noticed on the sunny threshold of the meetinghouse, and the honorable gentlemen from Plymouth walked in, and took their seats beside the speaker. The charge was given by elder Brewster, in which he principally dwelt on the awful responsibilities of his office, and the high honor Christ had done them, in sending them forth as laborers in his vineyard. Governor Bradford gave the right hand of fellowship with the dignified formality which was said to characterize him on public occasions.

"Well, what do you think of the sermon?" said Mr. Conant, as they mingled with the departing throng.

"Why, I think his tongue will never owe his mouth a penny's rent, if he never preaches such another," answered Mr. Oldham. "I trow that any godly man would be willing to lend his ears, scotfree, to such a sermon as that, seven days out of a week."

"I am suspicious some ears did not receive it very well," quoth another. "Didn't you see that Brown and his seditious company were vexed therewithal?"

"It's wosome to think," rejoined Mr. Oldham, "that there will so soon be difficulties among us. Here is Mr. Brown, now, whom I take to be a very comely sort of a personage in other respects, encouraging his people to chew the ratsbane of Satan, in that he privately readeth unto them the book of common prayer."

"Those were very savory words, which Mr. Higginson addressed to him," observed Mr. Conant. "I marvel that the Lord doth not send forth his javelin, and hurry such fellows from the earth."

"He is not given, like some people that I know of, to the abominable heresy of falling off from grace," interrupted Mr. Graves; "and he seemeth not to meddle with other people's matters."

"I tell you," returned Mr. Conant, "that whosoever is willing to tolerate any false religion, or discrepant way of religion, that his own may be tolerated, will for a need hang God's Bible on the devil's girdle. And as for other people's matters, I should like to know if God's glory is other people's matters;—and therefore to be given into the hands of the heathen and the papist? I should like to have Mr. Higginson hear such like sentiments."

"It is a small matter to me who heareth my sentiments," replied Mr. Graves; "forasmuch as I and my people are about to remove to Shawmut. They say the shipping hath far access into the land in that place; and that the woods are well stored with white oak, not a jot below our English timber."

"A new broom sweepeth clean," answered Mr. Conant; "but there is one thing I can tell you,—ours wore to a stub very quick. The Lord's work will go on at a grand rate carried on as it is by a race of wandering Jacobites, taking dislike at every little difficulty. The ploughable plains, forsooth, are too dry and sandy for them; and the rocky places, although more fruitful, yet to eat their bread with toil of hand, they deem it insupportable; and so away they hie to their new possessions. I tell you, Mr. Graves, bad as you found us, you know nothing at all, as it were, of the terrors of a new plantation."

"I think I have had some occasion to remember sickness and hard labor, though I have known but little concerning scarcity of bread," replied the man of dolorous countenance. "But though the Lord putteth his people to some trials, he upholdeth them in time of danger, and comforteth them in time of need. After all, it maketh but little difference what part of this wilderness a man chooseth. It all seems dismal enough to a body from the old countries."

"Yes," rejoined Mr. Oldham. "I often think of what a witty man at Plymouth once said. Quoth he, 'it may be said of the two Englands, as our Saviour said of the wine, "no man having tasted the old straightway desireth the new; for he saith the old is better."'"

All this while, Mary, who had taken a cross path with Mr. and Mrs. Collier, found means to linger behind, and hear many kind things from Brown. It was likewise observed, that Hopkins dined with his rival; although as some said, Sally's eyes sparkled with malicious exultation when his stentorian voice was heard far out of time and tune in his favorite Old Hundred. Buildings were not numerous enough to give shelter to all their visitors; so tents were erected in the fields, and the multitude were furnished with provisions, plentiful enough, though coarse, and homely in the preparation.

Various were the discussions which were held that day. Some sat apart and talked of state policy, in dark hints and mysterious insinuations; while others loudly and boldly deprecated the high-handed course of the second Stuart. Some dwelt on the great goodness of God in raising them up from their low estate, to the enjoyment of outward comfort, and gospel privileges; or entered into theological controversies, in which a penetrating eye might discover the embryo forms of Familism, Gortonism,[4] and divers other long forgotten sects, which in their day and generation had a reason for the faith that was in them. Many a rough, untutored swain paid his blunt compliments to a rosy cheek, and many a ruddy damsel "whispered, in biblical phrase, her soft words of encouragement and welcome."

CHAPTER X

Their judge was conscience, and her rule their law.
—*Cowper*

MEN SO ENTIRELY uncongenial as Brown and his companions could not long tolerate each other. To the talents and virtues of many of them he gave a voluntary tribute of respect and admiration; but some of them were so far below his intellectual standard, that nothing could have saved them from his contempt, save the strong bond of religious unity; and under no circumstances, and in no situation whatever, could Brown have been a Puritan. Perhaps he and his adversaries equally mistook the pride of human opinion, for conscientious zeal; but their contradictory sentiments owed their origin to native difference of character. Spiritual light, like that of the natural sun, shines from one source, and shines alike upon all; but it is reflected and absorbed in almost infinite variety; and in the moral, as well as the natural world, the diversity of the rays is occasioned by the nature of the recipient.

Brown had gradually grown more daring in the declaration of his belief; but it was not until the Sabbath after ordination that he publicly evinced his adherence to the rites of the Episcopal church. A meeting was held in a vacant building which had been erected as a common house until more convenient dwellings could be procured. Here a considerable number were collected; and the English ritual was read, and the sacrament administered by Mr. Blackstone in his full, canonical robes, according to the ceremonies prescribed by James and his Bishops at the council of Hampton House.

This was a thing not to be passed over. Mr. Blackstone living alone in his solitary hut at Tri-Mountain, was out of their jurisdiction; but Brown and his brother were the next morning ordered to appear before an assembly of the elders, to answer the charges brought against them. At 4 o'clock in the afternoon the inhabitants of Salem were seen again collecting at their meetinghouse to hear what could be said in defence of the culprits.

After a suitable pause, the Governor arose, as he said, "You Mr. Charles and Samuel Brown are accused of fomenting disturbance among the people, forasmuch as you have taught them that under the shadow of the mitre is the only place where men ought to worship. Do you plead guilty thereto?"

"That I bow with reverence before the holy mitre, is most true, Governor Endicott; but in no respect whatever have I bred disturbance among the people."

"Have you not," interrupted Mr. Conant, "have you not made them drink of the wine of Babylon? Yea, have you not made them drunk with her fornication? Have you not, like the red dragon, pursued the church into the wilderness, and poured out a flood after her, that you might cause her to be destroyed?"

"My answers are to Governor Endicott, and the elders of what you term the church," replied Brown, with respectful coldness.

"Mr. Conant," said the Governor, "these things should be done decently, and in order. It is the business of men in authority to inquire into this matter. Have you, young man, upheld the ritual of the first-born daughter of the church of Rome, and maintained that the arm of royal authority ought to enforce obedience thereto?"

"I have said," replied Brown, "that 'Religio docenda est, non coercenda,' was a bad maxim of state policy; and that 'Hæresis dedocenda est, non permittenda,' was a far better.[1] If by the first-born daughter of Rome, you mean that church descended in a direct line from Jesus Christ and his Apostles, a church at the feet of which the most sacred and virtuous Elizabeth bowed down her majestic head, and beneath the shelter of whose mighty arm the learned king James, and our liege prince Charles, have reposed their triple diadem—if you mean this church, I do say, her sublime ritual should be enforced, till every fibre of the king's dominions

yields a response thereto. Saints have worn her white robe, and her mitre
has rested on holy men. The sacred water hath been on my unworthy head,
and therewithal have their hands signed the mystic symbol of redemption.
And I would rather," continued he, raising the tones of his fine, manly
voice, "I would rather give my limbs to the wolves of your desert, than see
her sceptre broken by men like yourselves."

"Think you," said Governor Endicott, smiling, "that king James
cared aught for the church, save that he considered it the basis of the
throne? You forget his open declaration in the assembly at Edinburgh. 'The
church of Geneva,' saith he, 'keepeth pasche and yule; what have they for
them? They have no institution. As for our neighbour kirk of England, their
service is an evil said mass in English. They want none of the mass but the
liftings.'"

"King James had not then come to the English throne," answered
Brown. "He found cause to alter his opinion after he had felt the blessed
influence of that church, and seen many of her corner stones, elect and
precious."

"Nay, Mr. Brown," rejoined the Governor, "there is enow wherewithal to convince your reason, for you are not wanting in the light which
leadeth astray, that it was 'king craft,' which made James turn his back
upon a church whereunto he had given the name of the 'sincerest kirk in
the whole world;' and, with all reverence to his royal memory, I cannot but
think that his love of forms and ceremonies was but a taint of hereditary
evil from his Moabitish mother.[2] Forasmuch as I am a loyal subject of king
Charles, it is neither wise nor safe for me to find specks and blemishes in
his government; but to my thinking, there is but a fine-spun thread
between the crosier and the liturgy, the embroidered mantle and the
bishop's gown; and who does not know that the heart of the king is
fastened to the rosary of Henrietta Maria? And that the mummeries of
Rome are, at her instigation, heard within the palace of St. James? But after
all, Mr. Brown, there is one higher than princes. It was a cardinal truth,
which Cardinal Pole spake unto Henry the Eighth, 'Penes reges inferre
bellum, penes autem Deum terminare.'"[3]

"And I marvel that men of sense, like yourself, Governor Endicott,
can expect the sword of the Lord to be quiet in its scabbard, when the robe
of religion is torn, and her altars overturned," replied Brown; "and that

too, by men unto whom you give your countenance—a parcel of sepa-
ratists and anabaptists, covering their sins with the cloak of religion, and
concealing their own factious and turbulent spirit therewith."

Upon this Mr. Higginson and Mr. Skelton arose and made answer:

"Neither as factious men affecting a popular parity in the church, nor
as schismatics aiming at the dissolution of the church ecclesiastical, but as
faithful ministers of Christ, and liege subjects of king Charles, did we come
hither. We have suffered much for nonconformity in our native land, and
after much tribulation have we come to this place of liberty. Here the cap
and the gown may not be urged upon us, for we consider these things as
sinful abominations in the sight of God. So may the Almighty prosper us, as
we have, in all humility, spoken the truth."

"Credat Judæus, non ego,"[4] replied Brown, scornfully. "It is easy to
talk about conscience and humility, but wherein have you shown it, in that
you judge the consciences of your brethren?"

"We have but testified against what we conceived to be the errors
and abuses of the church," answered Mr. Higginson. "We have been made
the humble instruments to begin the good work, which God will go on to
perfect for his own praise and his people's peace. Let good men sit still and
behold his salvation. He that sitteth in the heavens, laugheth at the pride of
men. The Most High hath them in derision; and their folly shall certainly
be made known unto all."[5]

"Mr. Brown," said the Governor, "you need not reply to this; for
disrespectful words like unto those you have spoken, must not be repeated
in my presence. Inasmuch as gentle means have been in vain used to
convince you of your errors, it is our opinion that New England is no place
for such haughty spirits to dwell within. Therefore, in the first vessel
which departeth from these shores, we do order you to return from
whence you came; and, in the meantime, we do command you to desist
from convening the people together at any time; or in any wise calling their
attention to common prayer."

"Let them that scorn the mitre, fear the crown," replied the angry
young man. "Who is it that has wrought upon the minds of the people,
persuading them that they should not march under the king's colors,
pretending that his conscience is wounded by the popish sign of the cross,

and thereby concealing his traitorous purposes against his sovereign? Mayhap you had spoken less freely within the court of St. James; but the sceptre can reach you even here, and you may yet tremble at its touch. There are those who can tell of your evil practices, and they shall be told in a voice of thunder."

So saying, the young man and his brother, with stately step, departed from the house.

"The council will sit some time longer," said Brown to his brother; "for they have other heretical matters to discuss. If you will give me notice when they begin to disperse, I will go directly to Mr. Conant's; for I must see Mary to-night."

"I could hardly stoop to woo the daughter of that dogmatical rascal," replied Samuel; "though I will acknowledge, she is the very queen of women."

"Pride can endure much in such a cause," rejoined his brother; "but I must away."

The young man sprung over the log enclosure, ran across a meadow to conceal his intended route from those within the dwelling, and in a few moments coming out into the open footpath, he hurried along with the rapid pace of a man in whose bosom painful thoughts are struggling and busy.

"Well," thought he, "I shall at least see England again—again tread on her classic ground, and gaze on her antique grandeur and cultivated beauty. But, oh, to leave her in such a place, is the bitterest thought of all. And what would be her lot, if far away from her, I should go to 'that bourne from whence no traveller returns?'"[6]

But the heart of youth rebounds from the pressure of despondency—and presently brighter scenes were passing swiftly before him. One moment he was invested in the civil gown, the applause of princes and nobles resounding in his ears;—and the next presented Mary restored to her original rank, and shining amid the loveliest and proudest of the land. She too, had had many bitter thoughts; for she well knew the temper of the souls about her, and she felt that the decree of the assembly could not be otherwise than it had proved. When Brown entered, he received a cordial grasp both from the mother and daughter, as they anxiously inquired,

"What have they done?"

"A vessel sails for England in a week," replied Brown; "and Samuel and I depart from America, perhaps forever."

Whenever Mary thought of the possibility of separation, and of late she had frequently feared that the time would soon come, she had felt that the youth was still dearer and dearer to her heart. And now when she heard him announce the speedy certainty of this, her pale lip quivered, and in the silent unreserve of hearts long wedded to each other, she threw herself sobbing on his neck, her slender arms clinging around him, in all the energy of grief.

"I know not," said Mrs. Conant, dashing the tears from her cheek, "I know not that I ought to allow this. Remember, dear Mary, what I owe to your father."

"Madam Conant," replied Brown, "we have loved each other too long, and too purely, to stand upon idle ceremonies at this painful moment. Had I been treated with more moderation, perhaps I might never have been so hasty as to declare my religious opinions. Then these unhappy differences had never arisen, and with my Mary, I could happily have shared a log hut in the wilderness. But I have been spurned, goaded, trampled on, as a heretic—and worse than all, I have been doomed to hear every thing blasphemed which I held most sacred. As it is, you cannot deny us this sorrowful alleviation of our lot."

"It is the duty of woman to love and obey her husband," answered Mrs. Conant; "but had you known whereunto my heart has been inclined in this matter—" she would have said more, but something unbidden rose and prevented her utterance.

"I do know it," rejoined the young man; "and wherever I go, you will be in my pleasantest and most grateful thoughts. But, Mary, it will not be always thus—You will come to England and be my wife."

Mary looked at her mother and sighed.

"It may as well be said as not, my child," observed Mrs. Conant. "I shall not long hang a dead weight upon your young life. Nay, do not weep, Mary; I know that you are willing to bear the burden, and that you have been kind and cheerful beneath it; but the shadows of life are fleeting more dimly before me, and I feel that I must soon be gathered to my fathers."

The expression brought with it a flash of painful recollection.

"No," continued she, "like the wife of Abraham, I must be buried far from my kindred. If my grey-haired father could but shed one tear upon my grave, methinks it would furnish wherewithal to cheer my drooping heart. I loved my husband,—nor have I ever repented that I followed him hither; but oh, Mary, I would not have you suffer as I have suffered, when I have thought of that solitary old man. 'The heart knoweth its own sorrows, and a stranger intermeddleth not with its grief.'"[7]

"Dear mother," replied Mary, "you know that grandfather loves you, and has long since forgiven you. I have told you how often he used to take me in his lap and kiss me, as he said how much I looked like his dear child."

The mournful smile of consumption passed over the pale face of Mrs. Conant,—one of those smiles in which the glowing light of the etherial inhabitant seemed gleaming through its pale and broken tenement.

"Well, Mr. Brown," said she, "Mary will write a letter to her grandfather, and when you deliver it, give him therewith the duty and affection of his dying daughter. I could wish that Mary might be always with her father. He loves her, notwithstanding his conscientious scruples cause him to seem harsh; and perhaps she might feel happier when her days are numbered like mine. But I don't know—It is no doubt a painful sacrifice."

"Wherever I am," replied Brown, "my home shall be most gladly shared with Mary's father. Besides," continued he, smiling, "the prayer book should be hid, and not another word said about the surplice."

"I am glad to hear you speak so," interrupted Mary. "I was afraid you would be angry, inasmuch as I knew they would speak irreverently of our holy church."

"I was angry," answered Brown; "and I threatened that the king should be informed of heresy and treason."

"Oh, Charles, don't stir up their enemies in England," said Mary. "There are a great many good men among them; and I am sure they have difficulties enough already."

"I would not hurt a hair of their heads, if I could," rejoined her lover; "and sorry am I that my unruly tongue led me far beyond my reason in this matter. As you say, I believe some of them are conscientious; though the arch enemy of souls hath led them far from the true path of safety."

"I cannot think with you and Mary," observed Mrs. Conant, "about forms and ceremonies. But it appears to me that an error in judgment is nothing, if the life be right with God. I have lately thought that a humble heart was more than a strong mind, in perceiving the things appertaining to divine truth. Matters of dispute appear more and more like a vapor which passeth away. I have seldom joined in them; for it appears to me there is little good in being convinced, if we are not humbled; to know every thing about religion, and yet to feel little of its power—yea, even to feel burdened with a sense of sin and misery, and yet be content to remain in it."

"Why, I must say," replied Brown, "that I think the Bible is clear enough, as explained by our holy bishops. But to my mind, the view of God's works brings more devotion than any thing relating to controversy."

"Ah, Mr. Brown, the Bible is an inspired book; but I sometimes think the Almighty suffers it to be a flaming cherubim, turning every way, and guarding the tree of life from the touch of man. But in creation, one may read to their fill. It is God's library—the first Bible he ever wrote."

"Bless me," exclaimed Mary, "here is father at the very doors."

Her lover hastily relinquished her hand, and she sprang from his side; but there was no chance for him to retreat. Mrs. Conant's pulse throbbed high, for she saw that her husand was already in no pleasant humor. The old gentleman hung up his hat, and drew his chair forward, without being aware of the presence of any one but his own family, till Brown rose and stood before him. The countenance of Mr. Conant was flushed with anger, when he saw the bold intruder.

"Mr. Brown," said he, stamping his foot violently, "how came you hither?"

"*Why*, I came hither, you already know," replied the youth calmly; "and most gladly would I have had my last visit here, a peaceable one."

The tyrannical man opened the door, and pointed to it, as he said, "A man may not touch pitch, and remain undefiled.[8] I marvel if you bring not a curse on the whole house."

"I was about to depart," answered his guest; "but there is one thing I would say before I go. In my anger I spoke disrespectfully to men older and better than myself. It is a matter of choice as well as of necessity to leave New England, and be no more among you; and now, Mr. Conant, for the sake of those who are dear to me, I would fain have our parting, not that of churchman and non-conformist, but of christians."

"Out with you, and your damnable doctrines, you hypocritical son of a strange woman," exclaimed Mr. Conant.

Pride was struggling hard for utterance, as Brown moved towards the door; but for Mary's sake it was repressed—and before the old man was aware of his purpose, he stept back and took the hand of the mother and daughter, as he said,

"God bless you both. To me you have been all kindness."

He then made a formal, stately bow to Mr. Conant, who muttered, "Take my curse with you," and slammed the door after him.

Mary rushed into her apartment, and hiding her face in the bed clothes, gave free vent to her tears.

But the poor may not long indulge their grief. Her father's supper must be prepared, and her mother's wants must not be neglected; and, with as much serenity as she could assume, she again appeared in his presence. The tears of his sickly wife had allayed the first gust of passion, and perhaps even the heart of that rigid man reproached him for its violence. However that might be, pride would suffer no symptoms of remorse to appear before his family. Every thing went wrong through the whole evening. The cake was burned,—and the milk was not sweet,— and there had been too much fire to prepare their little repast; till wearied out with his continual fretfulness, they both retired to their beds at an early hour, and Mary sobbed herself into an uneasy slumber.

CHAPTER XI

Farewell!
Oh, in that word—that fatal word—howe'er
We promise—hope—believe—there breathes despair.
—*Byron*

THE INTERIM between Brown's sentence and his departure, seemed like "a hideous dream." In vain Mary tried to recognize its certainty enough to prepare the letter which he was to convey. It was not until the day before the dreaded event, that the solicitations of her mother prevailed on her to commence the task; and when she did, the pen remained uplifted, and the stainless sheet lay for a long time before her, while she pressed her hand upon her brow in a bewilderment of misery. She wrote "Deare Grandfather,"—but could proceed no further. The name of that fond, doting relation was encircled with painful thoughts. By him she had been reared with more than tenderness, like some fair and slender blossom in his gardens. There she had been the little idol of the brilliant circle. There too, she had first seen Charles Brown, and mingled with him in the graceful evolutions of the dance, while her young heart in vain strove to be proof against the intoxicating witchery of light and motion. And there, as she gazed on his lofty forehead, stamped with the proud, deep impress of intellect, and watched the changeful lustre of his dark, eloquent eyes, that alternately beamed with high or tender thoughts, she too became covetous of mental riches, and worshipped at the shrine of genius. Amid this fairy dream, the stern voice of duty was heard commanding her to depart from her country and her kindred, and to go to a land of strangers. It recks not how many sighs and tears it cost, the sacrifice was made; and Heaven in reward gave to her solitude the only being that could enliven its dreariness.

What was she now? A lily weighed down by the pitiless pelting of the storm; a violet shedding its soft, rich perfume on bleakness and desolation; a plant which had been fostered and cherished with mild sunshine and gentle dews, removed at once from the hot-house to the desert, and left to unfold its delicate leaves beneath the darkness of the lowering storm. And of the two, for whom she had cheerfully endured this change, one was already within sight of the mansions of the blest—and the other was soon to be like a bright and departed vision. 'Twas bitterness, all bitterness, and she bowed down her head and wept.

"It must not be thus," said she, as she thoughtfully walked across the room. "The painful sacrifice was made with serenity; and none shall say, that I at last shrunk from the trial—" and with steadier nerve, she wrote as follows:

"Deare Grandfather,

"I againe take up my penn to write upon the same paper you gave me when I left you, and tolde me thereupon to write my thoughts in the deserte. Alas, what few I have, are sad ones. I remember you once saide that Shakspeare would have beene the same greate poet if he had been nurtured in a Puritan wildernesse. But indeed it is harde for incense to rise in a colde, heavy atmosphere, or for the buds of fancie to put forth, where the heartes of men are as harde and sterile as their unploughed soile. You will wonder to hear me complain, who have heretofore beene so proud of my cheerfulnesse. Alas, howe often is pride the cause of things whereunto we give a better name. Perhaps I have trusted too muche to my owne strengthe in this matter, and Heaven is nowe pleased to send a more bitter dispensation, wherewithal to convince me of my weakness. I woulde tell you more, venerable parente, but Mr. Brown will conveye this to your hande, and he will saye much, that I cannot finde hearte or roome for. The settlement of this Western Worlde seemeth to goe on fast now that soe many men of greate wisdome and antient blood are employed therein. They saye much concerning our holie church being the Babylone of olde, and that vials of fierce wrath are readie to be poured out upon her.[1] If the prophecies of these mistaken men are to be fulfilled, God grante I be not on earthe to witnesse it. My dear mother is wasting awaye, though I hope she will long live to comforte me. She hath often spoken of you lately. A fewe dayes agone, she said she shoulde die happier if her grey-haired father coulde shed a tear upon her grave. I well know that when that daye does come, we shall both shed many bitter tears. I must leave some space in this paper for her feeble hande to fill. The Lord have you in His holie keeping till your dutifull grandchilde is againe blessed with the sighte of your countenance.

"With all love and reverence,
"Your Affectionate and Dutifull Childe,

"MARY CONANT."

"Deare and Venerable Sire,
"I knowe nott wherewithal to address you, for my hearte is full, and my hande trembleth with weaknesse. My kinde Mary is mistaken in thinking I shall long sojourne upon Earthe. I see the grave opening before me, but I feel that I cannot descend thereunto till I have humbly on my knees asked the forgiveness of my offended father. He who hath made man's hearte to suffer, alone knoweth the wretched-ness of mine when I have thought of your solitary old age. Pardon, I beseech you, my youthfull follie and disobedience, and doe not take offence if I write that the husbande for whose sake I have suffered much, hath been through life a kinde and tender helpe-meete; for I knowe it will comforte you to think upon this, when I am dead and gone. I would saye much more, but though my soule is strong in affection for you, my body is weake. God Almighty bless you, is the prayer of

"Your loving Daughtere,

"MARY CONANT."

The letter once finished, how was it to be delivered to the young man? Mr. Conant had given commands which his wife dared not disobey, and seemed more than ever inclined to keep watch upon Mary's motions. In this dilemma she resolved to tax the ready wit of her friend Sally; but when she sought Mrs. Collier for that purpose, she found her ready equipped for a journey.

"What, are you going to Plymouth so soon?" asked Mary. "I thought you told me you did go not till to-morrow."

"And so I supposed then," answered Sally; "but John hath heard that the boat will sail this afternoon, and he is coming for me shortly. I was just stepping in, to bid you good-bye."

"And you are going away from Salem then, for—always," said Mary, as the tears came to her eyes. "What shall I do, when you are gone?"

"You used to tell me to trust in God," replied her friend, "and perhaps I did wrong that I did not think more of such sober talk. I declare, I did not suppose any thing would have made me so sorry to go back to Plymouth," added she, and the ready tears of sympathy trickled down her cheeks.

"Well, good-bye," said Mary, as she threw her arms round her neck in the full tide of girlish affection. "I shall always love you for your kindness to me and my good mother. Peradventure when we are both ancient women, there will be a road cut through from hence, and I shall come and see you."

At another time Mary would have mourned bitterly over the loss of her old associate; but now in the selfishness of more weighty sorrows, she hardly expended a thought upon it. Her whole mind was occupied in devising a method of seeing Brown, free from interruption. We know that love now usually finds means to effect his purpose, and it seems he laughed as loudly at locksmiths in 1629, as he does in these degenerate days. At the instigation of Mr. Brown, the widow Willet (whose red cardinal gave such offence to Mr. Oldham), was induced to request Mary's company through the night, under pretence of her son's absence. The lonely woman had frequently asked the same favor, and it was, of course, granted without hesitation. Once arrived within her dwelling, the sorrowful young couple were left to an undisturbed discourse upon their present prospects and future plans. The night passed rapidly away, and the sun rose brightly on the pale and agitated pair, as if no hearts were there, to meet his rays with sickening desolation. Brown rested his arm upon Mary's shoulder, and pointed to the rising light, as he said,

"It is the signal of separation. The vessel sails at early sunrise. Would it had never been day."

"Oh," replied Mary, "were it not for the hope of speedy re-union, how gladly would I now lay down my aching head deep, deep, in the cold earth."

"Talk not so sadly, Mary," answered her lover. "If your mother lives long, I shall again come to America, at least for a season; and if she dies, you will soon return to your grandfather, who will make us both happy."

"Alas, Charles," replied she, "it makes me shudder to think of the wickedness of such devoted love. I did even wish to night that mother's earthly trials were all over, and I at liberty to follow you wheresoever you went, through storms or sunshine. It was a wicked thought, and I struggled till I overcame it."

"Be ever thus, my own dear girl," rejoined the young man. "I could not love you if you were otherwise. May the atmosphere of your mind be always so pure that a passing cloud has power wherewithal to disturb it."

For some moments he stood silently clasping her to his heart. He moved from her, and made a reluctant motion toward the table where he had placed his hat—walked across the room again and again—looked out upon the increasing light, and cursed its swiftness; at length, a loud, shrill blast came upon the morning air; "'Tis the last signal for all to be on board," exclaimed he; "and now I *must* depart."

She sprung to his embrace, and his arms twined round her, "and clung as they would cling forever." One deep, painful pause, one fervent long protracted kiss on that cold brow, and he was gone.

The maiden slowly returned to her father's house, sick, exhausted, and weary of life. The household duties were silently and serenely per-formed; and no outward token of anguish could be discovered save a death-like paleness. Two hours elapsed, and yet the gay pennon of the Queen Elizabeth was seen fluttering in the air. Mary could not follow the multitude to the beach, and give the sacredness of her grief to the vulgar gaze; but she sought a woody, retired hill, and watched the departure of her lover's vessel, which with spreading sails, was soon seen wheeling from the shore. A handkerchief was waving from the quarter deck; it was a farewell signal, and was speedily answered. It again waved toward the thicket, and Mary knew that her last token of love had not passed un-observed. Her intense and eager gaze was never turned from the object, until the red-cross flag indistinctly mingled with the horizon. Mary looked on the bright, blue expanse of water before her. The deep furrows, which had so lately marred its beauty, had all passed away, as suddenly as the tribulations of boyhood; and as she turned away from that smooth surface, she, for the first time, realized what she had as yet shrunk from acknowledging, the cheerless, utter solitude of the heart.

CHAPTER XII

Erewhile, where yon gay spires their brightness rear,
Trees waved, and the brown hunter's shouts were loud
Amid the forest; and the bounding deer
Fled at the glancing plume, and the gaunt wolf yelled near.
—*Bryant*

DURING THE LONG and dreary winter which followed, there was nothing to break the monotony of the scene, except the occasional visits of Hobomok, who used frequently to come up from Plymouth and join the hunters in their excursions. At such seasons, he was all vigor and elasticity; and none returned more heavily laden with furs and venison, than the tawny chieftain. The best of these spoils were always presented to the "child of the Good Spirit," as he used to call Mary; and never to Squantam or Abbamocho had he paid such unlimited reverence.

A woman's heart loves the flattery of devoted attention, let it come from what source it may. Perhaps Mary smiled too complacently on such offerings; perhaps she listened with too much interest, to descriptions of the Indian nations, glowing as they were in the brief, figurative language of nature. Be that as it may, love for Conant's daughter, love deep and intense, had sunk far into the bosom of the savage. In minds of a light and thoughtless cast, love spreads its thin, fibrous roots upon the surface, and withers when laid open to the scorching trials of life; but in souls of sterner mould, it takes a slower and deeper root. The untutored chief knew not the strange visitant which had usurped such empire in his heart; if he found himself gazing upon her face in silent eagerness, 'twas but adoration for so bright an emanation from the Good Spirit; if something within taught him to copy, with promptitude, all the kind attentions of the white man, 'twas gratitude for the life of his mother which she had preserved.

84

However, female penetration knew the plant, though thriving in so wild a soil; and female vanity sinfully indulged its growth. Sometimes a shuddering superstition would come over her, when she thought of his sudden appearance in the mystic circle, and she would sigh at the vast distance which separated her from her lover; but the probability of Brown's return, would speedily chase away such thoughts.

Hobomok seldom spoke in Mr. Conant's presence, save in reply to his questions. He understood little of the dark divinity which he attempted to teach, and could not comprehend wherein the traditions of his fathers were heathenish and sinful; but with Mary and her mother, he felt no such restraint, and there he was all eloquence.

It was in the middle of the "cold moon," by which name he used to designate January, that he arrived in Salem, on one of his numerous visits, bringing with him some skins of the beautiful grey fox of the Mississippi.

"Hobomok brought you fur for moccasins," said he, as he handed them to Mary.

"How very soft it is," said she, showing it to her mother. "It seems like the handsome fur, which grandfather had from Russia. You did not kill it yourself, Hobomok?"

The Indian shook his head. "His tracks are toward the setting sun," replied he. "Hobomok give beaver skins like sand to a warrior come in from the west. He say they call it Muzaham Shungush. There is a council-fire at Mount Haup. The chiefs think the hunter came not to trade for beaver skins, but to find how heavy the red men of Ossamequin,[1] Sassacus, Miantonimo, and Uncas."

"Have none of them been hither, heretofore?" inquired Mary.

"One warrior came among us in the moon of flowers,* and spread his blanket with us through the hunting moon.† I talked with him, like as with the Yengees. He told big stories about his tribe; but he say Great Spirit lay between us, and his back bone so high, make foot of the Indian weary. The chiefs said he counted red men then; but the cloud passed over."

"Well," rejoined Mary, "I hope they'll bring more such handsome fur hither. If they come to count the red men, peradventure they'll find them

* May.
† December.

too heavy. You see I am going to make you a wampum belt of the shells you brought, and I want you to tell me how to put them together."

"Hobomok glad," replied the Indian, his eyes sparkling with joy at such a proof of gratitude. "You see that shell, the color of the sky when the sun goes down? Put him in the big moose there," pointing to the middle of the belt. "Him like the rainbow, put on the back of the deer; and him like the heaped snow, put on the big snake. That's like Tatobam's wampum. Tatobam kill snakes—make great spirit snake very angry—That's reason the Indian from the west call him Tongoomlishcah." [2]

"And who is he?" asked Mary.

"The grass has now grown on Tatobam's grave, and trees are planted thereon," answered the savage. "He was the father of Sassacus, great Sachem of the Pequods. In council, cunning as the beaver, and quick-sighted as the eagle. His tribe were like swallows before a storm, and his wrath like the rising of a thunder cloud. Furious as a wounded buffalo in the fight, but true to his love as the star of the north."

"And was she good enough for so great a warrior?" rejoined Mary.

"His Mohegan squaw was bright and handsome as the wakon-bird [3] of the west. Her voice cheered the sachem, like the song of the muck-a-wiss, [4] that tells of frost gone by. In the dance she was nimble as the deer, and quick as the diving loon. But the quiver of Mohegan was sent to the Pequod, and it was wound with the skin of the snake."

"And then he made war upon his squaw's tribe, I suppose?"

"Tatobam's men were thick as leaves in autumn, his quiver was full, his bow was strong, and his arrow sharp as the lightning, when the Great Spirit sends it forth in his anger. There would have been few left among the Mohegans to black their faces for the dead. The voice of his tribe was for battle. The hunter heard their war-song far away in the desert, like the notes of the woodpecker, which tell of the tempest. So the council-fire was extinguished. The face of Tatobam was anointed, and his belt buckled for the fight. But Indian can love," said he, as he stooped low, and looked up in Mary's face.

"How did Tatobam prove it?" inquired Mrs. Conant.

"Grass never grows in the war-path of the Pequod. His warriors said they would bring home the scalps of their enemies before the rising of the sun. They called on Tatobam to lead to the fight, that they might drink the blood of Mohegan. Before the moon went behind the hills, his tracks were upon the sand; the rising tide washed them away. He rose up at the call of his tribe, and they knew not he had been forth alone. They found not a sleeping enemy. The ambush of the Pequod was broken. The tomahawk was changed for the peace pipe, and the marriage dance was seen in the wigwam of Tatobam."

"Hobomok," interrupted Mr. Conant, who entered at this moment, "it is a pity you were not out with your bow, forasmuch as a fine deer just ran through the settlement."

"There's a tribe of 'em, out on the plains to night," answered the Indian. "Their tracks are thick as flies in the Sturgeon moon.* Sagamore John's men are coming out with—with—" and unable to think of the English word, he pointed to the candle.

"Oh, they are coming out by torch-light," exclaimed Mary, "as Hobomok says the western Indians do. How I do wish I could see them hunt by torch-light."

"I shall go out with you," said Mr. Conant, "to see what success the Lord giveth us in this matter. I have heard wonderful stories appertaining to the taking of deer after this fashion. They say that in the lightest night that ever was made, the creatures are so bewitched, that they'll not move a jot, after they once get sight of the fire."

"And wherefore shouldn't I go, father?" asked Mary.

"A pretty sight truly," replied the old man, "to see you out at midnight with twenty hunters."

"But," rejoined his wife, "two or three horses can be procured; and if a few of the young folks will go, assuredly I see no harm therein; more especially as you will accompany Mary. You must remember," continued she, in an insinuating tone, "that there are few such like gratifications in this wilderness."

"No doubt there is enough of them; wherewithal to entice their wandering hearts," answered her husband; "but if you think it fitting the girl should go, verily I have no objection thereto."

Preparations were accordingly made. The widow Willet agreed to come up and stay with Mrs. Conant; and a few young women readily

* August.

consented to accompany Mary, on such horses as the settlement could afford. As for Hobomok, he was all eagerness to display his skill. His arrows were carefully selected, and the strength of his bow was tried again and again, as he occasionally turned to Mary, and boasted of the service it had always done him, in field and forest.

Winter seldom presents a night of such glittering beauty, as the one they chose for their expedition. The mellow light of moon and star looked down upon the woods, and as the trees danced to the shrill music of the winds, their light was reflected by ten thousand undulating motions, in all the rich varieties of frost work. It seemed as if the sylphs and fairies, with which imagination of old, peopled the mountain and the stream, had all assembled to lay their diamond offerings on the great altar of nature. Silently Mary gazed on the going down of that bright planet, and tree and shrub bowed low their spangled plumes in homage to her retiring majesty, till her oblique rays were only to be seen in faint and scattered radiance, on the cold, smooth surface of the earth.

At length the party were in motion, proceeding through the woods by the twinkling lustre of the stars. Mr. Conant held the rein of Mary's horse, and guided his footsteps along the rough and narrow path. Hobomok walked by her side, as silent and thoughtful as he usually was in the presence of her father. They soon came out upon the open plain; and a few moments after, six neighboring Indians were seen winding along from the opposite woods, with their torches carried upon poles high above their heads, casting their lurid glare on the mild, tranquil light of the evening. As they drew up, a few inquiries were made by Hobomok in his native tongue, and answered by his companions in scarcely an audible tone, as they significantly placed their fingers upon their lips. Mr. Conant and his ten associates formed a line and fell into the rear, while the Indians who carried the poles, did the same, and placed themselves forward. It was indeed a strange, romantic scene. The torches sent up columns of dense, black smoke, which vainly endeavoured to rise in the clear, cold atmosphere. Hobomok stood among his brethren, gracefully leaning on his bow, and his figure might well have been mistaken for the fabled deity of the chase. The wild, fitful light shone full upon the unmoved countenance of the savage, and streamed back unbroken upon the rigid features of the Calvinist, rendered even more dark in their expression by the beaver cap which deeply shaded his care-worn brow. The pale loveliness of Mary's face, amid the intense cold of the night, seemed almost as blooming as her ruddy companions; and the frozen beauty of the surrounding woods again flashed brightly beneath the unwonted glow of those artificial rays.

There, in that little group, standing in the loneliness and solitude of nature, was the contrast of heathen and christian, social and savage, elegance and strength, fierceness and timidity. Every eye bent forward, and no sound broke in upon the stillness, excepting now and then, the low, dismal growl of the wolf was heard in the distance. Whenever this fearful sound came upon the ear, the girls would involuntarily move nearer to their protectors, who repeatedly assured them that wolves would never approach a fire. Presently a quick, light step was heard, and a deer glided before them. The beautiful animal, with rapid and graceful motion, was fast hurrying to the woods, when his eye seemed caught by the singular light which gleamed around him. He paused, and looking back, turned his pert, inquiring gaze full upon the hunters. He saw the forms of men, and knew they were his enemies; but so powerful was the fascination of the torches, that his majestic antlers seemed motionless as the adjacent shrubbery.

The arrow of Hobomok was already drawn to the head, when Mary touched his shoulder, as she said, "Don't kill it, Hobomok—don't;" but the weapon was already on the wing, and from his hand it seldom missed its mark. The deer sprung high into the air, its beautiful white breast was displayed for an instant, a faint, mournful sound was heard—and Hobomok stept forward to seize the victim he had wounded. As he brought it up to Mary, the glossy brown of its slender sides was heaving with the last agonies of life, and she turned away from the painful sight.

But a short space ensued, ere another was seen sweeping across the plain. He too noticed the unnatural brightness, and stood bound by the same bewitching spell. One of the Indians gave his torch to Hobomok, and placing his eye on a level with his bow, took steady and deliberate aim. However, it seemed he had not effected his purpose entirely; for the creature uttered a piercing cry, and bounded forward with incredible swiftness. The next Indian handed his torch to one of the white men, and rushing before his companion, he buried his knife deep in the bosom of the wounded deer. A loud laugh of derision followed.

"It's mine," exclaimed he, in Indian language, "It's mine, for I killed it."

"'Tisn't yours," retorted the other, furiously; "the deer hadn't run ten rods; and a hunter never gave up a beast under that."

The girls could not understand what was spoken by the contending savages; but they saw that a quarrel was likely to ensue, and Mary whispered to her father to guide them homeward. The route they had taken was a short one, and the difficulties in retracing it were few. The maidens gladly welcomed their own quiet apartments, and Mr. Conant returned to the plain. The Indian who had first wounded the animal, had proudly relinquished his claim, and stood by, in sullen, offended majesty. The others were preparing a new set of flambeaux for a fresh attack.

CHAPTER XIII

Strong was the love to heaven, which bare
From their dear homes and altars far,
The old, the young, the wise, the brave,
The rich, the noble, and the fair,
And led them o'er the mighty wave,
Uncertain peril's front to dare.
—*Yamoyden*

NOTWITHSTANDING the occasional excitements which we have mentioned, the winter passed wearily away; and to Mary, the moral as well as the natural atmosphere, was chill and heavy. The earth, in this cold, northern climate, wore one uniform robe of state—her spotless ermine, studded with jewels. Even in this dress, she displayed much to excite a poetic imagination and a devotional heart; but the souls of men were not open to the influence of nature. Little thought they, amid the fierce contests of opinion, of the latent treasures of mind or the rich sympathies of taste. Still, their stern piety was lofty and genuine, though deeply colored with the ignorance and superstition of the times. A sound, doctrinal exposition of Romans brought more religious warmth into their hearts, than the nightly exhibition of the numerous hosts shining in the broad belt of the heavens, those mighty apostles, which God has sent forth to proclaim throughout creation, his majesty and power. Mary grew more and more weary of the loneliness of unreciprocated intellect; and when she thought of Brown, it seemed as if winter would never depart. But though the wings of time appeared clogged, and folded about him in heaviness, he wheeled the same course through the sky; and Spring was soon seen peeping from the sunny gates of heaven, and strewing her wild-flower wreath along the woods.

Intelligence had reached New England that a large company of godly brethren were coming out early in the season, among whom was Mrs.

Johnson, the favorite sister of the Earl of Lincoln.[1] Mary had known the lady Arabella in Lincolnshire, and she now kept an almost constant watch upon the seashore, in the eager anticipation of meeting with her friend. Perhaps even that friend was frequently forgotten in the thoughts of one still dearer; for she had heard nothing from Brown since his departure, and her heart grew sick with "hope deferred."

It was late in May, when, as she was walking by the seashore, gazing on the bright scene, to her so painfully associated, she espied two vessels under full sail, and her spirits danced with the certainty of intelligence from her lover, if not his actual presence. The news was hastily communicated, and all felt disappointed when they were discovered to be under foreign colors. The suspicion at once arose that they were Dunkirkers, and, of course, enemies to the English. The alarm was given, and every man seized his loaded gun, and prepared to give them a hostile reception. Luckily, however, the precaution was found unnecessary. The ships rode quietly into port, and proved to be merchantmen from the Netherlands, bringing a large supply of provisions and utensils of various kinds, to exchange for beaver skins. Another fortnight passed slowly away, and it was rumored that one of the Arabella company had safely arrived at Shawmut; but still there came no intelligence to hush the tumult of Mary's hopes and fears. At length, on the 12th of June 1630, the settlers had scarcely swung their axes over their shoulders, or fastened the plough to their oxen, at early sunrise, before the tall mast of the Arabella was seen careering above the waves, bending her prow, and "walking the waters like a thing of life."[2] And as she came within hearing, the cheerful note of the trumpet, proclaiming, "Capt. Millburn of the Arabella—sixty-five days from Yarmouth, Isaac Johnson, Esq. and the Lady Arabella on board," was answered by three loud and hearty shouts of welcome. A tall, dignified looking lady descended from the vessel, and scarcely had the exclamations, "My dear Mary," and "My dear Lady Arabella," escaped their lips, ere they were fast locked in each other's arms.

"Come," said Mary, "I know you will be glad to enter any dwelling, after this voyage; and my dear mother will be impatient to be introduced to you."

"Then she is yet spared?" asked Mrs. Johnson.

"Yes," replied Mary; "but she is sinking away, like a decaying lamp."

"This is my mother," continued she, as she entered and placed Lady Arabella's hand within Mrs. Conant's.

"I am glad to welcome you to New England, Lady Arabella," said the mother; "though perhaps we have both been used to better apartments," added she, as her eye glanced round the humble room, with a look of pride, which ill assorted with her broken fortunes.

"No doubt, no doubt, Lady Mary," answered her guest; "but there are strong hands and firm hearts, as well as noble blood, engaged in this cause. I have heard my husband say that our own mighty kingdom was once a remote province of the Roman empire,—and who knows where-unto these small beginnings may arrive?"

"It's little that I have to do with the thoughts of kings, empires, and nobles in these days," replied Mrs. Conant; "but I would fain ask whether the old man, my father, is yet alive?"

"The Earl of Rivers is alive and well," said the Lady Arabella. "When my chest arrives I can give you some further news."

"Well, Madam Conant," said Mr. Johnson, whom Mr. Conant intro-duced a few moments after, "I have taken the liberty of bringing my lady hither; inasmuch as there are no conveniences for us at Shawmut, whither we propose shortly to depart. Lady Arabella chose the rather to abide with you, on account of her sometime acquaintance with your daughter."

"Right glad we are to have a hand in helping forward the work of the Lord," replied Mr. Conant.

"Such as we have, we gladly give unto you," interrupted his wife; "but you see our velvet cushions are wooden benches, and our tapestry the rough bark of the forest tree. However, 'it is better to be a doorkeeper in the house of the Lord, than to dwell in the tents of the wicked.'"

"And is Mary cheerful under all these privations?" inquired Mr. Johnson. "Two or three years' residence so far from the busy world hath made her matronly before her time. Bless me, Lady Arabella, what would the Earl of Lincoln say to see his young favorite now?"

"How I wish I could see him," said Mary. "Is he married?"

"No," answered Mrs. Johnson; "but he is shortly to be united to the virtuous daughter of Lord Say; and a great blessing she will prove to our family, no doubt. It is said that Lord Say and Lord Brook are thinking of a settlement in New England."

"Yes," said her husband, "many godly men are turning their faces hitherward; and many of the wealthy and noble of our land are devoting their riches to the building up of Zion."

"And no doubt they'll be prospered," rejoined Mr. Conant. "'Media movent bonitate finis.'³ Well may they come out of England, when Episcopacy hath become such a religious jewel in the state that the king will sell all his coronets, caps of honor, and blue garters, for six and twenty cloth caps. And who cannot see the tempter which hath led him astray? I am bold to say, Mr. Johnson, that though the king sitteth highest on the bench, his papistical queen sitteth in a chair above; and though he is placed in the saddle, she hath her hand upon the bridle."

"Yes," replied his guest, "it is a great pity that 'no bishop, no king'⁴ hath become such an oraculous truth with him, that he is willing to pawn his crown and life thereupon. His oppression gallops so hard, that it outstrips the patience of his subjects; but it is well for princes to remember that *preces et lachrymæ*⁵ are not the only weapons of the people. Have you heard that bishop Laud is made Chancellor of Oxford?"

"Assuredly I have not," answered Mr. Conant; "and well pleased should I be, never to have heard thereof; but it is plain enough to see that there is nothing to which he and my Lord Treasurer Weston may not aspire in the kingdom. What is to become of poor old England, when the despotic Lewis and the subtle Richelieu have so powerful an emissary in the very bosom of king Charles?"⁶

"It's a dolorous truth indeed," replied Mr. Johnson. "But as I was saying, the Bishop of London came to the vacancy last April; and even before I departed, he straightway instituted copes, railings, and crucifixes within the university. St. Katherine's church, which was repaired as late as bishop Mountain's time, must likewise be closed, until his successor seeth fit to revive the ceremony of consecration therein; which he did, with many popish ceremonies; such as bowing and kneeling before the altar, wearing of hood and surplice, and so on; but the worst of the whole blasphemy you have yet to hear. As Laud approached the doors of the church, his attendants opened them wide, crying with a loud voice, 'Open, ye everlasting gates, that the King of Glory may come in.'"

"No doubt this was like sugar in the mouth of the queen," rejoined

Mr. Conant. "If the church of England, as it is in these days, be not the whorish woman of Babylon, I declare it requireth more than ordinary spirit of discerning to distinguish between them. Peradventure it may be the second beast, seen by St. John, who 'exerciseth all the power of the one before him, and causeth the earth and them which dwell therein, to worship the first beast whose deadly wound was healed.'"

"There is much reason to fear that 'God will soon put in his sickle and gather the vine of the earth, to cast into the great wine-press of his wrath,'"[7] observed Mr. Johnson. "I am glad that I have come out from among them; and I have no doubt we shall go on to complete the good work, though there are enemies on every side—yea, though Morton, and divers others, daily increase in zeal against us."

"Charles Brown found there was a Phinehas among us, to stand up and stay the plague,"[8] said Mr. Conant; "and no doubt he hath wielded his sword in the ranks of our adversaries?"

"I understand the testimony of Mr. Brown hath always been honorable to the colonies," answered Mr. Johnson; "and as for the mischief intended by others, he who discovered the plottings of the Assyrian king, even in his bed chamber, will no doubt turn it aside."[9]

Mary's face flushed with conscious triumph, at this mention of her lover's honorable conduct; and even her father was surprised into something like respect. However, that unyielding pride, which was at once the source of his greatest virtues and his greatest faults, prevented his making any reply.

"Well," said Mr. Johnson, after a moment's pause, "how do you succeed, outwardly and spiritually, in this heritage?"

"We speed as we can, as men must, who are no better shod," rejoined Mr. Conant. "As for worldly wisdom, we have been obliged to pay pretty roundly to dame experience for filling our heads with a little of her active after-wit; and as for the church, sects are springing up among us, like vipers in the sun. Many an honest mind hath been led away by sore temptations, and embittered by constant disputations."

"Weak wine becometh sour by fermentation, and strong wine is made better," replied Mr. Johnson. "I marvel if the Lord often suffereth the devices of Satan to lead away those who are firm in the faith;—I believe they are strengthened thereby. After all, most of the carping and controversy in the world is about matters of small moment, which tend much to the neglecting of the soul's salvation. 'Tis like unto a man's diving into a well to see the stars in broad sunlight."

"And what hath he for his pains but to be blinded when he cometh from thence?" said Mr. Conant. "The fact is, passengers to heaven are in haste, and will walk one way or the other. If a man doubts of his way, Satan is always ready at hand to help him to a new set of opinions at every stage; and if his infernal Majesty hath too much employment, he can always find helpers in such like men as Mr. Graves and Mr. Blackstone."

"Do you have any trouble with the latter gentleman, now-a-days?" asked Mr. Johnson.

"I know nothing concerning him," answered Mr. Conant, "except that he came hither at the instigation of Jereboam son of Nebat, and that he made Israel to sin.[10] I'll tell you a very singular story, Mr. Johnson, wherein the Lord shewed his indignation against the pride of prelacy. This Mr. Blackstone, living immured there at Tri-Mountain, hath not much communication with any one on the earth or above it; but those who have been within his dwelling, say that he hath many books, forgetting the excellent advice of Pliny, '*Multum* legendum est, non *multa*.'[11] This man, in the sinful pride of his heart, had the book of common prayer, that dud of the devil, bound up with the Testament of our blessed Lord. Now look at the miraculous manner in which God pointed out his sin unto him. There were many rats in the room wherein these books lay, but among three hundred, none were touched save the one I have mentioned. No, not even the Testament which was bound therewith. But the book of common prayer was probably savory to such filthy vermin, for it was clean devoured."[12]

"And had he no prickings of conscience on the occasion?" inquired Mr. Johnson.

"I doubt whether the minions of Babylon have a conscience," rejoined Mr. Conant. "If so be they have, you might as well skin a flint, as stick a pin therein."

"It is a matter of rejoicing that they are all in the hands of the Lord," observed Mr. Johnson. "In due time, he will no doubt 'drive the Canaanite out of the land.'"

"There is no reason to despair thereof," replied Mr. Conant; "but I marvel that England, which hath always been the staple of truth to the whole world, doth not rise and give him a helping hand. And now I think on't, can you tell me how the Protestant cause goes on in Europe?"

"You have heard of the success of Ferdinand the II. He has overrun all Saxony, and seems like to subdue the Protestants entirely. Urban hath swords and pens enough in his unrighteous service. Powerful kings are fighting in his cause; the Jesuits are stretching their arms north, south, east, and west, to hold up the reins of the falling church—and king Charles has caught the beast, and christened it Episcopacy, a cunning way, truly, to save him from the pursuit of his enemies. But Gustavus dares to stand out firmly against him; and I understand he is even now in arms, at the call of the reformers."[13]

"I wish he had plenty of such men as Governor Endicott among his army," replied Mr. Conant. "Though I am verily sorry that there is likely to be difficulty concerning what he hath said of the king's popish colors. Assuredly I am of his opinion that it is a sinful and shameful abomination among us. The Governor is a bold man, and withal discreet. He sheweth that he hath the fear of God in this matter, though he had none for man or devil."

"And yet," said Mary, "he is very courteous, and when he unbends the bow, you would think loving was all his trade. But come, Lady Arabella, your breakfast is, at last, ready. I have honored you more than we ever did any guests in America, for see mother's damask cloth is spread over our pine table."

"I have come into the wilderness too," rejoined her friend; "and I must learn to eat hominy and milk, and forget the substantial plum puddings of England. But 'sweet is a dinner of herbs where love is,'" said she, as her eye rested on her husband, with all the pride of woman's affection. She touched a sensitive chord, and Mary hastily turned away, to conceal the starting tears.

"Come, move to the table, Mr. Johnson," said her father; "and you too, Lady Arabella; and after we have craved a blessing thereon, we will partake of pilgrims' fare."

"I am sure this venison is good enough for an alderman," observed his guest. "Will you taste some, Lady Arabella?"

"No, thank you," answered his wife. "I am going to try some of Mary's pumpkin and milk."

"That's right, Lady Arabella," rejoined Mr. Conant. "They are a kind of food which has been much despised, but I trust hereafter nobody will speak disrespectfully of pumpkins, inasmuch as it hath pleased the Lord to feed his people thereupon for many years. Ah, Mr. Johnson, you have come among us in good time, for the Dutch ships you heard us speak of, not only brought comforting tidings from our godly brethren in the Netherlands, but likewise much that was needful for the sustenance of the body. But the time has been when our bread was measured out to us, and scanty weight too. And comfortless as you may think this hut looketh now, it hath been far worse; for there was a season that we had no doors wherewithal to keep out the Indians—but though their hunters used to come in among us, 'very mooch hungry,' as they would say, the Lord so disposed them, that they never harmed a hair of our heads."

Mr. Johnson looked at his wife, and smiled half mournfully, as if he was doubtful whether she could endure such trials; but he met the answering smile of a mind aware of its difficulties, and fortified against them.

"I have heard great reports about Hobomok," said she, turning to Mr. Conant. "They say he is a clever Indian and comely withal, and that he hath been of great use to our Plymouth brethren."

"You must ask Mary about him," replied Mrs. Conant, smiling. "She loves to hear his long stories about the Iroquois, which he learned of one of their chiefs who came hither many years ago; and his account of the ancestors of some neighboring tribe, who, as he saith, were dropped by an eagle on an island to the south."

"It's little I mind his heathenish stories," rejoined her husband; "but I have sat by the hour together, and gazed on his well fared face, till the tears have come into mine eyes, that the Lord should have raised us up so good a friend among the savages. Good morning to your honor," contined he, as Governor Endicott entered. "I trust you have not come to take our guests from us?"

"I have come in behalf of my good woman," answered the Governor, after he had returned the salutation of the strangers, "entreating that the Lady Arabella will abide with us during her stay in Salem."

"I shall most assuredly see madam Endicott, before I depart from hence," replied the noble lady; "but I chose the rather to abide with Lady Mary, as long as my husband seeth fit I should sojourn here, inasmuch as her daughter and I were some time acquainted across the water."

"It shall be as your ladyship says," rejoined the Governor; "but there are many godly women at my house, who came with you, and right glad should I be to have you added to them. At any event, I must carry away your good husband for the present, forasmuch as I have many important things whereof to inquire."

The gentlemen rose, and prepared to depart, and the ladies having returned the formal salutations of the courteous chief magistrate, were soon left to themselves.

CHAPTER XIV

Epistles, wet
With tears that trickled down the writer's cheeks
Fast as the periods from his fluent quill,
Or charg'd with am'rous sighs of absent swains.
 —*Cowper*

ON THIS DAY there was business and rejoicing through every corner of the settlement. Among all the daring souls, who left honor, comfort, and independence, for the sake of worshipping God according to the dictates of their own consciences, there was no one more highly or more deservedly respected than Mr. Johnson.[1] In the bloom of life, a gentleman, a scholar, and nearly allied to a noble family, he left his own wise, wealthy, and happy land, to join a poor, despised, and almost discouraged remnant in this western wilderness. Could his prophetic eye have foreseen that the wild and desolate peninsula where he first purchased, would become the proud and populous emporium of six flourishing states; could he have realized that the transfer of government from London to Massachusetts, was but the embryo of political powers, which were so soon to be developed before the gaze of anxious and astonished Europe; how great would have been the reward of the high-minded Englishman. But his self-denying virtue had not these powerful excitements. Who in those days of poverty and gloom, could have possessed a wand mighty enough to remove the veil which hid the American empire from the sight? Who would have believed that in two hundred years from that dismal period, the matured, majestic, and unrivalled beauty of England, would be nearly equalled by a daughter, blushing into life with all the impetuosity of youthful vigor? But though Johnson and his associates could not foresee the result of the first move which they were unconsciously making in the great game of nations—a game which has ever since kept kings in constant check—he, at least, was amply rewarded by an approving conscience, and the confiding admiration of his brethren, which almost amounted to idolatry. All was life and activity during the day of his arrival. In one place might be seen boats, passing and repassing from the vessel, the ripples breaking against their oars, as they glistened in the sun. In another, the hearty interchange of salutation between seamen and landsmen; or a group of gentlemen, busy in the delivery of letters, and already eagerly engaged in discussions concerning the extent of the government wherewith they had been entrusted.

While all this bustle was going on without doors, there were questions enough to be asked and answered by the female inmates of Mr. Conant's dwelling. Several hours past before the Lady Arabella's chest was brought on shore; and though Mary's heart was throbbing high with expectation, she made no inquiries concerning letters from England. At length, however, a sailor arrived with the long expected treasures.

"This is from your father, Lady Mary," said Mrs. Johnson as she placed a letter in her hand. With provoking delay, she handed another package to Mary, as she said, "This is from brother George."

It was a neat edition of Spenser's Fairy Queen, written within, in his lordship's own hand, "To Miss Mary Conant. This cometh to remind her of bye past daies, from her olde friend GEORGE—Earl Lincoln."

"And this," continued Lady Arabella, "is likewise from Earl Rivers, who desired that Mary would open it in her own apartment."

Every one acquainted with the mazes of love, is aware of a strange perversity in the female heart with regard to such matters. Mary half suspected that her friend noticed the painful suffusion which covered her face and neck, and the package which she supposed contained news, to her more important than any thing else in the world, was placed in her little bedroom with affected indifference, and was not touched till every article of household work was completed with even more deliberate neatness than usual. Not so Mrs. Conant—she eagerly caught her letter, and tearing open the envelope, devoured with painful pleasure the only words which her father had addressed to her since her marriage. They were as follows:

"Deare Daughtere,

"Manie thoughts crowde into my hearte, when I take upp my pen to write to you. Straightwaye my deare wife, long in her grave, cometh before me, and bringeth the remembrance of your owne babie face, as you sometime lay suckling in her arms. The bloode of anciente men floweth slow, and the edge of feeling groweth blunte: but heavie thoughts will rise on the surface of the colde streame, and memorie will probe the wounded hearte with her sharpe lancett. There hath been much wronge between us, my deare childe, and I feel that I trode too harshlie on your young hearte: but it maye nott be mended. I have had many kinde thoughts of you, though I have locked them up with the keye of pride. The visit of Mr. Brown was very grievious unto me, inasmuch as he tolde me more certainly than I had known before that you were going downe to the grave. Well, my child, 'it is a bourne from whence no traveller returns.' My hande trembleth while I write this, and I feel that I too am hastening thither. Maye we meete in eternitie. The tears dropp on the paper when I think we shall meete no more in time. Give my fervente love to Mary. She is too sweete a blossom to bloome in the deserte. Mr. Brown tolde me much that grieved me to hear. He is a man of porte and parts,² and peradventure she maye see the time when her dutie and inclination will meete together. The greye hairs of her olde Grandefather maye be laide in the duste before that time; but she will finde he hath nott forgotten her sweete countenance and gratious behaviour. I am gladd you have founde a kinde helpe-meete in Mr. Conant. May God prosper him according as he hath dealte affection-ately with my childe. Forgive your olde father as freelie as he for-giveth you. And nowe, God in his mercie bless you, dere childe of my youthe. Farewell.

"Your Affectionate fathere,

"RIVERS."

"N.B. I have sente you a Bible, (which please to accept as a token of love) by Mr. Isaac Johnson; whome I esteeme a right honorable gentleman, though it grieveth me to see the worthies and nobles of the lande giving their countenance to the sinn of Non-conformitie."

The unqualified kindness of her repenting father proved too much for the weak nerves of his disobedient child; and for a long time Mary and her friend hung over her in a fearful anxiety, lest the blow should hasten a departure, which they all saw must soon come. Lady Arabella brought forward some cordials which she had brought with her, and presently her highly excited system sunk exhausted into slumber. Mrs. Johnson laid herself down beside the sleeping invalid, and gladly sought repose after the fatigue of a long and wearisome voyage. Mary willingly improved this opportunity to examine the contents of her package. A prayer book, bound in the utmost elegance of the times, first met her view. It was ornamented with gold clasps, richly chased; the one representing the head of king Charles, the other the handsome features of his French queen; and the inside of both adorned with the arms of England. Mary hardly paused to look at the valuable present in her eagerness to read the following lines.

"Deare Mary,

"How many times I should have written to you, could I have devised any waye for it to come safely into your hands, I leave your own hearte to judge. God knoweth howe much more I have beene in the deserte since I came hither, than while I was in the wildernesse of Newe England. It was a trial I needed, to showe me howe very deare you were unto my soule. I often think of the sicknesse, wante, and misery I founde you in, when Hobomok first guided me from Plymouth to Naumkeak; and although since the company hathe sente many vessels, there hathe been an alteration in the state of affairs, yet my hearte is readie to burste when I thinke to what you are nowe exposed. God willing, I would have shared any difficulties with you, soe as I might have called you wife; but I loved you the better in that you forgot not your dutie to your mother in your love for me. I live only on the hope of againe seeing the lighte of your countenance, but I nowe feare it cannot be until a yeare from hence. Before this reacheth you, I shall be on my waye to the East Indies, where wealthe promiseth to pour forth many treasures. For your sake I will toyle for the glittering duste, and many hardships would I endure so as I might throwe it at your feete, and saye, 'Tis all for thee. Your grandfather received your letter with much kindnesse. He spoke with greate love, of your mother, but made no remarks concerning your father. He shooke his head mournfully when I parted from him, and saide, when he was in the grave peradventure you would finde you had not been forgotten by the olde Earle: and he added, 'I hope you will live long and be happie together.' You see there is no need of having any heavy thoughts; for in the Spring I shall return unto you, if God spares my life: and whenever it pleaseth him to take your goode mother (and I sincerely hope it be not soone, much as I desire to call you mine), you will come and share my home, in England or America, as circumstances may be. To that home your father will alwayes have a wellcome, and if he chooseth not to accept it, I know nott that your dutie extendeth furthere. Some time or other I maye make New England my abode. My hearte woulde incline to staye here; but England, like the pelican we have read of, is mangling her owne bosome: though unlike that birde, she doth not give nourishment to her childrene.[3] The Protestants banished by Mary, thirste for the bloode of Charles; sending out their poisoned arrows from Geneva and the Netherlands with all the acrimonie of exile. Our goode king Charles and his beautiful consorte are perplexed and embarrassed on every side, and it needeth no very keene eye to see that a terrible crisis draweth neare. For these reasons I would fain seeke tranquillity on the other side of the vaste ocean, if so be that an Episcopalian dove, flying from the deluge which he seeth approaching, and bringing an olive branch in his mouthe, maye there finde refuge. My hearte bleedeth for olde England, torne with religious commotions, as she hath beene, from the time of the second Tudor: but my feeble hande may not stop her wounds, gushing though they be at every pore. In the Spring I shall more certainlie knowe concerning what I have mentioned in general terms: but wheresoever I may abide, my hearte leapeth for joye, when I think I shall then be permitted to kiss your hande. I have sent a pipe to Hobomok, inasmuch as I thoughte it mighte please him to knowe that I remembered him in the big island across the water. In remembrance of our last interview at dame Willet's, I have likewise sent her a Bible, which I thought she would value more than anything wherewith I coulde furnish her. And to you my dear girle, I sende what I knowe will be more wellcome than anything but myself. Remember me kindly to Sally and dame Willet, and with much dutifull love to your mother. I remaine through life,

"Your affectionate and humble servante,

"CHARLES BROWN."

A pipe gaudily decorated, and carefully enveloped in several wrappings of paper, accompanied this package. Another contained a largely lettered Bible, written within "For my olde friende Mistress Willet." On the outside of the third parcel was written, "I had almoste forgotten my promise to Sally: if she be at Plimouth, sende this to her." It contained a handsome gown, which Brown had once playfully promised her for a wedding dress. A letter from the Earl of Rivers was bound up with the prayer book which he sent to his "Deare grandedaughtere;" but the import of it was so similar to her mother's, that I forbear to copy it. Last of all, though the first opened, was a miniature likeness of Brown; and Mary gazed upon it till the eyes seemed laughing and beaming, in all the brilliancy of life, then turned away and wept that the mockery of the pencil had such power to cheat the heart. There was a strange contrast between these presents, and every thing around them. A small rough box placed upon a trunk, was all Mary's toilette. And now there reposed upon it the miniature of her lover, in its glittering enclosure; and a splendid prayerbook printed for the royal family. As Mary looked upon them, and thought of her present situation, she felt that it was ill-judged kindness thus forcibly to remind her of what she had left. Her meditations were interrupted by the sound of Lady Arabella's footsteps, and she hastily removed the rich articles which covered her table. However, the precaution was needless; for Mr. Johnson and his wife were perfectly aware of Brown's reciprocated attachment; and both supposed that the earl's private parcel contained intelligence from him. No one could have more conscientious horror of the form of church worship established by the first defender of the faith, and either from opinion or policy, supported by three successive monarchs; but personal respect for Mr. Brown, and affectionate interest in

Mary, overcame in some degree the narrow prejudices of the times, and the secret was faithfully preserved.

In the evening Mr. Johnson brought up another package from the Earl of Rivers. It contained, as he had mentioned, a large, handsome Bible, written within, in the trembling hand of age, "For my beloved daughtere, the Ladye Mary." Beneath, a blistered spot announced that the name had aroused the cold sympathies of advanced years, and given to the stainless page the peace-offering of a father's heart. It were but mockery of nature's power, to define the complicated tissue of pain and pleasure, in the mind of mother or daughter. Even the stern nerves of Mr. Conant relaxed a little, when he read the old gentleman's letter. He turned to the window, and drummed a psalm tune for a few moments, then cast round an inquiring glance, to see if any one had noticed this moment of weakness. He met the anxious look of Mary, who was timidly watching the changes of his countenance. From his softened mood she argued that her grandfather's expressions concerning Brown, had met with no very unfavorable reception; but however the old man's worldly pride might have been affected by such honorable mention of his name, it was all concealed, beneath a deep shade of rigidity, as he said,

"I have but two things whereof to complain,—the one in the letter, the other in the book; and they are both things which my soul hateth. I mean the standing of the Apocrypha in the Bible, and what is said concerning that son of Belial."[4]

CHAPTER XV

Her eye still beams unwonted fires,
With a woman's love and a saint's desires;
And her last, fond, lingering look is given
To the love she leaves, and then to heaven,—
As if she would bear that love away,
To a purer world and a brighter day.
—*Percival*

DURING SEVERAL WEEKS Mr. Johnson continued almost constantly at Shawmut* and Tri-Mountain,† full of zeal and perseverance in his new enterprise. Lady Arabella in the mean time remained at Salem, and entered with enthusiasm into all the plans of her honored husband. She never spoke of the reverse in her situation, and scarcely seemed to think of it. Her character was indeed all that her countenance indicated. The expression of her eyes was gentle, but her high forehead, aquiline nose, and the peculiar construction of her mouth, all spoke intellect and fortitude, rather than tenderness. Firmness of purpose had been her leading trait from childhood; and now she tasked it to the utmost. But it was soon evident that the soul, in the consciousness of its strength, had too heavily taxed its frail, earth-born companion. The decline of each day witnessed a bright, shadowy spot upon her cheek, too delicate to be placed there by the pencil of health—her lips grew pale—and her eyes had lost all their lustre, save a transient beam of tenderness when she welcomed the return of her beloved partner. These changes could not escape the watchful eye of affection. The important business in which Mr. Johnson was engaged, rendered his frequent presence at Shawmut absolutely necessary; but notwithstanding the solitary and wearisome distance between them, eve-

* Charlestown.
† Boston.

ning seldom returned without seeing him by the side of Lady Arabella. Mrs. Conant too was fast drooping, and there seemed but a hair's breadth between her and the grave. It was interesting to observe the contrast between the two invalids. One, always weak and gentle, bended to the blast, and seemed to ask support from every thing around her. The other, struggling against decay, seemed rather to give assistance, than to require it. Their husbands watched over them, with the tender solicitude of a mother over her sickening infant. Mr. Conant, stern as he was, felt that a sigh or groan from the woman whom he had so long and sincerely loved, had power to stir up those deep recesses of feeling, which had for years been sealed within his soul; and Mary's heart was ready to burst with keen and protracted anguish, when she saw death standing with suspended dart, taking slow, but certain aim, at two endeared victims. But medicine, anxiety, and kindness, were alike unavailing; and soon they both retired to the same apartment, and laid themselves down on the beds from which they were never more to rise. Their feeble hold upon life daily grew more precarious, till at length nothing could tempt their anxious husbands from the pillow. Neither of them had spoken much for several days, when on the 24th of August the faint voice of Mrs. Conant was heard, as she whispered, "Roger—My dear Roger."

In a moment he was at her side.

"What would you say, Mary?" asked he.

"There are many things I would have spoken," she replied; "but I fear I have not strength wherewith to utter them. If Brown comes back, you must remember our own thwarted love, and deal kindly with Mary. She hath been a good child; and verily the God who had mercy on our unconverted souls, will not forsake her. Will you promise?"

"I will," answered the old man, in an agitated voice. "Verily, my dear wife, your dying request shall be obeyed."

"I would fain turn to the light," said she, "for I feel that my departure draweth nigh."

Mary and her father gently raised her, and turned her toward the little window. She looked on her husband, with the celestial smile of a dying saint, as she said,

"I die happy in the Lord Jesus. Sometimes I would fain tarry longer for your sake; but the Lord's will be done."

The agonized man pressed back the crowding tears, as he said,

"If in the roughness of my nature, I have sometimes spoken too harshly; say that you forgive me."

"I have nothing to forgive," she replied. "To me you have been uniformly kind."

She reached out her hand to Mary—"For my sake," added she, "be as dutiful to your good father as you have been to me."

"I will—I will," answered Mary, as she, sobbing, hid her face in the bedclothes.

She spoke no more for several hours. At length, Mr. Conant, who remained close by her side, heard her whisper, in low and broken tones, "My dear husband." She attempted to extend her hand toward him, but the blindness of death was upon her, and it feebly sunk down by her side. As her husband placed it within his, she murmured, "I cannot see you, dear Roger. Kiss me before I die." He stooped down—and oh, how deeply painful was that last embrace. Mary likewise bent over her, and kissed her cold cheek.

"My child—God—bless"—was heard from the lips of that dying mother; but the utterance was troubled and indistinct. Her breathings soon became shorter and more disturbed, and the last agonies seemed passing over her. No sound was heard in the room, till presently a short, quick gasp announced the soul's departure. Mr. Conant placed his hand upon her heart—its pulse no longer throbbed. He held the taper before her mouth—no breath was there to move the steady flame. Mary uttered an involuntary shriek, and sunk upon her knees. There is nothing like the chamber of death to still the turbulence of passion, and overcome the loftiness of pride. What now was the shame of human weakness to that bereaved old man? He stood by the corpse of her, who for twenty years had lain in his bosom, and he heeded not that the big, bright tears fell fast upon the bed. Nothing now remained but the last, sad offices of friendship; and they were silently performed. Not a word was spoken by father or daughter. The sheet was carefully drawn over that pale face; and both bowed down their weary, aching heads upon the pillow, in still communion with their own souls.

During this time, the Lady Arabella had sunk into a slumber so deep and tranquil that she seemed almost like her departed companion. Mr.

Johnson remained with her hand clasped in his, half doubtful whether it was not indeed the sleep of death. Towards morning she awoke; and resting her eyes upon her husband with a look of unutterable love, she feebly returned the pressure of his hand, as she said, "You are always near me, dear Isaac." After a thoughtful pause, she asked, "Is not the Lady Mary dead?"

"She is," answered Mr. Johnson.

"Assuredly I so thought," continued she. "I dreamed that angels came for her, and she said they must wait for me. They are standing by her bed-side now. Don't you see the light of their garments? Well, I shall soon be ready."

"My God, my God," exclaimed the young husband, "would that the bitterness of this cup might pass from me."

"But it may not pass," rejoined his wife, calmly; "and you must drink it like a christian. Let your whole trust be on the Rock of Ages."

"I could bear all, Arabella," replied he, "had I not brought you into trials too mighty for your strength. But for my selfish love, you might now be living in ease and comfort."

"My dear Isaac, does this sound like a follower of the Lamb?" said she. "The time of my departure hath come, and what matters it whether it be in England or America? In the short space we have been allowed to sojourn together, I have enjoyed more than all my life beside; and let this remembrance comfort you when I am gone. Remember me most kindly to my good brother. May his earthly union be as happy and more permanent than mine."

For a long time she seemed exhausted by the effort she had made. Then, taking the ring from her finger,

"Give this to Mary," said she; "and when she looks thereon, bid her think to what all human enjoyment must come. I know you will always wear my miniature. It would have been a great comfort, had I been permitted to leave a living image of myself; but it hath pleased the Lord to order otherwise. Faint not in the enterprise whereunto our blessed Lord has called you; and remember we meet again in Jesus."

The heart of her husband was too full to speak; and he could only kiss her emaciated hand in reply. She fixed her dying gaze upon him, and a faint smile hovered round her lips, shedding its unearthly light over her whole

countenance, as she said, "I hear the angels singing. 'Tis time for me to go."
Her look was still towards her husband, when her lids closed as if
in peaceful slumber. All was hushed. The flickering lamp of life was
extinguished.

There, in that miserable room, lay the descendants of two noble
houses. Both alike victims to what has always been the source of woman's
greatest misery—love—deep and unwearied love. The Lady Mary had in
her life time been so still and fair, that the smile on her placid countenance
seemed but a mockery of death; and whoever looked upon the Lady
Arabella would have judged that thought was still busy beneath those
closed eye-lids.

The next day all was still in that house of mourning. Each one spoke
in a subdued tone, and moved with light and cautious tread, as if fearful of
awakening the repose of the dead. All had passed a sleepless night, and as
they arose from the pillow which had for hours received their tears, a silent
grasp of the hand, strong in the first desperation of grief, was their only
salutation.

"My friend," said Mr. Conant, "it becometh not christians to be cast
down in time of tribulation. Let us pray to Him who is always a present
help in time of trouble."

Mary handed down the Bible; and her father read the 88th Psalm,
without evincing any other emotion than the slight quivering of his lip and
the gathering moisture of his eye. Mr. Johnson rose to prayer, and for
awhile his voice was clear and undisturbed; but in a few moments sobs
were alone audible. Even his exalted piety sunk in that dreadful conflict of
feeling. One burst of weakness, earth claimed as its own—the rest he gave
to heaven. His brethren were all eager to speak words of comfort. He
thanked them for their kindness, and tried to hear them calmly; but the
mourner only can tell how painful at such seasons, are well-meant offers of
consolation.

Few honors could there be paid to deceased nobility. The bodies
were placed in rough coffins, covered with black, and supported side by
side, even as they had expired. The procession stopped on a neighbouring
eminence, and after Mr. Higginson had dwelt long on the sufferings and
virtues of the departed, the earth closed over them forever.

Grief, like all violent emotions, is still when deepest. Mr. Johnson returned from that sad funeral, and not a sigh or tear was seen to escape him. The next day, he went to Shawmut, mingled in the debates of his associates, encouraged the settlers, and surveyed the tract he had purchased at Tri-Mountain. How to build up the church seemed to occupy his whole thoughts; and to that purpose he directed his active and constant exertions. But in the midst of this artificial strength, it was plain enough to be seen, that his heart was broken.

A few weeks after Lady Arabella's death, he was seen slowly proceeding through the forest, on his way to Salem. He paused not to rest his weary footsteps till he reached the place where he had last seen the features of his adored wife. Silently he laid down his head upon the ground, and wept. He arose, and for awhile rested his melancholy gaze on the bright sun and verdant earth. Then kneeling beside the grave, he prayed, "Heavenly Father, I beseech thee to forgive this worship of an earthly idol; and if it so pleaseth thee, take me from this world of sin and misery."

He entered Mr. Conant's dwelling, and slightly partook of the food which Mary's assiduous kindness prepared for him. No expostulations could prevail upon him to remain through the following day. He retraced his solitary path to Shawmut, and it soon became evident that the hand of death was upon him.

The day before his decease, he called Governor Winthrop to his bed-side.

"Let not the laborers of the vineyard mourn that I am removed," said he. "Tell them to go on, like brave soldiers of Christ Jesus, until they perfect the work wherewithal he hath entrusted them. I bless the Lord that he has called me to lay down my life in his service, inasmuch as he has suffered me to witness the gathering of one church in apostolic purity. I have but one request to make unto you. Bury me in the lot which I have laid out at Tri-Mountain;* that at the great judgment-day I may rise among the heritage which I have feebly endeavored to build up. I would fain have the Lady Arabella placed by my side; but it is a wearisome ways to Salem, and wheresoever our bodies may be, our souls will be united. God forgive

---

*This request was complied with; and the first burying-place in Boston was laid out around his grave.

me, if in sinful weakness, I have loved that dear woman even better than his righteous cause."

The excellent man soon after followed his young wife to the mansions of eternal rest; and on the same day that the news arrived at Salem, the pious and revered Mr. Higginson was likewise numbered with the dead. Misfortunes and discouragements seemed crowding upon the infant colonies, which had so lately been rejoicing at their prosperity and increase. "In all their streets was the voice of lamentation and wo." The countenances of men became disconsolate, and mournfully they passed each other, as they said, "Ichabod! Ichabod! Verily the Lord hath sorely smitten us."[1]

inglorious
son of Phineas
1 Samuel 4:19

Phinehas
negro

The deaths are very-romantic/religious tones

CHAPTER XVI

Nor think to village swains alone
Are these unearthly terrors known;
For not to rank nor sex confined
Is this vain ague of the mind.
—*Rokeby*

INDEPENDENT of universal public depression, a peculiar and settled gloom pervaded Mr. Conant's dwelling; and on every account it was a sad home for one in the freshness of existence. True, Mr. Conant seldom spoke with his former harshness, and even the tones of his voice had become more gentle; still his feelings were too rigid and exclusive to sympathize with a young heart almost discouraged by surrounding difficulties. One after another, she had been deprived of the cheering influence of Sally Oldham, the firm support of Lady Arabella, and the mild, soothing spirit of her mother; and no one was left to supply their place. As for Mrs. Oldham, the whole circle of her ideas might be comprised in one sentence, viz. "People will marry whom they are fore-ordained to marry, and die when they are appointed to die." The facetiousness of Mr. Oldham was sometimes amusing; but his feelings were blunt, and his wit too often partook of coarseness and vulgarity. There were some in the settlement in whom Mary might have found as much sympathy as she ever met from her old associate, but she knew them not; and when the heart is oppressed with many sorrows, it shrinks from the task of initiating a stranger into all its mysteries of thought and feeling. With none therefore, had Mary any thing like communion. Even Hobomok came unnoticed, and went away unheeded. Sometimes she would think of asking her father's permission to return to England; and then the prospect of Brown's arrival the ensuing spring, would determine her to await his motions. This hope enabled her to discharge her daily duties with tolerable cheerfulness; but twilight generally saw the melancholy maiden seated by her mother's grave. At such seasons her imagination would be busy with the light silvery clouds, as they hurried along the sky in every variety of form and hue. In one place might be seen a group rising side by side, like the sacred groves of the ancients; here, a stupendous column stood alone, like the magnificent pillar of some ruined edifice; and there, a large, shadowy cloud rested upon the horizon, like the aerial drapery of an angel's couch. It was a mild evening at the commencement of October, when, as she had seated herself as usual to pursue this fanciful amusement, her attention was suddenly arrested by the singular appearance of one of those capricious forms. It was a vessel— so perfect and distinct that the shrouds seemed creaking in the wind, and the canvass fluttering to the breeze. It slowly floated along the atmosphere, till it came over the place where she stood, when it gradually descended and melted into air. Mary had no small share of the superstition of the times, and shuddering at the fatal omen she hastily ran to inform her father. The figure was again seen in the west, and to Mr. Conant, it seemed even more plain than it had to his daughter. Mr. Oldham and two or three neighbours were now called in; and a third time did the strange appearance rise, sink, and disperse, even as at first.

"I marvel if some mishap be not about to befall the shipping which is coming hither," said Mr. Conant. "Forerunners like this, seldom appear but to warn us of some coming disaster."

"That's true enough," rejoined Mr. Oldham. "Don't you remember the story that Capt. Thurston told us about the Castor and Pollux lights on the mast of the Jewel, the night before she run against the Ambrose? A sad mishap that. They say the Jewel would assuredly have been torn in pieces, had it not been for the discreet counsel of Mr. Johnson. God rest his soul; he was the wisest and best man in the whole fleet; and no disparagement to them who are left behind."

"Them Castor and Pollux lights are bad things when one of them is seen alone," quoth another; "but they are nothing to what I have seen and heard in the line of forewarnings. The night before the godly Mr. Higginson died, I heard the tolling of a bell by the hour together, as plain as if I had been within bow-shot of St. Paul's."

"I'm thinking it could be no bell in this world that echoed in this wilderness," replied Mr. Oldham; "unless the devil is sexton now-a-days, and has the ringing of their English bells, which I trow is no very unlikely thing, while Bishop Laud sitteth at the helm."

"It's not well to use lightness of speech concerning such things," said his companion. "I knew a man in England who laughed at the power which it hath pleased the Lord to give unto Satan, and the self-same night a blow was heard on the side of his house as loud as a clap of thunder, and it was cracked to the very foundation, though none of his neighbours heard the report thereof."

"England has come to a dreadful pass in these days," observed Mr. Conant. "I have known some of their scholars who would fain judge of the doings of their Maker by their own reason, and they say that all such like things are the cunning devices of man's imagination."

"I should like to have such folks see a sight that I can tell them of," said a third. "On the night that Mr. Johnson died, though he was at Shawmut, and of course I couldn't know that his end drew near, I saw a light on the foot of my bed, about two in the morning. It burned a few minutes, and then went out. My wife straightway said, 'You may depend upon it, the pious Mr. Johnson hath departed,' and sure enough, as nigh as I can discover, he died just at that time."

The relation of such wonders continued for a long time, and perhaps would never have known an end, had not the lateness of the hour reminded them it was time to depart.

There is a great facility in appropriating any thing uncommon to our own situation and circumstances. Mary readily believed that the extraordinary phantom was meant for herself only; and she immediately conjectured it foreboded evil tidings from her lover. The more she indulged these thoughts, the more their power increased, till their unquiet influence entirely deprived her of rest. At that credulous period, it is not surprising that superstition exerted her full force over a mind so prone to revel in the etherial visions of imagination. And who, even in these enlightened days, when reason sits almost sole arbiter of the human mind, has not felt similar influences powerful and strong within him? Who among the wisest and the best, has not experienced states of feeling when the light sigh of the summer breeze, or the gentle pattering of midnight rain, or mayhap a passing shadow on the moonlight floor, or the rustling of the trees, as they bowed their foliage to the evening gale, has had power to quicken the pulse, and restrain the motion of the breath? But there are moments of weakness, which pride would hardly deign to bring before the tribunal of reason; and which, if brought there, would doubtless be found to originate in causes merely physical. Whatever is their source, they sometimes come suddenly upon the mind, striking with magic force, "the electric chain wherewith it's darkly bound;"[1] and in this instance, Mary's fearful augury was too soon realized. The next week Hobomok came to Salem, bearing a letter for Mr. Conant, and another for Governor Endicott. The first contained information of the death of Earl Rivers, written by his grandson; the other mentioned that an East India ship had been lately wrecked, with the loss of her whole crew and cargo; and added that Charles Brown, formerly of Salem, was among the passengers. No sooner had the news passed the lips of the Governor, than it spread through the whole settlement, like an electric shock through an united circle. The circumstance of Mary's attachment was well known, and the matrons and maidens paid a passing tribute of grief, as they asked,

"How will the poor damsel bear this? The Lord support her; for whatsoever be her errors in doctrine, she hath a sweet-favored face, and a disposition like an angel."

"Hold your blasphemous tongues," replied their rigid listeners. "Because the children of Belial have a comely form, a smooth skin, and noble blood, you forsooth straightway liken them to angels of light. Wot you not that all these things pass away as if they had never been? As for the untimely end of him who hath bred so much disturbance among us, 'tis but the visitation of the Lord, for his sinful upholding of the domineering prelates."

While people were busy with similar observations, an officious neighbour eagerly carried the unwelcome news to Mary.

For a moment her heart reeled, and the blow threatened to suspend her faculties. The next, there was a ray of hope. She had become accustomed to false alarms, and she trusted this would prove to be one. Fallacious as she felt this hope, she could not, and would not relinquish it. Whatever were her feelings, they were but briefly exposed to the unfeeling curiosity of her guest. Her father's supper was left half prepared, her cloak hastily thrown on, and an instant after, she entered Governor Endicott's.

"The Lord help you," exclaimed Mrs. Endicott, "how pale you look, and how you tremble. Do be seated, and let me give you some cordial."

"Has his Honor received a letter from England?" inquired the anxious girl, without taking notice of her kind offer.

"Bless your young heart," replied Mrs. Endicott, as she put the corner of her apron to her eyes, "I'm expecting him home every minute. But do take a drop of cordial. It grieves me to death to see you look so."

Her importunities were all useless, and the good woman would have attempted words of comfort, had not the misery of Mary's countenance made such an emphatic appeal to her forbearance. Mary spoke not; but fixed her wild and anxious gaze on the door, until the Governor entered, when she suddenly rose and inquired,

"Have you received a letter from Plymouth to day?"

She had always been a great favorite with the chief magistrate, for, zealous as he was, he was not the man to look on so fair and young a creature, and hate her for her creed. Her question awakened his deepest sympathy, and he cast a pitying glance upon her, as he replied,

"It is all too true, Mary."

There are things which the heart can never realize, be they ever so long in prospect. Come when they will, they come with crushing, agonizing power. The mother may listen for weeks, to the hushed moan of her dying infant; the bridegroom may watch the hectic flush, daily settling more deeply on the cheek of his young bride; but the chain is rivetted closer and closer, and terrible must be the force which rends it asunder.

Mary answered not. She pressed her hand hard upon her brow, and she who had been so gentle and childlike that a rough word would draw tears from her eyes, now neither wept nor sighed. She was about to depart, but the Governor grasped her hand affectionately as he said,

"Forgive me, my good girl, I know that your heart is full; but I would fain remind you that we are only sojourners in this world until we can find a better; and that whatsoever befalleth us, is meant for our eternal good. Cast therefore the burthen of your sorrows at the feet of Jesus."

Mary appreciated his kindness, but she could not attend to him; and, struggling to release her hand, she muttered an indistinct answer, and hastily quitted the house, to hide her grief from his view. She rested her head on a young tree which grew in the path, and tried to pray; but, in that whirl of feeling, she could not even think, and scarcely knowing what she did, she proceeded homeward.

Her father had finished his supper, and though he had found it unprepared, he uttered no complaint. He well knew the occasion of this neglect; and his own thoughts were not unmixed with bitterness. Conscience, cool and unbiassed, inquired whether he had not in some measure mistaken obstinacy and pride for conscientious zeal; and in the humbleness of the moment, he acknowledged that christians were too apt to mistake the voice of selfishness for the voice of God. His earliest enemies had been of the English church, and he had seen his wife drooping and dying amid the poverty which his religious opinions had brought upon her, and yet he tried hard to be convinced, and did at last verily believe, that earthly motives had nothing to do with his hatred of Episcopacy. He still retained all his abhorrence of Brown's sentiments, but since the death of his wife, he had thought, with a good deal of concealed pleasure, how very graciously he would make a sacrifice to the peace of her only child; and now that there was no hope of making this atonement for his past harshness, he felt more of disappointment than he would have been willing to acknowledge. In this softened state of feeling, one gentle expostulation would have driven him to the bosom of his child, there to impart comfort, and seek forgiveness. He did indeed speak feelingly of the death of her grandfather, and told her of the God who was alike the support of the young and the aged. While he dwelt upon the excellence of religious consolation, he called her "my dear child," and more than once his eyes filled with tears. Unfortunately, Mary was too absent, too distressed, to receive these tardy proofs of affection with the gratitude which kindness was always wont to excite; so after one or two efforts to mention the painful subject, he did as he too often had done—stifled the voice of nature, and hid all his better feelings beneath the cold mask of austerity. Mary, tortured with thoughts she could no longer endure in his presence, observed that she was going to dame Willet's, and then left him to his meditations.

CHAPTER XVII

The tempter speaks, when all is still,
And phantoms in the mind will raise,
That haunt the path of after days.

. . . .

On one sad night she left her home;
She parted with the tawny chief,
And left me lonely in my grief.
—*Yamoyden*

THE SAME RESTLESSNESS which had led Mary to dame Willet's, soon made that scene of former happiness insupportable. The loquacious old woman did not understand the nature of the human heart so well as the friends of Job, who "sat down on the ground, and none spake a word to him; for they saw that his grief was very great." Mary could not endure the good dame's blunt sympathy; beside, every object which there met her view, did but remind her of her lover's farewell interview; so she drew her cloak around her, and prepared to depart. The old lady followed her, and gently taking hold of her arm, looked in her face as if fearful of expressing her doubts.

"Mary," said she, "I have done all I could to comfort you; but verily, my dear child, I fear you are not altogether yourself."

"Assuredly I am," replied Mary; "but I cannot stay here, for when I stand at that little window, it seems as if I could see him as he looked the last time I ever saw him."

Notwithstanding this declaration, there was a partial derangement of Mary's faculties. A bewilderment of despair that almost amounted to insanity. She sat down by her mother's grave, and wished to weep. The sorrow that can be exhausted, however keen it may be, has something of luxury in it, compared with grief when her fountains are all sealed, and her stormy waters are dashing and foaming within the soul. Mary's heart refused to overflow, and she laid down her head on the cold sod, in hopes it would cool the burning agony of her brain. As she sat thus, insensible of the autumnal chilliness, she felt something lightly thrown over her. She looked up, and perceived that it was Hobomok, who had covered her with his blanket, and silently removed a short distance from her. He approached when he saw her rise.

"It's a cold night for Mary to be on the graves," said he.

"Ah, Hobomok," she replied, "I shall soon be in my own grave."

The savage turned away his head for some time, as if struggling with some violent emotion.

"How Hobomok wish he could make you happy," at length said he.

There was a chaos in Mary's mind;—a dim twilight, which had at first made all objects shadowy, and which was rapidly darkening into misery, almost insensible of its source. The sudden stroke which had dashed from her lips the long promised cup of joy, had almost hurled reason from his throne. What now had life to offer? If she went to England, those for whom she most wished to return, were dead. If she remained in America, what communion could she have with those around her? Even Hobomok, whose language was brief, figurative, and poetic, and whose nature was unwarped by the artifices of civilized life, was far preferable to them. She remembered the idolatry he had always paid her, and in the desolation of the moment, she felt as if he was the only being in the wide world who was left to love her. With this, came the recollection of his appearance in the mystic circle. A broken and confused mass followed; in which a sense of sudden bereavement, deep and bitter reproaches against her father, and a blind belief in fatality were alone conspicuous. In the midst of this whirlwind of thoughts and passions, she turned suddenly towards the Indian, as she said,

"I will be your wife, Hobomok, if you love me."

"Hobomok has loved you many long moons," replied he; "but he loved like as he loves the Great Spirit."

"Then meet me at my window an hour hence," said she, "and be ready to convey me to Plymouth."

She returned home; and Hobomok, overjoyed at this unexpected fortune, prepared to obey her injunctions. Her father was absent when she entered, and lighting a taper, she sat down in the solitary room, and alternately attempted to fix her attention on the prayer book and Bible. In a few moments Mr. Conant returned. He spoke but little; but his prayer that evening evinced much parental tenderness as well as lofty piety. Fervently did he beseech that God would heal the wounded and broken heart, and lead back all those who were wandering in errors to the true fold of Christ Jesus.

When Mary thought that she was perhaps hearing that venerable voice for the last time, her heart relented. She acknowledged that a sort of desperate resentment towards him, had partly influenced her late conduct; and she asked herself,

"What if he has been harsh and restrained in his intercourse with me? It is cruel to wrench from him his last earthly tie; and to prostrate the soul of a parent, because my own lies bleeding in the dust."

Perhaps this effort of dawning reason and gentler feeling would have prevailed; but her father angrily seized the prayer book, which she had carelessly left in his way, and would have thrown it upon the fire, had she not caught his arm and rescued it from his grasp.

"Have it out of my sight," exclaimed the old man, in a violent tone. "My soul abhorreth it, as it doth the spirits of the bottomless pit."

That single act decided the fluctuating fate of his child. Who can look back upon all the important events of his life, without acknowledging that the balance of destiny has sometimes been weighed down by the most trivial touch of circumstance. Mary's mind was just in that vacillating state when a breath would have turned her from her purpose, or confirmed it forever. Her heart writhing and convulsed as it was, was gentle still; and it now craved one look of tenderness, one expression of love. That soothing influence she in vain sought; and the feelings which had harrowed up her soul to that fatal resolution, again returned in their full force. In the unreasonableness of mingled grief and anger, she accused her father as the sole cause of her present misery; and again she sunk under the stupifying influence of an ill directed belief in the decrees of heaven, and the utter fruitlessness of all human endeavour. It was strange that trouble had power to excite her quiet spirit to so much irascibility; and powerful indeed must have been the superstition, which could induce so much beauty and refinement, even in a moment of desperation, to exchange the social band, stern and dark as it was, for the company of savages. Mary retired to her own room, resolved on immediate departure; but she was not sufficiently collected to make any necessary arrangements; she even neglected taking a change of apparel. However, Brown's miniature was not forgotten; and as it lay before her, she could think of nothing, only that the form, which once could boast so much dignified beauty, was now unshrouded and uncoffined in the deep, deep ocean,—and imagination shuddered over the thoughts which followed. She placed the miniature in her bosom, and looked out upon the scenes she was so soon to leave. Her eye first rested upon Endicott's Hollow, where, as she supposed, it had been first revealed to her that Hobomok was to be her husband; and falling on her knees,

"Oh, Charles," murmured she, "if thy pure spirit is looking down upon this action, forgive me, in that I do but submit to my fate."

Presently the low whistle of Hobomok was heard. She obeyed the signal, and in a few moments she was by his side, walking toward the seashore. Almost every thing in their path was, in some way or other, connected with Brown; and she would frequently pause, as she uttered some mournful and incoherent soliloquy. The Indian had witnessed the dreadful ruins of mind in his own tribe, and the fear of her insanity more than once occurred to him; then again her brief answers to his questions would be so prompt and rational, that he could not admit the doubt.

"She is communing with the Good Spirit," thought he.

And now might be seen the dark chieftain seated in his boat, exulting in his prize, and rowing with his whole strength, while the rays of a bright October moon shone full upon the contrast of their countenances. Neither of them spoke, save when Hobomok stooped on his oar, and drawing the blanket more closely around her, asked whether or not the cold was uncomfortable. He would often raise his loud, clear voice in some devotional boat-song, alternately English or Indian, among which the following seemed to be a favorite.

"Lend me, oh, moon, lend me thy light, that I may go back to my wigwam, and my wakon-bird may rest there in safety. I will rise with the sun, to see his fire consume the morning clouds. I will come back to my wakon-bird, laden with beaver and deer."

The whole scene was singularly melancholy. Nothing but the face of the Indian wore an expression of gladness. Mary, so pale and motionless, might have seemed like a being from another world, had not her wild, frenzied look revealed too much of human wretchedness. The moon, it is true, pursued her heavenly path as bright and tranquil as ever; but the passing clouds made her appear hurried and perturbed, even as the passions of men float before the mild rays of the Gospel, making them seem as troubled and capricious as their own. Nature too, was in her saddest robe; and the breeze, as it swept along the variegated foliage, sounded like the dismal roarings of the distant ocean. Mary's meditations were more dull, and cold, and dreary still. It is difficult to tell what the feelings could have been, half bewildered as they were, which led her to persevere in so strange a purpose. It is even doubtful if their victim could have defined them. But whatever they were, they were endured and cherished, until the boat drew up on the shore of Plymouth. Fortunately for Hobomok, none of the inhabitants had risen, and he guided her to his wigwam unobserved. In a few words, he explained to his mother the occasion of the visit. Full of astonishment, the grateful squaw danced, sung, and caressed Mary, with every demonstration of frantic joy. Hobomok endeavoured to calm her transports, and urged the necessity of forwarding the marriage immediately; for the savage had many fears that Mary would yet shrink from the strange nuptials. His arguments were readily assented to, and Hobomok asked his intended bride whether she was willing to be married in the Indian form.

"Yes," answered she, and turned from him, as if a sudden pang had passed through her heart.

"She is mad," whispered the old squaw.

Her son hesitated a moment, then taking some wine, which Governor Bradford had once given his sick mother, he offered it to her, as he said,

"If Mary sick, this will make her well."

"I am not sick," was the laconic reply.

Hobomok again convinced of her rationality, went forth to make arrangements for his marriage. In the course of an hour, he returned with four of his relations. They spoke no English, but each one lifted his hands as he looked at Mary, and seemed to utter some exclamation of surprise. Presently they joined in a dance, singing in a low tone, for fear of exciting the suspicion of their white neighbours. After this was concluded, Hobomok stept out, and looked cautiously in every direction, to see that none were approaching, then taking Mary by the hand, he led her round the wigwam, and again entered. In the mean time, a mat had been placed in the centre of the room, and thither the Indian led his bride. The eldest of the company then presented him with a witch-hazel wand of considerable length, and having placed one end of it in Mary's hand, the bridegroom stood waiting for the ceremony. The oldest Indian then uttered some short harangues, in which he dwelt upon the duty of a husband to hunt plenty of deer for his wife, to love her, and try to make her happy; and that the wife should love her husband, and cook his vension well, that he might come home to his wigwam with a light heart. To this Hobomok responded in a tone half way between singing and speaking,

"Hobomok love her like as better than himself. Nobody but Great Spirit know how well he loveth her."

The priest then looked toward Mary, as if waiting for her answer.

"Tell how well you love him," said the Indian woman, as she touched her arm. Mary raised her head with a look, which had in it much of the frightful expression of one walking in his sleep, as she replied,

"I love him better than any body living." *Her criterion for marriage*

Hobomok then took the rod, which they had held, and breaking it into five pieces, gave one to each of the witnesses. The married couple still continued standing, and the company formed a circle and danced round them three times, singing their marriage song. When this was finished, Hobomok took out his pipe and handed it to the priest. It was the one which Brown had sent, and when Mary saw it, she uttered a piercing shriek, as she pointed to it, and said, "Send it away! Send it away!" Her husband understood her meaning, and returning it to his pocket, he produced another. After each one had smoked, they again formed a ring, and danced and sung as before, each one, as he came near the door, dancing backward, and disappearing. After they had all gone, Hobomok went out and buried Brown's beautiful present in the earth. Mary continued listless and unmoved, apparently unconscious of any change in her situation. But the ceremony of that morning was past recall; and Mary Conant was indeed the wife of Hobomok.

CHAPTER XVIII

It was strange for him to show
Such outward signs of inward wo.
—*Yamoyden*

THE NEXT MORNING Mr. Conant arose, and, as usual, went out to his labors. He came in at his accustomed time, and found that no preparations had been made for their scanty morning meal. He knocked at Mary's door. No one answered. With dreadful apprehension he looked into her apartment. The lifeless object which he had expected, did not meet his view; and he saw at a single glance, that the bed had been unoccupied. A suspicion even more painful than the first, then flashed upon him, that his child had been driven to suicide. "Oh God," thought he, "have I likewise been called to offer my last remaining child upon thine altar." Then came the question, "Might I not have performed the work of the Lord as well, and shown less rigour to that poor thoughtless girl?" He felt that he had, in reality, known very little of Mary, except through the medium of her mother; and he now blamed himself that he had not given her his confidence and sympathy, instead of compelling her so cautiously to conceal her feelings. The words of his dying wife seemed to resound in his ears, as she said, "Be kind to Mary for my sake;" and with this remembrance came the sting of self-reproach, the keenest that can enter the human soul. For a few moments the old man sat down, and rested his head upon his hand, with more positive wretchedness than he had ever before felt, crushed as his heart had been in the battle of life. He stood for some time hesitating between the consciousness that something must be done, and a perplexity as to what course to pursue. At length the idea that she might have slept at

Mr. Oldham's, or Dame Willet's, occurred to his mind, and though he gave it little credence, it afforded a moment's relief.

Mr. Conant had persevered in his resolution to continue at Naum-keak, when but three of his discontented companions remained to share his poverty, and even those three threatened to desert him; when his family, unable to endure such hardships, were obliged to consent to a temporary separation; and when his young, vigorous boys were bowed down to the grave by labor and famine. In the midst of all these difficulties, the MS. states that "he made a vow to abide in Naumkeake as long as the Lorde pleased to spare his life, if he coulde finde a clam on the seacoaste, or an acorne on the trees." This same inflexible self-command had ever since made him the "very soul of counsel," in all times of danger; and it now induced him to chasten his heart, that its agitated feelings might not be betrayed to the wondering gaze of his neighbours. With his usual calm appearance he entered Mr. Oldham's dwelling, and inquired whether they had seen any thing of Mary the preceding night.

"Bless me, no," answered Mrs. Oldham. "I may safely say she has scarcely darkened my doors since the day Sally was married. But is she missing, Goodman?"

Mr. Conant briefly answered that she had not slept at home, and went out as he added,

"Peradventure she abode with Dame Willet."

"Poor man," said Mrs. Oldham. "I always knowed it would be so, from the very minute I heard of Brown's death. I said then she'd never live through it. There never any good come of crossing folks in love, to my knowledge. I'm sure I never would have said a word, if Sally had taken it into her head to marry a Pequod."

"I'm sure I would, though," rejoined her husband. "A pretty piece of business it would be of a truth, to have a parcel of tawny grandchildren at your heels, squeaking *powaw*, and *sheshikwee*, and the devil knoweth what all."

"I hope you don't mean that folks have a free will of their own in such matters," said his wife.

"To be sure I do. 'Tan't much that I should have done in the business, if I hadn't had my own way," rejoined he. "But now I have made out to get on my boots, I'll go out and inquire concerning this matter. Mary was as sweet a creature as ever man looked upon; and if she be indeed missing, the boats must be had out."

"You're a sinful wicked man to talk, considering you're a christian," said his wife, as he departed.

The application at dame Willet's was equally unsuccessful, and the report that Mary Conant was dead, spread like wildfire through the village. She had been so humble, kind, and cheerful among them, and had so seldom evinced any aversion to their sentiments, that she was a universal favorite. The young admired her as the loveliest being they had ever beheld; and the old, even while they held up her errors of doctrine as a warning to their children, could not refrain from adding,

"Assuredly, in many things she hath borne herself worthy of a woman professing godliness."

For some minutes, the settlement was one scene of commotion.

"Have out the boats—have out the boats," said one.

"Fire guns over the water," said another.

These orders were complied with, and boats were ordered out in several directions. As Mr. Oldham was entering one of these, he espied a ring lying close to the water's edge, and stepping back, he asked Mr. Conant if he had ever seen it.

"The Lady Arabella gave it to my child," answered the disconsolate father; and without further pause he passed through the crowd, who readily made way for him. He entered his desolate home, fastened the door of his little apartment, and threw himself down beside the bed. Hours passed away before the bitterness of affliction could be in any degree overcome; but at length the tears flowed plentifully, and fervently did he pray for support and assistance, to that God who had never forsaken him in his hour of need.

In the meantime the search of his brethren had of course proved useless, though the supposition that Mary was drowned amounted almost to absolute certainty. Now that the opinion was apparently so well proved, every one, as usual, had something to give as additional evidence. Mrs. Endicott made exaggerated reports of the wildness and paleness of her looks, when she came to inquire concerning the letter. Another remembered to have seen her go to her mother's grave at sun-down, and remain there till after the night closed in.

"For my part," says Dame Willet, "I couldn't go quietly to my bed till I went up and looked into Mr. Conant's to see that Mary was at home with her father; for she came down to my house in the evening, and she took hold of my hand till I thought it had been in a vice and she had a dreadful wild look about her. Poor creature, I couldn't help foreboding that all was not right, when she sighed so, and said that she little thought my house was the last place where she should ever see him; for you must know," continued she, "I gave the young folks a meeting without Goodman Conant's knowing of the same."

"And you should take shame and sorrow to yourself for such an action," replied Mr. Skelton. "I grant the maiden had many charms, and much seeming goodness in speech and behaviour, but so had that idolatrous woman of the house of Stuart, whom it pleased the Lord, in his righteousness, to bring to the block.[1] I tell you, woman, the Most High will visit their iniquity upon the heads of all such as bow the knee to Baal, and worship the golden calf of Episcopacy. Wot ye not that Mr. Conant was led by the fear of God in this matter?"

"Assuredly I think so," answered the dame; "but a body couldn't look upon the girl without loving her, and I meant no harm, your Reverence."

"I don't suppose you did, good woman; but it behoves us to give little heed to natural affection, when we are engaged in the work of the Lord Jesus. Forasmuch as it seems useless to waste more time and powder in this melancholy search, I will even go up and speak a word to Mr. Conant, in his troubles; though I doubt not he bears them like a christian."

When Mr. Skelton arrived on his errand of consolation, he distinctly heard the voice of his friend as he prayed,

"If in this thing, O Lord, I have acted from my own pride, rather than from zeal for thy glory, I beseech thee, spare me not—but pour out the vials of thy wrath upon my unworthy head, so that the sins of my child may be forgiven."

The voice ceased—and a few moments after Mr. Skelton knocked for admission. No answer was returned, until he said,

"I have come to see you, Mr. Conant, thinking it might comfort you to unite in prayer during this season of distress."

"I have much reason to thank you," replied Mr. Conant; "but I trust your Reverence will not be offended if I tell you that I would fain be left with God and my own heart for a season."

Before evening Mr. Conant had regained his wonted manner. All his necessary avocations were performed, and at night he went into Mr. Oldham's and said with his customary calmness, "I will partake of whatever you have for supper, if you are so inclined;" and at nine o'clock he performed the family devotions, in a voice so distinct and untroubled, that all who heard him wondered at the strength wherewith it pleased the Lord to support him. But quiet as all seemed on that unruffled surface, there was a tempest beneath, which threatened to uptear the very roots of existence; and even when his lips were opened in prayer at the footstool of divine grace, his thoughts were deep in the cold wave. Whatever were his concealed feelings, before three days had elapsed, none could judge by the most trifling external sign, that the waters of affliction had passed over him. During this time, he had invited Dame Willet and her son Jacob to take up their abode at his house, and they now constituted his whole family. On the third evening after Mary's departure, the good woman and her son were absent, and Mr. Conant seated alone by his solitary fire, when Mr. Collier arrived at Mr. Oldham's, bringing news of the lamentable fact. All were eager to ascertain how, when, and where, it had been discovered.

"It's a dismal story to tell her old father," observed Mr. Collier; "but my good woman hath seen her with her own eyes, and heard her acknowledge that she was married to Hobomok, so there can be no mistake about it. Our knowledge of the matter came after this fashion. Sally went in to see Hobomok's mother, as is often her custom, inasmuch as she is old, and frequently alone. The squaw had stept out when she first went in; but seeing somebody in the bed, Sally thought she had been sick, and so went up to speak to her, when behold, she found it was Mary Conant. She said she was so stupid that she did not seem to know her, and she wouldn't speak a word; only when she asked if what the old squaw said, was true, she answered, Yes. My good woman came home and went to bed sick about it, and she desired me straightway to come up and deliver the tidings."

Considerable altercation ensued, concerning who should inform

Mr. Conant. Mr. Oldham and his wife were as eager to undertake the unwelcome task, as their son-in-law was willing to decline it. Mr. Oldham was just preparing to execute the mission, when Mr. Skelton entered, and having heard the story, he put an end to all interfering claims, by saying that he thought it was his duty to impart the same.

As Mr. Conant sat alone, ruminating on the many sad events in his chequered life, a few reluctant tears had forced their way, and lay cold and undisturbed upon his furrowed cheek. Perhaps had he known the near approach of his minister, they had never been shed; as it was, they were hastily brushed away, when he returned the pressure of his hand.

"I'm glad to see you have borne this heavy affliction as becomes a follower of Christ Jesus," said Mr. Skelton.

"It doth but cause our enemies to blaspheme, when christians, who of all men ought to glory in affliction, are disposed to murmur at the weight thereof," replied Mr. Conant. "Whatsoever dispensation the Lord may send in his anger, I hope he will always give me strength to say, 'My trust is in thee, and in the shadow of thy wings will I take refuge.' Besides, Mr. Skelton, how would it beseem me to talk of my own sorrows, when the Lord hath so sorely smitten us all?"

"Of a truth," rejoined the clergyman, "he hath removed many goodly pillars from the land. Much could I wish that the godly Mr. Higginson were alive this day; inasmuch as he had a soul-ravishing, a soul-saving, and a soul-comforting speech. Alas, that he left not his mantle behind him."

"No doubt he was taken away from the evil to come," answered Mr. Conant. "But we have abundant need of his pious reproofs among us, notwithstanding you carry yourself much for the edification of those unto whom you are called to minister. These are trying times among us. Numbers are swept off by sickness; and the blight and mildew in our corn seemeth to forbode a famine; and as for the colony at Shawmut, I verily fear, their joyful beginning will have but a dolorous end."

"If every man bears his part of the public calamities as well as you have borne the death of your child, I have no doubt the Lord will smile upon our undertakings; though for a season 'He feedeth us with the bread of tears, and giveth us tears to drink in great measure,'"[2] rejoined Mr. Skelton.

"Why, I trust, I have not in vain heard your godly exhortations from the pulpit," said Mr. Conant; "nor yet the dying admonitions of Mr. Higginson, who told us in all times of trouble to lean upon the Lord of Hosts. Verily I will rest upon His promises, though 'mine own familiar friend, in whom my soul trusted, who did eat of my bread, should lift up his heel against me;' yea, though 'lover and friend be put far from me, and mine acquaintance into darkness.'"

"But what would you say," asked Mr. Skelton, "if Mary was yet alive?"

"What would I say?" exclaimed he, starting up eagerly. Then with more composure he added, "Verily, I would thank the Lord, in that the bitter cup had passed from me. Have you heard any news?"

"Mary is alive and well at Plymouth," answered Mr. Skelton.

"God be praised," said Mr. Conant—and now indeed the tears fell fast and unrestrained. He seized Mr. Skelton's hand, and repeated again and again, "The Lord be praised—The Lord be praised for all his goodness."

A stern, unbending sense of duty, a gloomy experience of human nothingness, all his strange obliquities of character had left him a father still. The clergyman said nothing to interrupt this burst of feeling, until Mr. Conant paused and inquired,

"But why went she thither without my knowledge?"

"That is what will be the hardest for you to bear like a christian," rejoined Mr. Skelton; "and I would not tell you thereof till you have strengthened your mind for the worst."

"I can bear any thing, if so be she is alive," answered the distressed father. "I beseech you, let me hear the worst."

"She is married to Hobomok," replied Mr. Skelton.

The unexpected information fell like a deadly blow on the heart of the old man; and those cheeks and lips grew pale, which no man had ever before seen blanched since his boyhood. He stood at the window a moment, firmly compressing his lips, to keep back some choking emotion; but finding the effort ineffectual, he took up his hat and went forth to seek a solitude where he might pour out his sorrows before his Maker. An hour elapsed before he returned, and could Mary have foreknown the agony of that hour, she had never left the parental roof. When he again entered his house, he found his friend still waiting for his return. He took his offered hand, as he said,

"I am more calm now, Sir. God forgive me, if in aught I have rebelled against his holy will; but assuredly I find I could more readily have covered her sweet face with the clods, than bear this; but the Lord's will be done."

"It behoves you to think what would have become of her unconverted soul if she had died in such a state," replied the minister. "Goodman Collier thinks she was bereaved of reason, when she did this deed; and peradventure the Lord may yet raise her up to be 'a burning and a shining light.'"[3]

"For her soul's salvation, God grant she may not be in her right mind," answered Mr. Conant. "I would fain have the poor stray lamb returned to the fold."

"Had you no suspicions concerning Hobomok's visits heretofore?" asked Mr. Skelton.

"I knew he was grateful to us for much we had done for him at Plymouth," rejoined Mr. Conant; "but verily, had I been told it extended further, I had never believed so unlikely a thing. I knew that Mary loved to hear his long stories, abounding as they were with metaphors, but then the thoughtless child was always given to vain imaginations, which profit not. Her good mother told me, the day before she died, that Mary's heart would always hanker after him who is now lost in the bowels of the ocean; and I promised that I would give my assent to their marriage. Peradventure this chastisement hath come upon me, because I thought in my heart, to countenance the doings of the unrighteous."

"Well," replied Mr. Skelton, "it is a mercy to receive the reward of our sins, in some sort, during this life; but you must not be tempted to forget Him in whom you said you would put your trust, 'though darkness overshadowed you, and the waters compassed you about.'"

Mr. Conant shook his head despairingly. "I had made up my mind to her watery grave," said he; "but to have her lie in the bosom of a savage, and mingle her prayers with a heathen, who knoweth not God, is hard for a father's heart to endure."

"Let us unite in prayer," said Mr. Skelton. "Verily at all seasons it is the best balm for a wounded soul."

Mr. Conant was indeed soothed and strengthened by the exercise. The next day saw him busy in his daily employments;—weeks and months past on, and witnessed the same unvaried fortitude. But the heart of the old man was bowed down within him. The widow Willet said, she often heard him groan bitterly in the night; and his neighbours frequently noticed him leaning upon his axe or his hoe, by the hour together, apparently lost in melancholy reflections.

CHAPTER XIX

Yes—it was love—if thoughts of tenderness,
Tried in temptation, strengthened by distress—
Which nor defeated hope, nor baffled wile,
Could render sullen, were she ne'er to smile,
Nor rage could fire, nor sickness fret to vent
On her one murmur of his discontent—
If there be love in mortals—this was love!
    —*Byron*

FOR SEVERAL WEEKS Mary remained in the same stupified state in which she had been at the time of her marriage. She would lie through the livelong day, unless she was requested to rise; and once risen, nothing could induce her to change her posture. Language has no power to shadow forth her feelings as she gradually awoke to a sense of her situation. But there is a happy propensity in the human mind to step as lightly as possible on the thorns which infest a path we are compelled to tread. It is only when there is room for hope, that evils are impatiently borne. Desolate as Mary's lot might seem, it was not without its alleviations. All the kind attentions which could suggest themselves to the mind of a savage, were paid by her Indian mother. Hobomok continued the same tender reverence, he had always evinced, and he soon understood the changing expression of her countenance, till her very looks were a law. So much love could not but awaken gratitude; and Mary by degrees gave way to its influence, until she welcomed his return with something like affection. True, in her solitary hours there were reflections enough to make her wretched. Kind as Hobomok was, and rich as she found his uncultivated mind in native imagination, still the contrast between him and her departed lover, would often be remembered with sufficient bitterness. Beside this, she knew that her own nation looked upon her as lost and degraded; and, what was far worse, her own heart echoed back the charge. Hobomok's connexion with her was considered the effect of witchcraft on his part, and even he was generally avoided by his former friends. However, this evil brought its own cure. Every wound of this kind, every insult which her husband courageously endured for her sake, added romantic fervor to her increasing affection, and thus made life something more than endurable. While all her English acquaintances more or less neglected her, her old associate, Mrs. Collier, firmly and boldly stemmed the tide, and seemed resolved to do all in her power to relieve the hardships of her friend. For a long time her overtures were proudly refused; for Mary could not endure that the visits of one, who had been so vastly her inferior, should now be considered an honor and obligation. However, persevering kindness did in time overcome this feeling, and in less than a year, Sally became a frequent inmate of her wigwam. To this, was soon likely to be added another source of enjoyment. Before two years passed away, she became the mother of a hopeful son. Under such circumstances, his birth was no doubt entwined with many mournful associations; still the smiles of her infant brought more of pleasure than of pain. As Mary looked on the little being, which was "bone of her bone, and flesh of her flesh," she felt more love for the innocent object, than she thought she should ever again experience.

During the period before his birth, nothing occurred of any importance to our story, excepting that Mr. Conant had written two letters to his daughter. The first conjured her not to consider a marriage lawful, which had been performed in a moment of derangement, and invited her to return to the arms of a parent who tenderly loved her. The second informed her of a considerable legacy left to her by the Earl of Rivers, and again offered her a welcome home and oblivion of all the past. Mary's heart was melted at these proofs of affection, when she had so little expected them; but she well knew she should only be considered an outcast among her brethren, and she could not persuade herself that her marriage vow to the Indian was any less sacred, than any other voluntary promise. So she wrote to her father, implored his forgiveness, hinted at the deplorable state of mind which had led her to this extremity, stated many reasons which now rendered it impossible for her to return, even if she were so disposed, and concluded by urging him to appropriate her property to his own comfort, as she should probably never be in a situation to enjoy it.

After this general view of things, we must now pass over to the 16th of September, 1633, and leave the interim to the reader's imagination. The old squaw had lately died of a fever, and symptoms of the same disorder began to appear in her little grandson, now nearly two years old. On the morning we have mentioned, Mrs. Collier took her own little blooming daughter in her arms, and went into the wigwam to inquire concerning the health of the boy. No sooner was she seated, than the children, accustomed to see each other, began to peep in each other's faces, and look up to their mothers, their bright, laughing eyes beaming with cherub love. Hobomok entered, and for a moment stood watching with delighted attention, the bewitching sports of childhood. He caught up the infant, and placing his little feet in the centre of his hand, held him high above his head.

"My boy, my brave hunter's boy," said he, and pressing him in his arms he half suffocated him with caresses. He placed him in his mother's lap, and took down his quiver, as he said, "Hobomok must be out hunting the deer." The child jumped down upon the floor, and tottling up to him, took hold of his blanket and looked in his face, as he lisped, "Fader come back gin to see 'ittle Hobomok."

Again the father stooped and kissed him, as he answered,

"Hobomok very much bad, if he didn't come back always to see little Hobomok, and his good Mary."

He went out, but soon returned and lifting the blanket, which served for a door, he again looked at his boy, who would alternately hide his head, and then reach forward to catch another glimpse of his father.

"Good bye, Hobomok—Good bye, Mary"—said the Indian. "Before the sun hides his face, I shall come home loaded with deer."

"Take care of yourself," said his wife, affectionately; "and see that Corbitant be not in your path."

"Sally, you have never said one word about my marrying Hobomok," continued she; "and I have no doubt you think I must be very miserable; but I speak truly when I say that every day I live with that kind, noble-hearted creature, the better I love him."

"I always thought he was the best Indian I ever knew," answered Sally; "and within these three years he has altered so much, that he seems almost like an Englishman. After all, I believe matches are foreordained."

"I don't know concerning that," rejoined Mary. "I am sure I am happier than I ever expected to be after Charles' death, which is more than I deserve, considering I broke my promise to my dying mother, and deserted my father in his old age."

While conversation of this nature was going on at home, Hobomok was pursuing his way through the woods, whistling and singing as he went, in the joyfulness of his heart. He had proceeded near half a mile in this way, when he espied an eagle, soaring with a flight so lofty, that he seemed almost like a speck in the blue abyss above. The Indian fixed his keen eye upon him, and as he gradually lowered his flight, he made ready his arrow, and a moment after the noble bird lay fluttering at his feet.

"A true aim that, Hobomok," said a voice which sounded familiar to his ears. He raised his head to see from whence it proceeded. Charles Brown stood by his side! The countenance of the savage assumed at once the terrible, ashen hue of Indian paleness. His wounded victim was left untouched, and he hastily retreated into the thicket, casting back a fearful glance on what he supposed to be the ghost of his rival. Brown attempted to follow; but the farther he advanced, the farther the Indian retreated, his face growing paler and paler, and his knees trembling against each other in excessive terror.

"Hobomok," said the intruder, "I am a man like yourself. I suppose three years agone you heard I was dead, but it has pleased the Lord to spare me in captivity until this time, and to lead me once more to New England. The vessel which brought me hither, lieth down a mile below, but I chose the rather to be put on shore, being impatient to inquire concerning the friends I left behind. You used to be my good friend, Hobomok, and many a piece of service have you done for me. I beseech you feel of my hand, that you may know I am flesh and blood even as yourself."

After repeated assurances, the Indian timidly approached—and the certainty that Brown was indeed alive, was more dreadful to him than all the ghosts that could have been summoned from another world.

"You look as if you were sorry your old friend had returned," said the Englishman; "but do speak and tell me one thing—Is Mary Conant yet alive?"

Hobomok fixed his eyes upon him with such a strange mixture of sorrow and fierceness, that Brown laid his hand upon his rifle, half fearful his intentions were evil. At length, the Indian answered with deliberate emphasis,

"She is both alive and well."

"I thank God," rejoined his rival. "I need not ask whether she is married?"

The savage looked earnestly and mournfully upon him, and sighed deeply, as he said,

"The handsome English bird hath for three years lain in my bosom; and her milk hath nourished the son of Hobomok."

The Englishman cast a glance of mingled doubt and despair towards the Indian, who again repeated the distressing truth. Disappointed love, a sense of degradation, perhaps something of resentment, were all mingled in a dreadful chaos of agony, within the mind of the unfortunate young man; and at that moment it was difficult to tell to which of the two, anguish had presented her most unmingled cup. The Indian gazed upon his rival, as he stood leaning his aching head against a tree; and once and again he indulged in the design of taking his life.

"No," thought he. "She was first his. Mary loves him better than she does me; for even now she prays for him in her sleep. The sacrifice must be made to her."

For a long time, however, it seemed doubtful whether he could collect sufficient fortitude to fulfil his resolution. The remembrance of the smiling wife and the little prattling boy, whom he had that morning left, came too vividly before him. It recks not now what was the mighty struggle in the mind of that dark man. He arose and touched Brown's arm, as he said,

"'Tis all true which I have told you. It is three snows since the bird came to my nest; and the Great Spirit only knows how much I have loved her. Good and kind she has been; but the heart of Mary is not with the Indian. In her sleep she talks with the Great Spirit, and the name of the white man is on her lips. Hobomok will go far off among some of the red men in the west. They will dig him a grave, and Mary may sing the marriage song in the wigwam of the Englishman."

"No," answered his astonished companion. "She is your wife. Keep her, and cherish her with tenderness. A moment ago, I expected your arrow would rid me of the life which has now become a burden. I will be as generous as you have been. I will return from whence I came, and bear my sorrows as I may. Let Mary never know that I am alive. Love her, and be happy."

"The purpose of an Indian is seldom changed," replied Hobomok. "My tracks will soon be seen far beyond the back-bone of the Great Spirit. For Mary's sake I have borne the hatred of the Yengees, the scorn of my tribe, and the insults of my enemy. And now, I will be buried among strangers, and none shall black their faces for the unknown chief. When the light sinks behind the hills, see that Corbitant be not near my wigwam; for that hawk has often been flying round my nest. Be kind to my boy."— His voice choked, and the tears fell bright and fast. He hastily wiped them away as he added, "You have seen the first and last tears that Hobomok will ever shed. Ask Mary to pray for me—that when I die, I may go to the Englishman's God, where I may hunt beaver with little Hobomok, and count my beavers for Mary."

Before Brown had time to reply, he plunged into the thicket and disappeared. He moved on with astonishing speed, till he was aware he must be beyond the reach of pursuit; then throwing himself upon the grass, most earnestly did he hope that the arrow of Corbitant would do the office it had long sought, and wreck upon his head deep and certain vengeance. But the weapon of his enemy came not. He was reserved for a fate that had more of wretchedness. He lay thus inactive for several hours, musing on all he had enjoyed and lost. At last, he sprung upon his feet, as if stung with torture he could longer endure, and seizing his bow, he pursued with delirious eagerness every animal which came within his view.

The sun was verging towards the western horizon, when he collected his game in one spot, and selecting the largest deer, and several of the handsomest smaller animals, he fastened them upon a pole and proceeded towards Plymouth.

It was dark, and the tapers were lighted throughout the village, when he entered Governor Winslow's dwelling. Whatever was the purpose of his visit, it was not long continued; and soon after, the deer was noiselessly deposited by the side of Mr. Collier's house, with a slip of paper fastened on his branching horns. Hobomok paused before the door of his wigwam, looked in at a small hole which admitted the light, saw Mary feeding her Indian boy from his little wooden bowl, and heard her beloved voice, as she said to her child, "Father will come home and see little Hobomok presently."

How much would that high-souled child of the forest have given for one parting embrace—one kind assurance that he should not be forgotten. Affection was tugging hard at his heart strings, and once his foot was almost on the threshold.

"No," said he; "it will distress her. The Great Spirit bless 'em both."

Without trusting another look, he hurried forward. He paused on a neighboring hill, looked toward his wigwam till his strained vision could hardly discern the object, with a bursting heart again murmured his farewell and blessing, and forever passed away from New England.

141

CHAPTER XX

God, the best maker of all marriages,
Combine your hearts in one.
—*King Henry V*

CHARLES BROWN had listened with respect and admiration to the farewell address of the Indian, and forgetful of every other sentiment, he eagerly pursued him, with the intention of restoring the happiness he had so nobly sacrificed. But there were few of the swiftest animals of the forest could outstrip the speed of Hobomok. His step was soon out of hearing, and Brown having at length lost sight of his track, reluctantly gave over the pursuit. In his anxiety to overtake the savage, and in the bewilderment of his own brain, he lost the path; and the sun was nearly setting, when he regained the road he had left. He seated himself upon a rock, in hopes of again meeting Hobomok, should he attempt to return to Plymouth. No sound was heard in those lone forests, save the rustling of the leaves as they bowed to the autumnal wind, or the shriek of some solitary bird as he flapped his wings above the head of the traveller. To these was now and then added the monotonous sound of the whippowill, answered by a strain of wild and varied melody from some far-off songster of the woods. The foliage of the trees was every where so thickly interlaced, excepting the narrow footpath which opened before him, that scarcely a single ray of light could be discerned among the branches. The brightness of the sun had already gone beyond the view, and a long train of sable clouds were gathering in the west, as if mourning his departure. The conflicting feelings of the young man were settled in deep melancholy; and the aspect of nature "suited the gloomy habit of his soul."

"Thus," thought he, "has been my ambitious course. Thus did the dawning rays of hope and imagination send forth their radiance, till the world seemed all light and joy. I have struggled through the clouds which have gathered around me, cheered by the thought that Mary's love would render the evening of my days tranquil and happy. Desperate must have been the temptations which beset the dear girl's mind, when she took the cruel step which has forever wrenched that hope from me. But the deed is done and God forbid that my resentment should rest on her unhappy head. Existence must now be as sad as those dull clouds which are so fast gathering."

The evening grew more dark, and still nothing betokened the approach of the hunter; and the dismal hooting of the owls, and the distant growling of the wolf, warned the traveller to seek safety in the haunts of men. He proceeded along his journey uninterrupted; and soon the well known wigwam of Hobomok met his view. He started with a sudden pang, and walked along rapidly, whistling lest he should hear the sound of that voice so dear to his memory. Immediately after the painful spot was passed, he met a little boy, hieing homeward, as merry and hardy as youth and poverty could make him.

"My boy," said he, "can you tell me where Mr. Collier lives?"

The child pointed to a new house that was hard by, and scampered home to tell his father there was a stranger in the settlement. Mr. Brown already had his hand upon the latch, when the recollection of Hobomok's terror induced him to ascertain who were the inmates of the dwelling, before he ventured to enter. Stepping round cautiously he looked in at the window. Sally sat there knitting by a dim taper, her foot gently moving the white pine cradle, which contained her sleeping infant.

"I shall no doubt alarm her if I go in so suddenly," thought he.

While he was deliberating, he heard the noise of coming footsteps, and presently a man stumbled, and fell directly before him.

"What have we here?" muttered the stranger, springing on his feet and looking back. "I'll go in and ask Sally for a light."

"Who are you, sir?" inquired he, as he noticed Brown standing before his door.

"Mr. Collier," replied the young man, "I would not willingly alarm you, therefore give me your hand, before I tell you my name. You suppose

Charles Brown to be dead, but he is alive, and you now have him by the hand."

"Charles Brown of Salem!" exclaimed Mr. Collier.

"The same," answered his visitor.

"If you are really the living Mr. Brown," said the other, "why do you stand outside of my door? Don't you suppose you'd have a welcome within, after all that's past and gone?"

This was the first expression of kindness which the disconsolate wanderer had heard since his arrival, and he shook the hand of his old acquaintance so cordially, that he could have no remaining doubts whether he was real flesh and blood.

"I knew I should frighten your wife," replied he. "I saw she was alone, and inasmuch as I knew she supposed me to be dead, I thought best to await your return. But if you will prepare her to see me, I will gladly enter, for I am overcome with weariness."

Mr. Collier entered, and drawing his chair towards the cradle, he looked in upon his infant, and smiled, as he said,

"Sally, I have some strange news to tell you, if you'll promise not to be frightened."

"What is it? What is it?" asked his wife, eagerly. "I'm sure you don't look as if it was very terrifying."

"It's bad enough though, for some folks that you love," replied he, thoughtfully. "Charles Brown is alive."

"Charles Brown alive!" screamed Sally. "Tell me how you know it."

"I have seen him, shook hands with him, and talked with him," rejoined her husband.

"What will poor Mary do?" asked his wife.

"That's the first thing I thought of," answered Mr. Collier. "Poor fellow, he little knoweth what is in reserve for him; but the Lord over-ruleth all things in infinite wisdom. I have one thing more to tell you; and you must be calm about it, for peradventure I should have been sorely frightened had I seen his face before he spoke. He standeth even now at the door."

"It can't be true," exclaimed she, jumping up, and looking out of the window.

The door opened, and Brown stood before her.

"Do you believe it now, Sally?" said he.

"Yes, I do; and I am glad to see you," she replied; "and since my good-man is here, I will kiss your hand."

She looked him in the face till the multitude of thoughts in her kind heart broke forth in tears.

"Do tell us," said Mr. Collier, "for I was so surprised that I never thought of it until now, how came you hither?"

"I came in an English vessel, which lies two miles below waiting for wind. My story is no uncommon one for an East India passenger. Our vessel was wrecked, and for nearly three years I have been a prisoner on the coast of Africa. How I effected my escape, I have neither strength nor spirits to tell you now."

"How wonderful are the doings of Providence," rejoined Mr. Collier; and he looked at his wife, as if he would add, "Poor fellow, his hardest fortune is yet to come."

"You need not look thus mournfully on each other, my good friends," observed the young man. "Had I not known the worst, I had not so long refrained from asking after my dear Mary."

"How could you have heard so soon?" inquired both.

"I met Hobomok soon after I landed," replied Brown; "and I have waited a long while, trusting to see him again as he returned; but if he came he must have taken a different route. He himself told me that Mary was his wife, and the mother of an Indian boy."

"Is it possible you have met Hobomok alone, and yet live to tell thereof?" asked Mr. Collier.

"I met him alone in the woods, and sincerely did I wish he would take my life," answered the young man. "I have a story to tell of that savage, which might make the best of us blush at our inferiority, Christians as we are; but I cannot tell it now."

"Speaking of hunting, makes me think of what I stumbled over, when I met you," replied Mr. Collier. "I'll take a light and go out to see what it was; for assuredly I thought it seemed like some large animal."

He soon returned, bringing in the pole, which had been left there by Hobomok.

"This is strange," exclaimed he. "Here is as handsome a deer as ever I put eyes on; and three clever foxes."

"What's that paper, fastened on the horns?" asked his wife.

Her husband untied it; and when opened, it proved to be as follows:

"This doth certifie that the witche hazel sticks, which were givene to the witnesses of my marriage are all burnte by my requeste: therefore by Indian laws, Hobomok and Mary Conant are divorced. And this I doe, that Mary may be happie. The same will be testified by my kinsmen Powexis, Mawhalissis, and Mackawalaw. The deere and foxes are for my goode Mary, and my boy. Maye the Englishmen's God bless them all.

The marke of ⟋⟍ Hobomok.

"Written by me, at the instigatione of the above Indian, who hath tolde me all, under an injunctione of secresie for three daies.

EDWARD WINSLOW.[1]
Governor of the jurisdictione of New Plimouth."

"His conduct is all of a piece, noble throughout," observed Brown. And he repeated to his friends, his singular interview with the Indian.

The behavior of the savage naturally drew forth many expressions of wonder and admiration; and the next question was, "How is Mary to be informed of all this? She will, no doubt, be alarmed at the absence of Hobomok."

"I am going to prepare some food for Mr. Brown," replied Sally; "and after I have done that, if you will take care of little Mary, I will go and spend the night with her. It is so near the fort, there can't be any danger when there are two of us; and perhaps to-morrow she will see Mr. Brown."

The young man insisted that he needed no food; and that he himself would stand sentinel near Mary's wigwam, and guard her through the night. Sally represented the impracticability of this plan, and the terrible alarm it would give Mary, should she chance to discover him; and after a good deal of friendly altercation, she carried her point. A small repast was set before Brown, and Mrs. Collier, having made all necessary arrangements for the comfort of her family, and having received repeated cautions, both from her husband and her guest, departed to the dwelling of her friend. She found her, as she expected, anxiously looking out for the hunter.

"What can be the reason he does not return?" said she, as Sally entered. "I was just thinking of coming in to ask you about him."

"Perhaps he did not find game plenty," replied Mrs. Collier.

"You know he seldom fails to find something," rejoined his anxious wife; "and besides he always comes home at night, whether he has been lucky or unlucky. He never would trust me and his boy to the mercy of Corbitant, after the night closed in; but perhaps, like every thing else that I ever loved, he is snatched away from me."

"I have thought a great deal of that trick you tried at Naumkeak," observed her friend. "It would be strange if Hobomok should die, and Brown should yet return alive and well; and yet we do sometimes hear of things as wonderful as that."

"How wildly you talk, dear Sally," she replied. "Charles has been dead these three years, and it is wicked in me to think of him so much as I do; for if ever a wife owed love to a husband, heathen or christian, I do to Hobomok. But have you heard any thing about my husband, that made you speak thus?"

Slowly did her friend prepare her mind for the reception of the tidings, and cautiously and gradually did she impart them, until she was made to comprehend the return of her lover, his meeting with Hobomok, and the exalted course which her husband had pursued.

The singular circumstances were so prudently revealed, and Mary had been so much accustomed to excitement, that no violent tumult was raised within her bosom; but she sobbed till Mrs. Collier thought her heart must break.

"I would willingly go down to the grave," said she, "willingly forfeit my hopes of heaven, if I could know they were both happy; but to have Hobomok a wanderer, for my sake, and to have him die among strangers, without one relation to speak those words of comfort and kindness, which he has so often uttered to me, I cannot—I cannot endure it. I only have sinned; and yet all the punishment has fallen upon his head. No; not quite all; for I know Brown must despise me."

Sally tried every gentle art to soothe her perturbed feelings, and before she departed, she extorted a promise that she would see Brown towards evening. A thousand times did Mary repent this resolution, notwithstanding her eagerness for the interview. Alternately would she weep, and then pray that blessings might rest on the head of him who had so lately been her husband; and if she regained any thing like composure, little Hobomok, who wandered about unused to such neglect, would ask, "What for make mamy ky so 'bout fader;" and his tone of infant melancholy would call forth all her sorrows afresh. At length the day drew toward a close; and Mary's pulse throbbed high when she heard those well-known footsteps approaching. In an instant she was at the feet of her lover, clasping his knees with a pale imploring countenance, as she said,

"Can you forgive me, Charles,—lost and humbled as I have been?"

"The Lord judge you according to your temptations, my dear Mary," replied he, as he raised her to his bosom, and wept over her in silence.

For a time both seemed afraid to trust each other with a second word or look.

"My temptations were many," said Mary, interrupting the silence. "I cannot tell you all now. But at home all was dark and comfortless; and when I heard you too were gone, my reason was obscured. Believe me I knew as little as I cared, whither I went, so as I could but escape the scenes wherewith you were connected; but to this hour, my love has never abated."

"I believe it, Mary; but where is your boy?"

The child moved before his mother, as he lisped, "Here's little Hobomok."

Mary caught him to her heart and kissed him, while the tears fell fast upon his cheeks.

"He is a brave boy," observed Brown, as he passed his fingers through the glossy black hair of the fearless young Indian.

"Those were the last words his father said to him," rejoined Mary, and she placed him in his arms, and turned away to conceal her emotion.

"Let's talk no more concerning this subject," said the young man. "The sacrifice that has been made is no doubt painful to us both; more especially to you, who have so long known his goodness; but it cannot now be remedied. You must go to Mr. Collier's to night; but will you first say that you will be my wife, either here or in England?"

"I cannot go to England," she replied. "My boy would disgrace me, and I never will leave him; for love to him is the only way that I can now repay my debt of gratitude."

"What is his name?" asked Brown.

"According to the Indian custom, he took the name of his mother," answered Mary. "I called him Charles Hobomok Conant."

"He shall be my own boy," exclaimed the young man. "May God prosper me according to my kindness towards him. But, my dear Mary, will you, as soon as possible, be my wife?"

"If you do not utterly despise me," rejoined she, in an agitated tone. "You well know how dear you are to my soul."

Mary and her son removed to Mrs. Collier's; and a letter was immediately despatched to Mr. Conant, informing him of existing circumstances, and requesting that the marriage might be performed at his house. The old gentleman returned this brief answer.

"Come to my arms, my deare childe; and maye God forgive us both, in aughte wherein we have transgressed."

The necessary arrangements were made; and a few days after, Mr. Brown, accompanied by Mary and her son, returned to Salem. It was the first time Mary had seen the town since her departure with the savage; and on many accounts the meeting could not be otherwise than one of mingled pain and pleasure.

Her father clasped her in a long, affectionate embrace, and never to the day of his death, referred to a subject which was almost equally unpleasant to both. A few weeks after their arrival, Mr. Skelton was sent for, and Mary stood beside her bridegroom, her hand resting on the sleek head of that swarthy boy. He, all unconscious of what was going forward, gave little heed to the hand which was intended to restrain his restless motions; for now he would be wholly concealed behind his mother's dress, and now, one roguish black eye would slily peep out upon his favorite companion, the laughing little Mary Collier.

Charles Brown and Mary Conant were pronounced husband and wife, in the presence of her father and Dame Willet, Mr. and Mrs. Oldham, and her two constant friends from Plymouth.

A new house was soon after erected near Mr. Conant's; and through the remainder of his life, the greater part of his evenings were spent by that fireside. Disputes on matters of opinion would sometimes arise; but Brown seldom forgot his promises of forbearance, and they were always brought to an amicable termination. Partly from consciousness of blame, and partly from a mixed feeling of compassion and affection, the little Hobomok was always a peculiar favorite with his grandfather. At his request, half the legacy of Earl Rivers was appropriated to his education. He was afterwards a distinguished graduate at Cambridge; and when he left that infant university, he departed to finish his studies in England. His father was seldom spoken of; and by degrees his Indian appellation was silently omitted. But the devoted, romantic love of Hobomok was never forgotten by its object; and his faithful services to the "Yengees" are still remembered with gratitude; though the tender slip which he protected, has since become a mighty tree, and the nations of the earth seek refuge beneath its branches.

OTHER WRITINGS

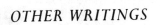

"The Lone Indian," the opening story of Child's *The Coronal* (1832), was first published in the inaugural issue of Samuel Goodrich's annual gift book, *The Token* (1828), and subsequently reprinted three times in *The Garland* (1830, 1839, 1840).

In the 1820s, the vogue of fiction exploiting Indian themes was at its peak. The Indian viewpoint Child assumes in this story, with its indictment of the "civilized destroyer"'s "ravages" and "insolence," is not typical, however. A thorough canvassing of *The Token* and its chief rival *The Atlantic Souvenir* reveals only one analogue: John Neal's "Otter-Bag, the Oneida Chief" (*The Token*, 1829). Instead, the dominant modes are captivity narratives and tales of Indian fighting, historical fiction about the French and Indian War, and Indian legends.

Such comparisons make it clear that "The Lone Indian," like Child's stories about Indians and blacks in her children's periodical, *The Juvenile Miscellany*—and like her antislavery stories of the 1840s—represents a conscious attempt to use fiction as a vehicle for mobilizing opposition to the United States government's racist policies. In 1828 Lydia Maria and David Lee Child were actively campaigning against Andrew Jackson's Cherokee removal scheme, as well as against the war still being waged on the Seminoles in Florida. Child ends her history book for children, *The First Settlers of New-England: or, Conquest of the Pequods, Narragansets and Pokanokets* . . . with a ringing plea for justice toward the Cherokees and Seminoles. Her peroration can serve as a gloss on "The Lone Indian": "It is, in my opinion, decidedly wrong, to speak of the removal, or extinction of the Indians as inevitable; it surely implies that the people of these states have not sufficient virtue or magnanimity to redeem their past offences, by affording the sad remnant, which still exist, succour and protection." In contrast, a poem by I. M'Lellan titled "Hymn of the Cherokee Indian" in *The Atlantic Souvenir* for 1831 puts these words into its Cherokee speaker's mouth:

> Let us yield our pleasant land
> To the stranger's stronger hand;
> Red men, and their realms must sever,
> They forsake them, and for ever!

THE LONE INDIAN

"A white man, gazing on the scene,
  Would say a lovely spot was here,
And praise the lawns so fresh and green,
  Between the hills so sheer.
I like it not—I would the plain
Lay in its tall old groves again."
  —*Bryant*

POWONTONAMO was the son of a mighty chief. He looked on his tribe with such a fiery glance, that they called him the Eagle of the Mohawks. His eye never blinked in the sunbeam, and he leaped along the chase like the untiring waves of Niagara. Even when a little boy, his tiny arrow would hit the frisking squirrel in the ear, and bring down the humming bird on her rapid wing. He was his father's pride and joy. He loved to toss him high in his sinewy arms, and shout, "Look, Eagle-eye, look! and see the big hunting-grounds of the Mohawks! Powontonamo will be their chief. The winds will tell his brave deeds. When men speak of him, they will not speak loud; but as if the Great Spirit had breathed in thunder."

The prophecy was fulfilled. When Powontonamo became a man, the fame of his beauty and courage reached the tribes of Illinois; and even the distant Osage showed his white teeth with delight, when he heard the wild deeds of the Mohawk Eagle. Yet was his spirit frank, chivalrous, and kind. When the white men came to buy land, he met them with an open palm, and spread his buffalo for the traveller. The old chiefs loved the bold youth, and offered their daughters in marriage. The eyes of the young Indian girls sparkled when he looked on them. But he treated them all with the stern indifference of a warrior, until he saw Soonseetah raise her long dark eye-lash. Then his heart melted beneath the beaming glance of beauty. Soonseetah was the fairest of the Oneidas. The young men of her tribe called her the Sunny-eye. She was smaller than her nation usually are; and her slight, graceful figure was so elastic in its motions, that the tall grass would rise up and shake off its dew drops, after her pretty moccasins had pressed it. Many a famous chief had sought her love; but when they brought the choicest furs, she would smile disdainfully, and say, "Soonseetah's foot is warm. Has not her father an arrow?" When they offered her food, according to the Indian custom, her answer was, "Soonseetah has not seen all the warriors. She will eat with the bravest." The hunters told the young Eagle, that Sunny-eye of Oneida was beautiful as the bright birds in the hunting-land beyond the sky; but that her heart was proud, and she said the great chiefs were not good enough to dress venison for her. When Powontonamo listened to these accounts, his lip would curl slightly, as he threw back his fur-edged mantle, and placed his firm, springy foot forward, so that the beads and shells of his rich moccasin might be seen to vibrate at every sound of his tremendous war song. If there was vanity in the act, there was likewise becoming pride. Soonseetah heard of his haughty smile, and resolved in her own heart that no Oneida should sit beside her, till she had seen the chieftain of the Mohawks. Before many moons had passed away, he sought her father's wigwam, to carry delicate furs and shining shells to the young coquette of the wilderness. She did not raise her bright melting eyes to his, when he came near her; but when he said, "Will the Sunny-eye look on the gift of a Mohawk? his barbed arrow is swift; his foot never turned from the foe;" the colour on her brown cheek was glowing as an autumnal twilight. Her voice was like the troubled note of the wren, as she answered, "The furs of Powontonamo are soft and warm to the foot of Soonseetah. She will weave the shells in the wampum belt of the Mohawk Eagle." The exulting lover sat by her side, and offered her venison and parched corn. She raised her timid eye, as she tasted the food; and then the young Eagle knew that Sunny-eye would be his wife.

There was feasting and dancing, and the marriage song rang merrily in Mohawk cabins, when the Oneida came among them. Powontonamo loved her as his own heart's blood. He delighted to bring her the fattest deers of the forest, and load her with the ribbons and beads of the English. The prophets of his people liked it not that the strangers grew so numerous in the land. They shook their heads mournfully, and said, "The moose and the beaver will not live within sound of the white man's gun.

They will go beyond the lakes, and the Indians must follow their trail." But the young chief laughed them to scorn. He said, "The land is very big. The mountain eagle could not fly over it in many days. Surely the wigwams of the English will never cover it." Yet when he held his son in his arms, as his father had done before him, he sighed to hear the strokes of the axe levelling the old trees of his forests. Sometimes he looked sorrowfully on his baby boy, and thought he had perchance done him much wrong, when he smoked a pipe in the wigwam of the stranger.

One day, he left his home before the grey mist of morning had gone from the hills, to seek food for his wife and child. The polar-star was bright in the heavens ere he returned; yet his hands were empty. The white man's gun had scared the beasts of the forest, and the arrow of the Indian was sharpened in vain. Powontonamo entered his wigwam with a cloudy brow. He did not look at Soonseetah; he did not speak to her boy; but, silent and sullen, he sat leaning on the head of his arrow. He wept not, for an Indian may not weep; but the muscles of his face betrayed the struggle within his soul. The Sunny-eye approached fearfully, and laid her little hand upon his brawny shoulder, as she asked, "Why is the Eagle's eye on the earth? What has Soonseetah done, that her child dare not look in the face of his father?" Slowly the warrior turned his gaze upon her. The expression of sadness deepened, as he answered, "The Eagle has taken a snake to his nest: how can his young sleep in it?" The Indian boy, all unconscious of the forebodings which stirred his father's spirit, moved to his side, and peeped up in his face with a mingled expression of love and fear.

The heart of the generous savage was full, even to bursting. His hand trembled, as he placed it on the sleek black hair of his only son. "The Great Spirit bless thee! the Great Spirit bless thee, and give thee back the hunting ground of the Mohawk!" he exclaimed. Then folding him, for an instant, in an almost crushing embrace, he gave him to his mother, and darted from the wigwam.

Two hours he remained in the open air; but the clear breath of heaven brought no relief to his noble and suffering soul. Wherever he looked abroad, the ravages of the civilized destroyer met his eye. Where were the trees, under which he had frolicked in infancy, sported in boyhood, and rested after the fatigues of battle? They formed the English boat, or lined the English dwelling. Where were the holy sacrifice-heaps of his people? The stones were taken to fence in the land, which the intruder dared to call his own. Where was his father's grave? The stranger's road passed over it, and his cattle trampled on the ground where the mighty Mohawk slumbered. Where were his once powerful tribe? Alas, in the white man's wars they had joined with the British, in the vain hope of recovering their lost privileges. Hundreds had gone to their last home; others had joined distant tribes; and some pitiful wretches, whom he scorned to call brethren, consented to live on the white man's bounty. These were corroding reflections; and well might fierce thoughts of vengeance pass through the mind of the deserted prince; but he was powerless now; and the English swarmed, like vultures around the dying. "It is the work of the Great Spirit," said he. "The Englishman's God made the Indian's heart afraid; and now he is like a wounded buffalo, when hungry wolves are on his trail."

When Powontonamo returned to his hut, his countenance, though severe, was composed. He spoke to the Sunny-eye with more kindness than the savage generally addresses the wife of his youth; but his look told her that she must not ask the grief which had put a woman's heart within the breast of the far-famed Mohawk Eagle.

The next day, when the young chieftain went out on a hunting expedition, he was accosted by a rough, square-built farmer. "Powow," said he, "your squaw has been stripping a dozen of my trees, and I don't like it over much." It was a moment when the Indian could ill brook a white man's insolence. "Listen, Buffalo-head!" shouted he; and as he spoke he seized the shaggy pate of the unconscious offender, and eyed him with the concentrated venom of an ambushed rattlesnake,—"Listen to the chief of the Mohawks! These broad lands are all his own. When the white man first left his cursed foot-print in the forest, the Great Bear looked down upon the big tribes of Iroquois and Abnaquis. The wigwams of the noble Delawares were thick, where the soft winds dwell. The rising sun glanced on the fierce Pequods; and the Illinois, the Miamies, and warlike tribes like the hairs of your head, marked his going down. Had the red man struck you then, your tribes would have been as dry grass to the lightning! Go—shall the Sunny-eye of Oneida ask the pale face for a basket?" He breathed out a quick, convulsive laugh, and his white teeth showed through his parted lips, as he shook the farmer from him, with the strength and fury of a raging panther.

After that, his path was unmolested, for no one dared to awaken his wrath; but a smile never again visited the dark countenance of the degraded chief. The wild beasts had fled so far from the settlements, that he would hunt days and days without success. Soonseetah sometimes begged him to join the remnant of the Oneidas, and persuade them to go far off, toward the setting sun. Powontonamo replied, "This is the burial place of my fathers;" and the Sunny-eye dared say no more.

At last, their boy sickened and died, of a fever he had taken among the English. They buried him beneath a spreading oak, on the banks of the Mohawk, and heaped stones upon his grave, without a tear. "He must lie near the water," said the desolate chief, "else the white man's horses will tread on him."

The young mother did not weep; but her heart had received its death-wound. The fever seized her, and she grew paler and weaker every day. One morning, Powontonamo returned with some delicate food he had been seeking for her. "Will Soonseetah eat?" said he. He spoke in a tone of subdued tenderness; but she answered not. The foot which was wont to bound forward to meet him, lay motionless and cold. He raised the blanket which partly concealed her face, and saw that the Sunny-eye was closed in death. One hand was pressed hard against her heart, as if her last moments had been painful. The other grasped the beads which the young Eagle had given her in the happy days of courtship. One heart-rending shriek was rung from the bosom of the agonized savage. He tossed his arms wildly above his head, and threw himself beside the body of her he had loved as fondly, deeply, and passionately, as ever a white man loved. After the first burst of grief had subsided, he carefully untied the necklace from her full, beautiful bosom, crossed her hands over the sacred relic, and put back the shining black hair from her smooth forehead. For hours he watched the corpse in silence. Then he arose and carried it from the wigwam. He dug a grave by the side of his lost boy; laid the head of Soonseetah toward the rising sun; heaped the earth upon it, and covered it with stones, according to the custom of his people.

Night was closing in, and still the bereaved Mohawk stood at the grave of Sunny-eye, as motionless as its cold inmate. A white man, as he passed, paused, and looked in pity on him. "Are you sick?" asked he. "Yes; me sick. Me very sick here," answered Powontonamo, laying his hand upon his swelling heart. "Will you go home?" "*Home!*" exclaimed the heart broken chief, in tones so thrilling, that the white man started. Then slowly, and with a half vacant look, he added, "Yes; me go home. By and by me go home." Not another word would he speak; and the white man left him, and went his way. A little while longer he stood watching the changing heavens; and then, with reluctant step, retired to his solitary wigwam.

The next day, a tree, which Soonseetah had often said was just as old as their boy, was placed near the mother and child. A wild vine was straggling among the loose stones, and Powontonamo carefully twined it around the tree. "The young oak is the Eagle of the Mohawks," he said; "and now the Sunny-eye has her arms around him." He spoke in the wild music of his native tongue; but there was none to answer. "Yes; Powontonamo will go home," sighed he. "He will go where the sun sets in the ocean, and the white man's eyes have never looked upon it." One long, one lingering glance at the graves of his kindred, and the Eagle of the Mohawks bade farewell to the land of his fathers.

FOR MANY a returning autumn, a lone Indian was seen standing at the consecrated spot we have mentioned; but, just thirty years after the death of Soonseetah, he was noticed for the last time. His step was then firm, and his figure erect, though he seemed old and way-worn. Age had not dimmed the fire of his eye, but an expression of deep melancholy had settled on his wrinkled brow. It was Powontonamo—he who had once been the Eagle of the Mohawks! He came to lie down and die beneath the broad oak, which shadowed the grave of Sunny-eye. Alas! the white man's axe had been there! The tree he had planted was dead; and the vine, which had leaped so vigorously from branch to branch, now, yellow and withering, was falling to the ground. A deep groan burst from the soul of the savage. For thirty wearisome years, he had watched that oak, with its twining tendrils. They were the only things left in the wide world for him to love, and they were gone! He looked abroad. The hunting land of his tribe was changed, like its chieftain. No light canoe now shot down the river, like a bird upon the wing. The laden boat of the white man alone broke its smooth surface. The Englishman's road wound like a serpent around the banks of the Mohawk;

and iron hoofs had so beaten down the war-path, that a hawk's eye could not discover an Indian track. The last wigwam was destroyed; and the sun looked boldly down upon spots he had visited only by stealth, during thousands and thousands of moons. The few remaining trees, clothed in the fantastic mourning of autumn; the long line of heavy clouds, melting away before the coming sun; and the distant mountain, seen through the blue mist of departing twilight, alone remained as he had seen them in his boyhood. All things spoke a sad language to the heart of the desolate Indian. "Yes," said he, "the young oak and the vine are like the Eagle and the Sunny-eye. They are cut down, torn, and trampled on. The leaves are falling, and the clouds are scattering, like my people. I wish I could once more see the trees standing thick, as they did when my mother held me to her bosom, and sung the warlike deeds of the Mohawks."

A mingled expression of grief and anger passed over his face, as he watched a loaded boat in its passage across the stream. "The white man carries food to his wife and children, and he finds them in his home," said he. "Where is the squaw and the papoose of the red man? They are here!" As he spoke, he fixed his eye thoughtfully upon the grave. After a gloomy silence, he again looked round upon the fair scene, with a wandering and troubled gaze. "The pale face may like it," murmured he; "but an Indian cannot die here in peace." So saying, he broke his bow string, snapped his arrows, threw them on the burial place of his fathers, and departed for ever.

NONE EVER KNEW where Powontonamo laid his dying head. The hunters from the west said, a red man had been among them, whose tracks were far off toward the rising sun; that he seemed like one who had lost his way, and was sick to go home to the Great Spirit. Perchance, he slept his last sleep where the distant Mississippi receives its hundred streams. Alone, and unfriended, he may have laid him down to die, where no man called him brother; and the wolves of the desert, long ere this, may have howled the death-song of the Mohawk Eagle.

"Chocorua's Curse," from Child's collection *The Coronal*, was first published in *The Token* for 1830 and subsequently reprinted in *The Lady's Cabinet Album* (1832, 1834, 1837, 1838). Child probably derived the idea for the story from Thomas Cole's 1829 painting *The Death of Chocorua*, an engraving of which, retitled *Chocorua's Curse*, likewise appears in *The Token*. Both Cole and Child drew inspiration from a legend of the Mount Chocorua region in New Hampshire, according to which an Indian chief killed by local whites had cursed the land with a bane making its waters deadly. "Chocorua's Curse" invites comparison with another story in the same issue of *The Token*: Timothy Flint's "The Indian Fighter," which follows the captivity narrative tradition of portraying Indians as bloodthirsty savages destined to be exterminated by a righteous God.

As in *Hobomok*, the white and Indian protagonists of "Chocorua's Curse" seem to be doubles. Here, however, the fusion of white and Indian eventuates in tragedy, as each blights the other. The source of this blight, the story suggests, is the white settlers' hostile relationship to nature, which they treat as an enemy to be subjugated, rather than as a source of life to be venerated or propitiated. Symbolizing the cycle of catastrophe the colonists set in motion through their war on nature, the poison they have prepared for a fox instead kills Chocorua's son, leading to the retaliatory murders, first of Caroline Campbell and her children, then of Chocorua himself. The story's pessimism about resolving the conflict between Indians and whites may reflect Child's assessment of the prospects for reversing the United States government's Cherokee removal policy.

"Chocorua's Curse" also makes an ambiguous statement about woman's sphere. Newly married and appreciative, like Caroline Campbell, of her husband's "intellectual energies," Child appears to reject the "modern doctrines of equality" currently being preached by Fanny Wright. Yet whether or not Caroline recognizes marriage as a "tyranny," she pays with her life for accepting her husband's decision to emigrate to a solitary frontier settlement.

CHOCORUA'S CURSE

✺✺✺✺✺✺

THE *ROCKY COUNTY* of Strafford, New-Hampshire, is remarkable for its wild and broken scenery. Ranges of hills towering one above another, as if eager to look upon the beautiful country, which afar off lies sleeping in the embrace of heaven; precipices, from which the young eagles take their flight to the sun; dells rugged and tangled as the dominions of Roderick Vich Alpine, and ravines dark and deep enough for the death scene of a bandit, form the magnificent characteristics of this picturesque region.

A high precipice, called Chocorua's Cliff, is rendered peculiarly interesting by a legend which tradition has scarcely saved from utter oblivion. Had it been in Scotland, perhaps the genius of Sir Walter would have hallowed it, and Americans would have crowded there to kindle fancy on the altar of memory. Being in the midst of our own romantic scenery, it is little known, and less visited; for the vicinity is as yet untraversed by railroads or canals, and no "Mountain House," perched on these tremendous battlements, allures the traveller hither to mock the majesty of nature with the insipidities of fashion. Our distinguished artist, Mr. Cole,[1] found the sunshine and the winds sleeping upon it in solitude and secrecy; and his pencil has brought it before us in its stern repose.

In olden time, when Goffe and Whalley[2] passed for wizards and mountain spirits among the superstitious, the vicinity of the spot we have been describing was occupied by a very small colony, which, either from discontent or enterprise, had retired into this remote part of New-Hampshire. Most of them were ordinary men, led to this independent mode of life from an impatience of restraint, which as frequently accompanies vulgar obstinacy as generous pride. But there was one master spirit among them, who was capable of a higher destiny than he ever fulfilled. The consciousness of this had stamped something of proud humility on the face of Cornelius Campbell; something of a haughty spirit, strongly curbed by circumstances he could not control, and at which he scorned to murmur. He assumed no superiority; but unconsciously he threw around him the spell of intellect, and his companions felt, they knew not why, that he was "among them, but not of them." His stature was gigantic, and he had the bold, quick tread of one who had wandered frequently and fearlessly among the terrible hiding-places of nature. His voice was harsh, but his whole countenance possessed singular capabilities for tenderness of expression; and sometimes, under the gentle influence of domestic excitement, his hard features would be rapidly lighted up, seeming like the sunshine flying over the shaded fields in an April day.

His companion was one peculiarly calculated to excite and retain the deep, strong energies of manly love. She had possessed extraordinary beauty; and had, in the full maturity of an excellent judgment, relinquished several splendid alliances, and incurred her father's displeasure, for the sake of Cornelius Campbell. Had political circumstances proved favourable, his talents and ambition would unquestionably have worked out a path to emolument and fame; but he had been a zealous and active enemy of the Stuarts, and the restoration of Charles the Second was the death-warrant of his hopes. Immediate flight became necessary, and America was the chosen place of refuge. His adherence to Cromwell's party was not occasioned by religious sympathy, but by political views, too liberal and philosophical for the state of the people; therefore Cornelius Campbell was no favourite with our forefathers, and being of a proud nature, he withdrew with his family to the solitary place we have mentioned.

It seemed a hard fate for one who had from childhood been accustomed to indulgence and admiration, yet Mrs. Campbell enjoyed more than she had done in her days of splendour; so much deeper are the sources of happiness than those of gaiety. Even her face had suffered little from time and hardship. The bloom on her cheek, which in youth had been like the sweet-pea blossom, that most feminine of all flowers, had, it is true, somewhat faded; but her rich, intellectual expression, did but receive additional majesty from years; and the exercise of quiet domestic love, which, where it is suffered to exist, always deepens and brightens with time, had given a bland and placid expression, which might well have atoned for the absence of more striking beauty. To such a woman as Caroline Campbell, of what use would have been some modern doctrines of equality and independence?

With a mind sufficiently cultivated to appreciate and enjoy her husband's intellectual energies, she had a heart that could not have found another home. The bird will drop into its nest though the treasures of earth and sky are open. To have proved marriage a tyranny, and the cares of domestic life a thraldom, would have affected Caroline Campbell as little, as to be told that pure, sweet atmosphere she breathed, was pressing upon her so many pounds to every square inch! Over such a heart, and such a soul, external circumstances have little power; all worldly interest was concentrated in her husband and babes, and her spirit was satisfied with that inexhaustible fountain of joy which nature gives, and God has blessed.

A very small settlement, in such a remote place, was of course subject to inconvenience and occasional suffering. From the Indians they received neither injury nor insult. No cause of quarrel had ever arisen; and, although their frequent visits were sometimes troublesome, they never had given indications of jealousy or malice. Chocorua was a prophet among them, and as such an object of peculiar respect. He had a mind which education and motive would have nerved with giant strength; but growing up in savage freedom, it wasted itself in dark, fierce, ungovernable passions. There was something fearful in the quiet haughtiness of his lip—it seemed so like slumbering power, too proud to be lightly roused, and too implacable to sleep again. In his small, black, fiery eye, expression lay coiled up like a beautiful snake. The white people knew that his hatred would be terrible; but they had never provoked it, and even the children became too much accustomed to him to fear him.

Chocorua had a son, about nine or ten years old, to whom Caroline Campbell had occasionally made such gaudy presents as were likely to attract his savage fancy. This won the child's affections, so that he became a familiar visitant, almost an inmate of their dwelling; and being unrestrained by the courtesies of civilized life, he would inspect everything, and taste of everything which came in his way. Some poison, prepared for a mischievous fox, which had long troubled the little settlement, was discovered and drunk by the Indian boy; and he went home to his father to sicken and die. From that moment jealousy and hatred took possession of Chocorua's soul. He never told his suspicions—he brooded over them in secret, to nourish the deadly revenge he contemplated against Cornelius Campbell.

The story of Indian animosity is always the same. Cornelius Campbell left his hut for the fields early one bright, balmy morning in June. Still a lover, though ten years a husband, his last look was turned towards his wife, answering her parting smile—his last action a kiss for each of his children. When he returned to dinner, they were dead—all dead! and their disfigured bodies too cruelly showed that an Indian's hand had done the work!

In such a mind grief, like all other emotions, was tempestuous. Home had been to him the only verdant spot in the wide desert of life. In his wife and children he had garnered up all his heart; and now they were torn from him, the remembrance of their love clung to him like the death-grapple of a drowning man, sinking him down, down, into darkness and death. This was followed by a calm a thousand times more terrible—the creeping agony of despair, that brings with it no power of resistance.

> "It was as if the dead could feel
> The icy worm around him steal."

Such, for many days, was the state of Cornelius Campbell. Those who knew and reverenced him, feared that the spark of reason was forever extinguished. But it rekindled again, and with it came a wild, demoniac spirit of revenge. The death-groan of Chocorua would make him smile in his dreams; and when he waked, death seemed too pitiful a vengeance for the anguish that was eating into his very soul.

Chocorua's brethren were absent on a hunting expedition at the time he committed the murder; and those who watched his movements observed that he frequently climbed the high precipice, which afterward took his name, probably looking out for indications of their return.

Here Cornelius Campbell resolved to effect his deadly purpose. A party was formed under his guidance, to cut off all chance of retreat, and the dark-minded prophet was to be hunted like a wild beast to his lair.

The morning sun had scarce cleared away the fogs when Chocorua started at a loud voice from beneath the precipice, commanding him to throw himself into the deep abyss below. He knew the voice of his enemy, and replied with an Indian's calmness, "The Great Spirit gave life to Chocorua; and Chocorua will not throw it away at the command of a white man." "Then hear the Great Spirit speak in the white man's thunder!" exclaimed Cornelius Campbell, as he pointed his gun to the precipice. Chocorua, though fierce and fearless as a panther, had never overcome his dread of fire-arms. He placed his hand upon his ears to shut out the stunning report; the next moment the blood bubbled from his neck, and he reeled fearfully on the edge of the precipice. But he recovered himself, and, raising himself on his hands, he spoke in a loud voice, that grew more terrific as its huskiness increased, "A curse upon ye, white men! May the Great Spirit curse ye when he speaks in the clouds, and his words are fire! Chocorua had a son—and ye killed him while his eye still loved to look on the bright sun, and the green earth! The Evil Spirit breathe death upon your cattle! Your graves lie in the war path of the Indian! Panthers howl, and wolves fatten over your bones! Chocorua goes to the Great Spirit—his curse stays with the white men!"

The prophet sunk upon the ground, still uttering inaudible curses—and they left his bones to whiten in the sun. But his curse rested on the settlement. The tomahawk and scalping knife were busy among them, the winds tore up trees and hurled them at their dwellings, their crops were blasted, their cattle died, and sickness came upon their strongest men. At last the remnant of them departed from the fatal spot to mingle with more populous and prosperous colonies. Cornelius Campbell became a hermit, seldom seeking or seeing his fellow men; and two years after he was found dead in his hut.

To this day the town of Burton, in New-Hampshire, is remarkable for a pestilence which infects its cattle; and the superstitious think that Chocorua's spirit still sits enthroned upon his precipice, breathing a curse upon them.

A landmark text, Child's *History of the Condition of Women, in Various Ages and Nations* (2 vols., 1835), from which the following excerpt on Indian women is drawn, attempted a task no writer had yet undertaken: a comprehensive survey of women's status in societies the world over, from ancient times to the mid-nineteenth century, from the remotest Siberian tribe to the United States. The project entailed sifting through innumerable travel accounts, treatises, histories, and missionary reports, most of which mentioned women only in passing. Child's sources on Indians, for example, included Captain John Smith's *The General History of Virginia* (1624); Cadwallader Colden's *History of the Five Indian Nations of Canada . . .* (1727); Joseph Gumilla's *El Orinoco ilustrado . . .* (1741); Nicholas Biddle's edition of *Travels to the Source of the Missouri River and Across the American Continent to the Pacific Ocean . . . By Captains Lewis and Clarke* (1814); John Heckewelder's *An Account of the History, Manners, and Customs of the Indian Nations Who Once Inhabited Pennsylvania and the Neighboring States* (1818); Edwin James's *Account of an Expedition from Pittsburgh to the Rocky Mountains . . . Compiled from the Notes of Major Long . . .* (1823); Charles Johnston's *A Narrative of the Incidents Attending the Capture, Detention, and Ransom of Charles Johnston . . . To Which Are Added, Sketches of Indian Character and Manners . . .* (1827); and William Joseph Snelling's *Tales of the Northwest; or, Sketches of Indian Life and Character* (1830).

Child's preface specifically denied that her monumental history of women was "an essay upon woman's rights, or a philosophical investigation of what is or ought to be the relation of the sexes." At the same time, her disclaimer hinted at an oblique strategy: "If any theories on this subject are contained in it, they are merely incidentally implied by the manner of stating historical facts." Readers so inclined, Child intimated, would find in the book "many materials for argument." Indeed her compendium proved an invaluable resource for the theorists of the women's rights movement. Among those it supplied with ammunition were Sarah Grimké, Margaret Fuller, and Elizabeth Cady Stanton.

Typifying both the political perspective that informs Child's *History* and the tactics of indirection she uses to convey her message, her discussion of Indian women comprises the opening section of the chapter "America," which covers "Women of the Arctic Regions," "South American Women," and "Women of the United States," black as well as white. Like most writers of the period, Child emphasizes the Indian woman's drudgery and subjection to male tyranny. Yet she also uses the Indian woman's physical strength, endurance, and hardy constitution to undermine culture- and class-bound notions of women's frailty. In the same vein, she notes all evidence indicating that Indian women exercise significant power and influence (e.g., as healers, prophets, participants in tribal councils and decisions), and she draws attention to practices showing how interchangeable male and female roles are from culture to culture (for example, Dacotah and Mexican marriage rituals). Her description of Indian weddings corresponds almost exactly to the account of Mary and Hobomok's wedding. The reference to a conversation with Penobscot Indians almost immediately afterwards raises the possibility that Child may actually have observed an Indian marriage ceremony during her sojourn in Maine; none of her identifiable sources describes such a ceremony.

❦❦❦❦❦❦

BEFORE AMERICA was settled by Europeans, it was inhabited by Indian tribes, which greatly resembled each other in the treatment of their women. Every thing except war and hunting was considered beneath the dignity of man. During long and wearisome marches, women were obliged to carry children, provisions, and hammocks on their shoulders; they had the sole care of the horses and dogs, cut wood, pitched the tents, raised the corn, and made the clothing. When the husband killed game, he left it by a tree in the forest, returned home, and sent his wife several miles in search of it. In most of the tribes, women were not allowed to eat and drink with men, but stood and served them, and then ate what they left.

When the Spaniards arrived in South America, the Indian women, delighted with attentions to which they had been entirely unaccustomed, often betrayed the conspiracies formed against them, supplied them with food, and acted as guides.

Father Joseph reproved a female savage on the banks of the Orinoco, because she destroyed her infant daughter. She replied, "I wish my mother had thus prevented the manifold sufferings I have endured. Consider, Father, our deplorable situation. Our husbands go out to hunt; we are dragged along with one infant at our breast, and another in a basket. Though tired with long walking, we are not allowed to sleep when we return, but must labor the whole night in grinding maize to make chica for them. They get drunk, and beat us, draw us by the hair of the head, and tread us under foot. And after a slavery of perhaps twenty years, what have we to comfort us? A young wife is then brought home, and permitted to abuse us and our children. What kindness can we show our daughters equal to putting them to death? Would to God my mother had put me under ground the moment I was born."

The Mexicans and Peruvians, particularly the latter, were more enlightened and refined than the other native tribes. The rich ornaments of gold and pearl worn by the Peruvians, surprised their European visiters, even more than the gentleness, modesty, and benevolence of their characters. They had a temple of the sun, to whose service young virgins were dedicated, and instructed in many accomplishments.

The parents of a young Mexican having selected a suitable wife, priests are consulted, and the match concludes or not, according to their predictions. If their answers are favorable, the girl is asked of her parents by certain women styled solicitors, who are chosen from the most respectable of the youth's kindred. The first demand is always refused; the second receives a more favorable answer; and when consent is finally obtained, the bride, after proper exhortation from her parents, is conducted to the house of her father-in-law. If wealthy, she is carried in a litter. The bridegroom and his relations receive her at the gate, where four women are stationed bearing torches. As soon as the young couple meet, they offer incense to each other. They then sit on a curiously wrought mat, in the centre of the hall, near the fire, and the priest ties the bride's gown to the bridegroom's mantle. They offer sacrifices to the gods, and exchange presents. The guests are then entertained with feasting and dancing in the open air; but the newly married are shut up in the house for four days. At the end of that period they appear in their richest attire, and give dresses to the company, in proportion to their wealth.

Gumilla, in his History of the River Orinoco, says there is one nation that marry old men to girls and old women to lads, that age may correct the petulance of youth. They say, to join together people equal in youth and imprudence, is to join one fool to another. The first marriage is however only a kind of apprenticeship; for after a while the young people are allowed to marry those of their own age.

Among several tribes of North American Indians, the lover begins his suit by going at midnight to the tent, or lodge, of his mistress. He lights a splinter of wood, and holds it to her face to awaken her. If she leaves the torch burning, it is a signal that she rejects him; but if she blows it out, he understands that he is at liberty to communicate his intentions.

In some places, when the lover approaches the hut of his mistress, he begs leave to enter it by signs. If permission is obtained, he goes in and sits down by her in silence. If she suffers him to remain, without any expression of disapprobation, it is an indication that she favors his suit; but if she offers him food or drink, he understands it as a refusal.

Indian marriages are generally performed in the following manner: The young couple are seated on a mat in the centre of the room. The bride, or bridegroom, hold a rod or wand between them, while some elderly person harangues them concerning their reciprocal duties. He tells the husband that he must catch plenty of venison and furs for his wife; and the bride is urged to cook his food well, mend his clothes, and take off his moccasins and leggins, when he comes home from hunting. The rod is then broken, and a piece given to the witnesses in testimony of the contract. The company form a circle and dance and sing around them. Before they separate, they partake of a plentiful feast provided for the occasion. A strap, a kettle, and a fagot, are put into the bride's apartment, in token of her employments. At Dacotah weddings, the bride is carried forcibly to her husband's dwelling, making resistance at every step. In some parts of Old Mexico, the bridegroom was carried off by his relations, as if he were the one forced into wedlock. A Dacotah lover puts on leggins of different colors, seats himself on a log near the wigwam of his beloved, and sings, or plays on some musical instrument. The following has been given as a sample of Indian love-songs, by a writer well acquainted with their manners:

> "She is handsomer than scarlet or wampum;
> I will put on a blue leggin and run after her;
> And she will flee as if afraid.
> But I see, as she turns her head over her shoulder,
> And mocks and laughs, and rails at me,
> That her fears are nothing but pretence.
> She is handsomer than scarlet and wampum;
> I will put on a blue leggin and run after her."

The Indians, both men and women, had great love of finery. Their caps, belts, and moccasins were plentifully embroidered with beads and shells, which they called wampum. The chiefs considered a coronet of feathers peculiarly beautiful; but this ornament, generally indicative of successful war, was seldom worn by women. But even among these rude people, jokes concerning female love of dress were not wanting. A few years since, the writer conversed with two Penobscot Indians, the one old, the other young, and very handsome. The youth wore a scarlet band upon his hat, and his wampum belt was curiously embroidered; the other had an old blanket carelessly wrapped about him. "Where is your wampum belt?" said I. With a look of quiet scorn, he replied, "What for me wear ribbons and beads? Me no want to catch 'em squaw."*

Among the Hohays are men who dress in a female garb, and perform all manner of female avocations. They are called *Winktahs*, and treated with the utmost contempt.

The Indian bridegroom generally pays his father-in-law for his bride; and even in their primitive form of society, he who can offer a large price is most likely to be acceptable to parents. Handsome Indian girls are not unfrequently disposed of contrary to their inclinations. They are not permitted to marry relations within so near a degree of consanguinity as cousins. Suicide is common among the women of these savage tribes. When thwarted in love, or driven to desperation by ill usage, they frequently hang themselves to the branch of a tree, rush into the sea, or throw themselves from a precipice. The men very rarely destroy their own lives. They seldom have more than one wife at a time; but they change just when they please, interchange with each other, and lend to visiters, without scandal. When a wife becomes old, a younger one is often purchased; and the first one may either kill her self, or tamely submit to be the drudge of the family. In several tribes, the pieces of stick given to the witnesses at the marriage are burnt, in sign of divorce. But, generally speaking, new connections are formed without any formal dissolution of the old one.

When the sachem of Saugus married the daughter of the chief of Pennakook, a great feast was given, and the bride and bridegroom escorted to their dwelling by some of the most honorable men of her father's tribe, who were feasted several days at the expense of the husband. Some time after, the wife expressed a wish to visit her father, and was permitted to do

*Indians call their women *squaws*, and infants *papooses*.

so, with a select escort to accompany her. When she desired to return, the old chief sent to the sachem to come and take her away. This offended the young man's pride. "I sent her to you in a manner that became a chief," he replied; "and now that she intends to return to me, I expect the same from you." The chief of Pennakook considered this an insolent message. He would not allow his daughter to return unless her husband sent for her; the sachem would not submit to the terms; and the young couple saw each other no more.

The Indians pride themselves on stoicism, and at no period of their history have been addicted to voluptuousness. Their sense of manliness and dignity prevents them from being immodest. In this respect, their deportment towards women is abundantly more praiseworthy than that of civilized nations.

When it was proposed (either facetiously or otherwise) that women should be members of parliament, an Englishman objected to it, on the ground that a lady, who sat with committees of gentlemen, might sometimes meet with a species of impoliteness that would be embarrassing. If *this* be a reason why women should not transact public business, it is a fact exceedingly disgraceful to civilized men. Female captives taken by Indians, though treated with the most diabolical cruelty, according to their savage mode of warfare, have travelled with powerful warriors days and weeks, through the loneliest paths of the forest, and never been subjected to the slightest personal insult.

Notwithstanding the habitual taciturnity of Indians, and their pride of concealing all emotion, the potent passion of love sometimes gets the mastery of them, as well as of other men. One of their strongest excitements to bravery, is the hopes of gaining favor in the bright eyes of some beautiful maiden; and it is often a matter of peculiar pride with them to obtain the handsomest furs to decorate a wife, and to furnish an abundant supply of venison for her comfortable subsistence. An Indian woman is always proud of having a good hunter for a husband; and a lover is often told that he must signalize himself by more daring exploits, before he can hope to be received into favor.

Mr. Heckewelder, in his interesting account of the American Indians, relates the following anecdote: "In the year 1762, I was witness to a remarkable instance of the disposition of Indians to indulge their wives. There was a famine in the land, and a sick Indian woman expressed a great desire for a mess of Indian corn. Her husband, having heard that a trader at Lower Sandusky had a little, set off on horseback for that place, one hundred miles distant, and returned with as much corn as filled the crown of his hat, for which he gave his horse in exchange, and came home on foot, bringing his saddle back with him.

"It very seldom happens that an Indian condescends to quarrel with his wife, or abuse her, though she has given him just cause. In such a case, the man, without replying, or saying a single word, will take his gun and go into the woods, and remain there a week, or perhaps a fortnight, living on the meat he has killed, before he returns home again; well knowing that he cannot inflict a greater punishment on his wife for her conduct to him, than by absenting himself for a while; for she is not only kept in suspense, uncertain whether he will return again, but is soon reported as a bad and quarrelsome woman; for, as on those occasions a man does not tell his wife on what day or at what time he will be back again, which he never, when they are on good terms, neglects to do, she is at once put to shame by her neighbors, who, soon suspecting something, do not fail to put such questions to her as she either cannot, or is ashamed to answer. When he at length does return, she endeavors to let him see, by her attentions, that she has repented, though neither speak to each other a single word on the subject of what has passed. And as his children, if he has any, will on his return hang about him, and soothe him with their caresses, he is on their account ready to forgive, or at least to say nothing unpleasant to their mother."

The women of these savage tribes, like the female peasantry of Europe, have very hardy constitutions. When an infant is a few hours old, they carry it to some neighboring stream and plunge it in the water, even if they have to break the ice for that purpose. Until it is old enough to crawl about, they lay it down on a clean piece of bark, while they attend to their customary avocations; when obliged to travel, they carry it swung at their backs, in a strip of cloth, or a basket. Some tribes have the habit of placing boys on the skin of a panther, and girls on that of a fawn, from an idea that they will imbibe the qualities of those animals. Names are usually bestowed to indicate some personal or moral quality; as *Parrot-nosed, Serpent-eyed, The Timid Fawn*, &c. These names are often added to others, signifying *The First Son, The Second Son, The First Daughter*, &c.

Most of the North American tribes make it a fundamental principle of education never to strike a child. When a fault is committed, the mother begins to cry; if her son or daughter ask what is the matter, she replies, "You disgrace me." This reproach is keenly felt, and generally produces amendment. If a young person is more obdurate than common, the parents throw a glass of water in his face, and this is considered a most disgraceful punishment. They seldom refuse a child any thing. Hence when the avenger of blood is implacable, the culprit is often led into his presence by a little child, prettily adorned, and taught to lisp a prayer for pardon; and a petition for mercy from such innocent lips, is rarely denied even by the sternest warrior. Pocahontas was only twelve years old when her intercession saved the life of captain Smith.

Both girls and boys are early taught to endure without a murmur the utmost rigors of climate, excess of labor, and the extremity of pain. It is common to try their fortitude by ordering them to hold their hands in the fire, till permission is given to withdraw them; and if even their countenances give indication of agony, it is deemed dishonorable. When taken captive in war they have need of their utmost powers of endurance; for their enemies exercise all their ingenuity in torture. Yet such is the force of education, that women, as well as men, will smile and utter jeering words, while their nails are pulled out by the roots, their feet crushed between stones, and their flesh torn with red-hot pincers.

It is an almost universal rule that women are more tender-hearted than men; but the North American Indians seem to furnish an exception. When a prisoner is tied to the stake, women are even more furious and active than men, in the work of cruelty. If any one of the tribe chooses to adopt the prisoner, his life is spared, and they cease to torment him. Parents, who have lost their own children in battle, often resort to this expedient, and bring up their adopted sons and daughters with great kindness.

The power of Indian husbands is absolute. If they detect a wife in unfaithfulness, they generally cut off her nose, or take off part of her scalp. In a sudden fit of anger they sometimes kill both her and her paramour;

and this goes unpunished, though it is considered more proper to call a council of the elders to decide the matter. Those stern old men do not approve of very furious transports on such occasions; because they deem it undignified to make such a fuss about a woman, so long as the world contains plenty of individuals to supply her place.

Dancing was a common amusement with the Indians. Their war-dances were performed by men; but there were others appropriated to women, or in which both sexes united. Captain Smith gives the following account of an "anticke" prepared by Pocahontas for his reception at her father's place of residence: "Thirty young women came out of the woods, covered onely with a few greene leaues, their bodies all painted, some of one colour, some of another, but all differing. Their leader had a fayre payre of bucks hornes on her head, and an otter-skinne at her girdle, and another at her arme, a quiver of arrowes at her backe, a bow and arrows in her hand. The next had in her hand a sword, and another a club, another a pot-sticke, all horned alike; the rest every one with their seuerall devises. These fiends, with most hellish shouts and cryes, rushing from among the trees, cast themselves in a ring about the fire, singing and dancing with most excellent ill varietie, oft falling into their infernall passions, and solemnly again to sing and dance. Having spent neare an houre in this mascarado, as they entred, in like manner they departed."

Captain Smith does not give a very gallant account of an entertainment intended as a particular compliment to his arrival. The dance, like most savage dances, was unquestionably a pantomime; and he probably did not understand what it was intended to represent.

The Indian women sometimes accompany the men on hunting excursions, for the purpose of bringing home the game; and in time of battle they often encourage and assist the warriors. In addition to the toilsome occupations already alluded to, they made garments of skins, sewed with sinews and thorns, wove neat mats and baskets, and embroidered very prettily with shells, feathers, and grass of various colors. When first visited by Europeans, they wore furs in winter, and mats tied about them in summer; but they soon learned to substitute blankets, and strips of cloth. Those that can afford it, have ears, neck, arms, and waist plentifully decorated with beads, pebbles, fishes' teeth, or shells. The Indians of California perforate the lobes of the ears, and insert pieces of wood five or six inches long, ornamented with feathers. On the North-West coast, the women make a horizontal incision in the lower lip, for the purpose of introducing a wooden plug, which makes the lip protrude in a hideous manner. In the neighborhood of Kotzebue's sound, they wear large beads suspended from the nose, and when they experience inconvenience from these ornaments, they stow them away in the nostrils. The Guiana females stick thorns, or pins, through the lower lip; the heads are inside, and the points rest upon the chin. They have likewise the habit of putting a band round the ankle and knee, when girls are ten or twelve years old; as this is never removed, it produces an unnatural compression, and the calf of the leg swells to an unwieldy size. Indians of both sexes paint themselves in various colors and patterns, and are more or less addicted to tattooing; though it is by no means practised to the extent that it is among the South Sea islanders.

Before America was visited by Europeans, the Indian tribes were universally temperate, healthy, and cleanly in their habits; but they have now acquired most of the evils of civilization, with few of its advantages. They have a reddish brown complexion, keen black eyes, regular white teeth, and sleek, shining black hair, which the women usually suffer to flow over the shoulders. Those who live near the sea never become bald, and their hair does not turn gray; perhaps this may be owing to the frequent habit of bathing in salt water, which always has a salutary effect on the hair.

The vigorous forms of their children may be attributed to active habits, and to the entire freedom of their limbs from all bands, ligatures, or clothing. Several tribes have the habit of flattening the forehead, by heavy pressure during infancy. To be childless is considered almost as great a misfortune as it was among the Jews. A man will never divorce a wife who has brought him sons, and though he may perchance marry several others, he always considers her as entitled to peculiar respect.

Indian women are usually well skilled in simple remedies, and are the physicians of their tribes. In some places, medicine is considered peculiarly efficacious if it is prepared and administered by the hand of a maiden. The healing art is intimately connected in their minds with magic, and medicines are seldom given without prayers and incantations, to avert the influence of evil spirits. There are in almost every tribe individuals who claim the gift of prophecy, and endeavor to foretel future events by conjurations and dreams. I am not aware that they consider women more frequently endowed with this supernatural power than men.

Some tribes bury their dead, others expose them on scaffolds suspended in high trees. The arms and horse of a warrior are buried with him for his use in another world; and a mortar, kettle, and other utensils of daily use accompany the corpse of a female. When a great chief dies, his wives, and many of his attendants, are sometimes obliged to follow him to the world of spirits. The tribe of Natchez is ruled by a chief called The Great Sun; and when any woman of the blood of the Suns dies, it becomes necessary that her husband and attendants should be sacrificed in honor of her decease. The widows of illustrious chiefs generally take pride in devoting themselves to death with stoical firmness. The wife of The Stung Serpent, who was brother to The Great Sun, thus addressed her children when she was about to leave them: "Your father waits for me in the land of spirits. If I were to yield to your tears, I should injure my love, and fail in my duty. You that are descended of his blood, and fed by my milk, ought not to weep. Rather rejoice that you are Suns and warriors, bound to give examples of firmness to the whole nation." The victims, having been made giddy by swallowing little balls of tobacco, are strangled, and placed near the corpse upon mats, ranged according to their rank.

The Indians, both men and women, lament for the dead with loud howling and lamentation, blacken their faces, and wound themselves with flints, knives, and splinters of wood. When the women are going out to work, or returning from their labors, the widows of the tribe often join in a sort of dirge, or mourning chorus.

As sailors have the superstition that it brings bad luck to have a woman on board a ship, so the Indians believe that the fleetest horse in the world would lose his speed, if a woman were suffered to mount him; hence when it becomes necessary for women to ride, they are placed on old worn-out animals.

Among the Dacotahs a particular lodge is set apart for councils, and the reception of strangers. The women supply it with wood and water, but are never permitted to enter it. This tribe have an institution called the

Lodge of the Grand Medicine, the ceremonies of which are celebrated in secret, and the members know each other by certain signs. It differs from Free-Masonry, in allowing women to be among the initiated.

The women of the Hurons and Iroquois seem to have had more influence than was common among other tribes. Huron women might appoint a member of the council, and one of their own sex if they chose. They could prevail upon the warriors to go to battle, or desist from it, according to their wishes. Among the Natchez, authority descended in an hereditary line both to male and female. It is a general rule with the American tribes that a man should be succeeded by his sister's children, not by his own.

The dwellings of the Indians are huts made of the interwoven boughs of trees, or tents covered with the skins of animals, without division of apartments. Whole villages of women and children are often left for weeks, while the men are absent on hunting expeditions.

The South American tribes were more docile, indolent, and soft-hearted than those of the north. They married at an earlier period; twelve or thirteen being the common age for a bride. It is said that the tribes about the isthmus of Darien considered it no impropriety for women to make the first declaration of love. When they preferred a young man, they told him so, and promised to be very faithful, good-tempered, and obedient, if he would take them to wife.

. . . .

. . . The North American Indians consider voluptuousness a despicable vice; and in cases of seduction, far more blame is attached to the man than the woman. The latter is forgiven; and, unless her conduct is very gross, finds no difficulty in subsequently forming a matrimonial connection; but her betrayer is treated with the utmost neglect and contempt. It may be questioned, whether Christian nations are in this respect so just as the Indians. While such severe blame and eternal infamy rests on women who have been deceived, it is obviously unjust that civilized society should so readily forgive the deceiver.

Beginning as a weekly newspaper column, first in the *National Anti-Slavery Standard*, which Child edited from 1841 to 1843, and later in the Boston *Courier*, Child's best seller *Letters from New York* (2 vols., 1843, 1845) introduced a new genre into American literature—the journalistic sketch. The style of free association, interweaving journalistic description, social criticism, and philosophical speculation, immediately charmed readers. "The letters from New York . . . created a literary sensation as they appeared," recalled the abolitionist-feminist Caroline Healey Dall after Child's death, in her 1883 *Unitarian Review* article: "The counting-room of the *Courier* was filled by an eager crowd, half an hour before the proper time, on the days when they were expected. . . . These letters were read aloud at the tea-table, and the next day everybody passed their bright sayings along."

Letter 36 records a visit to P. T. Barnum's wonder show, the American Museum, which exhibited Indians alongside such natural curiosities as the dwarf Tom Thumb and the Siamese Twins Chang and Eng. Typically, Child slides from colorful vignettes, serving to create sympathy for the Indians, into refutation of the racist theories recently advanced in works like Samuel G. Morton's influential *Crania Americana* (1839), which cited measurements of cranial capacity as "proof" of nonwhite races' intellectual inferiority. The new science of ethnology postulated that the various human races were distinct, permanently unequal species, originating from separate creations, and that biology, rather than environment, determined each race's character and rank in the scale of human development. In contrast, Child holds that racial differences are minor variations deriving from environmental causes, and that "savage" races are capable of evolving toward civilization. Although hardly less ethnocentric, her position represents the progressive side in the contemporary debate over the status nonwhite races ought to occupy in America's body politic.

The ideal of assimilation Child articulates here is no longer as monolithic as in *Hobomok*—now Child envisions a mingling of races that will result not in turning Indians and Africans into whites, but in enriching American culture: "They will be flutes on different notes, and so harmonize the better." Once again, however, she also expresses—this time explicitly—a fantasy quite at variance with the goal of "civilizing" the Indian: the fantasy of being "transmigrated" into the soul of an Indian "for a few days, that I might experience the fashion of their thoughts and feelings." Three years later she would translate this fantasy into the story "She Waits in the Spirit Land."

March, 1843

I WENT a few evenings ago, to the American Museum, to see fifteen Indians, fresh from the western forest. Sacs, Fox, and Iowas; really important people in their respective tribes. Nan-Nouce-Fush-E-To, which means the Buffalo King, is a famous Sac chief, sixty years old, covered with scars, and grim as a Hindoo god, or pictures of the devil on a Portuguese contribution box, to help sinners through purgatory. It is said that he has killed with his own hand one hundred Osages, three Mohawks, two Kas, two Sioux, and one Pawnee; and if we may judge by his organ of destructiveness, the story is true; a more enormous bump I never saw in that region of the skull. He speaks nine Indian dialects, has visited almost every existing tribe of his race, and is altogether a remarkable personage. Mon-To-Gah, the White Bear, wears a medal from President Monroe, for certain services rendered to the whites. Wa-Con-To-Kitch-Er, is an Iowa chief, of grave and thoughtful countenance, held in much veneration as the Prophet of his tribe. He sees visions, which he communicates to them for their spiritual instruction. Among the Squaws is No-Nos-See, the She Wolf, a niece of the famous Black Hawk, and very proud of the relationship; and Do-Hum-Me, the Productive Pumpkin, a very handsome woman, with a great deal of heart and happiness in her countenance.

> 'Smiles settled on her sun-flecked cheeks,
> Like noon upon the mellow apricot.'

She was married about a fortnight ago, at Philadelphia, to Cow-Hick-He, son of the principal chief of the Iowas, and as noble a specimen of manhood as I ever looked upon. Indeed I have never seen a group of human beings so athletic, well-proportioned, and majestic. They are a keen satire on our civilized customs, which produce such feeble forms and pallid faces. The unlimited pathway, the broad horizon, the free grandeur of the forest, has passed into their souls, and so stands revealed in their material forms.

We who have robbed the Indians of their lands, and worse still, of *themselves*, are very fond of proving their inferiority. We are told that the *facial angle* in the

Caucasian race is	85 degrees.
Asiatic	78 degrees.
American Indian	73 degrees.
Ethiopian	70 degrees.
Ourang Outang	67 degrees.

This simply proves that the Caucasian race, through a succession of ages, has been exposed to influences eminently calculated to develop the moral and intellectual faculties. That they started, *first* in the race, might have been owing to a finer and more susceptible nervous organization, originating in climate, perhaps, but serving to bring the physical organization into more harmonious relation with the laws of spiritual reception. But by whatever agency it might have been produced, the nation, or race that perceived even one spiritual idea in advance of others, would necessarily go on improving in geometric ratio, through the lapse of ages. For *our* Past, we have the oriental fervour, gorgeous imagery, and deep reverence of the Jews, flowing from that high fountain, the perception of the oneness and invisibility of God. From the Greeks, we receive the very Spirit of Beauty, flowing into all forms of Philosophy and Art, encircled by a glorious halo of Platonism, which

'Far over many a land and age hath shone,
And mingles with the light that beams from God's own throne.'

These have been transmitted to us in their own forms, and again reproduced through the classic strength and high cultivation of Rome, and the romantic minstrelsy and rich architecture of the middle ages. Thus we stand, a congress of ages, each with a glory on its brow, peculiar to itself, yet in part reflected from the glory that went before.

But what have the African savage, and the wandering Indian for *their* Past? To fight for food, and grovel in the senses, has been the employment of *their* ancestors. The Past reproduced in them, mostly belongs to the animal part of our mixed nature. They have indeed come in contact with the race on which had dawned higher ideas; but *how* have they come in contact? As *victims*, not as *pupils*. Rum, gunpowder, the horrors of slavery, the unblushing knavery of trade, these have been their teachers! And because these have failed to produce a high degree of moral and intellectual cultivation, we coolly declare that the negroes are made for slaves, that the Indians cannot be civilized; and that when either of the races come in contact with us, they must either consent to be our beasts of burden, or be driven to the wall, and perish.

That the races of mankind are different, spiritually as well as physically, there is, of course, no doubt; but it is as the difference between trees of the same forest, not as between trees and minerals. The facial angle and shape of the head, is various in races and nations; but these are the *effects* of spiritual influences, long operating on character, and in their turn becoming *causes*; thus intertwining, as Past and Future ever do.

But it is urged that Indians who have been put to schools and colleges, still remained attached to a roving life; away from all these advantages,

'His blanket tied with yellow strings, the Indian of the forest went.'

And what if he did? Do not white young men, who have been captured by savages in infancy, show an equally strong disinclination to take upon themselves the restraints of civilized life? Does anybody urge that this well-known fact proves the *white* race incapable of civilization?

You ask, perhaps, what becomes of my theory, that races and individuals are the product of ages, if the influences of half a life produce the same effects on the Caucasian and the Indian? I answer, that white children brought up among Indians, though they strongly imbibe the habits of the race, are generally prone to be the geniuses and prophets of their tribe. The organization of nerve and brain has been changed by a more harmonious relation between the animal and the spiritual; and this comparative harmony has been produced by the influences of Judea, and Greece, and Rome, and the age of chivalry; though of all these things the young man never heard.

Similar influences brought to bear on the Indians or the Africans, as a race, would gradually change the structure of their skulls, and enlarge their perceptions of moral and intellectual truth. The *same* influences cannot be brought to bear upon them; for *their* Past is not *our* Past; and of course never can be. But let ours mingle with theirs, and you will find the result variety, without inferiority. They will be flutes on different notes, and so harmonize the better.

And how is this elevation of all races to be effected? By that which worketh *all* miracles, in the name of Jesus— The LAW OF LOVE. We must not teach as superiors; we must *love as brothers*. Here is the great deficiency in all our efforts for the ignorant and the criminal. We stand apart from them, and expect them to feel grateful for our condescension in noticing them at all. We do not embrace them warmly with our sympathies, and put our souls into their soul's stead.

But even under this great disadvantage; accustomed to our smooth, deceitful talk, when we want their lands, and to the cool villany with which we break treaties when our purposes are gained; receiving gunpowder and rum from the very hands which retain from them all the better influences of civilized life; cheated by knavish agents, cajoled by government, and hunted with bloodhounds—still, under all *these* disadvantages, the Indians have shown that they *can* be civilized. Of this, the Choctaws and Cherokees are admirable proofs. Both these tribes have a regularly-organized, systematic government, in the democratic form, and a printed constitution. The right of trial by jury, and other principles of a free government, are established on a permanent basis. They have good farms, cotton-gins, saw-mills, schools, and churches. Their dwellings are generally comfortable, and some of them are handsome. The last annual message of the chief of the Cherokees is a highly interesting document, which would not compare disadvantageously with any of our governors' messages. It states that more than $2,500,000 are due to them from the United States; and recommends that this sum be obtained, and in part distributed among the people; but that the interest of the school fund be devoted to the maintenance of schools, and the diffusion of knowledge.

There was a time when *our* ancestors, the ancient Britons, went nearly without clothing, painted their bodies in fantastic fashion, offered up human victims to uncouth idols, and lived in hollow trees, or rude habitations, which we should now consider unfit for cattle. Making all due allowance for the different state of the world, it is much to be questioned whether they made more rapid advancement than the Cherokees and Choctaws.

It always fills me with sadness to see Indians surrounded by the false environment of civilized life; but I never felt so deep a sadness, as I did in looking upon these western warriors; for they were evidently the noblest of their dwindling race, unused to restraint, accustomed to sleep beneath the stars. And here they were, set up for a two-shilling show, with monkeys, flamingoes, dancers, and buffoons! If they understood our modes of society well enough to be aware of their degraded position, they would doubtless quit it, with burning indignation at the insult. But as it is, they allow women to examine their beads and children to play with their wampum, with the most philosophic indifference. In their imperturbable countenances, I thought I could once or twice detect a slight expression of scorn at the eager curiosity of the crowd. The Albiness, a short woman, with pink eyes, and hair like white floss, was the only object that visibly amused them. The young chiefs nodded to her often, and exchanged smiling remarks with each other, as they looked at her. Upon all the buffooneries and legerdemain tricks of the Museum, they gazed as unmoved as John Knox himself would have done. I would have given a good deal to know their thoughts, as mimic cities, and fairy grottoes, and mechanical dancing figures, rose and sunk before them. The mechanical figures were such perfect imitations of life, and went through so many wonderful evolutions, that they might well surprise even those accustomed to the marvels of mechanism. But Indians, who pay religious honours to venerable rocks, and moss-grown trees, who believe that brutes have souls, as well as men, and that all nature is filled with spirits, might well doubt whether there was not here some supernatural agency, either good or evil. I would suffer almost anything, if my soul could be transmigrated into the She Wolf, or the Productive Pumpkin, and their souls pass consciously in my frame, for a few days, that I might experience the fashion of their thoughts and feelings. Was there ever such a foolish wish! The soul *is* ME, and *is* Thee. I might as well put on their blankets, as their bodies, for purposes of spiritual insight. In that other world, shall we be enabled to know exactly how heaven, and earth and hell, appear to other persons, nations, and tribes? I would it might be so; for I have an intense desire for such revelations. I do not care to travel to Rome, or St. Petersburg, because I can only look *at* people; and I want to look *into* them, and *through* them; to know how things appear to *their* spiritual eyes, and sound to *their* spiritual ears. This is a universal want; hence the intense interest taken in autobiography, by all classes of readers. Oh, if any one had but the courage to write the *whole* truth of himself, undisguised as it appears before the eye of God and angels, the WORLD would read it, and it would soon be translated into all the dialects of the universe.

But these children of the forest do not even give us glimpses of their inner life; for they consider that the body was given to *conceal* the emotions of the soul. The stars look down into their hearts, as into mine; the broad ocean, glittering in the moonbeams, speaks to them of the Infinite; and doubtless the wild flowers and the sea-shells 'talk to them a thought.' But *what* thoughts, *what* revelations of the Infinite? This would I give the world to know; but the world cannot buy an answer.

How foreign is my soul to that of the beautiful Do-Hum-Me! How helpless should I be in situations where she would be a heroine; and how little could she comprehend my eager thought, which seeks the creative Three-in-one throughout the universe, and finds it in every blossom and every mineral. Between Wa-Con-To-Kitch-Er and the German Herder,[1] what a distance! Yet are they both prophets; and though one looks through nature with the pitch-pine torch of the wilderness, and the other is lighted by a whole constellation of suns, yet have both learned, in their degree, that matter is only the time-garment of the spirit. The stammering utterance with which the Iowa seer reveals this, it were worth a kingdom to hear, if we could but borrow the souls of his tribe, while they listen to his visions.

It is a general trait with the Indian tribes to recognise the Great Spirit in every little child. They rarely refuse a child anything. When their revenge is most implacable, a little one is often sent to them, adorned with flowers and shells, and taught to lisp a prayer that the culprit may be forgiven; and such mediation is rarely without effect, even on the sternest warrior. This trait alone is sufficient to establish their relationship with Herder, Richter,[2] and other spirits of angel-stature. Nay, if we could look back a few centuries, we should find the ancestors of Shakspeare, and the fastidiously-refined Goethe, with painted cheeks, wolves'-teeth for jewels, and boars'-hides for garments. Perhaps the universe could not have passed before the vision of those star-like spirits except through the forest life of such wild ancestry.

Some theorists say that the human brain, in its formation, 'changes with a steady rise, through a likeness to one animal, and then another, till it is perfected in that of man, the highest animal.' It seems to be so with the nations, in their progressive rise out of barbarism. I was never before so much struck with the animalism of Indian character, as I was in the frightful war-dance of these chiefs. Their gestures were as furious as wild-cats, they howled like wolves, screamed like prairie dogs, and tramped like buffaloes. Their faces were painted fiery red, or with cross-bars of green and red, and they were decorated with all sorts of uncouth trappings of hair, and bones, and teeth. That which regulated their movements, in lieu of music, was a discordant clash; and altogether they looked and acted more like demons from the pit, than anything I ever imagined. It was the natural and appropriate language of War. The wolfish howl, and the wild-cat leap, represent it more truly than graceful evolutions and the Marseilles hymn. *That* music rises above mere brute vengeance; it breathes in fervid ecstacy the *soul's* aspiration after freedom—the struggle of will with fate. It is the Future setting sail from old landings, and merrily piping all hands on board. It is too noble a voice to belong to physical warfare: the shrill howl of old Nan-Nouce-Fush-E-To is good enough for such brutish work: it clove the brain like a tomahawk, and was hot with hatred.

In truth, that war-dance was terrific both to eye and ear. I looked at the door, to see if escape were easy, in case they really worked themselves up to the scalping point. For the first time, I fully conceived the sacrifices and perils of the Puritan settlers. Heaven have mercy on the mother who heard those dreadful yells, when they really foreboded murder! or who suddenly met such a group of grotesque demons in the loneliness of the forest!

But instantly I felt that I was wronging them in my thought. Through paint and feathers, I saw gleams of right honest and friendly expression;

and I said, we are children of the same Father, seeking the same home. If the Puritans suffered from their savage hatred, it was because they met them with savage weapons, and a savage spirit. Then I thought of William Penn's treaty with the Indians; 'the only one ever formed without an oath, and the only one that was never broken.' I thought of the deputation of Indians, who some years ago visited Philadelphia, and knelt with one spontaneous impulse around the monument of Penn.

Again I looked at the yelling savages in their grim array, stamping through the war-dance with a furious energy, that made the floor shake as by an earthquake; and I said, These too would bow, like little children, before the persuasive power of Christian love! Alas, if we had but faith in this divine principle, what mountains of evil might be removed into the depths of the sea!

P.S. Alas, poor Do-Hum-Me is dead! so is No-Nos-See, Black Hawk's niece; and several of the chiefs are indisposed. Sleeping by hot anthracite fires, and then exposed to the keen encounters of the wintry wind; one hour, half stifled in the close atmosphere of theatres and crowded saloons, and the next driving through snowy streets and the midnight air; this is a process which kills civilized people by inches, but savages at a few strokes.

Do-Hum-Me was but nineteen years old, in vigorous health, when I saw her a few days since, and obviously so happy in her newly wedded love, that it ran over at her expressive eyes, and mantled her handsome face like a veil of sunshine. Now she rests among the trees, in Greenwood Cemetery; not the trees that whispered to her childhood. Her coffin was decorated according to Indian custom, and deposited with the ceremonies peculiar to her people. Alas, for the handsome one, how lonely she sleeps here! Far, far away from him, to whom her eye turned constantly as the sunflower to the light!

Sick, and sad at heart, this noble band of warriors, with melancholy steps, left the pestilential city last week, for their own broad prairies in the West. Do-Hum-Me was the pride and idol of them all. The old Iowa chief, the head of the deputation, was her father; and notwithstanding the stoicism of Indian character, it is said that both he and the bereaved young husband were overwhelmed with an agony of grief. They obviously loved each other most strongly. May the Great Spirit grant them a happy meeting in their 'fair hunting grounds' beyond the sky.

"She Waits in the Spirit Land," from *Fact and Fiction: A Collection of Stories* (1846), was first published in the March, 1846 issue of *The Columbian Lady's and Gentleman's Magazine*, Child's main outlet for fiction during the 1840s, and later reprinted in *The Gem of the Season* (1849).

As the epigraph indicates, one of Child's aims was to foster respect for "a brother's creed, though not like mine"—a persistent theme in her writings. The most remarkable aspect of the story, however, is its treatment of sexuality. Clearly, Child is using the romantic equation of Indians with nature and primitivism to protest against the repressiveness of Victorian sexual codes. What appeals to her in Indian life, as she understands it, is that "nature" is "subjected to no false restraints" and sexual impulses are not defined as sinful. It is the "self-consciousness" of "artificial society" that is "unclean," she insists, not the sexual impulses themselves. Daringly erotic, her depiction of the Indian lovers' first night together conjures up a vision of sexual ecstacy that culminates in dissolving the boundaries between matter and spirit, (wo)man and nature. In short, this story translates the latent sexual fantasies of *Hobomok* into a conscious plea for sexual freedom.

The progression correlates with several developments in Child's life: her move to New York to assume the editorship of the *National Anti-Slavery Standard*, a decision resulting in a nine-year informal separation from her husband; her Platonic, but highly charged relationships with two other men during this period; her activities on behalf of "fallen women," with whom she seems to have strongly identified, perhaps out of guilt over these relationships; and the recent publication of Margaret Fuller's *Woman in the Nineteenth Century* (1845), which Child hailed for its "bold" attack on the double standard.

SHE WAITS IN THE SPIRIT LAND

A Romance founded on an Indian Tradition

A bard of many breathings
Is the wind in sylvan wreathings,
O'er mountain tops and through the woodland groves
Now fifing and now drumming,
Now howling and now humming,
　　　　As it roves.

Though the wind a strange tone waketh
In every home it maketh,
And the maple tree responds not as the larch,
Yet harmony is playing
Round *all* the green arms swaying
　　　　Neath heaven's arch.

Oh, what can be the teaching
Of these forest voices preaching?
'Tis that a brother's creed, though not like mine,
May blend about God's altar,
And help to fill the psalter,
　　　　That's divine.

　　—*Eliza Cook*

PU-KEE-SHE-NO-QUA was famous among her tribe for her eloquent manner of relating stories. She treasured up all the old traditions, and though she repeated them truly, they came from her mouth in brighter pictures than from others, because she tipped all the edges with her own golden fancy. One might easily conjecture that there was poetry in the souls of her ancestry also; for they had given her a name which signifies, "I light from flying." At fourteen years old, she was shut up in a hut by herself, to fast and dream, according to the custom of the Indians. She dreamed that the Morning Star came down and nestled in her bosom, like a bird; therefore she choose it for the Manitou, or Protecting Spirit of her life, and named her first-born son Wah-bu-nung-o, an Indian word for the Morning Star. The boy was handsome, brave and gentle; and his childhood gave early indications that he inherited the spiritual and poetic tendencies of his mother. At the threshold of his young life, he too was set apart to fast and dream. He dreamed of a wild rose bush, in full bloom, and heard a voice saying, "She will wait for thee in the spirit-land. Do not forsake her." The Wild Rose was accordingly adopted as his Manitou.

In a neighbouring wigwam, was a girl named O-ge-bu-no-qua, which signifies the Wild Rose. When she, at twelve years old, was sent into retirement to fast and dream, she dreamed of a Star; but she could tell nothing about it, only that it was mild, and looked at her. She was a charming child, and grew into beautiful maidenhood. Her dark cheek looked like a rich brown autumn leaf, faintly tinged with crimson. Her large eyes, shaded with deep black fringe, had a shy and somewhat mournful tenderness of expression. Her voice seemed but the echo of her glance, it was so low and musical in tone, so plaintive in its cadences. Her well-rounded figure was pliant and graceful, and her motions were like those of some pretty, timid animal, that has always stepped to sylvan sounds.

The handsome boy was but two years older than the beautiful girl. In childhood, they swung together in the same boughs, hand in hand they clambered the rocks, and gathered the flowers and berries of the woods. Living in such playful familiarity with the deer and the birds, the young blood flowed fresh and strong, their forms were vigorous, and their motions flexile and free. The large dark eyes of Wah-bu-nung-o were tender and sad, and had a peculiarly deep, spiritual, inward-looking expression, as if he were the destined poet and prophet of his tribe. But the lofty carriage of his head, the Apollo curve of his parted lips, and his aquiline nose, with open well-defined nostrils, expressed the pride and daring of a hunter and a warrior.

It was very natural that the maiden should sometimes think it a beautiful coincidence that a Star was her guardian spirit, and this handsome friend of her childhood was named the Morning Star. And when he told her of the Wild Rose of his dream, had he not likewise some prophetic thoughts? Fortunately for the free and beautiful growth of their love, they lived out of the pale of civilization. There was no Mrs. Smith to remark how they looked at each other, and no Mrs. Brown to question the propriety of their rambles in the woods. The simple philosophy of the Indians had never taught that nature was a sin, and therefore nature was troubled with no sinful consciousness. When Wah-bu-nung-o hunted squirrels, O-ge-bu-no-qua thought it no harm to gather basket-stuff in the same woods. There was a lovely crescent-shaped island opposite the village, profusely covered with trees and vines, and carpeted with rich grasses and mosses, strewn with flowers. Clumps of young birches shone among the dark shrubbery, like slender columns of silver, and willows stooped so low to look in the mirror of the waters, that their graceful tresses touched the stream. Here, above all other places, did the maiden love to go to gather twigs for baskets, and the young man to select wood for his bows and arrows. Often, when day was declining, and the calm river reflected the Western sky, glowing with amber light, and fleckered with little fleecy rose-coloured clouds, his canoe might be seen gliding across the waters. Sometimes O-ge-bu-no-qua was waiting for him on the island, and sometimes he steered the boat for the grove of willows, while she urged it forward with the light swift stroke of her paddle.

Civilized man is little to be trusted under such circumstances; but nature, subjected to no false restraints, manifests her innate modesty, and even in her child-like abandonment to impulse, rebukes by her innocence the unclean self-consciousness of artificial society. With a quiet grave tenderness, the young Indian assisted his beautiful companion in her tasks, or spoke to her from time to time, as they met by brook or grove, in the pursuit of their different avocations. Her Manitou, the Morning Star of the sky, could not have been more truly her protecting spirit.

It was on her sixteenth birth day, that they, for the first time, lingered on the island after twilight. The Indians, with an untaught poetry of modesty, never talk of love under the bright staring gaze of day. Only amid the silent shadows do they yield to its gentle influence. O-ge-bu-no-qua was born with the roses; therefore this birth-night of their acknowledged love was in that beautiful month, named by the Indians "the Moon of Flowers." It was a lovely evening, and surpassingly fair was the scene around them. The picturesque little village of wigwams, on the other side of the river, gave a smiling answer to the sun's farewell. The abrupt heights beyond were robed in the richest foliage, through which the departing rays streamed like a golden shower. In the limitless forest, the tall trees were of noble proportions, because they had room enough to grow upward and outward, with a strong free grace. In the flowery glades of the islands, flocks of pigeons, and other smaller birds, cooed and chirped. Soon all subsided into moon-silence, and the elysian stillness was interrupted only by the faint ripple of the sparkling river, the lone cry of the whippowill, or the occasional plash of some restless bullfrog. The lovers sat side by side on a grassy knoll. An evening breeze gave them a gentle kiss as it passed and brought them a love-token of fragrance from a rose-bush that grew at their feet. Wah-bu-nung-o gathered one of the blossoms, by the dim silvery light, and placing it in the hand of O-ge-bu-no-qua, he said, in a voice tender and bashful as a young girl's, "Thou knowest the Great Spirit has given me the wild rose for a Manitou. I have told thee my dream; but I have never told thee, thou sweet rose of my life, how sadly I interpret it."

She nestled closer in his bosom, and gazing earnestly on a bright star in the heavens, the Manitou of her own existence, she murmured almost inaudibly, "How *dost* thou?" His brave strong arm encircled her in a closer embrace, as he answered with gentle solemnity, "The Rose will go to the spirit-land, and leave her Star to mourn alone." The maiden's eyes filled with tears, as she replied, "But the Rose will wait for her Star. Thus said the voice of the dream."

They sat silently leaning on each other, till Wah-bu-nung-o took up the pipe, that lay beside him, and began to play. Birds sing only during their mating season; their twin-born love and music pass away together, with the roses; and the Indian plays on his pipe only while he is courting. It is a rude kind of flute, with two or three stops, and very limited variety of tone. The life of a savage would not be fitly expressed in rich harmonies; and life in any form never fashions to itself instruments beyond the wants of the soul. But the sounds of this pipe, with its perpetual return of sweet simple chords, and its wild flourishes, like the closing strain of a bob o'link, was in pleasing accord with the primeval beauty of the scene. When the pipe paused for awhile, O-ge-bu-no-qua warbled a wild plaintive little air, which her mother used to sing to her, when she swung from the boughs in her queer little birch-bark cradle. Indian music, like the voices of inanimate nature, the wind, the forest, and the sea, is almost invariably in the minor mode; and breathed as it now was to the silent moon, and with the shadow of the dream interpretation still resting on their souls, it was oppressive in its mournfulness. The song hushed; and O-ge-bu-no-qua, clinging closer to her lover's arm, whispered in tones of superstitious fear, "Does it not seem to you as if the Great Spirit was looking at us?" "Yes, and see how he smiles," replied Wah-bu-nung-o, in bolder and more cheerful accents, as he pointed to the sparkling waters: "The deer and the birds are not sad; let us be like them."

He spoke of love; of the new wigwam he would build for his bride, and the game he would bring down with his arrow. These home-pictures roused emotions too strong for words. Stolid and imperturbable as the Indian race seem in the presence of spectators, in these lonely hours with the beloved one, they too learn that love is the glowing wine, the exhila-rating "fire-water" of the soul.

WHEN THEY RETURNED, no one questioned them. It was the most natural thing in the world that they should love each other; and natural politeness respected the freedom of their young hearts. No marriage settlements, no precautions of the law, were necessary. There was no person to object, whenever he chose to lead her into his wigwam, and by that simple circumstance she became his wife. The next day, as O-ge-bu-no-qua sat under the shadow of an elm, busily braiding mats, Wah-bu-nung-o passed by, carrying poles, which he had just cut in the woods. He stopped and spoke to her, and the glance of her wild melancholy eye met his with a beautiful expression of timid fondness. The next moment, she looked down and blushed very deeply. The poles were for the new wigwam, and so were the mats she was braiding; and she had promised her lover that as soon as the wigwam was finished, she would come and live with him. He conjectured her thoughts; but he did not smile, neither did he tell her that her blush was as beautiful as the brilliant flower of the Wickapee; but that bashful loving glance filled him with an inward warmth. Its beaming, yet half-veiled tenderness passed into his soul, and was never afterward forgotten.

That afternoon, all the young men of the tribe went a few miles up the river to fish. Sad tidings awaited their return. Ong-pa-tonga, the Big Elk, chief of a neighbouring tribe, in revenge for some trifling affront, had attacked the village in their absence, wounded some of the old warriors, and carried off several of the women and children. The blooming Wild Rose was among the captives. Wah-bu-nung-o was frantic with rage and despair. A demon seemed to have taken possession of his brave, but usually gentle soul. He spoke few words, but his eyes gleamed with a fierce unnatural fire. He painted himself with the colours of eternal enmity to the tribe of Big Elk, and secretly gloated over plans of vengeance. An opportunity soon offered to waylay the transgressors on their return from a hunting expedition. Several women accompanied the party, to carry their game and blankets. One of these, the wife of Big Elk, was killed by an arrow, and some of the men were wounded. This slight taste of vengeance made the flames of hatred burn more intensely. The image of his enemy expiring by slow tortures was the only thought that brought pleasure to the soul of Wah-bu-nung-o. Twice he had him nearly in his power, but was baffled by cunning. In one of the skirmishes between the contending tribes, he took captive a woman and her two children. Being questioned concerning the fate of O-ge-bu-no-qua, she said that Big Elk, in revenge for the loss of his wife, had killed her with his war club. For a moment, Wah-bu-nung-o stood as if suddenly changed to stone; then his Indian firmness forsook him, he tore his hair, and howled in frantic agony. But in the midst of this whirlwind of grief, the memory of his dream came like a still small voice, and whispered, "She waits for thee in the spirit land. Do not forsake her." The mad fire of his eye changed to the mildest and deepest melancholy. He promised the captive that she and her children should be treated kindly, and allowed to return to her tribe, if she would guide him to the maiden's grave.

Leaving her children in his own village, as a security against treachery, he followed her through the forest, till they came to a newly-made mound, with a few stones piled upon it. This she said was O-ge-bu-no-qua's grave. The young warrior gazed on it silently, with folded arms. No cry, or groan, escaped him; though in the depths of his soul was sorrow more bitter than death. Thus he remained for a long time. At last, he turned to take a careful inspection of the scene around him, and marked a tree with the point of his arrow. Then commanding the woman to walk before him, he strode homeward in perfect silence. A monotonous accompaniment of tree-whispering alone responded to the farewell dirge in his heart. As he looked on the boundless wilderness, and gazed into its dark mysterious depths, wild and solemn reveries came over him; vast shadowy visions of life and death; but through all the changes of his thought sounded the ever-recurring strain, "She waits for thee in the spirit-land." Then came the dread that Big Elk would go there before him, and would persecute his beloved, as he had done during her life in the body. An impatient shudder went over him, and he longed for death; but he had been taught to consider suicide a cowardly act, and he was awe-stricken before the great mystery of the soul. The dreadful conflict terminated in one calm fixed resolution. He determined to relinquish all his cherished plans of vengeance, and during the remainder of his life to watch over Big Elk, and guard him from danger, that he might not go to the spirit-land till he himself was there to protect his beloved.

The day after his return home, he told his mother that he must go away to fulfil a vow, and he knew not when he should return. He earnestly conjured his brothers to be kind and reverent to their mother; then bidding them a calm but solemn farewell, he stepped into his canoe, and rowed over to the Isle of Willows. Again he stood by the grassy knoll where the loved one had lain upon his breast. The rose-bush was there, tall and vigorous, though the human Rose had passed away, to return no more. He shed no tears, but reverently went through his forms of worship to the tutelary spirit of his life. With measured dance, and strange monotonous howls, he made a vow of utter renunciation of everything, even of his hopes of vengeance, if he might be permitted to protect his beloved in the spirit-land. He brought water from the brook in a gourd, from which they had often drunk together; he washed from his face the emblems of eternal enmity to Big Elk, and with solemn ceremonial poured it on the roots of the rose. Then he rowed far up the river, and landed near the grave, on which he kindled a fire, that the dear departed might be lighted to the spirit-land, according to the faith of his fathers. He buried the gourd in the mound, saying, "This I send thee, my Rose, that thou mayest drink from it in the spirit-land." Three nights he tended the fire, and then returned for the rose-bush, which he planted at the head of the grave. He built a wigwam near by, and dwelt there alone. He feared neither wild beast nor enemies; for he had fulfilled his duties to the dead, and now his only wish was to go and meet her. Big Elk and his companions soon discovered him, and came upon him with their war-clubs. He stood unarmed, and quietly told them he had consecrated himself by a vow to the Great Spirit, and would fight no more. He gazed steadily in the face of his enemy, and said, if they wanted his life, they were welcome to take it. The deep, mournful, supernatural expression of his eyes inspired them with awe. They thought him insane; and all such are regarded by the Indians with supersititious fear and reverence. "He has seen the door of the spirit-land opened," they said; "the moon has spoken secrets to him; and the Great Spirit is angry when such are harmed." So they left him in peace. But he sighed as they turned away; for he had hoped to die by their hands. From that time he followed Big Elk like his shadow; but always to do him service. At first, his enemy was uneasy, and on his guard; but after awhile, he became accustomed to his presence, and even seemed to be attached to him. At one time, a fever brought the strong man to the verge of the grave. Wah-bu-nung-o watched over him with trembling anxiety, and through weary days and sleepless nights tended him as carefully as a mother tends her suffering babe. Another time, when Big Elk was wounded by an enemy, he drew out the arrow, sought medicinal herbs, and healed him. Once, when he was about to cross a wide deep ditch, bridged by a single tree, Wah-bu-nung-o perceived a rattle-snake on the bridge, and just as the venomous reptile was about to spring, his arrow nailed him to the tree.

Thus weary months passed away. The mourner, meek and silent, held communion with his Manitou, the rose-bush, to which he repeated often, "Bid her look to the Morning Star, and fear nothing. I will protect her. Tell her we shall meet again in the spirit-land, as we met in the Isle of Willows." Sadly but mildly his eye rested on the murderer of his beloved, and he tended upon him with patient gentleness, that seemed almost like affection. Very beautiful and holy was this triumph of love over hatred, seeking no reward but death. But the "twin-brother of sleep" came not where he was so much desired. Others who clung to life were taken, but the widowed heart could not find its rest. At last, the constant prayer of his faithful love was answered. By some accident, Big Elk became separated from his hunting companions, late in the afternoon of a winter's day. There came on a blinding storm of wind and snow and sleet. The deep drifts were almost impassable, and the keen air cut the lungs, like particles of sharp-ened steel. Night came down in robes of thick darkness. Nothing interrupted her solemn silence, but the crackling of ice from the trees, and the moaning and screaming of the winds. The very wolves hid themselves from the fury of the elements. While light enough remained to choose a shelter, the wanderers took refuge in a deep cleft screened by projecting rocks. The morning found them stiff and hungry, and almost buried in snow. With much difficulty they made their way out into the forest, completely bewildered, and guided only by the sun, which glimmered gloomily through the thick atmosphere. Two days they wandered without food. Toward night, Wah-bu-nung-o discovered horns projecting through the snow; and digging through the drift, he found a few moose bones, on which the wolves had left some particles of flesh. He resisted the cravings of hunger, and gave them all to his famishing enemy. As twilight closed, they took shelter in a large hollow tree, near which Wah-bu-nung-o, with the watchful eye of love and faith, observed a rose-bush, with a few crimson seed-vessels shining through the snow. He stripped some trees, and covered Ong-pa-tonga with the bark; then piling up snow before the entrance to the tree, to screen him from the cold, he bade him to sleep, while he kept watch. Ong-pa-tonga asked to be awakened, that he might watch in his turn; but to this his anxious guardian returned no answer. The storm had passed away and left an atmosphere of intense cold. The stars glittered in the deep blue sky, like points of steel. Weary, faint, and starving, Wah-bu-nung-o walked slowly back and forth. When he felt an increasing numbness stealing over his limbs, a disconsolate smile gleamed on his countenance, and he offered thanks to the Manitou bush by his side. It was the first time he had smiled since his Wild Rose was taken from him. Presently, the howl of wolves was heard far off. He kept more carefully near the tree where his enemy slept, and listened to ascertain in what direction the ravenous beasts would come. "They shall eat me first, before they find their way to him," he said; "She would be so frightened to see his spirit, before mine came to protect her." But the dismal sounds died away in the distance, and were heard no more. Panting and staggering, the patient sufferer fell on the ground, at the foot of the rose-bush, and prayed imploringly, "Let not the wild beasts devour him, while I lie here insensible. Oh, send me to the spirit-land, that I may protect her!" He gasped for breath, and a film came over his eyes, so that he could no longer see the stars. How long he remained thus, no one ever knew.

Suddenly all was light around him. The rose-bush bloomed, and O-ge-bu-no-qua stood before him, with the same expression of bashful love he had last seen in her beautiful eyes. "I have been ever near thee," she said; "Hast thou not seen me?"

"Where am I, my beloved?" he exclaimed: "Are we in the Isle of Willows?"

"We are in the spirit-land," she answered: "Thy Rose has waited patiently for the coming of her Morning Star."

"A Legend of the Falls of St. Anthony," from Child's second collection of stories, *Fact and Fiction* (1846), is actually a revised version of a story from *The Coronal*, first published in *The Legendary* (1828) under the title "The Indian Wife." A comparison of the two versions reveals Child's increased mastery of her craft, as well as her heightened political consciousness after more than a decade of antislavery activism. Everywhere Child has pruned florid rhetoric, toned down melodramatic scenes, and substituted realistic detail for abstract phraseology. For example, the lament "I am a poor daughter of the Sioux; oh! why did you marry me?" disappears in the second version, and "a more careful arrangement of her rude dress" becomes "her dress of soft beaver-skins was more coquettishly garnished with porcupine quill-work, and her moccasins were embroidered in gayer patterns."

Most interesting are the revisions that emphasize the Indians' national pride and promote a positive view of their culture. A derogatory reference to Indians' failure to show "deference and courtesy" toward women gives way to the neutral comment that Zah-gah-see-ga-quay had been "hitherto unaccustomed" to such "graceful gallantry toward women." The pointed observation, "According to Indian custom, the mother's right to her offspring amounts to unquestioned law," highlights an aspect of Indian culture that many nineteenth-century women would have viewed with envy. The Sioux chief's "reluctance to mix his proud race with foreign blood" implicitly rebukes the assumption that it is the white person who "stoop[s]" in an interracial alliance. The Indian heroine, characterized in the first version as a "creature" of "infantile beauty" and "timidity," "all formed for love," becomes more mature in the second version, where she displays "uncommon intelligence." And in the opening scenes, the focus shifts from the heroine to her father and his concern to protect her against white treachery.

The political thrust of Child's story emerges most clearly when contrasted with a story in a similar vein, "The Indian Bride," which appeared in *The Atlantic Souvenir* for 1832. There the Frenchman who aspires to marry an Indian chief's daughter is portrayed sympathetically, but falls victim to her father's enmity. After their elopement, the lovers are captured by the chief's war party and die together at the stake.

A LEGEND

OF THE FALLS OF ST. ANTHONY

Founded on Indian Tradition

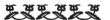

From all its kind
  This wasted heart,
This moody mind
  Now drifts apart;
It longs to find
  . The tideless shore,
Where rests the wreck
  Of Heretofore—
The great heart-break
  Of loves no more.

I drift alone,
For all are gone,
Dearest to me;
And hail the wave
That to the grave
  On hurrieth me:
Welcome, thrice welcome, then,
  Thy wave, Eternity.
    —Motherwell

WEE-CHUSH-TA-DOO-TA was a powerful Sioux chief. He numbered many distinguished warriors among his ancestors, and was as proud of his descent as was ever feudal noble. His name simply signified The Red Man; but he was "a great brave," and the poet of his tribe, whose war-songs were sung on all great occasions. In one of the numerous battles of the Sioux with their enemies the Chippewas, he took prisoner a very handsome little girl. A widowed woman begged to adopt her, to supply the place of a daughter, who had gone to the spirit-land; and thus the pretty young creature was saved from the general massacre of prisoners. As she approached womanhood, the heart of the poet-chieftain inclined towards her, and he made her his wife.

Their first-born was a daughter. When she was two years old, the mother, struck by a peculiarity in the expression of her eyes, named her Zah-gah-see-ga-quay, which, in her own language, signified Sunbeams breaking through a Cloud. As she grew older, this poetic name became more and more appropriate; for when she raised her large deeply-shaded eyes, their bright lucid expression was still more obviously veiled with timidity and sadness. Her voice, as usual with young Indian women, was low and musical, and her laugh was gentle and childlike.

There was a mixed expression in her character, as in her eyes. She was active, buoyant, and energetic, in her avocations and amusements; yet from childhood she was prone to serious moods, and loved to be alone in sequestered places, watching the golden gleam of sunset on the green velvet of the hills, till it passed away, and threw their long twilight-shadows across the solitude of the prairies.

Her father, proud of her uncommon intelligence and beauty, resolved to mate her with the most renowned of warriors, and the most expert of hunters. In the spring of 1765, when she had just passed her fourteenth birth-day, she attracted the attention of one worthy to claim the prize. Nee-hee-o-ee-woo, The Wolf of the Hill, was a noble-looking young chief, belonging to the neighbouring tribe of Shiennes. He was noted for bold exploits, superb horsemanship, and the richness of his savage attire. The first time he saw the beautiful Sioux, he looked at her with earnest eyes; and he soon after returned, bringing Wee-chush-ta-doo-ta a valuable present of furs. The maiden understood very well why his courting-flute was heard about the wigwam till late into the night, but the sounds excited no lively emotions in her heart. The dashing young warrior came too late. The week previous, a Frenchman, drawn thither by thirst for new adventures, had arrived with a company of fur traders from Quebec. He was a handsome man; but Zah-gah-see-ga-quay was less attracted by his expressive face and symmetrical figure, than by his graceful gallantry toward women, to which she had been hitherto unaccustomed. His power of fascinating was increased by the marked preference bestowed upon herself. She received his attentions with childish delight and pretty bashfulness, like a coy little bird. The lustrous black hair, which he praised, was braided more neatly than ever; her dress of soft beaver-skins was more coquettishly garnished with porcupine quill-work, and her moccasins were embroidered in gayer patterns.

The beauty of this forest nymph pleased the Frenchman's fancy, and his vanity was flattered by the obvious impression he had made on her youthful imagination. He was incapable of love. A volatile temperament, and early dissipation, had taken from him that best happiness of human life. But Indian lands were becoming more and more desirable to his ambitious nation, and Wee-chush-ta-doo-ta had the disposal of broad and valuable tracts. He had an aversion to marriage; but this he knew would be but the shadow of a fetter, for he could dissolve the bond at any moment, with as little loss of reputation as if it were a *liaison* in Paris. Thus reasoned civilized man, while the innocent child of the woods was as unconscious of the possibility of such selfish calculations, as is a robin in the mating season.

Her father had encountered white men, and was consequently more on his guard. When Jerome de Rancé offered rich presents, and asked his daughter in marriage, he replied, "Zah-gah-see-ga-quay must mate with a chieftain of her own people. If a paleface marries an Indian woman, he calls her his wife while he likes to look upon her, but when he desires another, he walks away and says she is not his wife. Such are not the customs of the red men."

Though Jerome de Rancé had secretly rejoiced over the illegality of an Indian marriage, being highly civilized, he of course made the most solemn protestations of undying love and everlasting good faith. But the proud chieftain had set his heart upon an alliance with the magnificent Wolf of the Hill, and he listened coldly. Obstacles increased the value of the prize, and the adventurous Frenchman was determined to win his savage bride at any price. With the facility of his pliant nation, he accommodated himself to all the customs of the tribe; he swore to adopt all their friendships and all their enmities; he exercised himself in all performances requiring strength and skill, and on all possible occasions he exhibited the most reckless courage. These things made him very popular, and gained the admiration of the chief more than was shown by his grave countenance and indifferent manner. Still he could not easily overcome a reluctance to mix his proud race with foreign blood.

De Rancé, considering himself the one who stooped in the proposed alliance, was piqued by what seemed to him a ridiculous assumption of superiority. Had it not been for the tempting Indian lands, of which he hoped to come in possession, he would have gained the loving maiden on his own terms, and left her when he chose, without seeking to conciliate her father. But the fulfilment of his ambitious schemes required a longer probation. With affected indifference, he made arrangements for departure. He intended to re-appear among them suddenly, in a few weeks, to test his power over the Clouded Sunbeam; but he said he was going to traffic with a neighbouring tribe, and it was doubtful whether he should see them again, or return to Canada by a different route. That she would pine for him, he had no doubt; and he had observed that Wee-chush-ta-doo-ta, though bitter and implacable to his enemies, was tender-hearted as a child toward his own family.

He was not mistaken in his calculations. Zah-gah-see-ga-quay did not venture to dispute the will of her father; but her sweet voice was no more heard in songs; the sunbeam in her eyes went more and more behind the cloud, and the bright healthy colour of her cheek grew pale. Her listless movements and languid glance pained her mother's heart, and the stern father could not endure the mournfulness of their beseeching looks. He spoke no words, but called together a few of his companions, and went forth apparently to hunt in the forest. Before the moon had traversed half her monthly orbit, he and Jerome entered the wigwam together. Zah-gah-see-ga-quay was seated in a dark corner. Her head leaned despondingly on her hand, and her basket-work lay tangled beside her. As she looked up, a quick blush mantled her face, and her eyes shone like stars. Wee-chush-ta-doo-ta noticed the sudden change, and, in tones of deep tenderness, said, "My child, go to the wigwam of the stranger; that your father may again see you love to look on the rising sun and the opening flowers." There was mingled joy and modesty in the upward glance of The Clouded Sunbeam, and when she turned away bashfully from his triumphant gaze, the Frenchman smiled with a consciousness of unlimited power over her simple heart.

That evening, they rambled alone, under the friendly light of the moon. When they returned, a portion of the scarlet paint from her brown cheek was transferred to the face of her lover. Among his Parisian acquaintance, this would have given rise to many a witty jest; but the Indians, with more natural politeness, observed it silently. A few days after, the gentle daughter of the Sioux passed into the tent of the stranger, and became his wife.

Years passed on, and she remained the same devoted, submissive friend. In all domestic avocations of the Indians, she was most skilful. No one made more beautiful matting, or wove into it such pretty patterns. The beaver skins she dressed were as soft and pliable as leather could be. She rowed her canoe with light and vigorous stroke, and the flight of her arrow was unerring. Her husband loved her as well as was possible for one of his butterfly temperament and selfish disposition; but the deferential courtesy of the European lover gradually subsided into something like the lordly indifference of the men around him. He was never harsh; but his affectionate bride felt the change in his manner, and sometimes wept in secret. When she nestled at his feet, and gazed into his countenance with her peculiarly pleading plaintive look, she sometimes obtained a glance such as he had given her in former days. Then her heart would leap like a frolicsome lamb, and she would live cheerfully on the remembrance of that smile through wearisome days of silence and neglect. Her love amounted to passionate idolatry. If he wished to cross the river, she would ply the oar, lest he should suffer fatigue. She carried his quiver and his gun through the forest, and when they returned at twilight, he lounged indolently on the bottom of the boat, while she dipped her oars in unison with her low sweet voice, soothing him with some simple song, where the same plaintive tones perpetually came, and went away in lullaby-cadence.

To please him, she named her son and daughter Felicie and Florimond, in memory of his favourite brother and sister. On these little ones, she could lavish her abundant love without disappointment or fear. The children inherited their parents' beauty; but Felicie, the eldest, was endowed with a double portion. She had her mother's large lucid eye, less deeply shaded with the saddening cloud; but her other features resembled her handsome father. Her oval cheeks had just enough of the Indian tint to give them a rich warm colouring. At thirteen years old, her tall figure combined the graceful elasticity of youth, with the rounded fulness of womanhood. She inherited her father's volatile temperament, and was always full of fun and frolic. As a huntress, she was the surest eye, and the fleetest foot; and her pretty canoe skimmed the waters like a stormy petrel. It was charming to see this young creature, so full of life, winding about among the eddies of the river, or darting forward, her long black hair streaming on the wind, and her rich red lips parted with eagerness. She sported with her light canoe, and made it play all manner of gambols in the water. It dashed and splashed, and whirled round in pirouettes, like an opera-dancer; then, in the midst of swift circles, she would stop at once, and laugh, as she gracefully shook back the hair from her glowing face. Jerome de Rancé had never loved anything, as he did this beautiful child. But something of anxiety and sadness, mingled with his pride, when he saw her caracoling on her swift little white horse of the prairies, or leaping into the chase, or making her canoe caper like a thing alive. Buoyant and free was her Indian childhood; but she was approaching the period, when she would be claimed as a wife; and he could not endure the thought, that the toilsome life of a squaw, would be the portion of his beautiful daughter. He taught her to dance to his flute, and hired an old Catholic priest to instruct her in reading and writing. But these lessons were irksome to the Indian girl, and she was perpetually eluding her father's vigilance, to hunt squirrels in the woods, or sport her canoe among the eddies. He revolved many plans for her future advancement in life; and sometimes, when he turned his restless gaze from daughter to mother, the wife felt troubled, by an expression she did not understand. In order to advance his ambitious views, it was necessary to wean Felicie from her woodland home; and he felt that his Clouded-Sunbeam, though still beautiful, would be hopelessly out of place in Parisian saloons. Wee-chush-ta-doo-ta and his wife were dead, and their relatives were too much occupied with war and hunting, to take particular notice of the white man's movements. The acres of forest and prairie, which he had received, on most advantageous terms, from his Indian father-in-law, were sold, tract after tract, and the money deposited in Quebec. Thither, he intended to convey first his daughter, and then his son, on pretence of a visit, for the purposes of education, but in reality, with the intention of deserting his wife, to return no more.

According to Indian custom, the mother's right to her offspring amounts to unquestioned law. If her husband chooses to leave the tribe, the children must remain with her. It was therefore necessary to proceed artfully. De Rancé became more than usually affectionate; and Zah-gah-see-ga-quay, grateful for such gleams of his old tenderness, granted his earnest prayer, that Felicie might go to Quebec, for a few moons only. The Canadian fur-traders made their annual visit at this juncture, and he resolved to accept their escort for himself and daughter. His wife begged hard to accompany them; humbly promising, that she would not intrude among his white friends, but would remain with a few of her tribe, hidden in neighbouring woods, where she could now and then get a glimpse of their beloved faces. Such an arrangement, was by no means pleasing to the selfish European. The second time she ventured to suggest it, he answered briefly and sternly, and the beautiful shaded eyes filled with unnoticed tears. Felicie was the darling of her heart; she so much resembled the handsome Frenchman, as she had first known him. When the parting hour came, she clung to her daughter with a passionate embrace, and then starting up with convulsive energy, like some gentle animal when her young is in danger, she exclaimed, "Felicie is *my* child, and I will not let her go." De Rancé looked at her, as he had never looked before, and raised his arm to push her away. Frightened at the angry expression of his eye, she thought he intended to strike her; and with a deep groan she fell on the earth, and hid her face in the long grass.

Felicie sobbed, and stretched out her arms imploringly towards her mother; but quick as a flash, her father lifted her on the horse, swung himself lightly into the same saddle, and went off at a swift gallop. When the poor distracted mother rose from the ground, they were already far off, a mere speck on the wide prairie. This rude parting would perhaps have killed her heart, had it not been for her handsome boy of seven summers. With a sad countenance, he gravely seated himself by her side. She spoke no word to him, but the tears rolled slowly down, as she gazed at him, and tried to trace a resemblance to his unkind father.

The promised period of return arrived; but moon after moon passed away, and nothing was heard from the absent ones. A feeling that she had been intentionally deceived gradually grew strong within the heart of the Indian mother; and the question often arose, "Will he seek to take my boy away also?" As time passed on, and suspicion changed into certainty, she became stern and bitter. She loved young Florimond intensely; but even this love was tinged with fierceness, hitherto foreign to her nature. She scornfully abjured his French name, and called him Mah-to-chee-ga, The Little Bear. Her strongest wish seemed to be to make him as hard and proud as his grandfather had been, and to instil into his bosom the deadliest hatred of white men. The boy learned her lessons well. He was the most inveterate little savage that ever let fly an arrow. Already, he carried at his belt the scalp of a boy older and bigger than himself, the son of a chief, with whom his tribe were at war. The Sioux were proud of his vigour and his boldness, and considered his reckless courage almost a sufficient balance to the disadvantage of mixed blood.

Such was the state of things, when Jerome de Rancé returned to the shores of the Mississippi, after an absence of three years. He was mainly induced to make this visit by a wish to retain some hold upon his Indian boy, and preserve a good understanding with the tribe, as an advantage in future speculations. He had some dread of meeting the Clouded Sunbeam, and was not without fear that she might have exasperated her people against him. But he trusted much to her tenderness for him, and still more to his own adroitness. He was, however, surprised at the cold indifference with which she met him. He had expected deep resentment, but he was not prepared for such perfect apathy. He told a mournful and highly-wrought story of Felicie's sudden death, by being thrown from her horse, in their passage through the forest; and sought to excuse his long absence, by talking of his overwhelming grief, and his reluctance to bring sad tidings. The bereaved mother listened without emotion; for she did not believe him. She thought, and thought truly, that Felicie was in her father's native land, across the wide ocean. All his kind glances and endearing epithets were received with the same stolid indifference. Only when he talked with her Little Bear, did she rouse from this apparent lethargy. She watched over him like a she-wolf, when her young are in danger. She hoped that the hatred of white men, so carefully instilled, would prove a sufficient shield against all attempts to seduce him from her. But in the course of a few weeks, she saw plainly enough that the fascinating and insidious Frenchman was gaining complete power over the boy, as he had over her own youthful spirit. She was maddened with jealousy at her own diminished influence; and when Mah-to-chee-ga at last expressed a wish to go to Canada with his father, the blow was too severe for her deeply lacerated soul. The one thought that he would be enticed away from her took complete possession of her mind, and night and day she brooded over plans of vengeance. More than once, she nearly nerved her hand to murder the father of her son. But his features recalled the image of the handsome young Frenchman, who had carried her arrows through the woods, and kissed the moccasin he stooped to tie; and she could not kill him.

As the time approached for de Rancé to return to Canada with the traders, her intense anxiety increased almost to frenzy. One day, when he had gone to a neighbouring tribe to traffic for furs, she invited Mah-to-chee-ga to go up the river with her, to fish. She decked herself in her most richly embroidered skins, and selected the gaudiest wampum-belt for her Little Bear. When the boy asked why they were dressed so carefully, she replied, "Because we are going to meet your grandfather, who was a great brave, and a mighty hunter." He was puzzled by the answer, but when he questioned her meaning, she remained silent. When they came to the waterside, she paused and looked back on the forest, where she had spent her happy childhood, and enjoyed her brief dream of love. The beautiful past, followed by a long train of dark shadows, rushed through memory, and there seemed no relief for her but death.

She entered the boat with a calm countenance,, and began to chant one of those oppressively mournful songs, which must have been suggested to her people by the monotonous minor cadences of the rustling forest. As they approached the Falls of St. Anthony, and heard more and more plainly the rush of waters, she gazed on her child with such a wild expression of vehement love, that the boy was frightened. But his eye was spell-bound to hers, and he could not escape its concentrated magnetic power. At length, his attention was roused by the violent motions of the boat; and he screamed, "Mother! mother! the canoe is going over the rapids!"

"We go to the spirit-land together," she replied: "he cannot come there to separate us."

With whirl and splash, the boat plunged down the cataract. The white foam leaped over it, and it was seen no more.

The sky soon after darkened, and the big rain fell in torrents.

The Indians believe that the spirits of the drowned ones, veiled in a winding-sheet of mist, still hover over the fatal spot. When they see the vapour rising, they say, "Let us not hunt to-day; a storm will certainly come; for Zah-gah-see-ga-quay and her son are going over the Falls of St. Anthony."

Felicie was informed of the death of her mother and brother, and wept for them bitterly, though she never knew the painful circumstances of their exit. She married a wealthy Frenchman, and was long pointed out in society as "*La Belle Indienne*."

An Appeal for the Indians, first published in the *National Anti-Slavery Standard* (April 11 and 18, 1868) and reissued as a pamphlet later that year, represents Child's most complete statement of her thinking on the Indian question, as it had matured over forty-five years. It also illustrates the strengths and limitations of the abolitionist approach toward solving America's race problem.

Abolitionist racial theory had developed in response to twin programs aimed at turning the United States into a nation of whites only: the colonization scheme for repatriating American blacks in Africa and the Indian removal policy formulated by Presidents James Monroe and Andrew Jackson. Repudiating as unchristian the assumption on which these programs were based—that "inferior" or "savage" races could not be incorporated into the American body politic on equal terms—abolitionists insisted that all races had the capacity to attain the level of "civilization" whites had reached through favorable historical circumstances, and that education and assimilation were the only solutions consistent with American democratic principles. Unfortunately, abolitionists shared their adversaries' ethnocentric belief in the superiority of white civilization. Thus their concept of racial equality did not include the right to maintain a separate cultural identity, which they viewed merely as another form of the racial segregation they were committed to eradicating.

As Child's own career attests, abolitionists had begun championing the cause of the Indians before taking up the issue of slavery, and they continued to plead for justice toward both Indians and blacks until the intensifying crisis over slavery absorbed all their energies. By the end of the Civil War, however, the accelerating pace of road and railway construction across the tribal lands of the Plains Indians, threatening the buffalo herds on which they depended for food and causing frequent clashes with white settlers, forced the Indian problem back to the forefront of national attention. In 1864, after the bloody Sand Creek Massacre of Cheyenne Indians at Fort Lyon had provoked an outbreak of Indian hostilities throughout the Southwest, which could only be quelled by diverting troops from the Southern theater, Congress recognized the need for a new Indian policy. The result was the creation of the Indian Peace Commission, empowered to negotiate with the warring Sioux. Humanitarian reformers opposed to military action against Indians played a prominent role in the commission, a reflection of the government's change in policy. It is to their report of January 7, 1868, that Child responds in her *Appeal for the Indians*.

Tragically, the Peace Commission Report denounced white Americans' two-hundred-year war of extermination against the Indians, only to advocate in its stead what amounted to a war of extermination against Indian culture. Shaping national policy for almost a century thereafter, the report recommended confining the Indians to reservations governed by benevolent, but firm, white authorities; weaning them from hunting to "agriculture and manufactures," from collective to individual modes of life; and compelling Indians to abandon their cultural and tribal identity. "The object of greatest solicitude," the commissioners spelled out, "should be to break down the prejudices of tribe among the Indians; to blot out the boundary lines which divide them into distinct nations, and fuse them into one homogeneous mass. Uniformity of language will do this—nothing else will."

Contemporary opinion recognized only two alternatives—civilization or extermination. Western settlers, who vociferously attacked the Peace Commission's "sentimentality," called for extermination. Social theorists argued that the Indians' inevitable progress toward civilization could best be hastened not by direct intervention, but by such indirect means as cutting off their traditional game supply and witholding annuities from recalcitrant tribes. Humanitarian reformers embraced the more active and seemingly benevolent approach recommended by the Peace Commission Report—compulsory schooling in civilization.

Thus in criticizing the report for exhibiting "our haughty Anglo-Saxon ideas of force," and in suggesting that educationists seek not to "blot out" Indian culture, but to use it as a medium for uplifting the Indians, Child showed an unusual degree of sensitivity. In fact, she had herself designed a reader for the ex-slaves precisely along the lines she prescribed for the Indians—*The Freedmen's Book* (1865), which featured many selections by and about blacks who could serve their people as

inspiring role models. Ultimately, however, she differed from the commissioners on means, rather than ends. An ideology that defined Indians
and blacks as "younger members of the same great human family, who
need to be protected, instructed and encouraged, till they are capable of
appreciating and sharing all our advantages," made it impossible for
Child to move beyond racial egalitarianism to cultural pluralism. In this
respect, as well as in its persisting fascination with "intermarriages," *An
Appeal for the Indians* reveals continuities with *Hobomok*.

AN APPEAL FOR THE INDIANS

I EARNESTLY DESIRE to call the attention of humane and thinking people to the recent "Report of the Indian Peace Commission." I know not who wrote this report; but whoever he may be, he is obviously a just and humane man, with opinions concerning the relations of the human race more enlightened and liberal, than is common with public men. Gen. Terry[1] is one of the signers, and I am always ready to believe that any good thing may come from him.

I welcomed this Report almost with tears of joy. "Thank God!" I exclaimed, "we have, at last, an Official Document which manifests something like a right spirit toward the poor Indians! Really, this encourages a hope that the Anglo-Saxon race are capable of civilization?"

That those who have not seen it may judge of its spirit, I will make a few extracts somewhat condensed: "In April, 1864, when the Indians were confessedly at peace, a man named Ripley came into Camp Sanborn and stated that the Indians had taken his stock; he did not know what tribe. Who or what Ripley was, we know not. That he *owned* stock we have *his own* word, and the word of no one else. He asked for troops, and forty men were placed under his guidance, with instructions to disarm the Indians and take possession of Ripley's stock. In the course of the day, Indians were found, and Ripley claimed some of the horses. The Lieutenant ordered the herd to be stopped, and called to the Indians to come and talk with him. As soon as they rode forward, the soldiers were ordered to disarm them. The Indians of course resisted and a fight ensued. . . .

"In May following, Major Downing asked for a force to attack the Indians; for what reason we do not know. Soldiers were given him, and his own account is: 'I captured an Indian and ordered him to go to the village of Cheyenne with us, or I would kill him. We rode all day and night, and about daylight succeeded in surprising the Cheyenne village. We commenced shooting. They lost some twenty-six killed, and thirty wounded. I burnt up their lodges and everything I could get hold of. I took a hundred of their ponies and distributed them among the boys. That is the usual way in New Mexico.' During the Summer, similar occurrences were frequent. In the Fall, several prominent Chiefs sent word to Major Wynkoop,[2] Commander of Fort Lyon, that war had been *forced* upon them and that they desired peace. The Major accompanied seven of the Chiefs to the house of the Governor of Colorado, to communicate their wishes for peace and protection. The Governor replied, 'I am sorry you brought them here. I have nothing to do with them. They are in the hands of the military authorities. But I don't think it is policy, anyhow, to make peace with them, till they are properly punished; for, if we did, the United States would be acknowledging themselves whipped. In consequence of my representations at Washington, the Third Colorado Regiment was raised to kill Indians, and Indians they *must* kill.' Major Wynkoop then ordered the Indians to move nearer to the Fort, and bring their women and children; promising them military protection. They accordingly encamped near the Fort, to the number of about five hundred. A new commander, who soon after took the place of Major Wynkoop, renewed the promise to protect them. But while they imagined themselves secure under this pledge, the Third Colorado Regiment surrounded their Camp at daylight and commenced indiscriminate slaughter. The heart-rending particulars of this massacre are too well known to need repetition. It is enough to say that it scarcely has its parallel in the records of Indian barbarity. Fleeing women, holding up their hands, and praying for mercy, were brutally shot down; infants were killed and scalped in derision; and men were tortured and mutilated in a manner that would put to shame the ingenuity of savages. No one will be astonished that a war ensued which cost the government thirty millions of dollars, and carried conflagration and death to our border settlements. During the Spring and Summer of 1865, no less than eight thousand troops were withdrawn from the effective force engaged in suppressing the Rebellion, to meet this Indian war. The result of the year's campaign satisfied all reasonable men that war with Indians was useless and expensive. Fifteen or twenty Indians had been killed, at the expense of more than a million dollars apiece, while hundreds of our soldiers had lost their lives, many of our border settlers had been butchered, and much property destroyed. To those who reflected on the subject, *knowing the facts*, the war was something more than useless and expensive; it was dishonorable to the nation, and disgraceful to those who originated it."

The Report goes on to say: "As soon as Treaties were signed, the war which had been waged for nearly two years instantly ceased. During the Summer and Winter of 1866, General Sherman[3] travelled without escort to the most distant posts of his command, with a feeling of perfect security. To say that no outrages were committed by the Indians, would be claiming for them more than can be justly claimed by the most moral and religious communities. Many bad men are found among the whites, who commit outrages despite all social restraints, and often escape punishment. Is it to be wondered at that Indians are no better than we? . . . If it be said that because they are savages they should be exterminated, we answer that aside from the *humanity* of the suggestion it would prove exceedingly difficult. If money considerations are permitted to weigh, it costs less to civilize than to kill. Among civilized men, war usually springs from a sense of injustice. The best possible way, then, to avoid war is to do no act of injustice. When we learn that the same rule holds good with Indians, the chief difficulty is removed. It is said our wars with them have been almost constant. Have we been uniformly unjust? We answer, unhesitatingly, yes." . . .

"The white and Indian must jointly occupy the country, or one of them must abandon it. If they could have lived together, the Indian would have become civilized, and war prevented. All admit this would have been beneficial to the Indian; and if we grant that it would have proved a little inconvenient as well as detrimental to the white, it is questionable whether the policy that *has* been adopted has not been *more* injurious. What prevented their living together? First, the antipathy of race; second, difference of customs and manners; third, difference of language, which in a great measure prevented a proper understanding of each other's motives and intentions. Now, by educating their children in the English language, these differences would have disappeared, and civilization would have followed. Nothing would then have been left but the antipathy of race; and that, too, is always softened in the beams of a higher civilization." . . .

"Naturally, the Indian has many noble qualities. He is the very embodiment of courage. If he is cruel and revengeful, it is because he is outlawed, and the companion of wild beasts. Let civilized man be his companion, and the association warms into life virtues of the rarest worth. Civilization has driven him away from the home he loved; it has often tortured and killed him; but it could never make him a slave. Considering we have had so little respect for those we did enslave, we ought, for consistency's sake, to admire *this* element of Indian character."

Cordially as I approve of this Report, I dissent from it in a few particulars. It proposes that the tribes should be collected into some Territory, indicated by Congress, and "a man of unquestioned integrity and purity of character should be placed over them as Governor, with salary sufficient to place him above temptation." I would ask what salary *would* place a white Governor of Indians above temptation? I imagine the Treasury of the United States, in its most plethoric condition, would prove insufficient for such a purpose, unless the Governor was subject to a great deal of careful overseeing.

The Report says that schools should be established to instruct the children in English, and "their barbarous dialects should be blotted out." This partakes too much of our haughty Anglo-Saxon ideas of force. I would say, let their books, at first, be printed in Indian, with English translations; and let them contain selections from the best of their own traditionary stories, and records of such things as have been truly honorable in the history of their "braves." Give them pleasant associations with the English language by making it constantly the medium of just principles and kindly feelings. Let proficiency in English, and the habit of speaking it, be rewarded with some peculiar privileges and honors. The Report says, "Let Polygamy be punished." I would rather say let it be discountenanced, and reasoned against, and privileges conferred on those who live with one wife. In this way, the fixed habit of many generations might be weakened, and the way prepared for wise laws on the subject. Indians, like other human beings, are more easily led by the Angel Attraction, than driven by the Demon Penalty. But, alas, Force is the Anglo-Saxon God; and thus we are practically "Devil Worshippers." We have so long indulged in feelings of pride and contempt toward those whom we are pleased to call "the subject races," that we have actually become incapable of judging of them with any tolerable degree of candor and common sense. How *ought* we to view the peoples who are less advanced than ourselves? Simply as younger members of the same great human family, who need to be protected, instructed and encouraged, till they are capable of appreciating and sharing all our advantages.

I know it is an almost universal opinion that Indians are incapable of civilization; but I see no rational ground for such an opinion. Their mode of warfare is certainly barbarous; but, then, all wars are barbarous to a shocking degree. The difference between Indian and civilized warfare is, that we take prisoners, while it is their custom to kill all they conquer. To give no quarter in battle is the international law of their tribes. If this proves incapacity for civilization, the Greeks and Romans were incapable of it; for they did the same. The Lacedemonians slaughtered three thousand Athenians, taken by them at the naval battle of Ægospotami, four hundred years B.C., and all ancient history is full of such examples.

Do we say that their modes of torture indicate irreclaimable barbarism? Let us glance at the record of modern nations, and see whether it proves *our* natures to be essentially different from *theirs*. The Inquisition was in full operation, for centuries, in several Catholic countries. In the course of three hundred years, three hundred and forty-one thousand victims were prosecuted by the Inquisition, *in Spain alone*. Thirty-one thousand nine hundred and twelve of them were burnt alive; and uncounted numbers were subjected to tortures more or less cruel and protracted. The limbs of these poor creatures were stretched by an infernal machine called the rack, till the bones started from their sockets; they were compressed into iron hoops, till the blood gushed from eyes and nostrils, and sometimes from feet and hands; their hands were broken to pieces with thumb-screws and iron gauntlets; and their legs were forced into iron boots, into which wedges were driven, till flesh and bones became a clotted mass; they were confined for days in cages so constructed that they could neither walk, stand, sit, or lie down at full length. I might fill columns with similar monstrosities practiced by nations of the white race. The tortures of the Inquisition were almost entirely for differences of belief concerning theological doctrines; an insanity of cruelty of which Indians were never guilty.

The civil laws of all European countries authorized tortures in various forms. People were legally pinched to death with red hot pincers; they were slowly pressed to death by great weights; they were sawed in pieces alive; they were crucified, head downward; they were torn and devoured by wild beasts; their limbs were pulled asunder by wild horses. Prisoners in the Tower of London had their bones cracked on the rack, and their hands mutilated with thumb-screws. Such things continued to be common during the reign of Elizabeth, called "the Augustan Age of England." By the laws of that country, a person who was proved guilty of high treason was hung by the neck, cut down alive, his entrails taken out and burnt while yet alive, his head cut off, his legs and arms cut off, and exposed in public places. It is little more than two hundred years ago, that the Earl of Montrose was beheaded by the Covenanters for his adherance to the cause of Charles the 1st. His body was dismembered, and his limbs exposed over the gates of various cities, infecting the air with putrefaction, and depraving the moral instincts of mankind. England has ceased to do such things now; but even within a few years she placed Hindoo rebels before the muzzle of cannon, and scattered the blood and brains of the poor wretches in all directions.[4] The English newspapers were ferociously barbarous concerning that rebellion; and Mr. Spurgeon[5] preached a sermon denouncing vengeance against the Hindoos, in terms that seemed less in accordance with the education of a Christian minister than with the savage training of "Black-Hawk," "Pouncing-Eagle," or "Wild-Cat."

We Americans came upon the stage when the world had advanced so far in civilization that our record ought to be much cleaner than it is. The plain truth is, our relations with the red and black members of the human family have been one almost unvaried history of violence and fraud. Our ancestors, whether Catholics or Puritans, were accustomed to regard heathen tribes as Philistines, whom "the Lord's people" were commissioned to exterminate root and branch, or to hold them as bondmen and bondwomen. The early settlers of this country, with the exception of William Penn, treated the native tribes in this spirit. Benevolent individuals tried, from time to time, to ameliorate this state of things; but their efforts availed little, because the spirit of pride and violence pervaded all the laws, all the customs, and all the churches. In 1646, the Apostle Elliot[6] began to labor as a Christian missionary among the Indians in towns around Boston. Very touching is the question they asked him: "The English have been among us twenty-six years. If they thought the knowledge of their God so important, why did they not teach it to us sooner? If they had done so, we might have known much of God by this time, and many sins might have been prevented." The theological teaching of that time must have been bewildering to unsophisticated minds. Mr. Elliot, however, succeeded in gathering congregations in various towns, until there were over a thousand styled by him "praying Indians." They reverenced their teacher, and seemed glad to open their minds to such gleams of light as they could receive from the white man's religion. But while a few were engaged in this good work, multitudes were continually abusing and cheating the natives. King Philip,[7] driven to desperation by the continual encroachments of white men, went to war to defend his territories from invaders, just as white monarchs do. This was considered sufficient warrant for a general crusade against Indians. It did not occur to them that a course of strict honesty and impartial justice would have been a safer, cheaper, and better process. There was a camp of "praying Indians," called Wamesits, near the town now called Chelmsford. A barn, filled with corn and hay, was burned in the neighborhood. The Wamesits had nothing to do with it; but the white settlers, filled with the prevailing prejudice against Indians, determined to make them suffer for it. They accordingly went to their encampment and called them out to talk with them. The Wamesits being known as peaceable Christians, and, as they supposed, under the protection of Christians, came forth without hesitation. As soon as they made their appearance, a volley was fired at them. One was killed and seven wounded. Those who could, escaped to the woods, where several of them perished with hunger. The wigwams were set on fire, and seven, who were too old and infirm to get out, were burned alive. Subsequently, some of the fugitives were captured and sold for slaves. Under such circumstances, the teaching of the Apostle Elliot, of course, left no more trace than smoke in the air. How could those simple people believe in a religion whose professors manifested no sense of justice or of mercy toward them?

An Appeal for the Indians

In consequence of a feud between the French and the English, an Indian village in Norridgewock, Maine, was stealthily attacked by a band of English settlers, in 1724. Men, women and children were all massacred. Their Catholic priest, to whom they were devotedly attached, was shot and scalped, his skull smashed with hatchets, and his limbs broken and mangled in many different ways.

Indians are at least more consistent than white men. They profess to believe in revenge, and practice accordingly; while we profess a religion of love and forgiveness, and do such things as these!

The Seminole war, which cost the United States forty or fifty millions of dollars, was caused by the forcible carrying off of the wives and children of Florida Indians, who had intermarried with fugitive slaves, or with the descendants of fugitive slaves. The Indians paid a large sum, by way of compromise, but the Georgia slaveholders, not content with making them pay for their wives and children, demanded and took from the Creeks one hundred and forty-one thousand dollars, as payment for children that the slaves *might* have borne to their masters, if they had not escaped from bondage. Lawless bands were continually going into Florida, capturing whomsoever they pleased, and selling them into slavery, without attempting to establish any claim to them by law; and our government, if it did not connive at these wicked proceedings, neglected to furnish any redress. How can we blame the Indians for fighting, when we ourselves should have fought with half the provocation? Osceola,[8] whose beautiful wife had been torn from him and sold into slavery, fought like a tiger. Is it any wonder that he hated white men? At last, pacified by fair promises, he and other Chiefs agreed to meet the officers of the United States for the purpose of negotiating a treaty of peace. They met *under a flag of truce* and were immediately seized and thrown into prison, where Osceola lingered miserably a while, and died. Such are the methods we take to make the Indians in love with Christianity!

Similar atrocities continue to be perpetrated up to the present time. The record of Fremont's[9] pathfinders in California is enough to fill any humane soul with horror. By their own showing, his band were accustomed to shoot down Indians in mere sport, wherever they came in sight. The gold-hunters in Oregon burn wigwams and shoot the inmates whenever they want to take possession of any spot. They have claimed pay for such barbarities, under the name of military service in subduing the Indians; and they have actually received three millions of dollars from the United States government. If we wish to redeem the American name from everlasting infamy, something must be done to prevent the repetition of such wrongs.

⌐ Good Father Beeson,[10] who had lived in the Northwest, bore public testimony concerning the outrages committed within his own knowledge. It was painful to hear him tell how thoroughly dejected and hopeless the poor Indians were. I do not suppose the United States government have intended to sanction such proceedings; but they have been unpardonably careless. Rascals and swindlers have often been employed in various departments of Indian service. They have put a great part of the funds intrusted to them into their own pockets. Instead of the good articles stipulated by treaty, the Indians have received moth-eaten blankets, damaged guns, etc., in payment for their lands. Worse than this, soldiers and agents have often treated the Indian women as overseers are accustomed to treat negro slaves; and if an Indian seeks to revenge the violence done to wife or daughter, a hue and cry is raised that the savages are making war upon the whites, troops are called for to put them down, and, without inquiry into the cause of the difficulty, troops are sent.

In view of the facts I have presented, it seems to me that the Indians, even if judged from the most unfavorable side of their character, are no more barbarous than our own ancestors were a few centuries ago; and if *their* descendants have become civilized, why should we consider it impossible for Indians to become so? But are we civilized? When I reflect upon what we *have* done, and *are* doing toward our red brethren, I cannot in conscience answer yes. When I remember how professed Christians, claiming to be the model gentlemen of the nineteenth century have, in the mere wantonness of power, burned negroes alive, hunted them with blood-hounds, seared them with red-hot irons, blistered them with perforated paddles, and lacerated them with wire-pointed whips, I cannot, for very shame, say yes. When I remember how that same "chivalry" stabbed dying soldiers when the battle was over, how they deliberately starved helpless prisoners, and let them perish with cold in sight of acres of forest, from which they begged leave to cut a little fuel;[11] when I remember these things, I cannot say that Indians are the worst savages.

Still, the world has moved, and does move, though it is but slowly. One encouraging fact distinctly proves this. In former ages, the masses of the people were utterly ignored; now, the weakest cannot be outraged without finding powerful voices to proclaim their wrongs.

Good Father Beeson tried his utmost to obtain a hearing from the people concerning the wicked oppressions practiced upon our red brethren. But a death-grapple with Slavery was then coming upon the republic, and all felt that one or the other must die. There was too much excitement and anxiety to admit of attention to any other topic. But I think the time has now come when, without intermitting our vigilant watch over the rights of black men, it is our duty to arouse the nation to a sense of its guilt concerning the red men. Legislators are bound to examine, carefully and candidly into the dealings with that much-abused race, and to see that justice is done, for the good fame of the nation, if for no better reason. Lecturers should urge the removal of such a stain on an age of progress. Ministers and missionaries should exert their influence to prevent the name of Christianity from being further disgraced by such diabolical doings. I especially hope that the Quakers will put their hands to the work; for they, better than any others, can "reach the witness" in untutored minds, because they let alone incomprehensible doctrines of theology, and inculcate those great principles of morality, easily understood and recognized by all men. But little can be accomplished either by missionaries or schools, unless government is careful to employ none but honest, just and humane men in their transactions with these poor people. Hitherto, it has been the misfortune and disgrace of the nation that the very offscouring of society have generally been employed in our Indian affairs.

BRITAIN derives its name from an ancient word signifying parti-colored; because the inhabitants painted their bodies with various pigments. None of them cultivated the ground; they all lived by hunting and raising herds of cattle. They wore no other dress than the skins of beasts, and they lived in small huts of wicker-work covered with rushes. How little descriptive is this of Great Britain now.

I have no doubt that every nation and tribe on earth is capable of being softened and refined if brought under the right influences. But the great, the almost insurmountable difficulty in the way of universal civilization has always been that Christian nations, in their transactions with peoples of other religions, have never considered themselves bound by the same moral principles which regulate their conduct toward those of similar faith and equal power. They are more savage toward "heathens" in war, they are more fraudulent with them in trade, and in personal intercourse they treat them with less civility. Their philanthropic labors among them are nearly deprived of efficacy by an assumption of superiority, a pride of condescension, which is so ingrained in their habits that they are unconscious of it. When Moravian Missionaries attempted to convert the Delawares to Christianity, one of the Chiefs said: "There are two ways that lead to God; one is for the white man, the other for the red man; but the red man's path is the straighter and shorter of the two. If the Great Spirit came down into this world, and was treated as you say, I assure you the Indians are not to blame for it, but white men alone. As for your Book, we cannot understand it; it is too difficult for us." To which the Missionary replied, "I will tell you the reason of that. The Devil is the Prince of Darkness. Where *he* reigns all is dark; and he reigns in *you*; therefore, you cannot comprehend anything about God, or his Word." The missionaries were accustomed to repeat this conversation, with entire unconsciousness that such a method of conversion was ill-adapted to gain proselytes.

Contempt, whether expressed or implied, alienates all men; but it operates with peculiar force upon Indians, because they have by nature great pride of independence; a pride capable of producing glorious results, if rightly developed and applied. Nothing keeps down individuals, or races, like the consciousness of being considered inferior by those around them. It is not only mortifying and discouraging in its effects, but it produces a feeling of isolation, that builds up a complete wall of separation. An Indian of the Kennebec tribe, who had gained a high character by uniform good conduct, had a grant of land from the State, in a new township where a number of white families were settled. He applied himself to the cultivation of it, and was orderly and industrious. But his neighbors, though they found no pretext for molesting him, had the common prejudice against Indians, and they habitually treated him as an outcast. When his only child sickened and died, not one of them went near him. Soon afterward, he said to some of them: "When white man's child die, Indian sorry. He help bury him. When my child die, nobody speak to me. I make his grave all alone. I can no live here." He abandoned his farm, dug up the body of his child, and carried it two hundred miles through the forest, to join a Canadian tribe.

In reading Dr. Livingston's Travels in Africa,[12] the perfect feeling of human brotherhood which he invariably manifests toward those rude tribes is cheering to my heart. His dealings with them are uniformly just and kind, and his estimate of them always rests as a basis on the thought, "Thus should I do and be, if I had grown up under such circumstances; and they would be as I am, if they had received the same education." This spirit everywhere inspired confidence and attachment. Tribes accustomed to regard (with abundant reason) all white men with suspicion, fear and abhorrence, welcomed Dr. Livingston as a friend, and were zealous to serve him. Speke, the traveller,[13] seems to have been actuated by a different spirit. He was always ready to assert superiority and intimidate by threats; and the natural result was, that the native Chiefs were always wrangling with him and seeking to annoy him.

The native tribes of America are doubtless much more revengeful than those of Africa; but so much has been said of their horrid cruelties, and they have taken such deep hold of the popular mind, that it would be like throwing petroleum on a flaming village for me to repeat them. I will, therefore, pass them by, and endeavor to show that their character has its bright side.

Much as we are accustomed to abhor and despise them, they are in some respects, decidedly superior to white men. Gen. Houston,[14] who lived two years among them, said in the Senate of the United States, "I never knew an Indian to break a promise, or violate a treaty." Mr. Schoolcraft,[15] who was for twenty-five years an agent of the United States among the Chippewas and Ottawas, told Mrs. Jameson,[16] "I have never known an Indian to break a promise or violate a treaty." He regretted his inability to say as much in favor of his own government. At the very time he spoke those words he was troubled by orders to require the Indians to take goods instead of the money promised them in exchange for their lands. They needed the money to pay for articles they had obtained on credit, founded on the promise of it. They were indignant at what they justly considered a violation of the treaty; but so little did the United States regard their rights that a contract had actually been made with a trader to supply the goods, and he was there ready to deliver them, before the form was gone through of asking the Indians whether they consented or not. Mrs. Jameson, who was there at the time, says: "The mean petty-trader style in which American officials make and break treaties with the Indians is shameful. I met with no one who attempted to deny or excuse it." In this case, the Indians, after remonstrating in vain, became so exasperated that they killed some of the men who tried to force goods upon them in lieu of the promised money; and, as usual, a general hue and cry was raised about "Indian atrocities," without inquiring into the cause. I pass over the long record of similar facts. The amount of the whole is that the Indians never broke a treaty, and the white man never kept one. William Penn is an exception. His dealings with the natives were uniformly just and kind; and the consequence was that his little Colony lived in the midst of the numerous and warlike Delawares as safely as they could now live in his "City of Brotherly Love." Only one Quaker was ever killed by the Indians, and that was by mistake; his dress, and the gun he carried, having led them to suppose he did not belong to Penn's Colony.

The Indians have one marked trait of character, which is much less universal among the whites. They never return kindness with treachery; their gratitude is as lasting as their revenge. Edwin Corey, once an officer in the United States army, joined the Society of Friends, and was sent by them on a mission to the Indians. After residing among them for some years, he returned to transact some business. People were surprised that he did not bring his wife with him, and inquired anxiously, "Won't she be very much afraid there in the woods without you to protect her?" "O no, she won't be afraid," replied he. "She is perfectly safe. I left nine Indians with her."

Had the views of William Penn been faithfully carried out, we should doubtless see a very different state of things from that which now exists. But emigrants whose opinions and practices were different from the Quakers settled in that region, and his plans for the civilization and comfort of the natives all fell through. The Delawares have been three times removed from their lands, and are now about being removed again from the tract reserved for them in Kansas.

There is another trait in Indian character, which contrasts favorably with the frequent practices of white nations. They never, not even in their wildest moments of revenge, offend the modesty of female captives. Mr. Schoolcraft says: "The whole history of Indian warfare might be challenged in vain for a solitary instance of this kind. They think it would be degrading to a warrior to take dishonorable advantage of female prisoners; that it would render him unfit for manly achievements, and unworthy of them." Compare this with the disgusting details of towns and cities sacked by Christian nations! Compare it with the brutal treatment that Indian women receive from United States soldiers, agents, gold-diggers, fur-traders, and other lawless adventurers!

One would hardly expect to find enlightened views of education among the Indians; but I think one of their maxims on that subject is the wisest I ever read. They never strike children, giving this as a reason for it: "Before a child is old enough to understand, there is no *use* in striking him; and when he is old enough to understand, no one has a *right* to strike him." It is but a short time ago that an orthodox minister in New York whipped to death his child of three years old, to compel it to repeat a prayer. It would have been well for him if he had learned the maxim of the Indians, and practised it. Mrs. Jameson, describing her short sojourn with some of these uncivilized tribes, says: "I never heard the children scolded or threatened, and their mothers told me such language was never used. I saw no evil results from this mild system. The general reverence and affection of the children for their parents was delightful to witness."

Theologians and politicians have been prone to adduce the enslavement of negroes as sufficient proof of their natural inferiority. Judged by this standard, there is no justice in classing Indians among "the subject races." White men have outnumbered them, as a thousand to one, they have tortured and slaughtered them, they have hunted them like wild beasts, they have brutified them with drink, they have heaped enough of discouragement and contempt upon them to crush all manhood out of them; but they could never succeed in making them slaves.

The quiet decorum of Indians imparts a dignity to their deportment rarely met with in the most elegant drawing-rooms. Mrs. Jameson, after describing strange costumes, grotesque finery, rags and dirt, adds, "But in *manners* they are the most perfect gentlemen I ever saw. We are twenty white people, with three thousand seven hundred of these wild creatures around us, and I never in my life felt more security. I never met with people more genuinely polite."

The stoicism of their manners has given rise to the idea that they are deficient in feeling; but in reality their affections are very strong. This is especially indicated by their tender memories of the dead, and their longing to rejoin them. When a delegation from the Chippewas visited Washington, in 1849, a babe that was brought with them sickened and died. The grief of the parents knew no bounds. A person who pitied their distress caused a daguerreotype likeness of the dead child to be taken. The bereaved mother carried it in her bosom, and ever and anon she would take it out, cry over it, kiss it, and offer it to her husband, whose keen black eyes would fill with tears as he kissed it also. Every morning, they bowed their heads solemnly over the little picture, and uttered a brief prayer before they entered upon the duties of the day. Another proof that their natures are emotional is that they are extremely fond of music, which missionaries have found peculiarly useful in arresting their attention and touching their feelings.

Notwithstanding the many discouragements that weigh them down, there have been not a few individuals among them, who have proved, beyond dispute, their capability for moral and intellectual culture. Miss Brandt, daughter of a Mohawk Chief, attracted attention by her intelligence and lady-like manners. The mother of Mrs. Schoolcraft was an unmixed Indian, who married a white trader by the name of Johnson. These intermarriages are by no means rare; and they prove, as plainly as the complexions of mulattoes and quadroons, that the "antipathy of races" is not a *natural* antipathy. Mrs. Johnson was an uncommon woman. Her father, a Chippewa Chief, was celebrated among his tribe for his talent in making allegories and stories. She inherited the gift, and some of her productions are quite poetic. Mrs. Jameson says: "Her habits and manners are those of a genuine Indian squaw, but her talents and domestic virtues command the highest respect. Her two sons-in-law, Mr. MacMurray, and Mr. Schoolcraft, both educated in good society, the one a clergyman, and the other a man of science and literature, look up to this remarkable woman with sentiments of affection and veneration. In her own language she is eloquent, and her voice, like that of her people, is low and musical. Many kind words were exchanged between us, mostly, in French, for she understood English but little. When I said anything that pleased her, she laughed softly, like a little child. I was not well, and she took me in her arms, laid me on a couch, and began to soothe and caress me. She had the strongest marked Indian features, but her countenance was open, benevolent, and intelligent. Her manners were easy and simple, yet with something of motherly dignity. She set before us the best dressed and best served dinner I had seen since I left Toronto, and presided at her table with unembarrassed, unaffected propriety."

It is generally supposed that the Indians knew nothing of agriculture, till they saw it practised by the whites; but this is not true. In our war with the Indians, 1794, Gen. Wayne [17] destroyed many settlements of the Wyandots and Miamis on the shores of Lake Erie. In an official dispatch, he wrote thus: "The very extensive and cultivated fields and gardens show the work of many hands. The margins of the rivers appear like one continued village for miles. I have never beheld such immense fields of corn in any part of America, from Canada to Florida." All this was laid waste by white men. The Cherokee tribe in Georgia, numbering about twenty thousand, resolved to adopt our mode of life. They made good progress in Agriculture and various mechanic arts, and were as orderly as any other citizens. But the State of Georgia coveted their lands, and they were driven off to a Territory beyond Arkansas, by a series of insupportable persecutions, at which the government of the United States winked, if it did nothing worse. How *can* people improve, who are never secure in the possession of their lands? Yet, while we are perpetually robbing them, and driving them "from post to pillar," we go on repeating, with the most impudent coolness, "They are *destined* to disappear before the white man." And we "nail it with Scripture," just as we did our enslavement of the negroes; "Japhet shall be enlarged, and inhabit the tents of Shem, and Canaan shall be his servant." If the white man is Japhet, all I have to say is, he has behaved in a rascally manner toward Shem and Canaan.

Presented from such points of view, how must our religion appear to the Indians, who have always believed in One Great Spirit, the Father of the whole human race? No wonder there has been so little success in attempts to convert them to Christianity. Their ideas of politeness prevent them from ever ridiculing or contradicting the theological opinions of other people; but when missionaries told them of a hell, where sinners were punished to all eternity, perhaps there was some latent sarcasm in their reply, "If there be such a place, it must be for white men only."

One of two stories Child wrote about the Norridgewock massacre, the other being "The Adventures of a Bell" (*Juvenile Miscellany*, March 1827), "The Church in the Wilderness" led off Nathaniel Willis's 1828 gift book, *The Legendary*. Although Child inexplicably chose not to include it in her collection *The Coronal*, it ranks with her best early fiction.

The historical incident on which Child based "The Church in the Wilderness"—the English obliteration of an Abenaki Indian hamlet in Norridgewock, Maine, served by the French Jesuit priest, Sebastian Rale—took place in 1724. Because she spent her youth in the modern town of Norridgewock, located seven miles down river from the razed Abenaki settlement, the massacre held a special fascination for Child. The very year she arrived in Norridgewock—1815—a storm that uprooted an ancient oak tree, disinterring Father Rale's long-buried church bell in the process, revived public memory of the murdered priest and his slaughtered Abenaki congregation. Child would subsequently consult many accounts of Rale's confrontation with his British foes.

A comparison of "The Church in the Wilderness" with its sources reveals that Child revised Anglo-American testimony to produce a more sympathetic portrayal of Rale and to explore the viability of cultural syncretism and intermarriage with Indians—promoted by the French— as alternatives to the genocide practiced by the English. These themes also distinguish Child's fictionalization of the Norridgewock saga from other literary renditions the episode inspired: the anonymous story "Narantsauk" in *The Atlantic Souvenir* for 1829; the play *Carabasset* by Nathaniel Deering (1830); and the narrative poem "Mogg Megone" by John Greenleaf Whittier (1836). Child's most interesting contributions are her insights into the role of repressed sexuality in undermining the Jesuit's relationship with his Abenaki congregation and her use of mixed-blood characters to suggest the benefits Europeans might have derived from intermingling racially and culturally with the Indians.

There stood the Indian hamlet, there the lake
Spread its blue sheet, that flashed with many an oar,
Where the brown otter plunged him from the brake,
And the deer drank—as the light gale blew o'er,
The twinkling maze-field rustled on the shore;
And while that spot, so wild, and lone, and fair,
A look of glad and innocent beauty wore,
And peace was on the earth and in the air,
The warrior lit the pile and bound his captive there.
Not unavenged the foeman from the wood
Beheld the deed, and when the midnight shade
Was stillest, gorged his battle-axe with blood;
All died—the wailing babe—the shrieking maid—
And in the flood of fire, that scathed the glade,
The roofs went down; but deep the silence grew,
When on the dewy woods the day-beam played;
No more the cabin smokes rose wreathed and blue,
And ever by their lake, lay moored the light canoe.
  —*Bryant*[1]

THERE IS a solitary spot, in a remote part of Maine, known by the name of Indian Old Point. The landscape has no peculiar beauty, save the little sparkling river, which winds gracefully and silently among the verdant hills, as if deeply contented with its sandy bed; and fields of Indian corn, tossing their silken tresses to the winds, as if conscious of rural beauty. Yet there is a charm thrown around this neglected and almost unknown place, by its association with some interesting passages in our earliest history. The soil is fertilized by the blood of a murdered tribe. Even now the spade strikes against wampum belts, which once covered hearts as bold and true, as ever beat beneath a crusader's shield, and gaudy beads are found, which once ornamented bosoms throbbing with as deep and fervent tenderness, as woman ever displayed in the mild courtesies of civilized life.

Here, one hundred years ago, stood the village of the Norridge-wocks, one of the many tribes of the scattered Abnakis. These Indians have been less celebrated than many of their brethren; for they had not the fierce valor of the Pequods, the sinewy strength of the Delawares, or the bell-toned language of the Iroquois. They were, however, an influential nation; of consequence on account of their numbers, as well as their subtilty. The Jesuits, too, had long been among them, led by their zeal to fasten the strong girdle of an imposing faith around the habitable globe; and they had gained over the untutored minds of these savages, their usual mysterious and extraordinary power. The long continued state of efferves-cence, produced by the Reformation, tended to settle this country with rigid, restless, and ambitious spirits. Our broad lands were considered an ample tract of debatable ground, where the nations of the earth might struggle for disputed possession; and terrible indeed was the contest for religious supremacy between France and England, during the early part of the eighteenth century. Of the energy and perseverance displayed in this cause, there are few more striking examples than Sebastian Rallè, the apostle of the Norridgewocks. His rude, cross-crowned church, standing in the heart of the American wilderness, proved the ambition and extent of that tremendous hierarchy, 'whose roots were in another world, and whose far stretching shadow awed our own.'' Surrounded by the wigwams of the Abnakis, it seemed like an apostle of Antioch descended among savages, pointing out to them the heaven he had left. Our forefathers indeed thought it wore a different, and most unholy aspect; but to roman-tic minds, the Catholic church, even in its most degraded state, must ever be an object of interest. The majestic Latin, so lofty in its sound, and yet so soulless now to all save the learned, seems like the fragments of a mighty ruin, which Rome, in her decaying pride, scattered over the nations of the earth; and the innumerable ceremonies, more voiceless than the language in which they are preserved, forcibly remind one of the pomp and power rivalled only by attendant corruption. In this point of view only could the humble church of the Norridgewocks kindle the imagination; for it had little outward proportion, or inward splendor. It stood in a sheltered spot, between two small, verdant hills, with one graceful feathery elm at its side, bending forward, at every signal from the breeze, and half shading the cross, as if both bowed down in worship.

Various opinions were formed of the priest, who there administered the rites of a mysterious religion. All agreed that he was a learned man; some said he was benevolent and kind; while others pronounced him the most subtle and vindictive of hypocrites. The English settlers, who resided about three miles from the village of the Abnakis, regarded him with extreme aversion; but to the Indians he was the representative of the Good Spirit. It is true the maxims of the Jesuits had given something of sternness and cunning to a character naturally mild and frank; but he verily thought he was doing God's service, and he did it with a concentration of power and purpose well worthy of the respect it inspired. For thirty years he lived in the wilderness, sharing the dangers and privations incident to savage life. The languages of all the neighbouring tribes were familiar to him; and his utterance could not have been distinguished from that of a native, had it not been for a peculiarly softened cadence, and rapid enunciation. A restless light in his small, hazel eye, and the close compression of his lips, betokened one, who had, with a strong hand, thrown up dykes against the overflowing torrent of his own mad passions. The effort had likewise turned back many a gentle current of affection, which might have soothed and refreshed his heart; but let man do his worst, there are moments when nature will rebound from all the restraints imposed on her by pride, prejudice, or superstition.

There were two objects in the secluded residence of the self-denying Jesuit, on whom he poured forth in fulness the love he could not wholly stifle within him. When he came to America, he found among the savages the orphan son of the Baron de Castine,[3] by a beautiful young Abnakis. The child was remarkably pretty and engaging; and the lonely priest, finding his heart daily warming toward him, induced the squaw who nursed him, to take up her abode in his own wigwam. The Indians called him Otoolpha, 'The Son of the Stranger,' and seemed to regard the adopted one with quite as much interest as their own offspring. Not a year after Otoolpha and his nurse were domesticated in the dwelling of the Jesuit, some of the tribe, on their return from Canada, found a nearly famished female infant in the wood. Had not Sebastian Rallè been of the party, its sufferings would, probably, have met a violent end; but at his suggestion, comfortable nourishment, and such care as they could give it were afforded. A nose slightly approaching to aquiline, and a complexion less darkly colored than usual, betrayed an origin half European; but as her parentage and tribe were unknown, they gave her the emphatic name of Saupoolah, 'The Scattered Leaf,' and engrafted her on the tree of Abnakis. From the first dawn of reason she gave indications of an impetuous, fearless, and romantic spirit. The squaw who nursed her, together with the little Otoolpha, tried in vain to curb her roving propensities. At four and five years old, she would frequently be absent several days, accompanied by her foster brother. The duties of the missionary often called him far from home, and it was absolutely impossible for him always to watch over them, either in kindness, or authority. Their long excursions during his absence, at first occasioned many anxious and wretched thoughts; but when he found his wayward protégés invariably returned, and when he saw they could cross streams, leap ditches, and thread their way through the labyrinths of the wilderness, with the boldness and sagacity of young hunters, he ceased to disturb himself on their account.

During the whole of their adventurous childhood but one accident ever happened to them. They had been at the English settlement to beg some beads in exchange for their little baskets, and on their return, they took a fancy to cross the Kennebec, when recent rains had swollen its deep and beautiful waters. Saupoolah's life nearly fell a sacrifice to the rapidity of the current; but her foster brother ran, with the speed of lightning, to call assistance from the village they had just left. A muscular, kind hearted woman, by the name of Allan, lived in a log-house, very near the river. In the midst of his terror, Otoolpha remembered this circumstance, and went there for succor. His frightened looks told his story, even more plainly than his hurried exclamation;—'Ogh! Saupoolah die—the Great Spirit drink her up!' Mrs. Allan saved the Indian child at the risk of her own life, dried her clothes, gave them something warm and comfortable to eat, and conducted them into their homeward path in safety. To this woman and her children Otoolpha and Saupoolah ever after clung with singular intensity of affection. During their childish summers, it was a daily occupation to fill baskets with berries for her little ones, whom they always chose to feed with their own hands, watching every morsel of the fruit as it disappeared between their rosy lips, with the most animated expressions of delight; and when they arrived at maturer years, they used the great influence they had with the tribe, to protect Mrs. Allan from a thousand petty wrongs and insults, with which her white brethren were not unfrequently visited.

Educated by the learned priest, as far as such fetterless souls could be educated, and associating only with savages, these extraordinary young people grew up with a strange mixture of European and aboriginal character. Both had the rapid, elastic tread of Indians; but the outlines of their tall, erect figures possessed something of the pliant gracefulness of France. When indignant, the expression of their eyes was like light from a burning-glass; but in softer moments, they had a melting glance, which belongs only to a civilized and voluptuous land. Saupoolah's hair, though remarkably soft and fine, had the jet black hue of the savage; Otoolpha's was brown, and when moistened by exercise, it sometimes curled slightly around his high, prominent forehead. The same mixture of nations was shown in their costume, as in their personal appearance. Otoolpha usually wore a brown cloth tunic, with tight sleeves, and large buttons, under which appeared a scarlet kilt falling to his knees, in heavy folds, edged with the fur of the silver fox, and fastened at the waist by a broad girdle, richly ornamented with Indian hieroglyphics. A coronet of scarlet dyed fur, to which were fastened four silver bells, gave indication of his noble descent; and from his neck were suspended a cross and rosary of sandal wood, which Sebastian Rallè declared to have been sanctified by the blessed touch of Innocent the Eleventh. Saupoolah's dress was nearly similar. Her tunic was deep yellow; and her scarlet kilt touched the fur edge of her high, closely fitted, and very gaudy moccasins. Her cap was not shaped unlike a bishop's mitre; gaily ornamented with shells and beadwork, and surmounted by the black feathers of three eagles her own arrow had slain. In the chase, she was as eager and keen eyed as Otoolpha. It was a noble sight to see them, equipped for the chase, bounding along through the forest. The healthful and rapid blood, coursing beneath their smooth, brown cheeks, gave a richness and vividness of beauty, which a fair, transparent complexion can never boast; and their motions had that graceful elasticity produced only by activity, unconsciousness, and freedom. Sebastian Rallè had been several years at Rome, in the service of the Pope, and had there acquired a refinement of taste uncommon at that early period. His adopted children sometimes accompanied him on his missionary expeditions to Canada and elsewhere, on which occasions the game they killed served for his support. When he saw them with their dark eyes fixed on a distant bird, arrows ready for flight, their majestic figures slightly bending backward, resting on one knee, with an advancing foot firmly fixed on the ground, displaying, by a natural bend of the limb, outlines most gracefully curved, he gazed upon them with uncontrolled delight; and he could not but acknowledge that the young savages, in their wild and careless beauty, rivalled the Apollos and woodnymphs to which classic imaginations had given birth. Such endowments are rare in Indian women; for the toils imposed upon them, usually weigh down the springs of the soul, till the body refuses to rebound at its feeble impulses; but when it does occur, it is the very perfection of ideal loveliness. Otoolpha would suffer no one to curb Saupoolah in her wildness and inspiration. To him and the Jesuit, she was docile and affectionate; to all others, haughty and impetuous. The Norridgewocks regarded them both with wonder and superstition, and frequently called them by a name, which signified the 'Children of the Prophet.' The distant tribes, who frequently met them in their hunting excursions, were lost in admiration of their swiftness and majesty, and called them, by one consent, the 'Twin Eagles of Abnakis.'

Contemptuously as some think of our red brethren, genius was no rare endowment among them; and seldom have souls been so rich in the wealth of nature, as the two powerful and peculiar beings, whom we have described. Many were the bold and beautiful thoughts which rushed upon their untutored imaginations, as they roamed over a picturesque country, sleeping in clefts where panthers hid themselves, and scaling precipices from which they scared the screaming eagles. Perhaps cultivated intellect never received brighter thoughts from the holy rays of the evening star, or a stormier sense of grandeur from the cataract, than did these children of the wilderness. Their far leaping ideas, clothed in brief, poetic language, were perhaps more pleasant to the secluded priest, than frequent intercourse with his own learned, but crafty order. To him they were indeed as 'diamonds in the desert;' and long and painful were the penances he inflicted upon himself, for an all-absorbing love, which his erring conscience deemed a sin against that God, who bestowed such pure, delicious feelings on his mysterious creatures. The Jesuit was deeply read in human nature, and it needed but little sagacity to foresee that Saupoolah would soon be to her brother 'something than sister dearer.' When Otoolpha was but seventeen, and his companion not quite fifteen, their frank and childish affection had obviously assumed a different character. Restlessness when separated, and timidity and constraint when they met, betrayed their slavery to a new and despotic power. Sebastian Rallè observed it with joy. Early disappointment and voluntary vows had made the best and most luxurious emotions of our nature a sealed fountain within his own soul; but the old man had not forgotten youthful hopes and feelings, and for these beloved ones he coveted all earth had of happiness. They were married in presence of the whole tribe, with all the pomp and ceremony his limited means afforded. This event made no alteration in the household of the Jesuit. The old squaw, who had taken care of his adopted children from their infancy, performed all the services their half civilized way of life required, and the young hunters led the same wandering and fearless life as before. At the hour of sunset, it was the delight of the lonely priest to watch for their return, from a small opening, which served as a window to his study. It was a time he usually devoted to reflection and prayer; but the good man had virtues, which he called weaknesses and sins, and a spirit of devotion would not always remain with him at such seasons. The vine covered hills of France, his mother's kiss, and a bright, laughing girl, who had won his heart in early youth, would often rise before him with the distinctness of visions. The neglected rosary would fall from his hand, and love, as it first stole over a soul untainted by sensuality or selfishness, was the only heaven of which he dreamed. Such were the feelings with which he awaited the return of Otoolpha and Saupoolah, on the eleventh of December, 1719. Notwithstanding the lateness of the season, the day had been as mild as the first weeks of September. The drowsy sunshine dreaming on the hemlocks, pines, and cedars, had drawn forth an unusual fragrance; the children were at rest in the wigwams; most of the sanups[*] had gone to Moose Head Lake, on a hunting expedition; and the few old men who remained, sat at the doors of their huts smoking their pipes in lazy silence.

Wautoconomese, an aged prophet among them, declared this unnatural warmth to be a prelude of terrible things. He had gained his power of judging by a close observation of electrical phenomena and all the various changes of the weather, and it was no difficult matter to make his tribe mistake experience for inspiration. The women were all in alarm at his predictions; nor is it strange that the learned Jesuit, living as he did in a superstitious age, and believing doctrines highly calculated to excite the imagination, should be more affected by their terrors than he was willing to acknowledge, even to himself. These feelings naturally embodied themselves in anxiety concerning the two eccentric beings, whose presence was as morning sunshine in his dreary dwelling. The hour at which they usually returned, had long since passed; and strong and vigilant as he knew them to be, fearful thoughts of panthers and wolves crowded on his heart. Waking, he knew the fiercest prowlers of the wilderness would have shunned them; but they might have slept where loup-cerviers[5] were in ambush, and roused too late for safety.

While philosophy was struggling with these harassing ideas, and every moment growing weaker in the contest, he observed in the north a flash more brilliant then ever precedes the rising sun. For a moment it was stationary; then it moved, quivered, hurtled, and flashed, as if there had been 'war in heaven,' and the clouds, rolling themselves up 'as a scroll,' showed the gleaming of javelins, thrown thick and fast along the embattled line.[6] All at once, a vivid stream of light from the south towered up, like Lucifer in his terrific greatness, and rushed onward with a mighty noise. The fiery forces, nearly meeting at the zenith, were separated only by a clear, deep spot of blue, surrounded by a few fleecy clouds. The effect was awful. It seemed as if the All-seeing Eye were looking down upon a sinful world, in mingled wrath and pity. The Catholic bowed his head, and his subdued spirit was mute in worship and fear. His solitude was soon interrupted by Wautoconomese, whose trembling agitation betrayed how little he had foreseen that his pompous prophecies would be thus sublimely fulfilled. Next the aged squaw, who, from fear of interrupting her master in his devotions, had long been crouching in her own corner of the wigwam, more dead than alive, came in, and reverentially crossing herself, implored permission to remain. To these were soon added an accession of almost all the women in the hamlet. Perhaps Sebastian Rallè was hardly aware how much the presence of these rude, uninformed beings relieved his spirit. His explanations to them, mixed with the consolations of religion, nerved his mind with new strength; and he began to look upon the awful appearance in the heavens with a calmness and rationality worthy of him. By degrees the light grew dim, then closed upon the speck of blue sky, which had appeared to keep watch over the souls of superstitious men, and the glorious scene seemed about to end. But suddenly a luminous bow shot from north to south with the rushing sound of a rocket, and divided the heavens with a broad belt of brightness. The phenomena of that night had been more extraordinary than any the Jesuit had ever witnessed; but until that moment he had known their name and nature; and, with that strange tendency to a belief in supernatural agency, which the greatest and wisest minds have, in a state of high excitement, his cheek now turned pale, and his heart dropped heavily within him, at what he deemed a sure presage of ruin to those he loved. Reason would have indeed told him that it did not comport with the economy of Providence to change the order of creation for so insignificant a thing as man; but who is not more under the influence of feeling than of reason?

Unable to endure the terrific creations of his own fancy, he left the house, followed only by one of the tribe, and entered the path by which the young hunters usually returned. He pursued this route, for nearly a mile, without seeing any traces of the objects of his anxiety. At last he heard a loud 'Willoa.' The source of the clear, ringing sound could not be mistaken; for Saupoolah alone could give the shrillest tones of the human voice such depth and smoothness of melody. The Jesuit, by his long residence with the savages, had acquired their quickness of eye and ear, and a few moments brought him within view of his adopted child. She was standing in a thickly shaded part of the wood, her hand resting on her brow, looking backward, apparently listening with eagerness to the coming footsteps. A slight shade of disappointment passed over her face when she saw Otoolpha was not with her father; but it soon gave place to an affectionate smile, at his enthusiastic demonstrations of joy. From her brief account it appeared they had early in the evening heard distressed noises apparently proceeding from a human voice; that they had separated in search of those from whom it came, and had thus lost each other. As she finished her story, another loud shout sent echoing through the forest, betrayed more anxiety than was common to her fearless nature. Yet even amid her doubt and perplexity, her romantic soul was open to the influence of the sublime scene above her. As they wound along through the forest, ever and anon shouting with their united voices, in hopes the echo would arouse Otoolpha, she occasionally fixed her eye on the bright arch, which still preserved its wavy radiance, though a little softened by light flashes of clouds, through which the stars were distinctly visible. 'The arrows have been flying fast among the tribes of heaven to night,' said she. 'The stars have chased their enemies over the hills. They are returning victorious; and the moon has spread her mantle in their war path.'

When such thoughts as these came over her, Saupoolah's eyes had a brightness totally different from the keenness and outward brilliancy common to fine looking Indians; it was a light that came from within, gleaming up from fires deep, deep down in the soul. It was probably this peculiarity, which had so universally gained for her the title of 'Daughter of a Prophet;' and its effect on the savage, who had attended the Jesuit, was instantly observable; for he devoutly crossed himself, and walked at a great distance from the object of his veneration. Sebastian Rallè, accustomed as he was to the wild freaks, and almost infantile tenderness of his adopted children, had often smiled at their power over the tribe; yet something of pride, almost of deference, mingled with his own love of them. Saupoolah's remark, and the look of inspiration, with which she fixed her eye on the heavens, awakened in his mind the remembrance of many a season, when he had listened to their wild eloquence with wonder and delight. This train of thought betrayed itself in an eagerly affectionate glance at Saupoolah, and a loud shout to Otoolpha, that made the woods ring again. The young wife suddenly assumed the Indian attitude of intense listening; and joy flushed her whole face, like a sunbeam, as she exclaimed, 'It is answered!' Another shout! there could be no mistake. It could not be the reverberation of an echo, for it was repeated louder and louder, at irregular intervals. A rapid and devious walk, guided by sounds which evidently grew nearer, brought Otoolpha in sight. Quick as a young fawn, overflowing with life and frolic, Saupoolah bounded forward, and sprang upon his neck. But the eye of the Jesuit, always rapid and restless in its movements, quickly glanced from his new found treasure to the objects around. A European lady, possessed of much matronly beauty, lay lifeless at his feet; and a fragile looking boy, apparently eight or nine years old, was bending over her, and weeping bitterly. This child, alone in the wilderness with his dead mother, had uttered those cries of distress and terror, which had startled

Otoolpha and his companion. The sight of a white man seemed to the
desolate boy a pledge of safety. He nestled close to the side of the priest,
and looking up in his face imploringly, burst into tears. The heart of the
Jesuit was touched. There was something in the boy's voice and the lady's
features, that troubled the waters of a long sealed fountain. The Indians
exchanged whispers with that air of solemnity, which the presence of the
dead always inspires. They read a mixed feeling of agony and doubt in the
countenance of Sebastian Rallè, but they did not ask, and they never knew
its origin. After a moment's silence, during which he seemed struggling
with powerful emotion, he placed his hand gently on the boy's head, and
spoke soothing words in French, which the child understood with perfect
facility. No sigh, no outward sign of despair escaped him; but there was a
marble stillness, which, like the ominous quiet of a volcano, betrayed that
raging materials were at work within.

He ordered the corpse to be borne to his wigwam with all possible
gentleness; and when the unevenness of the path occasioned the least
violence of motion, he would cringe, as if an adder had stung him. It was in
vain that Wautoconomese and his frightened companion sought protection from him, on his return. Remarkable electrical appearances, in every
variety of form, continued during the whole night; but the miserable man
regarded them not. The lifeless mother was placed in his study, and he
knelt down beside it with the boy, and spoke not a word. The old squaw
brought in her tallest bayberry wax candles, and tried to prolong her stay
in the room by a thousand little officious arts; but a gentle signal to
withdraw was all she could gain from her heart stricken master. Day
dawned, and found him unchanged in countenance or position. The boy,
weary with grief and fatigue, had fallen asleep, and lay on the floor in a
slumber as deep and peaceful as if unalloyed happiness had been his portion.
The sight of his tranquil innocence, as the daylight shone upon his childish
features, brought tears to the eyes of the rigid priest. It was a charm that
broke the spell of agony which had bound down his spirit. The terribly
cold and glassy look departed from him; but never, after that night, was
Sebastian Rallè as he had been. Affliction did not soften and subdue him. It
deepened the gloom with which he had long looked upon the world, and
seemed to justify him in giving up his whole soul to the stern dictates of
Jesuitical maxims. Even Otoolpha and Saupoolah met with occasional

harshness; and William Ponsonby, the English boy, alone received uniform mildness and affection at his hands. He was a fair and delicate blossom; such a being as the heart would naturally cling to for its very fragility and dependence; but to none on earth, save Sebastian Rallè, was it known that there were other and deeper reasons for his peculiar tenderness.

The lady, whom he had loved in early youth, had been induced by her parents to marry a wealthy Englishman, in preference to the unportioned Frenchman, whom alone she had truly loved. Her husband lost much of his fortune, and joined his countrymen against the French, during the troubled period between 1690 and 1762. He was taken by the Indians, and his wife saw him suffer a horrid and lingering death. By the humanity of one of the savages, she made her escape, with her youngest son, the only one remaining of eight fine boys. She well knew the residence of that devoted lover, whom her weakness of purpose had driven to a life of solitude and self-denial; and to him she resolved to appeal for protection. Worn out with wandering and privation, she died suddenly in the wilderness, when her arduous journey was well nigh completed; and the conscientious priest, even in the anguish of a breaking heart, felt that it was well for him she had died; for to have seen the widowed one depending upon him for protection, when the solemn vows of his order had separated them forever, would have been worse than death to endure. The affection he had borne the mother rested on the child; and in him he found, what he had in vain wished for since his residence in the New World, a docile and intelligent scholar.

The boy was indeed a sort of 'young Edwin;' a sad, imaginative child, fond of his books, and still more fond of rambling far and wide with the wayward Saupoolah. The log-house of good Mrs. Allan was the only place where William spoke in the language of his father; for English was a hateful sound to the ear of the Jesuit. The troubles between the neighbouring villages of English and Abnakis increased daily; and not a few of the latter were induced to revolt against their spiritual ruler. Distrust, jealousy, and weakness characterized all their councils. Their deep, but fluctuating feelings alternately showed themselves in insults to the priest, and acts of violence on their neighbours. Representatives were sent from the English villages on the Kennebec to the government at Boston, who protested against Sebastian Rallè, for constantly using his influence to excite Indian revenge to its utmost rancor; and letters filled with charges of this nature may still be seen in the records of the Historical Society. It is probable that they were, in some measure, well founded; for it was the dangerous creed of the Jesuits, that all human power, good or bad, should be made subservient to one grand end. Yet the Norridgewocks had so much reason to complain of the fraud and falsehood of the English, that it is difficult to decide to whom the greatest share of blame rightfully belongs. Be that as it may, affairs went from bad to worse. Mutual dislike became every day more inveterate; and Mrs. Allan was the only one who had not in some way or other suffered from the powerful arm of the implacable Otoolpha. His French origin, the great influence he had over his tribe, and his entire submission to the will of the Jesuit, procured for him a double portion of hatred. Dislike was returned with all the fierceness and impetuosity of his savage nature; and English mothers often frightened their children into obedience by the use of his terrible name. In the autumn of 1724, these discontents were obviously approaching a fearful crisis. A Council Fire was kindled at the village of the Abnakis; and fierce indeed were the imprecations uttered, and terrible the resolutions taken against the English.

Wautoconomese in his fury said, that the Evil Spirit had governed them ever since William Ponsonby⁷ came among them; and he demanded that the boy should at once be sacrificed to an offended Deity. The lip of the venerable priest quivered and turned pale for an instant; but it passed quickly, and so carefully had even the muscles of his face been trained in obedience to the Society of Jesus, that rigid indifference could alone be read there, as he carelessly asked, 'Wherefore should the child die?' The fierce old prophet watched his emotions as the snake fixes her infernal eye on the bird she is charming unto death. 'Because the Great Spirit, who dwells among the windy hills, and covers himself with the snow mantle, has whispered it in the ear of the wise man,' said he proudly. 'Wherefore else did he breathe softly on the wood, for four sleeps, and take his garments from the sun, that it might give warmth to the pale papoose, on his way through the wilderness? I tell you, he sent him to Wautoconomese, that he might sacrifice him instead of the young fawn and the beaver; for he loves not the white face and the double tongue of the Yengees.'

'And the love I bear them is such as the panther gives the stricken deer,' replied the Jesuit. 'Ye are all one! ye are all one!' answered the raging prophet. 'The Yengees say their king has counted more scalps than any other chief; and you say he is but a boy to the great king, who lives where the vines run with oil. Ye both have faces pale as a sick woman. One hisses like a snake, and the other chatters like a mad cat bird; but both hunt the poor Indian like a buffalo to his trap. Wautoconomese was once a very big prophet. The Great Spirit spoke to him loud, and his tribe opened their eyes wide, that they might look on him. What is Wautoconomese now? He speaks the words of the Great Spirit; and ye laugh when ye tell the young men of his tribe that his ears are old, and he cannot hear.'

His stormy eloquence awakened the slumbering pride of his warlike nation; and against the whole race of white men they inwardly breathed a vow of extermination.

The boy was bound for sacrifice, and evil eyes were cast upon the Jesuit. The ingratitude of those for whom he had toiled thirty long years, and the threatened loss of the dearest object which God had left to cheer his lonely pilgrimage, seemed to freeze the faculties of the old man; and that day would have ended his trials with his life, had not Otoolpha stepped into the centre of the Council Circle, and, with a low bow to Wautoconomese, demanded to be heard. He spoke reverently of the prophet; but, by all the sufferings and kindness of their French Father, he conjured them not to be ungrateful to him in his old age. He begged for the boy's life, and promised to lead his tribe to war against every white man, woman, and child, from Corratwick Falls to the Big Sea, if they would thus reward his victory.

He was a favorite with his tribe, and they listened to him. After much consultation, they determined on midnight marches at the end of three weeks, by which means they intended to surprise and put to death all the English settlers on the Kennebec. If successful in this attempt, William Ponsonby was safe; if not, the innocent child must fall a victim to their savage hatred.

Saupoolah slept little the night after she listened to the Council of her tribe. She thought of Mrs. Allan's kind looks, when she saved her from drowning; and she remembered the happy hours when she used to feed the children from her little berry basket. Could she not save her from the general ruin? She asked Otoolpha if no stratagem could be devised. He told her it would lead to detection, and the life of William and the priest would be forfeited. In her uneasy slumbers she dreamed of the murder of her benefactress; and she started up, declaring she would save Mrs. Allan's life at the peril of her own. Otoolpha resolutely and somewhat harshly forbade her to do it. It was the first time he had ever spoken to her in a tone of authority; and her proud spirit rose against him. 'I have loved him,' thought she, 'but not with the tameness of a household drudge; if such is the service he wants, let him leave Saupoolah, and find a mate among the slaves of Abnakis.' Her manner the next day was cold, suspicious, and constrained towards her husband. She said no more to him of her plans, but sought advice from the priest. The heart broken old man was roused into sudden energy, and solemnly and vehemently forbade her project. Saupoolah's soul struggled in cords to which she had been entirely unaccustomed. She was silent, but determined. That night she left Otoolpha in a sound sleep, and effected her dangerous purpose secretly. She told Mrs. Allan all the plans of the Norridgewocks, beseeching her to make no other use of the knowledge, than to save herself and family. The terrified matron promised she would not. But could, or ought, such a promise to be kept?

TIME PASSED ON, and threw no light on the dangerous deed Saupoolah had dared to perform. Fears of its consequences haunted her own soul, like a restless demon; and again and again did she extort from Mrs. Allan a vow never to betray her. More than half of her fault sprang from a kind and generous nature; but she could not forgive herself for the vexation that had mingled with better feelings. Her pride and her buoyancy were both gone; and upon Otoolpha, Sebastian Rallè, and William Ponsonby, she lavished the most anxious fondness.

The old priest cared little whether life or death were his portion; for he was old, and disappointment had ever been the shadow of his hopes. But for the dead mother's sake, his heart yearned for the life of the boy. Saupoolah, ever enthusiastic and self-sacrificing, promised to convey him away secretly, and place him under the protection of a Canadian priest. The time appointed was four days before the intended massacre of the English, when a Council Fire of one of the neighbouring tribes would induce most of the Norridgewocks to be absent. The night preceding his departure was a weary one to Sebastian Rallè. He spent it at William's couch in wakefulness and prayer. Affections, naturally intense, were all centered on this one object; and he had nerved himself to think that he must part with him, and then lay him down and die.

The gray tints of morning rose upon him, showing the whole of his miserable little apartment in cheerless obscurity. The old priest, stern, philosophic, and rigid elsewhere, was in the seclusion of his own apartment, as wayward and affectionate as a child. He stooped down, and parting William's soft hair, imprinted a kiss on his forehead. The boy, half unconscious what he did, fondly nestled his cheek into the hand that rested on him. Sebastian Rallè looked upward with an expression that seemed to say, 'O Father, would that this cup might pass from me.' Just then the church bell, with feeble but sweet tones, announced the hour of early mass. William was on his feet in an instant, and as quickly knelt to his venerable friend to receive his customary benediction. In a few minutes, every living soul in the hamlet was within the walls of the church. Wigwams were all quiet, and canoes were wimpling about in Sandy river. The savages had all bowed down and crossed themselves before the unseen God. The broken voice of the Jesuit was heard loudly beseeching, '*Ora, ora pro nobis*,' when armed men rushed in amid their peaceful worship. The clashing of swords, the groans of the dying, and the yells of the frantic, mingled in one horrid chaos of clamor. Not one escaped; not one. Some called out, 'Save William Ponsonby and the priest!' Others aimed at the breast of the Jesuit, as if he had been the only victim desired. The English boy threw himself forward and received a stab, aimed at the heart of his old friend; and the priest, with one convulsive bound, and one loud shriek of agony, withdrew the sword and plunged it deeply in his own breast.

Saupoolah's noble heart broke with intensity of suffering. She fell lifeless by the side of the murdered William, and a dozen swords at once were pointed at her. Otoolpha cast one hurried glance upon her; and man has no power to speak the mingled rage, despair, and anguish, which that wild glance expressed. With the concentrated strength of fifty savages, he forced his way unhurt to the river side, and sprung into Saupoolah's favorite canoe. The boat filled with water; and he found that even here the treacherous revenge of his enemies would reach his life. With desperate strength he gained the shore, and ran toward the forest. His coronet and belt made him a conspicuous victim; multitudes were in pursuit; and he died covered with wounds. * * * Before the setting of the sun, the pretty hamlet was reduced to ashes; and the Indians slept their last sleep beneath their own possessions. * * * For many years two white crosses marked the place where the Jesuit and his English boy were buried; but they have long since been removed. The white man's corn is nourished by the bones of the Abnakis; and the name of their tribe is well nigh forgotten.

Published in the *Atlantic Monthly* of March 1863, "Willie Wharton" seems to have been written in early 1861, possibly under the inspiration of a Convention for the Indians, which Child either attended or read about in the abolitionist newpaper, *The Liberator* (8 March 1861). She repeatedly quotes John Beeson, the reformer who presided over this convention, in *An Appeal for the Indians* and "The Indians," both reprinted in this volume. In a letter to Oliver Johnson of 3 June 1861, Child reports having submitted to the *Knickerbocker* a story titled "Willie and Wikanee," which she had expected to appear in the March or April number. Apparently after a rejection by the *Knickerbocker*, she resubmitted it to the *Atlantic Monthly* in February 1862, changing the title and adding an introductory paragraph at the request of publisher James T. Fields.

"Willie Wharton" explores in fiction the solution to the Indian problem that Child would offer in *An Appeal for the Indians* five years later. Reconceptualizing assimilation not as the obliteration of Indian culture but as a mutually enriching process of cultural interchange, the story reflects the evolution of Child's views on interracial marriage since *Hobomok*. Unlike Mary Conant, Willie Wharton undergoes a profound cultural transformation during his sojourn among Indians, actually losing his white identity, and when he rejoins white society, he does not leave his Indian spouse behind. The adjustment to white ways proves as difficult for the Indianized Willie as for his Native bride, and both retain elements of their Indian upbringing that Child suggests Anglo-Americans might do well to adopt. Betraying none of the ambivalence toward interracial marriage that one finds in *Hobomok*, moreover, "Willie Wharton" endorses it as essential to the goal of incorporating Indians into the American body politic.

Though the story shows cultural traits to be acquired, not innate, and though it promotes a style of acculturation characterized by "judicious non-interference," Child's objective remains assimilationist—to guide Indians into "increasing conformity with civilized habits." Still, the methods of Indian education she advocates contrast sharply with the prevailing model. An 1869 article in the *National Anti-Slavery Standard* by a Quaker missionary, for example, advised removing Indian children from their families, immuring them in mission boarding schools, cutting off their hair, washing off their "paint and dirt," confiscating their earrings and bracelets, dressing them in "decent" clothes, and forcing them to "drop their lingo, and acquire our language."

Would you like to read a story which is true, and yet not true? The one I am going to tell you is a superstructure of imagination on a basis of facts. I trust you are not curious to ascertain the exact proportion of each. It is sufficient for any reasonable reader to be assured that many of the leading incidents interwoven in the following story actually occurred in one of our Western States, a few years ago.

IT WAS a bright afternoon in the spring-time; the wide, flowery prairie waved in golden sunlight, and distant tree-groups were illuminated by the clear, bright atmosphere. Throughout the whole expanse, only two human dwellings were visible. These were small log-cabins, each with a clump of trees near it, and the rose of the prairies climbing over the roof. In the rustic piazza of one of these cabins a woman was sewing busily, occasionally moving a cradle gently with her foot. On the steps of the piazza was seated a man, who now and then read aloud some paragraph from a newspaper. From time to time, the woman raised her eyes from her work, and, shading them from the sunshine with her hand, looked out wistfully upon the sea of splendor, everywhere waving in flowery ripples to the soft breathings of the balmy air. At length she said,—

"Brother George, I begin to feel a little anxious about Willie. He was told not to go out of sight, and he is generally a good boy to mind; but I should think it was more than ten minutes since I have seen him. I wish you would try the spy-glass."

The man arose, and, after looking abroad for a moment, took a small telescope from the corner of the piazza, and turned it in the direction the boy had taken.

"Ah, now I see the little rogue!" he exclaimed. "I think it must have been that island of high grass that hid him from you. He has not gone very far; and now he is coming this way. But who upon earth is he leading along? I believe the adventurous little chap has been to the land of Nod to get him a wife. I know of no little girl, except my Bessie, for five miles round; and it certainly is not she. The fat little thing has toppled over in the grass, and Willie is picking her up. I believe in my soul she's an Indian."

"An Indian!" exclaimed the mother, starting up suddenly. "Have you heard of any Indians being seen hereabouts? Do blow the horn to hurry him home."

A tin horn was taken from the nail on which it hung, and a loud blast stirred the silent air. Moles stopped their digging, squirrels paused in their gambols, prairie-dogs passed quickly from one to another a signal of alarm, and all the little beasts wondered what could be the meaning of these new sounds which had lately invaded the stillness of their haunts.

George glanced at the anxious countenance of his sister, and said,—

"Don't be frightened, Jenny, if some Indians do happen to call and see us. You know you always agreed with me that they would be as good as Christians, if they were treated justly and kindly. Besides, you see this one is a very small savage, and we shall soon have help enough to defend us from her formidable blows. I made a louder noise with the horn than I need to have done; it has startled your husband, and he is coming from his plough; and there is my wife and Bessie running to see what is the matter over here."

By this time the truant boy and his companion approached the house, and he mounted the steps of the piazza with eager haste, pulling her after him, immediately upon the arrival of his father, Aunt Mary, and Cousin Bessie. Brief explanation was made, that the horn was blown to hurry Willie home; and all exclaimed,—

"Why, Willie! who is this?"

"Found her squatting on the grass, pulling flowers," he replied, almost out of breath. "Don't know her name. She talks lingo."

The whole company laughed. The new-comer was a roly-poly, round enough to roll, with reddish-brown face, and a mop of black hair, cut in a straight line just above the eyes. But *such* eyes! large and lambent, with a foreshadowing of sadness in their expression. They shone in her dark face like moonlit waters in the dusky landscape of evening. Her only garment was a short kirtle of plaited grass, not long enough to conceal her chubby knees. She understood no word of English, and, when spoken to, repeated an Indian phrase, enigmatical to all present. She clung to Willie, as if he were an old friend; and he, quite proud of the manliness of being a protector, stood with his arm across her brown shoulders, half offended at their merriment, saying,—

"She's *my* little girl. *I* found her."

"I *thought* he'd been to the land of Nod to get him a wife," said Uncle George, smiling.

Little Bessie, with clean apron, and flaxen hair nicely tied up with ribbons, was rather shy of the stranger.

"She'th dirty," lisped she, pointing to her feet.

"Well, s'pose she is?" retorted William. "I guess *you*'d be dirty, too, if you'd been running about in the mud, without any shoes. But she's pretty. She's like my black kitten, only she a'n't got a white nose."

Willie's comparison was received with shouts of laughter; for there really was some resemblance to the black kitten in that queer little face. But when the small mouth quivered with a grieved expression, and she clung closer to Willie, as if afraid, kind Uncle George patted her head, and tried to part the short, thick, black hair, which would not stay parted, but insisted upon hanging straight over her eyebrows. Baby Emma had been wakened in her cradle by the noise, and began to rub her eyes with her little fists. Being lifted into her mother's lap, she hid her face for a while; but finally she peeped forth timidly, and fixed a wondering gaze on the new-comer. It seemed that she concluded to like her; for she shook her little dimpled hand to her, and began to crow. The language of children needs no interpreter. The demure little Indian understood the baby-salutation, and smiled.

Aunt Mary brought bread and milk, which she devoured like a hungry animal. While she was eating, the wagon arrived with Willie's older brother, Charley, who had been to the far-off mill with the hired man. The sturdy boy came in, all aglow, calling out,—

"Oh, mother! the boy at the mill has caught a prairie-dog. Such a funny-looking thing!"

He halted suddenly before the small stranger, gave a slight whistle, and exclaimed,—

"Halloo! here's a funny-looking prairie-puss!"

"She a'n't a prairie-puss," cried Willie, pushing him back with doubled fists. "She's a little girl; and she's *my* little girl. I found her."

"She's a great find," retorted the roguish brother, as he went behind her, and pulled the long black hair that fell over her shoulders.

"Now you let her alone!" shouted Willie; and the next moment the two boys were rolling over on the piazza, pommelling each other, half in play, half in earnest. The little savage sat coiled up on the floor, watching them without apparent emotion; but when a hard knock made Willie cry out, she sprang forward with the agility of a kitten, and, repeating some Indian word with strong emphasis, began to beat Charley with all her might. Instinctively, he was about to give blows in return; but his father called out,—

"Hold there, my boy! Never strike a girl!"

"And never harm a wanderer that needs protection," said Uncle George. "It isn't manly, Charley."

Thus rebuked, Charley walked away somewhat crestfallen. But before he disappeared at the other end of the piazza, he turned back to sing,—

"Willie went a-hunting, and caught a pappoose."

"She a'n't a pappoose, she's a little girl," shouted Willie; "and she's *my* little girl. I didn't hunt her; I found her."

Uncle George and his family did not return to their cabin till the warm, yellow tint of the sky had changed to azure-gray. While consultations were held concerning how it was best to dispose of the little wanderer for the night, she nestled into a corner, where, rolled up like a dog, she fell fast asleep. A small bed was improvised for her in the kitchen. But when they attempted to raise her up, she was dreaming of her mother's wigwam, and, waking suddenly to find herself among strangers, she forgot the events of the preceding hours, and became a pitiful image of terror.

Willie, who was being undressed in another room, was brought in in his nightgown, and, the sight of him reassured her. She clung to him, and refused to be separated from him; and it was finally concluded that she should sleep with her little protector in his trundle-bed, which every night was rolled out from under the bed of his father and mother. A tub of water was brought, and as Willie jumped into it, and seemed to like to splash about, she was induced to do the same. The necessary ablutions having been performed, and the clean nightgowns put on, the little ones walked to their trundle-bed hand in hand. Charley pulled the long hair once more, as they passed, and began to sing, "Willie went a-hunting"; but the young knight-errant was too sleepy and tired to return to the charge. The older brother soon went to rest also; and all became as still within-doors as it was on the wide, solitary prairie.

The father and mother sat up a little while, one mending a harness, the other repairing a rip in a garment. They talked together in low tones of Willie's singular adventure; and Mrs. Wharton asked her husband whether he supposed this child belonged to the Indians whose tracks their man had seen on his way to the mill. She shared her brother's kindly feeling toward the red men, because they were an injured and oppressed race. But, in her old New-England home, she had heard and read stories that made a painful impression on the imagination of childhood; and though she was now a sensible and courageous woman, the idea of Indians in the vicinity rendered the solitude of the wilderness oppressive. The sudden cry of a night-bird made her start and turn pale.

"Don't be afraid," said her husband, soothingly. "It is as George says. Nothing but justice and kindness is needed to render these wild people firm friends to the whites."

"I believe it," she replied; "but treaties with them have been so wickedly violated, and they are so shamefully cheated by Government-agents, that they naturally look upon all white men as their enemies. How can they know that we are more friendly to them than others?"

"We have been kind to their child," responded Mr. Wharton, "and that will prevent them from injuring us."

"I would have been just as kind to the little thing, if we had an army here to protect us," she rejoined.

"They will know that, Jenny," he said. "Indian instincts are keen.

Your gentle eyes and motherly ways are a better defence than armies would be."

The mild blue eyes thanked him with an affectionate glance. His words somewhat calmed her fears; but before retiring to rest, she looked out, far and wide, upon the lonely prairie. It was beautiful, but spectral, in the ghostly veil of moonlight. Every bolt was carefully examined, and the tin horn hung by the bedside. When all preparations were completed, she drew aside the window-curtain to look at the children in their trundle-bed, all bathed with silvery moonshine. They lay with their arms about each other's necks, the dark brow nestled close to the rosy cheek, and the mass of black hair mingled with the light brown locks. The little white boy of six summers and the Indian maiden of four slept there as cozily as two kittens with different fur. The mother gazed on them fondly, as she said,—

"It is a pretty sight. I often think what beautiful significance there is in the Oriental benediction, 'May you sleep tranquilly as a child when his friends are with him!'"

"It is, indeed, a charming picture," rejoined her husband. "This would be a text for George to preach from; and his sermon would be, that confidence is always born of kindness."

The fear of Indians vanished from the happy mother's thoughts, and she fell asleep with a heart full of love for all human kind.

The children were out of their bed by daylight. The little savage padded about with naked feet, apparently feeling much at home, but seriously incommoded by her night-gown, which she pulled at restlessly, from time to time, saying something in her own dialect, which no one could interpret. But they understood her gestures, and showed her the kirtle of plaited grass, still damp with the thorough washing it had had the night before. At sight of it she became quite voluble; but what she said no one knew. "What gibberish you talk!" exclaimed Charley. She would not allow him to come near her. She remembered how he had pulled her hair and tussled with Willie. But two bright buttons on a string made peace between them. He put the mop on his head, and shook it at her, saying, "Moppet, you'd be pretty, if you wore your hair like folks." Willie was satisfied with this concession; and already the whole family began to outgrow the feeling that the little wayfarer belonged to a foreign race.

Early in the afternoon two Indians came across the prairie. Moppet saw them first, and announced the discovery by a shrill shout, which the Indians evidently heard; for they halted instantly, and then walked on faster than before. When the child went to meet them, the woman quickened her pace a little, and took her hand; but no signs of emotion were perceptible. As they approached the cabin, Moppet appeared to be answering their brief questions without any signs of fear. "Poor little thing!" said Mrs. Wharton. "I am glad they are not angry with her. I was afraid they might beat her."

The strangers were received with the utmost friendliness, but their stock of English was so very scanty that little information could be gained from them. The man pointed to the child, and said, "Wik-a-nee, me go way she." And the woman said, "Me tank." No further light was ever thrown upon Willie's adventure in finding a pappoose alone on the prairie. The woman unstrapped from her shoulder a string of baskets, which she laid upon the ground. Moppet said something to her mother, and placed her hand on a small one brightly stained with red and yellow. The basket was given to her, and she immediately presented it to Willie. At the same time the Indian woman offered a large basket to Mrs. Wharton, pointing to the child, and saying, "Wik-a-nee. Me tank." Money was offered her, but she shook her head, and repeated, "Wik-a-nee. Me tank." The man also refused the coin, with a slow motion of his head, saying, "Me tank." They ate of the food that was offered them, and received a salted fish and bread with "Me tank."

"Mother," exclaimed Willie, "I want to give Moppet something. May I give her my Guinea-peas?"

"Certainly, my son, if you wish to," she replied.

He ran into the cabin, and came out with a tin box. When he uncovered it, and showed Moppet the bright scarlet seeds, each with a shining black spot, her dark eyes glowed, and she uttered a joyous "Eugh!" The passive, sad expression of the Indian woman's countenance almost brightened into a smile, as she said, "Wik-a-nee tank."

After resting awhile, she again strapped the baskets on her shoulder, and taking her little one by the hand, they resumed their tramp across the prairie,—no one knowing whence they came, or whither they were going.

As far as they could be seen, it was noticed that the child looked back from time to time. She was saying to her mother she wished they could take that little pale-faced boy with them.

"So Moppet is gone," said Charley. "I wonder whether we shall ever see her again." Willie heaved a sigh, and said, "I wish she was my little sister."

Thus met two innocent little beings, unconscious representatives of races widely separated in moral and intellectual culture, but children of the same Heavenly Father, and equally subject to the attractions of great Mother Nature. Blessed childhood, that yields spontaneously to those attractions, ignoring all distinctions of pride or prejudice! Verily, we should lose all companionship with angels, were it not for the ladder of childhood, on which they descend to meet us.

It was a pleasant ripple in the dull stream of their monotonous life, that little adventure of the stray pappoose. At almost every gathering of the household, for several days after, something was recalled of her uncouth, yet interesting looks, and of her wild, yet winning ways. Charley persisted in his opinion that "Moppet would be pretty, if she wore her hair like folks."

"Her father and mother called her Wik-a-nee," said Willie; "and I like that name better than I do Moppet." He took great pains to teach it to his baby sister; and he succeeded so well, that, whenever the red-and-yellow basket was shown to her, she said, "Mik-a-nee,"—the W being beyond her infant capabilities.

Something of tenderness mixed with Mrs. Wharton's recollections of the grotesque little stranger. "I never saw anything so like the light of an astral lamp as those beautiful large eyes of hers," said she. "I began to love the odd little thing; and if she had stayed much longer, I should have been very loath to part with her."

The remembrance of the incident gradually faded; but whenever a far-off neighbor or passing emigrant stopped at the cabin, Willie brought forward his basket, and repeated the story of Wik-a-nee,—seldom forgetting to imitate her strange cry of joy when she saw the scarlet peas. His mother was now obliged to be more watchful than ever to prevent him from wandering out of sight and hearing. He had imbibed an indefinite idea that there was a great realm of adventure out there beyond. If he could only get a little nearer to the horizon, he thought he might perhaps find another pappoose, or catch a prairie-dog and tame it. He had heard his father say that a great many of those animals lived together in houses under ground,—that they placed sentinels at their doors to watch, and held a town-meeting when any danger approached. When Willie was summoned from his exploring excursions, he often remonstrated, saying, "Mother, what makes you blow the horn so *soon?* You never give me time to find a prairie-dog. It would be capital fun to have a dog that knows enough to go to town-meeting." Charley took particular pleasure in increasing his excitement on that subject. He told him he had once seen a prairie-dog standing sentinel at the entrance-hole of their habitations. He made a picture of the creature with charcoal on the shed-door, and proposed to prick a copy of it into Willie's arm with India-ink, which was joyfully agreed to. The likeness, when completed, was very much like a squash upon two sticks, but it was eminently satisfactory to the boys. There was no end to Willie's inquiries. How to find that hole which Charley had seen, to crawl into it, and attend a dogs' town-meeting, was the ruling idea of his life. Unsentimental as it was, considering the juvenile gallantry he had manifested, it was an undeniable fact, that, in the course of a few months, prairie-dogs had chased Wik-a-nee almost beyond the bounds of his memory.

Autumn came, and was passing away. The waving sea of verdure had become brown, and the clumps of trees, dotted about like islands, stood denuded of their foliage. At this season the cattle were missing one day, and were not to be found. A party was formed to go in search of them, consisting of all the men from both homesteads, except Mr. Wharton, who remained to protect the women and children, in case of any unforeseen emergency. Charley obtained his father's permission to go with Uncle George; and Willie began to beg hard to go also. When his mother told him he was too young to be trusted, he did not cry, because he knew it was an invariable rule that he was never to have anything he cried for; but he grasped her gown, and looked beseechingly in her face, and said,—

"Oh, mother, do let me go with Charley, just this once! Maybe we shall catch a prairie-dog."

"No, darling," she replied. "You are not old enough to go so far. When you are a bigger boy, you shall go after the cattle, and go a-hunting with father, too, if you like."

"Oh, dear!" he exclaimed, impatiently, "when *shall* I be a bigger boy? You *never* will let me go far enough to see the prairie-dogs hold a town-meeting!"

The large brown eyes looked up very imploringly.

Mr. Wharton smiled and said,—

"Jenny, you do keep the little fellow tied pretty close to your apron-string. Perhaps you had better let him go this time."

Thus reinforced, the petted boy redoubled his importunities, and finally received permission to go, on condition that he would be very careful not to wander away from his brother. Charley promised not to trust him out of his sight; and the men said, if they were detained till dark, they would be sure to put the boys in a safe path to return home before sunset. Willie was equipped for the excursion, full of joyous anticipations of marvellous adventures and promises to return before sunset and tell his parents about everything he had seen. His mother kissed him, as she drew the little cap over his brown locks, and repeated her injunctions over and over again. He jumped down both steps of the piazza at once, eager to see whether Uncle George and Charley were ready. His mother stood watching him, and he looked up to her with such a joyful smile on his broad, frank face, that she called to him,—

"Come and kiss me again, Willie, before you go; and remember, dear, not to go out of sight of Uncle George and Charley."

He leaped up the steps, gave her a hearty smack, and bounded away.

When the party started, she stood a little while gazing after them. Her husband said,—

"What a pet you make of that boy, Jenny. And it must be confessed he is the brightest one of the lot."

"And a good child, too," she rejoined. "He is so affectionate, and so willing to mind what is said to him! But he is so active, and eager for adventures! How the prairie-dogs do occupy his busy little brain!"

"That comes of living out West," replied Mr. Wharton, smiling. "You know the miller told us, when we first came, that there was nothing like it for making folks know everything about all *natur'*."

They separated to pursue their different avocations, and, being busy, were consequently cheerful,—except that the mother had some occasional misgivings whether she had acted prudently in consenting that her darling should go beyond sound of the horn. She began to look out for the boys early in the afternoon; but the hours passed, and still they came not. The sun had sunk below the horizon, and was sending up regular streaks of gold, like a great glittering crown, when Charley was seen coming alone across the prairie. A pang like the point of a dagger went through the mother's heart. Her first thought was,—

"Oh, my son! my son! some evil beast has devoured him."

Charley walked so slowly and wearily that she could not wait for his coming, but went forth to meet him. As soon as she came within sound of his voice, she called out,—

"Oh, Charley, where's Willie?"

The poor boy trembled in every joint, as he threw himself upon her neck and sobbed out,—

"Oh, mother! mother!"

Her face was very pale, as she asked, in low, hollow tones,—

"Is he dead?"

"No, mother; but we don't know where he is. Oh, mother, do forgive me!" was the despairing answer.

The story was soon told. The cattle had strayed farther than they supposed, and Willie was very tired before they came in sight of them. It was not convenient to spare a man to convey him home, and it was agreed that Charley should take him a short distance from their route to a log-cabin, with whose friendly inmates they were well acquainted. There he was to be left to rest, while his brother returned for a while to help in bringing the cattle together. The men separated, going in various circuitous directions, agreeing to meet at a specified point, and wait for Charley. He had a boy's impatience to be at the place of rendezvous. When he arrived near the cabin, and had led Willie into the straight path to it, he charged him to go into the house, and not leave it till he came for him; and then he ran back with all speed to Uncle George. The transaction seemed to him so safe that it did not occur to his honest mind that he had violated the promise given to his mother. While the sun was yet high in the heavens, his uncle sent him back to the log-cabin for Willie, and sent a man with him to guide them both within sight of home. Great was their alarm when the inmates of the house told them they had not seen the little boy. They searched, in hot haste, in every direction. Diverging from the road to the cabin was a path known as the Indian trail, on which hunters, of various tribes, passed and repassed in their journeys to and from Canada. The prints of Willie's shoes were traced some distance on this path, but disappeared at a wooded knoll not far off. The inmates of the cabin said a party of Indians had passed that way in the forenoon. With great zeal they joined in the search, taking with them horns and dogs. Charley ran hither and thither, in an agony of remorse and terror, screaming, "Willie! Willie!" Horns were blown with all the strength of manly lungs; but there was no answer,—not even the illusion of an echo. All agreed in thinking that the lost boy had been on the Indian trail; but whether he had taken it by mistake, or whether he had been tempted aside from his path by hopes of finding prairie-dogs, was matter of conjecture. Charley was almost exhausted by fatigue and anxiety, when his father's man guided him within sight of home, and told him to go to his mother, while he returned to give the alarm to Uncle George. This was all the unhappy brother had to tell; and during the recital his voice was often interrupted by sobs, and he exclaimed, with passionate vehemence,—

"Oh, father! oh, mother! do forgive me! I didn't think I was doing wrong,—indeed, I didn't!"

With aching hearts, they tried to soothe him; but he would not be comforted.

Mr. Wharton's first impulse was to rush out in search of his lost child. But the shades of evening were close at hand, and he deemed it unsafe to leave Jenny and Mary and their little girls with no other protector than an overtired boy.

"Oh, why did I advise her to let the dear child go?" was the lamenting cry continually resounding in his heart; and the mother reproached herself bitterly that she had consented against her better judgment.

Neither of them uttered these thoughts; but remorseful sorrow manifested itself in increased tenderness toward each other and the children. When Emma was undressed for the night, the mother's tears fell fast among her ringlets; and when the father took her in his arms to carry her to the trundle-bed, he pressed her to his heart more closely than ever before; while she, all wondering at the strange tearful silence round her, began to grieve, and say,—

"I want Willie to go to bed with me. Why don't Willie come?"

Putting strong constraint upon the agony her words excited, the unhappy parents soothed her with promises until she fell into a peaceful slumber. As they turned to leave the bedroom, both looked at the vacant pillow where that other young head had reposed for years, and they fell into each other's arms and wept.

Charley could not be persuaded to go to bed till Uncle George came; and they forbore to urge it, seeing that he was too nervous and excited to sleep. Stars were winking at the sleepy flowers on the prairie, when the party returned with a portion of the cattle, and no tidings of Willie. Uncle George's mournful face revealed this, before he exclaimed,—

"Oh, my poor sister! I shall never forgive myself for not going with your boys. But the cabin was in plain sight, and the distance so short I thought I could trust Charley."

"Oh, don't, uncle! don't!" exclaimed the poor boy. "My heart will break!"

A silent patting on the head was the only answer; and Uncle George never reproached him afterward.

Neither of the distressed parents could endure the thoughts of discontinuing the search till morning. A wagon was sent for the miller and his men, and, accompanied by them, Mr. Wharton started for the Indian trail. They took with them lanterns, torches, and horns, and a trumpet, to be sounded as a signal that the lost one was found. The wretched mother traversed the piazza slowly, gazing after them, as their torches cast a weird, fantastic light on the leafless trees they passed. She listened to the horns resounding in the distance, till the *tremolo* motion they imparted to the air became faint as the buzz of insects. At last, Charles, who walked silently by her side, was persuaded to go to bed, where, some time after midnight, he cried himself into uneasy, dreamful slumber. But no drowsiness came to the mother's eyelids. All night long she sat watching at the bedroom-window, longing for the gleam of returning torches, and the joyful *fanfare* of the trumpet. But all was dark and still. Only stars, like the eyes of spirits, looked down from the solemn arch of heaven upon the desolate expanse of prairie.

The sun had risen when the exploring party returned, jaded and dispirited, from their fruitless search. Uncle George, who went forth to meet them, dreaded his sister's inquiring look. But her husband laid his hand tenderly on her shoulder, and said,—

"Don't be discouraged, Jenny. I don't believe any harm has happened to him. There are no traces of wild beasts."

"But the Indians," she murmured, faintly.

"I am glad to hear you say that," said Uncle George. "My belief is that he is with the Indians; and for that reason, I think we have great cause to hope. Very likely he saw the Indians, and thought Wik-a-nee was with them, and so went in pursuit of her. If she, or any of her relatives, are with those hunters, they will be sure to bring back our little Willie; for Indians are never ungrateful."

The mother's fainting heart caught eagerly at this suggestion; and Charley felt so much relieved by it that he was on the point of saying he was sure it must have been either Moppet or a dogs' town-meeting that lured Willie from the path he had pointed out to him. But everybody looked too serious for jesting; and memory of his own fault quickly repressed the momentary elasticity.

Countless were the times that the bereaved parents cast wistful glances over the prairie, with a vague hope of descrying Indians returning with their child. The search was kept up for days and weeks. All the neighbors, within a circuit of fifteen miles, entered zealously into the work, and explored prairie and forest far and wide. At last these efforts were given up as useless. Still Uncle George held out the cheerful prospect that the Indians would bring him, when they returned from their long hunting-excursion; and with this the mother tried to sustain her sinking hopes. But month after month she saw the snowy expanse of prairie gleaming in the moonlight, and no little footstep broke its untrodden crust. Spring returned, and the sea of flowers again rippled in waves, as if Flora and her train had sportively taken lessons of the water-nymphs; but no little hands came laden with blossoms to heap in Emma's lap. The birds twittered and warbled, but the responsive whistle of the merry boy was silent; only its echo was left in the melancholy halls of memory. His chair and plate were placed as usual, when the family met at meals. At first this was done with an undefined hope that he might come before they rose from table, and afterward they could not bear to discontinue the custom, because it seemed like acknowledging that he was entirely gone.

Mrs. Wharton changed rapidly. The light of her eyes grew dim, the color faded from her cheeks, and the tones of her once cheerful voice became plaintive as the "Light of Other Days."¹ Always, from the depths of her weary heart, came up the accusing cry, "Oh, why did I let him go?" She never reproached others; but all the more bitterly did Mr. Wharton, Uncle George, and above all poor Charley, reproach themselves. The once peaceful cabins were haunted by a little ghost, and the petted child became an accusing spirit. Alas! who is there that is not chained to some rock of the past, with the vulture of memory tearing at his vitals, screaming forever in the ear of conscience? These unavailing regrets are inexorable as the whip of the Furies.

Four years had passed away, when some fur-traders passed through that region, and told of a white boy they had seen among the Pottawatomie Indians. Everybody had heard the story of Willie's mysterious disappearance, and the tidings were speedily conveyed to the Wharton family. They immediately wrote the United-States Agent among that tribe. After waiting awhile, they all became restless. One day, Uncle George said to his sister,—

"Jenny, I have never forgiven myself for leaving your boys to take care of themselves, that fatal day. I cannot be easy. I must go in search of Willie."

"Heaven bless you!" she replied. "My dear James has just been talking of starting on the same journey. I confess I want some one to go and look for the poor boy; but it seems to me selfish; for it is a long and difficult journey, and may bring fresh misfortunes upon us."

After some friendly altercation between Mr. Wharton and the brother, as to which should go, it was decided that George should have his way; and brave, unselfish Aunt Mary uttered no word of dissuasion. He started on his arduous journey, cheered by hope, and strong in a generous purpose. It seemed long before a letter was received from him, and when it came, its contents were discouraging. The Indian Agent said he had caused diligent search to be made, and he was convinced there was no white child among the tribes in that region. Uncle George persevered in efforts to obtain some clue to the report which had induced him to travel so far. But after several weeks, he was obliged to return alone, and without tidings.

Mrs. Wharton's hopes had been more excited than she was herself aware of, and she vainly tried to rally from the disappointment. This never-ending uncertainty, this hope forever deferred, was harder to endure than would have been the knowledge that her dear son was dead. She thought it would be a relief, even if fragments of his clothes should be found, showing that he had been torn to pieces by wild beasts; for then she would have the consolation of believing that her darling was with the angels. But when she thought of him hopelessly out of reach, among the Indians, imagination conjured up all manner of painful images. Deeper and deeper depression overshadowed her spirits and seriously impaired her health. She was diligent in her domestic duties, careful and tender of every member of her household, but everything wearied her. Languidly she saw the seasons come and go, and took no pleasure in them. A village was growing up round her; but the new-comers, in whom she would once have felt a lively interest, now flitted by her like the shadows in a magic-lantern. "Poor woman!" said the old settlers to the new ones. "She is not what she was. She is heart-broken."

Eight years more passed away, and Mrs. Wharton, always feeble, but never complaining, continued to perform a share of household work, with a pensive resignation which excited tenderness in her family and inspired even strangers with pitying deference. Her heartstrings had not broken, but they gradually withered and dried up, under the blighting influence of this life-long sorrow. It was mild October weather, when she lay down to rise no more. Emma had outgrown the trundle-bed, and no one occupied it; but it remained in the old place. When they led her into the bedroom for the last time, she asked them to draw it out, that she might look upon Willie's pillow once more. Memories of her fair boy sleeping there in the moonlight came into her soul with the vividness of reality. Her eyes filled with tears, and she seemed to be occupied with inward prayer. At a signal from her, the husband and brother lifted her tenderly, and placed her in the bed, which Aunt Mary had prepared. The New Testament was brought, and Mr. Wharton read the fourteenth chapter of John. As they closed the book, she said faintly, "Sing, 'I'm going home.'" It was a Methodist hymn, learned in her youth, and had always been a favorite with her. The two families had often sung it together on Sabbath days, exciting the wonderment of the birds in the stillness of the prairie. They now sang it with peculiar depth of feeling; and as the clear treble of Aunt Mary's voice, and the sweet childlike tones of Emma, followed and hovered over the clear, strong tenor of Uncle George, and the deep bass of Mr. Wharton, the invalid smiled serenely, while her attenuated hand moved to the measure of the music.

She slept much on that and the following day, and seemed unconscious of all around her. On the third day, her watchful husband noticed that her countenance lighted up suddenly, like a landscape when clouds pass from the sun. This was followed by a smile expressive of deep inward joy. He stooped down and whispered,—

"What is it, dear?"

She looked up, with eyes full of interior light, and said,—

"Our Willie!"

She spoke in tones stronger than they had heard from her for several days; and after a slight pause, she added,—

"Don't you see him? Wik-a-nee is with him, and he is weaving a string of the Guinea-peas in her hair. He wears an Indian blanket; but they look happy, there where yellow leaves are falling and the bright waters are sparkling."

"It is a flood of memory," said Mr. Wharton, in a low tone. "She recalls the time when Wik-a-nee was so pleased with the Guinea-peas that Willie gave her."

"She has wakened from a pleasant dream," said Uncle George, with the same subdued voice. "It still remains with her, and the pictures seem real."

The remarks were not intended for her ear, but she heard them, and murmured,—

"No,—not a dream. Don't you *see* them?"

They were the last words she ever uttered. She soon dozed away into apparent oblivion; but twice afterward, that preternatural smile illumined her whole countenance.

At that same hour, hundreds of miles away, on the side of a wooded hill, mirrored in bright waters below, sat a white lad with a brown lassie beside him, among whose black shining tresses he was weaving strings of scarlet seeds. He was clothed with an Indian blanket, and she with a skirt of woven grass. Above them, from a tree glorious with sunshine, fell a golden shower of autumn leaves. They were talking together in some Indian dialect.

"A-lee-lah," said he, "your mother always told me that I gave you these red seeds when I was a little boy. I wonder where I was then. I wish I knew. I never understood half she told me about the long trail. I don't believe I could ever find my way."

"Don't go!" said his companion, pleadingly. "The sun will shine no more on A-lee-lah's path."

He smiled and was silent for a few minutes, while he twined some of the scarlet seeds on grasses round her wrist. He revealed the tenor of his musings by saying,—

"A-lee-lah, I wish I could see my mother. Your mother told me she had blue eyes and pale hair. I don't remember ever seeing a woman with blue eyes and pale hair."

Suddenly he started.

"What is it?" inquired the young girl, springing to her feet.

"My mother!" he exclaimed. "Don't you see her? She is smiling at me. How beautiful her blue eyes are! Ah, now she is gone!" His whole frame quivered with emotion, as he cried out, in an agony of earnestness, "I want to go to my mother! I *must* go to my mother! Who can tell me where to find my mother?"

"You have looked into the Spirit-Land," replied the Indian maiden, solemnly.

Was the mighty power of love, in that dying mother's heart, a spiritual force, conveying her image to the mind of her child, as electricity transmits the telegram? Love photographs very vividly on the memory; when intensely concentrated, may it not perceive scenes and images unknown to the bodily eye, and, like the sunshine, under favorable circumstances, make the pictures visible? Who can answer such questions? Mysterious beyond comprehension are the laws of our complex being. The mother saw her distant son, and the son beheld his long-forgotten mother.

How it was, neither of them knew or thought; but on the soul of each, in their separate spheres of existence, the vision was photographed.[2]

In the desolated dwelling on the prairie, they were all unconscious of this magnetic transmission of intelligence between the dying mother and her far-off child. As she lay in her coffin, they spoke soothingly to each other, that she had passed away without suffering, dreaming pleasantly of Willie and the little Indian girl. Their memories were excited to fresh activity, and the sayings and doings of Willie and the pappoose were recounted for the thousandth time. Emma had no recollection of her lost brother, and the story of his adventure with Moppet always amused her young imagination. But such reminiscences never brought a smile to Charley's face. When he heard the clods fall on his mother's coffin, heavier and more dismally fell on his heart the remembrance of his broken promise, which had so dried up the fountains of her life.

Four times had the flowers bloomed above that mother's grave, and still, for her dear sake, all the memorials of her absent darling remained as she had liked to have them. The trundle-bed was never removed, the Indian basket remained under the glass in the bedroom, where his own little hands had put it, and his chair retained its place at the table. Out of the family he was nearly forgotten; but parents now and then continued to frighten truant boys by telling them of Willie Wharton, who was carried off by Indians and never heard of after.

The landscape had greatly changed since Mr. Wharton and his brother-in-law built their cabins in the wilderness. Those cabins were now sheds and kitchens appended to larger and more commodious dwellings. A village had grown up around them. On the spire of a new meeting-house a gilded fish sailed round from north to south, to the great admiration of children in the opposite schoolhouse. The wild-flowers of the prairie were supplanted by luxuriant fields of wheat and rye, forever undulating in wave-like motion, as if Nature loved the rhythm of the sea, and breathed it to the inland grasses. Neat little Bessie was a married woman now, and presided over the young Squire's establishment, in a large white house with green blinds. Charley had taken to himself a wife, and had a little Willie in the cradle, in whose infant features grandfather fondly traced some likeness to the lost one.

Such was the state of things, when Charles Wharton returned from the village-store, one day, with some articles wrapped in a newspaper from Indiana. A vague feeling of curiosity led him to glance over it, and his attention was at once arrested by the following paragraph:—

"A good deal of interest has been excited here by the appearance of a young man, who supposes himself to be twenty-three years old, evidently white, but with the manners and dress of an Indian. He says he was carried away from his home by Indians, and they have always told him he was then six years old. He speaks no English, and an Indian interpreter who is with him is so scantily supplied with words that the information we have obtained is very unsatisfactory. But we have learned that the young man is trying to find his mother. Some of our neighbors regard him as an impostor. But he does not ask for money, and there is something in his frank physiognomy calculated to inspire confidence. We therefore believe his statement, and publish it, hoping it may be seen by some bereaved family."

Charles rushed into the field, and exclaimed,—

"Father, I do believe we have at last got some tidings of Willie!"

"Where? What is it?" was the quick response.

The offered newspaper was eagerly seized, and the father's hand trembled visibly while he read the paragraph.

"We must start for Indiana directly," he said; and he walked rapidly toward the house, followed by his son.

Arriving at the gate, he paused and said,—

"But, Charles, he will have altered so much that perhaps we shouldn't know him; and it may be, as the people say, that this youth is an impostor."

The young man replied, unhesitatingly,—

"I can tell whether he is an impostor. I shall know my brother."

His voice quivered a little, as he spoke the last word.

Mr. Wharton, without appearing to notice it, said,—

"You have a great deal of work on hand at this season. Wouldn't it be better for Uncle George and me to go?"

He answered impetuously,—

"If all my property goes to ruin, I will hunt for Willie all over the earth, so long as there is any hope of finding him. I always felt as if mother couldn't forgive me for leaving him that day, though she always tried to

make me think she did. And now, if we find him at last, she is not here
to"——

His voice became choked.

Mr. Wharton replied, impressively,——

"She will come with him, my son. Wherever he may be, they are not
divided now."

The next morning Charles started on his expedition, having made
preparations for an absence of some months, if so long a time should prove
necessary. The first letters received from him were tantalizing. The young
man and his interpreter had gone to Michigan, in consequence of hearing
of a family there who had lost a little son many years ago. But those who
had seen him in Indiana described him as having brown eyes and hair, and
as saying that his mother's eyes were the color of the sky. Charles hastened
to Michigan. The wanderer had been there, but had left, because the family
he sought were convinced he was not their son. They said he had gone to
Canada, with the intention of rejoining the tribe of Indians he had left.

We will not follow the persevering brother through all his travels.
Again and again he came close upon the track, and had the disappointment
of arriving a little too late. On a chilly day of advanced autumn, he
mounted a pony and rode toward a Canadian forest, where he was told
some Indians had encamped. He tied his pony at the entrance of the wood,
and followed a path through the underbrush. He had walked about a
quarter of a mile, when his ears were pierced by a shrill, discordant yell,
which sounded neither animal nor human. He stopped abruptly, and
listened. All was still, save a slight creaking of boughs in the wind. He
pressed forward in the direction whence the sound had come, not altogether free from anxiety, though habitually courageous. He soon came in
sight of a cluster of wigwams, outside of which, leaning against trees, or
seated on the fallen leaves, were a number of men, women, and children,
dressed in all sorts of mats and blankets, some with tufts of feathers in their
hair, others with bands and tassels of gaudy-colored wampum. One or two
had a regal air, and might have stood for pictures of Arab chiefs or
Carthaginian generals; but most of them looked squalid and dejected.
None of them manifested any surprise at the entrance of the stranger. All
were as grave as owls. They had, in fact, seen him coming through the

woods, and had raised their ugly war-whoop, in sport, to see whether it would frighten him. It was their solemn way of enjoying fun. Among them was a youth, tanned by exposure to wind and sun, but obviously of white complexion. His hair was shaggy, and cut straight across his forehead, as Moppet's had been. Charles fixed upon him a gaze so intense that he involuntarily took up a hatchet that lay beside him, as if he thought it might be necessary to defend himself from the intruder.

"Can any of you speak English?" inquired Charles.

"Me speak," replied an elderly man.

Charles explained that he wanted to find a white young man who had been in Indiana and Michigan searching for his mother.

"*Him* pale-face," rejoined the interpreter, pointing to the youth, whose brown eyes glanced from one to the other with a perplexed expression.

Charles made a strong effort to restrain his impatience, while the interpreter slowly explained his errand. The pale-faced youth came toward him.

"Let me examine your right arm," said Charles.

The beaver-skin mantle was raised; and there, in a dotted outline of blue spots, was the likeness of the prairie-dog which in boyish play he had pricked into Willie's arm. With a joyful cry he fell upon his neck, exclaiming, "My brother!" The interpreter repeated the word in the Indian tongue. The youthful stranger uttered no sound; but Charles felt his heart throb, as they stood locked in a close embrace. When their arms unclasped, they looked earnestly into each other's faces. That sad memory of the promise made to their gentle mother, and so thoughtlessly broken, brought tears to the eyes of the elder brother; but the younger stood apparently unmoved. The interpreter, observing this, said,—

"Him sorry-glad; but red man he no cry."

There was much to damp the pleasure of this strange interview. The uncouth costume, and the shaggy hair falling over the forehead, gave Willie such a wild appearance, it was hard for Charles to realize that they were brothers. Inability to understand each other's language created a chilling barrier between them. Charles was in haste to change his brother's dress, and acquire a stock of Indian words. The interpreter was bound farther north; but he agreed to go with them three days' journey, and teach them on the way. They were merely guests at the encampment, and no one claimed a right to control their motions. Charles distributed beads among the women and pipes among the men; and two hours after he had entered the wood, he was again mounted on his pony, with William and the interpreter walking beside him. As he watched his brother's erect figure striding along, with such a bold, free step, he admitted to himself that there were some important compensations for the deficiencies of Indian education.

Languages are learned rapidly, when the heart is a pupil. Before they parted from the interpreter, the brothers were able, by the aid of pantomime, to interchange various skeletons of ideas, which imagination helped to clothe with bodies. At the first post-town, a letter was despatched to their father, containing these words: "I have found him. He is well, and we are coming home. Dear Lucy must teach baby Willie to crow and clap his hands. God bless you all! Charley."

They pressed forward as fast as possible, and at the last stage of their journey travelled all night; for Charles had a special reason for wishing to arrive at the homestead on the following day. The brothers were now dressed alike, and a family-likeness between them was obvious. Willie's shaggy hair had been cut, and the curtain of dark brown locks being turned aside revealed a well-shaped forehead whiter than his cheeks. He had lost something of the freedom of his motions; for the new garments sat uneasily upon him, and he wore them with an air of constraint.

The warm golden light of the sun had changed to silvery brightness, and the air was cool and bracing, when they rode over the prairie so familiar to the eye of Charles, but which had lost nearly all the features that had been impressed on the boyish mind of William. At a little distance from the village they left their horses and walked across the fields to the back-door of their father's house; for they were not expected so soon, and Charles wished to take the family by surprise. It was Thanksgiving day. Wild turkeys were prepared for roasting, and the kitchen was redolent of pies and plum-pudding. When they entered, no one was there but an old woman hired to help on festive occasions. She uttered a little cry when she saw them; but Charles put his finger to his lip, and hurried on to the family sitting-room. All were there,—Father, Emma, Uncle George, Aunt Mary, Bessie and her young Squire, Charles's wife, baby, and all. There was a universal rush, and one simultaneous shout of, "Willie! Willie!" Charles's young wife threw herself into his arms; but all the rest clustered round the young stranger, as the happy father clasped him to his bosom. When the tumult of emotion had subsided a little, Charles introduced each one separately to his brother, explaining their relationship as well as he could in the Indian dialect. Their words were unintelligible to the wanderer, but he understood their warmth of welcome, and said,—

"Me tank. Me no much speak."

Mr. Wharton went into the bedroom and returned with a morocco case, which he opened and placed in the stranger's hand, saying, in a solemn tone,—

"Your mother."

Charles, with a tremor in his voice, repeated the word in the Indian tongue. Willie gazed at the blue eyes of the miniature, touched them, pointed to the sky, and said,—

"Me see she, time ago."

All supposed that he meant the memories of his childhood. But he in fact referred to the vision he had seen four years before, as he explained to them afterward, when he had better command of their language.

The whole family wept as the miniature passed from hand to hand, and, with a sudden outburst of grief, Charles exclaimed,—

"Oh, if *she* were only here with us this happy day!"

"My son , she *is* with us," said his father, impressively.

William was the only one who seemed unmoved. He did not remember his mother, except as he had seen her in that moment of clairvoyance; and it had been part of his Indian training to suppress emotion. But he put his hand on his heart, and said,—

"Me no much speak."

When the little red-and-yellow basket was brought forward, it awakened no recollections in his mind. They pointed to it, and said, "Wik-a-nee, Moppet"; but he made no response.

His father eyed him attentively, and said,—

"It surely *must* be our Willie. I see the resemblance to myself. We cannot be mistaken."

"I *know* he is our Willie," said Charles; and removing his brother's coat, he showed what was intended to be the likeness of a prairie-dog. His father and Uncle George remembered it well; and it was a subject of regret that William could not be made to understand any jokes about his boyish state of mind on that subject. Mr. Wharton pointed to the chair he used to occupy, and said,—

"It seems hardly possible that this tall stranger can be the little Willie who used to sit there. But it *is* our Willie. God be praised!" He paused a moment, and added, "Before we partake of our Thanksgiving dinner, let us all unite in thanks to our Heavenly Father; 'for this my son was dead and is alive again, he was lost and is found.'"[3]

They all rose, and he offered a prayer, to which heart-felt emotion imparted eloquence.

Charles had taken every precaution to have his brother appear as little as possible like a savage, when he restored him to his family; and now, without mentioning that he would like raw meat better than all their dainties, he went to the kitchen to superintend the cooking of some Indian succotash, and buffalo-steak *very* slightly broiled.

For some time, the imperfect means of communicating by speech was a great impediment to confidential intercourse, and a drawback upon their happiness. Emma, whose imagination had been a good deal excited by the prospect of a new brother, was a little disappointed. In her own private mind, she thought she should prefer for a brother a certain Oberlin student, with whom she had danced the last Thanksgiving evening. Bessie, always a stickler for propriety, ventured to say to her mother that she hoped he would learn to use his knife and fork, like other people. But to older members of the family, who distinctly remembered Willie in his boyhood, these things seemed unimportant. It was enough for them that the lost treasure was found.

The obstacle created by difference of language disappeared with a rapidity that might have seemed miraculous, were it not a well-known fact that one's native tongue forgotten is always easily restored. It seems to remain latent in the memory, and can be brought out by favorable circumstances, as writing with invisible ink reappears under the influence of warmth. Tidings of the young man's restoration to his family spread like fire on the prairie. People for twenty miles round came to see the Willie Wharton of whose story they had heard so much. Children were disappointed to find that he was not a little rosy-cheeked boy, such as had been described to them. Some elderly people, who prided themselves on their sagacity, shook their heads when they observed his rapid improvement in English, and said to each other,—

"It a'n't worth while to disturb neighbor Wharton's confidence; but depend upon it, that fellow's an impostor. As for the mark on his arm that they call a prairie-dog, it looks as much like anything else that has legs."

To the family, however, every week brought some additional confirmation that the stranger was their own Willie. By degrees, he was able to make them understand the outlines of his story. He did not remember anything about parting from his brother on that disastrous day, and of course could not explain what had induced him to turn aside to the Indian trail. He said the Indians had always told him that a squaw, whose pappoose had died, took a fancy to him, and decoyed him away; and that afterward, when he cried to go back, they would not let him go. From them he also learned that he called himself six years old, at the time of his capture; but his name had been gradually forgotten, both by himself and them. He wandered about with that tribe eight summers and winters. Sometimes, when they had but little food, he suffered with hunger; and once he was wounded by a tomahawk, when they had a fight with some hostile tribe; but they treated him as well as they did their own children. He became an expert hunter, thought it excellent sport, and forgot that he was not an Indian. His squaw-mother died, and, not long after, the tribe went a great many miles to collect furs. In the course of this journey they encountered various tribes of Indians. One night they encamped near some hunters who spoke another dialect, which they could partly understand. Among them was a woman, who said she knew him. She told him his mother was a white woman, with eyes blue as the sky, and that she was very good to her little pappoose, when she lost her way on the prairie. She wanted her husband to buy him, that they might carry him back to his mother. He bought him for ten gallons of whiskey, and promised to take him to his parents the next time the tribe travelled in that direction,— because, he said, their little pappoose had liked them very much.

"We remember her very well," said Mr. Wharton. "Her name was Wik-a-nee."

"'That not *name*," replied William. "Wik-a-nee mean little small thing."

"You were a small boy when you found the pappoose on the prairie," rejoined his father. "You took a great liking to her, and said she was *your* little girl. When she went away, you gave her your box of Guinea-peas."

"Guinea-peas? What that?" inquired the young man.

"They are red seeds with black spots on them," replied his father. "Emma, I believe you have some. Show him one."

The moment he saw it, he exclaimed,—

"Haha! A-lee-lah show me Guinea-peas. Her say me give she."

"Then you know Wik-a-nee?" said his father, in an inquiring tone.

The wanderer had acquired the gravity of the Indians. He never laughed, and rarely smiled. But a broad smile lighted up his frank countenance, as he answered,—

"Me know A-lee-lah very well. She not Wik-a-nee now."

Then he became grave again, and told how he was twining the red seeds in A-lee-lah's hair, when his mother came and looked at him with great blue eyes and smiled. Most of his auditors thought he was telling a dream. But Mr. Wharton said to his oldest son,—

"I told you, Charles, that mother and son were not separated now."

William seemed perplexed by this remark; but he comprehended in part, and said,—

"Me see into Spirit-Land."

When asked why he had not started in search of his mother then, he replied,—

"A-lee-lah's father, mother die. A-lee-lah say not go. Miles big many. Me not know the trail. But Indians go hunt fur. Me go. Me sleep. Me dream mother come, say go home. Me ask where mother? Charles come. Him say brother."

The little basket was again brought forth, and Mr. Wharton said,—

"Wik-a-nee gave you this, when she went away; but when we showed it to you, you did not remember it."

He took it and looked at it, and said,—

"Me not remember"; but when Emma would have put it away, he held it fast; and that night he carried it with him to his chamber.

Some degree of restlessness had been observed in him previously to this conversation. It increased as the weeks passed on. He became moody, and liked to wander off alone, far from the settlement. The neighbors said to each other,—"He will never be contented. He will go back to the Indians." The family feared it also. But Uncle George, who was always prone to look on the bright side of things, said,—

"We shall win him, if we manage right. We mustn't try to constrain him. The greatest mistake we make in our human relations is interfering too much with each other's freedom. We are too apt to think *our* way is the *only* way. It's no such very great matter, after all, that William sometimes uses his fingers instead of a knife and fork, and likes to squat on the floor better than to sit in a chair. We mustn't drive him away by taking too much notice of such things. Let him do just as he likes. We are all creatures of circumstances. If you and I were obliged to dance in tight boots, and make calls in white kid gloves, we should feel like fettered fools."

"And *be* what we felt like," replied Mr. Wharton; "and the worst part of it would be, we shouldn't long have sense enough to *feel* like fools, but should fall to pitying and despising people who were of any use in the world. But really, brother George, to have a son educated by Indians is not exactly what one could wish."

"Undoubtedly not, in many respects; but it has its advantages. William has already taught me much about the habits of animals and the qualities of plants. Did you ever see an eye so sure as his to measure distances, or to send an arrow to the mark? He never studied astronomy, but he knows how to make use of the stars better than we do. Last week, when we got benighted in the woods, he at once took his natural place as our leader; and how quickly his sagacity brought us out of our trouble! He will learn enough of our ways, by degrees. But I declare I would rather have him always remain as he is than to make a city-fop of him. I once saw an old beau at Saratoga,—a forlorn-looking mortal, creeping about in stays and tight boots; and I thought I should rather be the wildest Ojibbeway that ever hunted buffaloes in a ragged blanket."

The rational policy recommended by Uncle George was carefully pursued. Everything was done to attract William to their mode of life, but no remark was made when he gave a preference to Indian customs. Still, he seemed moody, and at times sad. He carried within him a divided heart. One day, when he was sitting on a log, looking absent and dejected, his father put his hand gently upon his shoulder, and said,—

"Are you not happy among us, my son? Don't you like us?"

"Me like very much," was the reply. "Me glad find father, brother. All good."

He paused a moment, and then added,—

"A-lee-lah's father, mother be dead. A-lee-lah alone. A-lee-lah did say not go. Me promise come back soon."

Mr. Wharton was silent. He was thinking what it was best to say. After waiting a little, William said,—

"Father, me not remember what is English for squaw."

"Woman," replied Mr. Wharton.

"Not that," rejoined the young man. "What call Charles's squaw?"

"His wife," was the reply.

"Father, A-lee-lah be my wife. Me like bring A-lee-lah. Me fraid father not like Indian."

Mr. Wharton placed his hand affectionately on his child's head, and said,—

"Bring A-lee-lah, in welcome, my son. Your mother loved her, when she was Wik-a-nee; and we will all love her now. Only be sure and come back to us."

The brown eyes looked up and thanked him, with a glance that well repaid the struggle those words had cost the wise father.

So the uncivilized youth again went forth into the wilderness, saying, as he parted from them, "Me bring A-lee-lah." They sent her a necklace and bracelets of many-colored beads, and bade him tell her that they remembered Wik-a-nee, and had always kept her little basket, and that they would love her when she came among them. Charles travelled some distance with his brother, bought a new Indian blanket for him, and returned with the garments he had worn during his sojourn at home. They felt that they had acted wisely and kindly, but it was like losing Willie again; for they all had great doubts whether he would ever return.

He was incapable of writing a letter, and months passed without any tidings of him. They all began to think that the attractions of a wild life had been strong enough to conquer his newly awakened natural affections. Uncle George said,—

"If it prove so, we shall have the consciousness of having done right.

We could not have kept him against his will, even if we had wished to do it. If anything will win him to our side, it will be the influence of love and freedom."

"They are strong agencies, and I have great faith in them," replied Mr. Wharton.

Summer was far advanced, when a young man and woman in Indian costume were seen passing through the village, and people said, "There is William Wharton come back again!" They entered the father's house like strange apparitions. Baby Willie was afraid of them, and toddled behind his mother, to hide his face in the folds of her gown. All the other members of the family had talked over the subject frequently, and had agreed how they would treat Wik-a-nee, if she came among them again. So they kissed them both, as they stood there in their Indian blankets, and said, "Welcome home, brother! Welcome, sister!" A-lee-lah looked at them timidly, with her large moonlight eyes, and said, "Me no speak." Mr. Wharton put his hand gently on her head, and said, "We will love you, my daughter." William translated the phrase to her, heaved a sigh, which seemed a safety-valve for too much happiness, and replied, "Me thank father, brother, sister, all." And A-lee-lah said, "Me tank," as her mother had said, in years long gone by.

All felt desirous to remove from her eyebrows the mass of straight black hair, which she considered extremely becoming, but which they regarded as a great disfigurement to her really handsome face. However, no one expressed such an opinion, by word or look. They had previously agreed not to manifest any distaste for Indian fashions.

Mr. Wharton, apart, remarked to Charles,—

"When you were a boy, you said Moppet would be pretty, if she wore her hair like folks. It was true then, and is still more true now."

"Let us have patience, and we shall see her handsome face come out of that cloud by-and-by," rejoined Uncle George. "If we prove that we love her, we shall gain influence over her. Wild-flowers, as well as garden-flowers, grow best in the sunshine."

Emma tried to conform to the wishes of the family in her behavior; but she did not feel quite sure that she should ever be able to love the young Indian. It was not agreeable to have a sister who was clothed in a blanket and wore her hair like a Shetland pony. Cousin Bessie thought

stockings, long skirts, and a gown ought to be procured for her immediately. Her father said,—

"Let me tell you, Bessie, it would be far more rational for you to
follow *her* fashion about short skirts. I should like to see *you* step off as she
does. She couldn't move so like a young deer, if she had long petticoats to
trammel her limbs."[4]

But Bessie confidentially remarked to Cousin Emma that she thought
her father had some queer notions; to which Emma replied, that, for her
part, she thought A-lee-lah ought to dress "like folks," as Charley used to
say, when he was a boy. They could not rest till they had made a dress like
their own, and had coaxed William to persuade her to wear it. In a tone of
patient resignation, she at last said, "Me try." But she was evidently very
uncomfortable in her new habiliments. She often wriggled her shoulders,
and her limbs were always getting entangled in the folds of her long, full
skirts. She finally rebelled openly, and, with an emphatic "Me no like," cast
aside the troublesome garments and resumed her blanket.

"I suppose she felt very much as I should feel in tight boots and white
kid gloves," said Uncle George. "You will drive them away from us, if you
interfere with them so much."

It was agreed that Aunt Mary would understand how to manage
them better than the young folks did; and the uncivilized couple were
accordingly invited to stay at their uncle's house. Emma cordially approved
of this arrangement. She told Bessie that she did hope Aunt Mary would
make them more "like folks," before the Oberlin student visited the
neighborhood again; for she didn't know what he *would* think of some of
their ways. Bessie said,—

"I feel as if I ought to invite William and his wife to dine with us; but
if any of my husband's family should come in, I should feel *so* mortified to
have them see a woman with a blanket over her shoulders sitting at my
table! Besides, they like raw meat, and that is dreadful."

"Certainly it is not pleasant," replied her father; "but I once dined in
Boston, at a house of high civilization, where the odor of venison and of
Stilton cheese produced much more internal disturbance than I have ever
experienced from any of their Indian messes."

This philosophical way of viewing the subject was thought by some
of the neighbors to be assumed, as the best mode of concealing wounded

pride. They said, in compassionate tones, that they really did pity the Whartons; for, let them say what they would, it must be dreadfully mortifying to have that squaw about. But if such a feeling was ever remotely hinted to Uncle George, he quietly replied,—

"So far from feeling ashamed of A-lee-lah, we are truly grateful to her; and we are deeply thankful that William married her. His love for her safely bridges over the wide chasm between his savage and his civilized life. Without her, he could not feel at home among us; and the probability is that we should not be able to keep him. By help of his Indian wife, I think we shall make him contented, and finally succeed in winning them over to our mode of life. Meanwhile, they are happy in their own way, and we are thankful for it."

The more enlightened portion of the community commended these sentiments as liberal and wise; but some, who were not distinguished either for moral or intellectual culture, said, sneeringly,—

"They talk about his Indian wife! I suppose they jumped over a stick together in some dirty wigwam, and that they call being married!"

Uncle George and Aunt Mary had been so long in the habit of regulating their actions by their own principles, that they scarcely had a passing curiosity to know what such neighbors thought of their proceedings. They never wavered in their faith that persevering kindness and judicious non-interference would gradually produce such transformations as they desired. No changes were proposed, till they and their untutored guests had become familiarly acquainted and mutually attached. At first, the wild young couple were indisposed to stay much in the house. They wandered far off into the woods, and spent most of their time in making mats and baskets. As these were always admired by their civilized relatives, and gratefully accepted, they were happier than millionaires. They talked to each other altogether in the Indian dialect, which greatly retarded their improvement in English. But it was thus they had talked when they first made love, and it was, moreover, the only way in which their tongues could move unfettered. Her language no longer sounded to William like "lingo," as he had styled it in the boyish days when he found her wandering alone on the prairie. No utterance of the human soul, whether in the form of language or belief, is "lingo," when we stand on the same spiritual plane with the speaker, and thus can rightly understand it.

The first innovation in the habits of the young Indian was brought about by the magical power of two side-combs ornamented with colored glass. At the first sight of them, A-lee-lah manifested admiration almost equal to that which the scarlet peas had excited in her childish mind. Aunt Mary, perceiving this, parted the curtain of raven hair, and fastened it on each side with the gaudy combs. Then she led her to the glass, put her finger on the uncovered brow, and said,—

"A-lee-lah has a pretty forehead. Aunt Mary likes to see it so."

William translated this to his simple wife, who said,—

"Aunt Mary good. Me tank."

Mr. Wharton happened to come in, and he kissed the brown forehead, saying,—

"Father likes to have A-lee-lah wear her hair so."

The conquest was complete. Henceforth, the large, lambent eyes shone in their moonlight beauty without any overhanging cloud.

Thus adroitly, day by day, they were guided into increasing conformity with civilized habits. After a while, it was proposed that they should be married according to the Christian form, as they had previously been by Indian ceremonies. No attempt was made to offer higher inducements than the exhibition of wedding-finery, and the assurance that all William's relatives would be made very happy, if they would conform to the custom of his people. The bride's dress was a becoming hybrid between English and Indian costumes. Loose trousers of emerald-green merino were fastened with scarlet cord and tassels above gaiters of yellow beaver-skin thickly embroidered with beads of many colors. An upper garment of scarlet merino was ornamented with gilded buttons, on each of which was a shining star. The short, full skirt of this garment fell a little below the knee, and the border was embroidered with gold-colored braid. At the waist, it was fastened with a green morocco belt and gilded buckle. The front-hair, now accustomed to be parted, had grown long enough to be becomingly arranged with the jewelled side-combs, which she prized so highly. The long, glossy, black tresses behind were gathered into massive braids, intertwined on one side with narrow scarlet ribbon, and on the other with festoons of the identical Guinea-peas which had so delighted her when she was Wik-a-nee. The braids were fastened by a comb with gilded points, which made her look like a crowned Indian queen. Emma was decidedly struck by her picturesque appearance. She said privately to Cousin Bessie,—

"I should like such a dress myself, if other folks wore it; but don't you tell that I said so."

Charles smiled, as he remarked to his wife,—

"The grub has come out of her blanket a brilliant butterfly. Uncle George and Aunt Mary are working miracles."

After the wedding-ceremony had been performed, Mr. Wharton kissed the bride, and said to the bridegroom,—

"She is handsome as a wild tulip."

"Bright as the torch-flower of the prairies," added Uncle George.

When William made these compliments intelligible to A-lee-lah, she maintained her customary Indian composure of manner, but her brown cheeks glowed like an amber-colored bottle of claret in the sunshine. William, though he deemed it unmanly to give any outward signs of satisfaction, was inwardly proud of his bride's finery, and scarcely less pleased with his own yellow vest, blue coat, and brass buttons; though he preferred above them all the yellow gaiters, which A-lee-lah had skilfully decorated with tassels and bright-colored wampum.

The next politic movement was to build for them a cabin of their own, taking care to preserve an influence over them by frequent visits and kind attentions. They would have been very happy in the freedom of their new home, had it not been for the intrusion of many strangers, who came to look upon them from motives of curiosity. The universal Yankee nation is a self-elected Investigating Committee, which never adjourns its sessions. This is amusing, and perhaps edifying, to their own inquiring minds; but William and A-lee-lah had Indian ideas of natural politeness, which made them regard such invasions as a breach of good manners.

By degrees, however, the young couple became an old story, and were left in comparative peace. The system of attraction continued to work like a charm. As A-lee-lah was never annoyed by any assumption of superiority on the part of her white relatives, she took more and more pains to please them. This was manifested in many childlike ways, which were extremely winning, though they were sometimes well calculated to excite a smile. As years passed on, they both learned to read and write English very well. William worked industriously on his farm, though he never lost his predilection for hunting. A-lee-lah became almost as skilful at her needle as she was at weaving baskets and wampum. Her talk, with its slightly foreign arrangement, was as pretty as the unformed utterance of a little child. Her taste for music improved. She never attained to Italian embroidery of sound, still less to German intonations of intellect; but the rude, monotonous Indian chants gave place to the melodies of Scotland, Ireland, and Ethiopia. Her taste in dress changed also. She ceased to delight in garments of scarlet and yellow, though she retained a liking for bits of bright, warm color. Nature guided her taste correctly in this, for they harmonized admirably with her brown complexion and lustrous black hair. She always wore skirts shorter than others, and garments too loose to impede freedom of motion. Bonnets were her utter aversion, but she consented to wear a woman's riding-hat with a drooping feather. Those outide the family learned to call her Mrs. William Wharton; and strangers who visited the village were generally attracted by her handsome person and the simple dignity of her manners. Her father-in-law regarded her with paternal affection, not unmixed with pride.

"Who, that didn't know it," said he, "could be made to believe this fine-looking woman was once little Moppet, who coiled herself up to sleep on the floor of our log-cabin?"

Uncle George replied,—

"You know I always told you it was the nature of all sorts of flowers to grow, if they had plenty of genial air and sunshine."

As for A-lee-lah's little daughter, Jenny, she is universally admitted to be the prettiest and brightest child in the village. Mr. Wharton says her busy little mind makes him think of his Willie, at her age; and Uncle Charles says he has no fault to find with her, for she has her mother's beautiful eyes, and wears her hair "like folks."

The lead article in the May 1870 inaugural issue of *The Standard*, the ephemeral successor of the *National Anti-Slavery Standard*, "The Indians" condemns a massacre perpetrated against the Piegan Blackfeet Indians of Montana in January 1870. This attack by U.S. troops on the tribe's winter camp claimed the lives of 173 Piegans, "all but 15 [of whom] were women, children, and old men," and at least 50 of whom were "children under twelve years of age," "many of them in their mother's arms." Besides being vulnerable in the absence of their warriors, the Piegans were already decimated by a smallpox epidemic.

News of the massacre did not leak out until March. When it did, the Army justified the incident as a reprisal to punish the Piegans for their (falsely) alleged role in a bloody raid the previous summer led by Cheyenne Indians belonging to the band of Chief Black Kettle. In a widely quoted statement to which Child refers, former Civil War General Philip Sheridan, now commanding U.S. troops against the Plains Indians, accused Black Kettle's band of having "murdered, without mercy, men, women, and children; in all cases ravishing the women—sometimes as often as forty and fifty times in succession." Child's surmise that the Cheyennes may have been avenging "similar outrages on Indian women" is borne out by descriptions of the 1864 Sand Creek massacre in Colorado, to which she also refers. There U.S. soldiers had "mutilated the living and the dead, cut off and displayed as trophies the sexual organs of [Cheyenne] Indian men, women, and children," and ripped fetuses out of pregnant women, according to eyewitness testimony cited by historians Richard Slotkin and Dee Brown.

Blunting Child's protest against U.S. Army policies and the atrocities they license, however, is her recognition of Anglo-American settlers' right to occupy land traditionally held by Indian tribes and to claim protection of "life or property." The only long-term solution she can envisage to Indian-white conflict remains the assimilation of Indians into the U.S. body politic. In calling for the elimination of "independent tribes," Child has adopted a key recommendation of the Peace Commission, which she had criticized in her *Appeal for the Indians*. The analogy she sees between Indian tribes and Scottish clans inevitably leads her to equate all manifestations of tribalism, clannishness, and ethnic separatism with the barriers of race, caste, class, gender, and religion that she has spent a lifetime trying to dismantle. Yet Child also applies her abolitionist ideology to the Indian question in a more positive way when she advocates extending to Indians the citizenship and suffrage rights that had just been conferred on African-Americans.

The U.S. government would in fact cease acknowledging Indian tribes as independent nations in March 1871, but not until 1924 would an act making all Indians U.S. citizens be signed into law.

IF I SHOULD EVER enter a pulpit to preach, I would take for my text, "When the Son of Man cometh, shall he find *faith* on the earth?" Whenever trying emergencies occur in human affairs, we find men prone to shuffle off responsibility by compromise, or to transfer it to posterity by resorting to temporary expedients, admitted to be wrong in themselves, but advocated as the necessity of the moment. Whenever a new occasion for the application of old truths arrives, men in this way betray their total want of faith in eternal principles of right and wrong; which is, in reality, a distrust of God's government of the world by universal and invariable laws. In whatever form Truth makes its advent, it meets this want of faith on the earth.

One would think we might have learned by this time that there is the same ground-work of human nature in all varieties of the human race, and that the same influences which tend to develop what is good or evil in one class of men will have a similar effect on another class; that being dealt with justly and humanely tends to make men just and humane; that having truth and honesty practiced toward them, inspires men with respect for truth and honesty; that deriving profit from labor makes men industrious; and that having sure protection for life and property renders them peaceable. Yet men thought that the whip was more efficient than wages to get work out of the black man; and now the approved method of teaching red men not to commit murder is to slaughter their wives and children! General

Sheridan' officially reports that the troops under his command killed "ninety women and fifty children; none of the children twelve years old, and many of them in their mothers' arms." From other sources we learn that most of these little ones were sick with small-pox. Yet he seems to expect great credit because his soldiers spared "eighteen women and nineteen children; none of the children under three years old; some of whom were wounded."

Shame on General Sheridan! Everlasting shame! If I were to pass him in the street, I would avoid even the touch of his shadow. Some of the Indians had committed horrid atrocities, and the safety of frontier settlements required that they should be punished; but indiscriminate slaughter of helpless women and innocent babies is not war—it is butchery; it is murder. The rebels practiced cruelties on our soldiers unsurpassed by the worst babarities of the Indians. Would General Sheridan have slaughtered *their* women and babies? Would he have adopted such a mode of warfare with *any* white people upon earth, under *any* amount of provocation? Shame on General Sheridan for perpetrating such outrages on a people because they were poor, and weak, and despised! Shame on General Sherman' for sanctioning it! They have tarnished their laurels and disgraced the epaulets they wear. It behooves the American people, if they have any respect for the laws of humanity, or any regard for the reputation of their country, to proclaim aloud that such reckless butchery is not according to their ideas of civilized warfare. The annals of our country have received an indelible stain by this transaction, like the ineffaceable blot on English history occasioned by the wholesale slaughter of Highlanders at Glencoe;' including aged men and little boys, and the turning out of women to perish with hunger and cold. That onslaught, of infamous memory, occurred nearly two hundred years ago, and it is to be hoped that England could not now muster a sufficient number of Governors of Jamaica' and Captains of the Bombay to undertake another such a murderous job. If she can, let *us*, at least, not enter into competition with her for such black and bloody pages of history. I did think we had advanced considerably in civilization; but lo! here, in the last half of the nineteenth century, our model military heroes are found shooting defenseless women and sick babies! And a still more discouraging symptom is that the press is not roused by universal indignation. The Boston *Journal* quotes without comment General Sully's[5] remark that he "hopes the Piegan massacre will teach the Indians some respect for the government." An admirable method, assuredly, for teaching respect for government! Such a remark is indeed a *Sully*.

Do not suppose for a moment that I have no feeling for the white settlers of the frontier. They are in a horrible situation, surrounded by savages, whom we have exasperated by generations of wrong, and degraded by many years of whisky-guzzling. They *must* be protected! But let Justice be blind to color, and hold her scales with an even hand. Let an Indian who murders a white be punished in the same way that a white is punished who murders an Indian; and let both have the same fair chance for lawful trial. If their depredations and outrages make military interference necessary, let war be carried on as it is with white people who commit outrages on life or property. It is more than can be expected of human nature that the white frontier settlers, living as they do in the midst of deadly peril, should think dispassionately of the Indians, or treat them fairly. It is not in the nature of things, that they should coolly reflect upon the antecedent causes which have made the Indian what he is, or upon the present influences which inevitably keep him what he is. If a white settler finds his family murdered by an Indian, he does not ask himself, "Was this man's family murdered by a white man? and if so, is it not natural that the same revengeful feelings should be excited in *his* bosom which are now excited in *mine*?" He asks himself no such questions. He is filled with hatred to the Indians, and he shoots the first Indian he sees, without knowing whether he is at all implicated in the murder or not. Indeed, the shooting of Indians is habitual sport with white adventurers in that region. When General Fremont[6] and his companions were exploring California, their own record shows that when they spied an Indian it was their habit to aim a rifle at him, the same as they would at a wild beast. Perhaps the stranger thus ruthlessly shot had never done any injury to the whites; no matter—he had a red skin, and that was sufficient justification. This is the legitimate result of Anglo-Saxon arrogance, which brands all the rest of the human family as "inferior races," and treats them as if they had no rights which high civilization is bound to respect.

It is said, over and over again, that the Indians are devils. If they are, it is no wonder; for the course we have pursued toward them has been well adapted to make them so. Years ago, I was at an Anti-Slavery meeting in Boston when somebody repeated the threadbare assertion that the negro slaves were "a lazy set of liars and thieves." "And if they are," retorted George Thompson,[7] "whose fault is it? You push people into hell, and then complain that they smell of brimstone." It was a bold metaphor, not suited to ears polite; but I quote it because it exactly describes our relations with the Indians. The tribes, as we found them in this country, had many noble traits mixed with their savageness. They never broke their word or violated a treaty; they never ceased to be grateful for any kindness they had received; and they never treated female prisoners with indecency. They were terribly revengeful; but that trait of human nature has been conspicuous always and everywhere among uncivilized or half-civilized people. It is the natural indication of the undeveloped growth of society. The Highland clans that were at feud pursued each other with unrelenting fury, from generation to generation; but they are a peaceable, law-abiding people now. In Corsica, families that were at enmity were universally branded with infamy if they failed to kill each other's descendants, down to the remotest generations; but this horrible custom, called The Vendetta, has nearly disappeared. The North-American Indians, being divided into numerous tribes, constantly at war with each other, were systematically trained to be ferocious, cruel, and revengeful, because they supposed it to be a necessity of their situation; and it is much to be regretted that our mode of warfare with them has not been calculated to imbue them with better ideas. From the earliest times to the present day, we have never observed the same rules of warfare with them that we do with civilized people. There might be some plausible pretext for imitating their savage ways in the early settlement of the country, when they were numerous and powerful, and white settlers were few and weak; but no such excuse is admissible now that we are million-handed, and they are a poor miserable remnant. The New-York *Evening Post* says of Sheridan's massacre, "There is nothing like it in the annals of our country." For the honor of the United States, I wish it were so; but unfortunately it is not. When General Harney[8] attacked the Sioux Indians, at Ash Hollow, women and children were massacred. General Harney says it was done by one of his subordinates, unauthorized; but I find no record that the unauthorized subordinate was punished, as he would have been if he had tried such an experiment on any civilized people. When the Cheyenne village of Indians was sacked and burned by soldiers in Colorado, Major Wynkoop⁹ ordered the remnant of the Indians to move near to the United States fort, promising them military protection; and about five hundred of those hunted wretches encamped near the fort. A new commander soon came, who renewed the promise that they should be protected. But the Third Colorado Regiment dashed down upon them at daylight, and slaughtered them indiscriminately. Women praying piteously for mercy were shot, and babies were stabbed and scalped. In view of such facts, can we deny that we have stimulated the Indians to barbarity?

General Sheridan states that Black Kettle¹⁰ and his band always ravished their female prisoners; but he does not inform us whether it was done in reprisal for similar outrages on Indian women. It certainly is a new feature in the history of the red men. The early settlers of New-England were disposed to paint Indians in very black colors; but they testified that, while they were infernally cruel to captured women, they invariably treated them with decency. This was, in fact, a natural result of their stoical training, which taught them to be ashamed of being mastered by the senses. On this subject, also, I am sorry to believe that the influence of white men has been the worst possible. Father Beeson¹¹ told me that white traders and soldiers violated the wives and daughters of Indians with entire impunity. Husbands and fathers could obtain no redress at law, if they sought it; and if they attempted to resist, troops were called, and a massacre followed. Father Beeson testified not merely what he had heard, but what he positively knew, as a resident in the region where such outrages were perpetually occurring. Of course, such *must* be the state of things wherever one class in the community looks down upon another as an inferior race. We all know what protection negro women received at the hands of their masters and drivers. What reason Indians have for trusting to our laws for redress of their wrongs may be inferred from General Sully's own statement. He says "a harmless old man and a boy" were shot in the streets, in open daylight, by some citizens of Montana; and adds, "I think I can arrest the murderers, but I doubt very much whether I can convict them in any court." Is it wonderful that rapes and murders, for which the law affords no redress, and public opinion offers no sympathy, should be revenged by similar outrages?

Even the good we have tried to do these unfortunate tribes has been done most injudiciously. They have been kept in a perpetual state of dependence on our bounty—national paupers, in fact; and whoever submits to be a pensioner necessarily parts with his manhood. Dishonest agents have systematically defrauded them of the promised goods and provisions, and thus added perpetual distrust and wrangling to the inevitable bad effects of habitual dependence. General Sheridan says: "The Indian is a lazy vagabond; he never labors." Certainly our mode of dealing with him is ingeniously contrived to make him so. What little he has, he holds on sufferance, and with a continual feeling of insecurity. General Sheridan says: "The government has always been very liberal to the Indians. The lands allotted to them have always been of the very best character." But the Indians have learned by bitter experience that whenever their lands are wanted by white men they will surely be routed, by one process or another. In such cases, treaties have always proved mere ropes of sand. The inhabitants of Bozeman City bring it as a grave accusation against the Indian, that "he has no faith in treaties." He must have a marvelous capacity for belief if he *does* put any faith in our treaties, after the accumulated experience of two hundred years. They add, "He makes pledges and promises, with intent to disregard them whenever interest or caprice shall dictate." In what school did he learn that? No trait of Indian character has been so generally commended as their observance of treaties. General Houston, who lived much among them, testified heartily to that effect; and we are told that General Harney, "who has had fifty years' experience with the Indians, frequently declared that he never knew one of them to violate his plighted faith, or the rites of hospitality."

The plain truth is, our influence has made the Indians worse, instead of better, than we found them. The question is, what can be done to bring any thing like order out of this frightful chaos? Shall we, in good faith, try to raise them out of their forlorn and desperate condition, or shall we allow them to be exterminated at the point of the bayonet? General Sherman signed his name to a "Report of the Indian Peace Commission," published some two years ago, from which I make the following extract: "If it be said that, because they were savages, they should be exterminated, we answer that, aside from the *humanity* of the suggestion, it would prove extremely difficult. If money considerations are permitted to weigh, it costs less to civilize than to kill. Among civilized men, war usually springs from a sense of injustice. *The best possible way, then, to avoid war, is to do no act of injustice.* When we learn that the same rule holds good with Indians, the chief difficulty is removed. It is said our wars with them have been almost constant. Have we been uniformly unjust? We answer unhesitatingly, Yes."

Yet General Sherman sanctioned General Sheridan's massacre of women and babies!

That Indians are incapable of civilization, I believe to be as untrue as the assertion that negroes will not work without the driver's whip. Individuals among them have become highly civilized and educated. When the Cherokees were harried out of Georgia, they had brought their farms under good cultivation, had established schools and manufactories, and printed a newspaper in Cherokee, with an English translation. The Indian Agricultural Fair[13] in New-York, a year ago, proved them fully capable of excelling in various mechanical and manufacturing branches of industry; and the Indian schools in the same State manifested most encouraging progress. How shall the demoralized tribes of the West be brought into a similar state? First and foremost, by laws at once strict and impartial. The crimes of individuals must not be visited on whole villages. The Indian must feel assured that he will certainly suffer for crimes against white people, and that white people will be just as certainly equally punished for crimes against *him*. The whisky-dealers must be driven away. The Indians must be incited to agricultural and mechanical labor, and be rewarded with premiums for success. They must have reason to feel perfectly secure about the possession of the land they cultivate. If certain benefits were granted as a reward for substituting the English language in place of Indian dialects, it might have a good effect. Missionaries ought to pay particular attention to these people, and try to adapt their teaching to their ignorant condition. If some of the civilized Indians could help in such mission-work, they might do more than others to change hunters into farmers.

But I do not believe that harmony will prevail so long as they exist as independent tribes in our midst. There was never peace on the borders of England and Scotland till clans were abolished, and they all became one people, under one government. There has been no trouble with the Indians in Canada, because they are not divided into tribes, but all form an integral part of the body politic. If the Indian could earn his bread, and be secure in

296

the possession of it; if he could vote for the laws that govern him, and feel that he is really and truly acknowledged as an American citizen, it would make a man of him; and his vicinity would prove a blessing instead of a curse. Mr. Nast,[14] whose illustrations in *Harper's Weekly* evince as much moral rectitude as they do artistic ingenuity, has made a picture of General Grant[15] investing an Indian with a coat, which has a vote in one pocket and a tax-bill in the other. Tomahawk and whisky-bottle are laid on the shelf, and plow, hoe, spelling-book, and newspaper have taken their place. That picture presents the true solution of the problem. So far, General Grant has manifested great wisdom and humanity in the agencies he has employed for the improvement of these degraded people; and I trust the counsel of violent and reckless men will have no power to change his judicious course.

This subject is painful and wearisome to me; and there is so much prejudice and passion in the field, that I write with little hope. But when I think of the good monk Telemachus,[16] his example inspires me with fresh courage. When enslaved gladiators were killing each other, upon compulsion, for the entertainment of the Roman populace, he sprang on the arena and loudly proclaimed that the custom was wicked, cruel, and brutalizing. The populace were accustomed to think that gladiators had no rights or feelings which Romans were bound to respect, and the man who pleaded for them was killed on the spot. But the words he had uttered sank into some hearts, and took root there; and the fruit they bore was the abolition of these barbarous gladiatorial shows. Would that my weak voice could do something to arrest the insane and cruel disregard of Indian rights and feelings.

EXPLANATORY NOTES

HOBOMOK

CHAPTER I

1. Gen. 1.2: ". . . and darkness was upon the face of the deep. And the Spirit of God moved upon the face of the waters."

2. Conant is applying the Exodus story to the Puritans, the theological practice known as typology. The relevant passage is Exod. 15.27–16.3: "And they came to Elim, where were twelve wells of water, and three score and ten palm trees: and they encamped there by the waters. . . . And the whole congregation of the children of Israel murmured against Moses and Aaron in the wilderness: And the children of Israel said unto them, Would to God we had died by the hand of the LORD in the land of Egypt, when we sat by the flesh pots, and when we did eat bread to the full; for ye have brought us forth into this wilderness, to kill this whole assembly with hunger."

3. Thomas Morton was the founder of the nearby settlement of Merrymount, infamous for the maypole around which his followers danced with Indians in Bacchanalian revels. Morton made the settlement "a marrying-ground for two worlds and two races." Its name, which he also spelled Mary-mount, Marry-mount, and Mare-mount, was a triple pun evoking the popish worship of the Virgin Mary, the fertility goddesses and festivals of the Greeks and Indians, and the links between the human and animal worlds (see Slotkin 61). The Plymouth colonists feared Morton's immoral influence and objected to his sales of arms to the Indians. In 1628, troops from Plymouth under the leadership of Miles Standish destroyed Merrymount and captured Morton, whom they exiled to England.

4. King Charles I (1600–49) was blamed by the Puritans for yielding to the influence of his Catholic queen, Henrietta Maria of France (1609–69).

5. besom: an implement for sweeping, a broom; hence any agent that cleanses, purifies, or sweeps away things material or immaterial.

6. Isa. 17.9–11: "In that day shall his strong cities be as a forsaken bough, and an uppermost branch, which they left because of the children of Israel: and there shall be desolation. Because thou hast forgotten the God of thy salvation, and hast not been mindful of the rock of thy strength, therefore shalt thou plant pleasant plants, and shalt set it with strange slips."

7. Lev. 10.1–2: "And Nadab and Abihu, the sons of Aaron, took either of them his censer, and put fire therein, and put incense thereon, and offered strange fire before the LORD, which he commanded them not. And there went out fire from the LORD, and devoured them, and they died before the LORD."

8. Ps. 18.29: "For by thee I have run through a troop; and by my God have I leaped over a wall."

9. Amos 5.18–19: "Woe unto you that desire the day of the LORD! to what end is it for you? the day of the LORD is darkness, and not light. As if a man did flee from a lion, and a bear met him; or went into the house, and leaned his hand on the wall, and a serpent bit him."

10. flip: a mixture of beer and spirit sweetened with sugar and heated with a hot iron.

CHAPTER II

1. Ps. 76.2–3: "In Salem also in his tabernacle, and his dwelling place in Zion. There brake he the arrows of the bow, the shield, and the sword, and the battle. Selah."

2. Cf. 2 Peter 2.1–3: "But there were false prophets also among the people, even as there shall be false teachers among you, who privily shall bring in damnable heresies, even denying the Lord that bought them, and bring upon themselves swift destruction. And many shall follow their pernicious ways; by reason of whom the way of truth shall be evil spoken of. And through covetousness shall they with feigned words make merchandise of you: whose judgment now of a long time lingereth not, and their damnation slumbereth not."

3. Eccles. 7.6: "For as the crackling of thorns under a pot, so is the laughter of the fool: this also is vanity."

4. The London and Bristol Company was formed in 1610 for the settlement of Newfoundland. A joint stock company, it represented a milestone on the road toward capitalism—until then, private individuals had put up the funds for

colonial ventures. One of the company's founders was Sir Ferdinando Gorges, mentioned in chapter 6. Sally's complaint about the "great folks in London" reflects the class conflict between the Plymouth pilgrims, who provided the labor power, and the London adventurers and adventurer-planters who provided the capital and owned shares in the company.

CHAPTER III

1. lope-staff: a pole used for leaping dikes in the fens and Low Countries (an image reflecting the Pilgrims' long sojourn in the Netherlands).

2. Mr. Oldham is referring to Sally's friend Mary Conant and her preference for Episcopalianism. The Moabites, eternal enemies of the Israelites, supposedly originated from the incest of Lot and his daughter (Gen. 19.37). Like the Sodomites and Babylonians, they are frequently cited as symbols of vice and corruption.

3. According to Puritan theology, God had made a covenant, or compact, with the Congregational churches of New England, just as he had with the Israelites. By accepting the covenant, church members enabled themselves to submit willingly to God's law. Church membership was open only to those who could demonstrate that they had had a religious conversion, but children of church members were considered to be under the covenant. The historical Oldham had left Plymouth because he disagreed with the doctrines of the ruling elders.

4. In 2 Kings 14.23–24 King Jeroboam of Israel "did that which was evil in the sight of the LORD." Gen. 9.22–25 tells the story of Ham, son of Noah, who looked on his drunken father's nakedness. On awakening, Noah cursed Ham by dooming his son Canaan to be "a servant of servants . . . unto his brethren." These two examples serve to prove Oldham's point that contrary to the Plymouth community's interpretation of the covenant, "not every child of a righteous man . . . is among the elect."

5. Gen. 29 tells the story of Jacob's toiling fourteen years for Laban to win the hand of Laban's daughter Rachel.

6. In Gen. 24 Abraham sent his servant to find a wife for Isaac among Abraham's kindred in Mesopotamia. The criterion the servant used to choose the right wife was that she should offer both him and his camels water at the well. Rebecca, the daughter of Bethuel, a nephew of Abraham's brother, met this test.

7. A parallel episode occurs much later in Longfellow's *Courtship of Miles Standish* (1858). I have been unable to find a historical source for the Collier-Oldham courtship or the ensuing dispute with Hopkins.

CHAPTER IV

1. Gen. 30–31 tell of how Jacob and Laban divide the herds, allotting the speckled sheep, goats, and cattle to Jacob, when Jacob decides to return home after a twenty-year sojourn with Laban in Padanaram. Laban tries to cheat by removing the speckled animals, but Jacob outwits his father-in-law by magically inducing the white animals to bring forth spotted young.

2. Corbitant was a sachem (chief) of the Pocasset, subject to Massasoit, chief sachem of the Wampanoags, the tribe to which Hobomok belonged. The Wampanoags allied themselves with the English as a means of freeing themselves from the dominion of the Narragansetts, who had defeated them in battle. At the behest of the Narragansett sachems, anxious to keep control of the Wampanoags, Corbitant undertook to stir up Massasoit's subjects against him and to incite the Indians generally against the English. Mount Haup was the Wampanoags' domain. Sagamore John was a sachem of the Massachusetts Indians on the north side of the bay. They were tributaries of the Narragansetts.

3. Miantonimo was chief sachem of the Narragansetts, who helped the English to destroy the Pequots. Later the English played the Narragansetts off against the Mohegans. When the Mohegan chief Uncas took Miantonimo prisoner, the English advised Uncas to put Miantonimo to death with "mercy and moderation" (Bradford 331).

4. The Tarentines, or Abnakis, occupied the shores of Maine and part of New Brunswick. They reputedly descended on the other tribes at harvest time and stole their corn.

5. The Nipnets, or Nipmucs, were tributaries of the Narragansetts and later sided with them during King Philip's War, led by Massasoit's son Metacom (Philip).

6. Sassacus, chief of the Pequots, was the most powerful sachem in southern New England, dominating the territory from Narragansett Bay to the Hudson. At the end of the Pequot War, he fled to the Mohawks for protection, but was beheaded by them. Pokanecket was the home of the Wampanoags, hence a term meaning Wampanoag.

7. Ninigret was a sachem of the Niantics, united by marriage with their overlords the Narragansetts.

8. usually spelled sannup (der. Abnaki and Algonquian): a married Indian brave.

9. Rev. 21.10–24 describes the New Jerusalem, where the saints are to reside with God and the lamb forever after the apocalyptic destruction of the world. Child's version is a loose paraphrase.

CHAPTER V

1. Another Indian ally, Squanto, actually did spread a false rumor that Massasoit had joined with Corbitant and the Narragansetts in a conspiracy against the English (Morton 76–78).

2. Conant is quoting Christ's apocalyptic prophecies in Matt. 24.23–26: "Then if any man shall say unto you, Lo, here is Christ, or there; believe it not. For there shall arise false Christs, and false prophets, and shall shew great signs and wonders; insomuch that, if it were possible, they shall deceive the very elect. . . . Wherefore if they shall say unto you, Behold, he is in the desert; go not forth: behold, he is in the secret chambers; believe it not."

3. Cf. 1 Samuel 17.4–9, where Goliath, giant champion of the Philistines, challenges the Israelites with these words.

4. Cf. Eccles. 3.1–9: "To everything there is a season, and a time to every purpose under the heaven. . . . A time to weep, and a time to laugh. . . ."

5. In 1 Samuel 14.24–30, after the victory over the Philistines, Saul adjured the people of Israel not to eat any food until evening, but his son Jonathan, being unaware of the injunction, ate honey that he found on the ground, by dipping "the end of the rod that was in his hand . . . in an honeycomb," upon which his eyes were "enlightened."

6. Gen. 3.24: After the Fall, God drives Adam and Eve out of Eden and places "at the east of the garden of Eden Cherubims, and a flaming sword which turned every way, to keep the way of the tree of life."

7. The doctrine of "inward outpouring" holds that the Holy Ghost dwells in the sanctified believer, making him or her privy to direct revelations from the Deity. Among the groups who espoused some version of this doctrine were the Quakers, the Familists, and the followers of Anne Hutchinson (see chapter 8, note 2). The Puritans referred to the doctrine of inward outpouring as the antinomian heresy. Through Endicott's prophecy that "the viper will hereafter spring out of its shell, and aim at the vitals of the church," Child is anticipating the controversy that would arise in the Boston church a decade later, when the popular and venerated church member Anne Hutchinson (1591–1643) was indicted and driven out of the Massachusetts Bay colony for preaching a creed of "Inner Light."

CHAPTER VI

1. Oldham is referring to the hated William Laud, archbishop of Canterbury under Charles I. In 1629, Laud was still bishop of London. His promotion to

chancellor of Oxford in 1630 is referred to in chapter 13. Laud sought to root Calvinism out of the Anglican Church and to impose a High Church version of Anglicanism, very close to Catholicism, on the country. The Puritans fled to America largely to escape his persecution.

2. In 1620, Sir Ferdinando Gorges and other members of the Northern Virginia Company were given a charter to the Plymouth region. The charter created a new corporation, called the Council for New England, which was granted jurisdiction over the North Atlantic region. The patent that legalized the Plymouth Colony was issued by this corporation. In 1629–30 the Plymouth Pilgrims managed to obtain from Sir Ferdinando and the Earl of Warwick a patent that confirmed and enlarged the bounds of the Plymouth Colony. During the same period, the New England Company, formed to expand the settlement at Naumkeak, was trying to secure its title to the land by going over the heads of Sir Ferdinando and the council and obtaining a charter of incorporation directly from the king. The maneuver succeeded, and in March, 1629, the Massachusetts Bay Company received a royal charter. Mrs. Conant may be referring to either of these efforts to secure legal status for the Puritans' New England settlements. Sir Ferdinando Gorges played an obstructionist role in both of them. Judg. 6.1–4 tells of how the Amalekites attacked the Israelites by surprise and destroyed their harvest, leaving them no sustenance.

3. Cf. 1 Kings 18.44. After a long drought and famine in Samaria under the reign of Ahab, the prophet Elijah prays for rain, the first sign of which is "a little cloud out of the sea, like a man's hand." Mrs. Conant is applying this passage typologically to the Puritans' mission in New England.

4. Rev. 18.2: "Babylon the great is fallen . . . and is become the habitation of devils, and the hold of every foul spirit, and a cage of every unclean and hateful bird." Typologically, the Puritans identified Babylon with Rome and England. Now Conant fears that by tolerating religious dissenters, New England, too, will degenerate into Babylon.

5. Edmund Spenser, *The Faerie Queene*, I.i.7.4–6 and I.i.10.3–5.

CHAPTER VIII

1. *All's Well That Ends Well*, II.iii.112.

2. The Familists, or Family of Love, were a sixteenth-century sect professing love for all human beings, however wicked. The Puritans accused them of depending on personal revelations rather than on the revealed truth of the Bible. Familism was one of the heresies Anne Hutchinson was later charged with.

3. William Blaxton, or Blackstone, a Low Church Anglican, was one of two Episcopal clergymen who arrived in 1623 with a party led by Robert Gorges, Sir Ferdinando's son and governor general of New England. He lived as a recluse on the peninsula of Shawmut (Boston), but left in 1635 for Rhode Island, finding the Puritan magistrates too intolerant.

4. *Quae* (interrogative adjective meaning which) is feminine nominative singular or plural and neuter nominative or accusative plural. *Genus* (noun meaning class or type) is neuter nominative singular. They do not agree and so cannot be used together; they must "stand by themselves." The correct form would be *Quod Genus*.

CHAPTER IX

1. The arrival and ordination of Higginson and Skelton is mentioned by Morton, Bradford, and other Puritan chroniclers, but Child's version of the ceremony and sermon is fictitious.

2. "No day without a line." A quotation from Pliny, usually applied to writers.

3. Phil. 3.20: "For our conversation is in heaven; from whence also we look for the Saviour, the Lord Jesus Christ."

4. Samuel Gorton of Shawmut reputedly denied the humanity of Christ, teaching that Christ was simply a manifestation of God and that God was similarly manifested in the true believer. The Puritans interpreted that to mean that the Gortonists professed to be personally Christ.

CHAPTER X

1. " 'Religion is to be taught, not forced'. . . . 'Heresy must be unlearned, not permitted.' "

2. James I was the son of the Catholic Mary Queen of Scots.

3. " 'It is the function of kings to make war; however it is the function of God to end it.' "

4. "Let the Jew believe, not I."

5. Ps. 2.4.

6. *Hamlet*, III.i.79–80: "death, / The undiscover'd country from whose bourn / No traveller returns . . ."

7. Prov. 14.10: "The heart knoweth his own bitterness; and a stranger doth not intermeddle with his joy."

8. Sirach 13.1. "He that toucheth pitch shall be defiled therewith." It may be significant that this passage is from an apocryphal book, not from the Bible proper.

CHAPTER XI

1. Mary is reporting the Puritans' interpretation of Rev. 16–18, in which seven angels pour out "the vials of the wrath of God upon the earth." The pouring out of the seventh vial brings about the fall of Babylon, representing ancient Rome in this allegorical apocalypse. Protestants extended the allegory to papal Rome, and the Puritans extended it still further to the papistic Anglican church and to England.

CHAPTER XII

1. Ossamequin, chief sachem of the Wampanoags, was better known as Massasoit.

2. Tongoomlishcah remains obscure, but Heckewelder explains that the Indians considered the rattlesnake an ancestor, and hence a sacred animal, which they were forbidden to kill (252). It may be relevant that the Indian devil-god Hobomok frequently appeared in the form of a snake.

3. A note in *Yamoyden* translates "wakon bird" as "bird of the great Spirit" (Eastburn and Sands 66, 295n).

4. A bird resembling the whippoorwill, but with a different song.

CHAPTER XIII

1. This was the famous arrival on June 12, 1630, of John Winthrop and his company aboard the *Arbella*, named for Lady Arbella Johnson.

2. Byron, *The Corsair*, I.iii.11: "She walks the waters like a thing of life."

3. "'The end dictates the means,'" or more literally, "'The means move by grace of the end (purpose).'"

4. An aphorism attributed to James I of England.

5. Prayers and tears.

6. Sir Richard Weston, lord high treasurer, blocked the Plymouth Pilgrims' efforts to obtain a royal charter confirming their land grant and converting their colony into a legal corporation. Together with Laud and other enemies of the Puritans, he also supported a scheme to deprive the Massachusetts Bay Company

of its charter. The Puritans believed Charles I to be under the domination of the Catholic Louis XIII and his premier, Cardinal Richelieu.

7. Mr. Conant and Mr. Johnson are applying the prophecies in the Book of Revelation to the current situation in England, in order to judge how close the world is to the end of time. As an alternative to the usual identification of the English church with the whore of Babylon (Rev. 17), Mr. Conant suggests an identification with the second beast described in Rev. 13.11–12. The first beast would thus represent the Roman Church, the second the Anglican. Mr. Johnson is referring to the passage in Rev. 14.14–20, in which the Son of man and his angels begin the harvest of the evils to be cast into "the great winepress of the wrath of God."

8. Num. 25.1–8 tells of how, during a period when "the people began to commit whoredom with the daughters of Moab," Phinehas, the grandson of Aaron, kills an Israelite and his Midianite paramour: "So the plague was stayed from the children of Israel." In this case Phinehas would be Governor Endicott, who banished the Brown brothers.

9. In 2 Kings 19.32–36 God sent an angel to destroy the Assyrian armies, thus repelling the invasion of Jerusalem by the Assyrian king, Sennacherib.

10. See 1 Kings 11.26–14.20 for the story of Solomon's servant Jeroboam, the son of Nebat, to whom God gives the kingdom of Israel, after dividing it from Judah, as a punishment for Solomon's transgressions. Fearing that if the people continue to go to Jerusalem to perform sacrifices, his kingdom will "return to the house of David," Jeroboam decides to substitute the worship of golden calves in his own temples. Apparently Mr. Conant considers Blackstone an emissary of King Charles, whom he identifies here with Jeroboam.

11. "'*The great* should be selected, not *the many*.'"

12. A similar anecdote appears in a much anthologized passage of Winthrop's journal (2.24), dated 1640. There the book in question belongs to Winthrop's own son, who is not to blame for the inclusion of the Book of Common Prayer in a volume containing the New Testament and Psalms, though the same moral is drawn from the incident.

13. Ferdinand II (1578–1637), Holy Roman Emperor, educated by the Jesuits, attempted to put down Protestantism by force in Europe during the Thirty Years War. He was opposed by the Protestant King Gustavus Adolphus of Sweden (1594–1632). Urban VIII, pope from 1623 to 1644, supported the Catholic forces.

CHAPTER XIV

1. Isaac Johnson, brother-in-law of the Earl of Lincoln and an influential member of the Massachusetts Bay Company, was one of the men responsible for the decision to build up the settlement Roger Conant had established at Naumkeak.

2. "A man of porte and parts": a man of good carriage and social position, possessing abilities and talents.

3. According to legend, the pelican opens its breast with its beak and feeds its young with its blood. Charles goes on to discuss the worsening political crisis in England which would culminate in civil war between the Puritans and Royalists in the 1640s, and eventually the execution of Charles I by the Puritans in 1649. The origins of the civil strife go back to Henry VIII's break with Catholicism in the 1530s, when the pope refused to annul Henry's marriage with Catherine of Aragon, so as to permit him to marry Anne Boleyn. After the brief reign of Henry's young son by yet another marriage, Edward VI, during which the Protestant clergy ruled the country, Catherine's daughter Mary succeeded to the throne (1553–58). She tried to restore Catholicism, burning three hundred Protestants in four years. Protestant leaders and their congregations fled to Calvin's Geneva and to the Netherlands. Some remained in exile even after Mary's half sister Elizabeth I, daughter of Anne Boleyn, succeeded to the throne and restored Episcopal Protestantism. Meanwhile strife continued between Catholics and Protestants on the one hand, and between Episcopalians and various Protestant sects who wanted to purify the English church of all papistic tendencies on the other. Charles Brown attributes the Puritans' rancour toward Charles I and his Catholic queen to the "acrimonie of exile."

4. Mr. Conant is objecting to the inclusion in the Episcopal Bible of the Apocryphal books, which the Puritans rejected. And he is once again identifying the Episcopalian Brown as a "son of Belial," another name for the prince of devils.

CHAPTER XV

1. "Ichabod," meaning "where is the glory?" or "alas the glory," was the name the wife of Phinehas gave her son, born prematurely as a result of her shock on learning that the Philistines had captured the ark of God, Israel's glory (1 Sam. 4.21). The preceding quotation appears to be a loose paraphrase of passages prophesying the destruction of Moab in Jer. 48.38 and of Jerusalem in Amos 5.16.

CHAPTER XVI

1. Byron, *Childe Harold's Pilgrimage*, IV.23.9. "Striking the electric chain wherewith we are darkly bound."

CHAPTER XVIII

1. The Catholic Mary Queen of Scots, beheaded by Elizabeth I in 1587, was reputed for her beauty and charm.

2. Ps. 80.5

3. John 5.35. Jesus is speaking here of John the Baptist. The reference thus hints at Mary's role in heralding a new dispensation.

CHAPTER XX

1. It is a nice touch to have Winslow sign this letter, since his *Good News from New England* contains the fullest historical account of Hobomok's services to the English.

CHOCORUA'S CURSE

1. The English-born artist Thomas Cole, who emigrated to America in 1819, was famous for his American landscapes. Child is referring here to a Cole landscape used as an illustration to "Chocorua's Curse" in the 1830 *Token*.

2. William Goffe and his father-in-law Edward Whalley were among the regicides who signed Charles I's death warrant in 1649. After Charles II's restoration in 1660, they fled to New England, where they went into hiding. They appear frequently in nineteenth-century historical fiction.

LETTERS FROM NEW-YORK

1. Johann Gottfried von Herder (1744–1803), born in Mohrungen, was a philosopher, theologian, poet, and critic. He was an important source of nineteenth-century romantic ideas about inbred national character—ideas Child echoes in this letter.

2. Johann Paul Friedrich Richter, often known as Jean Paul (1763–1825), was a German novelist much appreciated by nineteenth-century American intellectuals.

AN APPEAL FOR THE INDIANS

1. General Alfred Howe Terry (1827–90), won fame for capturing Fort Fisher, North Carolina, during the Civil War. Child's high opinion of him is probably based on reports that he treated the black troops in his division well. Ironically, he later played a leading role in the Sioux War of 1876, perhaps bearing some responsibility for Custer's Last Stand.

2. Major Edward W. Wynkoop, special agent to the southern Cheyenne, tried to steer a middle course between his contradictory responsibilities as a military man and as an Indian agent; he later resigned from the Indian Commission to avoid being used against the Indians he was supposed to protect.

3. Civil War General William Tecumseh Sherman (1820–91), was famous for his march through Georgia in 1864, which left a trail of destruction and introduced into military history the concept of total war—the attempt to break the will of the enemy by making war on the civilian population. As commander of the Division of the Mississippi after the Civil War, he conducted an equally brutal campaign against the Plains Indians in the fall and winter of 1868. He was one of several military men who served on the Peace Commission.

4. The Indian Mutiny of 1857–59, ignited by a rumor that the rifle cartridges distributed to Indian troops were greased with beef and pork fat (unclean to Hindus and Muslims), spread rapidly across North India and was put down with great severity by the British.

5. Charles Haddon Spurgeon, (1834–92), English Baptist preacher, was famous for his oratorical powers, which made him "the most popular preacher of the day" (DNB).

6. John Eliot (1604–90), known as the Apostle to the Indians, began preaching to the Indians at Nonantum, near Roxbury, Massachusetts, in 1646. His converts numbered around 3600 at the height of his mission, but diminished rapidly after King Philip's War.

7. King Philip (Metacom), sachem of the Wampanoags, led a general uprising of Indian tribes in 1675–76. The bloodiest Indian war in New England's history, it was provoked by the Puritans' execution of three Wampanoag warriors.

8. The Seminole warrior Osceola led tribal resistance in Florida to the

U.S. government's Indian removal policy. His wife was a runaway slave. Child gives accounts of Osceola and the Seminole War in *SL* 301 and 514–15.

9. John C. Frémont (1813–90), explorer, politician, soldier, made several expeditions to California in 1844–46 with the scout Kit Carson and played a major role in the conquest of California during the Mexican War in 1846–47.

10. John Beeson, Illinois Methodist and abolitionist, settled in Oregon in 1853 and began agitating for Indian rights—an activity that subjected him to harassment by white settlers and night riders. Child may be referring either to his *Plea for the Indians* (New York, 1858) or to his speech at a public meeting in Faneuil Hall on October 9, 1859, in which a number of leading abolitionists also participated.

11. Child is probably referring to the scandal aroused by conditions at the Confederate prison of Andersonville, Georgia, where some 13,000 Union prisoners of war died.

12. David Livingstone (1813–73), celebrated Scottish traveler and missionary, discovered the Victoria Falls of the Zambezi. His *Missionary Travels and Researches in South Africa* was published in London in 1857.

13. John Hanning Speke (1827–64), British explorer. His *Journal of the Discovery of the Source of the Nile* was published in Edinburgh in 1863.

14. Samuel Houston (1793–1863), Mexican War hero and statesman, spent three years among the Cherokees from 1829 on and later served as president of the republic of Texas and governor of that state.

15. Henry Rowe Schoolcraft (1793–1864), explorer, ethnologist, and Indian agent, produced many influential books on Indians, including *Algic Researches* (2 vols. New York, 1839), which was Longfellow's source for *The Song of Hiawatha*. The Mrs. Schoolcraft to whom Child refers is his part-Chippewa wife, whom he married in 1823.

16. Anna Brownell Jameson (1794–1860), prolific English author of travelogues, art books, and literary criticism, took a feminist perspective in her works. Child is quoting from her *Winter Studies and Summer Rambles in Canada* (3 vols. London, 1838), whose feminist commentary also attracted Margaret Fuller's attention.

17. General Anthony Wayne (1745–96) defeated the Indian tribes of the Ohio region at Fallen Timbers (1794). His victory has been attributed to the Indians' half-starved condition, resulting from the destruction of their crops.

THE CHURCH IN THE WILDERNESS

1. From William Cullen Bryant, "The Ages," stanzas 30–31, the opening piece in his first published volume, *Poems* (Cambridge, Mass.: Hilliard and Metcalf, 1821). According to Bryant's son-in-law Parke Godwin, the editor of his collected *Poetical Works*, "The Ages" was commissioned by the Phi Beta Kappa Society of Harvard and read before it at the 1821 commencement ceremony, contributing more to securing Bryant's reputation than any of his other early poems, including "Thanatopsis." In a note that appears in all collections of his poems from 1832 on, Bryant writes: "In this poem . . . the author has endeavored, from a survey of past ages of the world, and of the successive advances of mankind in knowledge, virtue, and happiness, to justify and confirm the hopes of the philanthropist for the future destinies of the human race." The stanzas that follow describe a miraculous transformation of the wilderness into fertile agricultural land and populous cities as white colonists replace Indians.

2. From Bryant's "The Ages," stanza 23 (referring to the Catholic Church).

3. Jean-Vincent d'Abadie, Baron de St. Castin (spelled Castine by English writers), a French nobleman who had married an Abenaki woman and left his children in the care of their mother's people, is mentioned both in Child's sources and in the anonymous story, "Narantsauk," in the *Atlantic Souvenir* for 1829. See the accounts of Rale cited under Sources and Further Readings.

4. sannup, derived from the Abenaki word *senanbe*: a married Indian male.

5. loup-cervier: lynx.

6. See Rev. 6.14 and 12.7: "And the heaven departed as a scroll when it is rolled together. . . ."; "And there was war in heaven: Michael and his angels fought against the dragon. . . ." See also *Paradise Lost*, Book 1.

7. William Ponsonby: a fourteen-year-old English boy, who had been captured by the Indians six months before the English raid on Norridgewock, was found among the wounded and was said to have been shot and stabbed by Rale himself. None of Child's sources mentions his name. Her account of the boy's parentage is fictitious.

WILLIE WHARTON

1. The "Light of Other Days": apparently an allusion to the line "The light of other days is faded," from *The Maid of Artois* by Alfred Bunn (1796?–1860).

2. "the vision was photographed": Child wrote repeatedly about clairvoyant phenomena, notably in her novel *Philothea* (1836), Letters 4 and 22 of *Letters from New York, Second Series* (1845), *The Progress of Religious Ideas* (1855), "The Ancient Clairvoyant" and "Spirit and Matter" in her collection *Autumnal Leaves* (1857), and her article "Spirits," published in the *Atlantic* of May 1862. Her own leaning toward mysticism gave her an intuitive sympathy for the visionary aspect of American Indian culture; see, for example, "She Waits in the Spirit Land," reprinted in the present volume.

3. From the story of the Prodigal Son, Luke 15:24, the words in which the father expresses his joy over the return of his long lost son.

4. "long petticoats to trammel her limbs": women's rights advocates—among them Amelia Bloomer, Elizabeth Cady Stanton, and the Grimké sisters—were currently agitating for dress reform, a movement with which Child sympathized. The "hybrid between English and Indian costumes" that A-lee-lah eventually adopts resembles the feminist Bloomer garb.

THE INDIANS

1. Philip Henry Sheridan (1831–1888), won fame during the Civil War by reconquering the Shenandoah valley for the Union and making it a "barren waste" in the process. Shifted to the West after the Civil War, he conducted campaigns against the Plains Indians with even greater ruthlessness. The saying "The only good Indian is a dead Indian" is commonly attributed to Sheridan.

2. See *An Appeal for the Indians*, note 3.

3. The Massacre of Glencoe (13 February 1692), which victimized the MacDonald clan of Glencoe, Scotland, was conducted by troops under

Archibald Campbell, tenth Earl of Argyll. The MacDonalds were among the Scottish clans loyal to the deposed James II, king of England and Scotland, and the pretext for the massacre was that their chief had not yet taken the loyalty oath to James's successor, William III. Ancient clan animosities seem to have been the real motivation, however.

4. Child is apparently referring to Edward John Eyre, governor of Jamaica from 1861 to 1866, whose brutal suppression of a revolt by blacks in October 1865, culminating in hundreds of summary executions, triggered a heated controversy among British intellectuals. John Stuart Mill, Herbert Spencer, and Thomas Henry Huxley advocated trying Eyre for murder, while Thomas Carlyle, John Ruskin, and Alfred, Lord Tennyson defended him. "Captains of the Bombay" remain unidentified.

5. Alfred Sully (1821–1879), took part in campaigns against the Cheyenne in 1860–61, fought in the Civil War on the Union side, and was responsible for punitive expeditions against the Sioux in the Dakota territory in 1863 and 1864.

6. See An Appeal for the Indians, note 9.

7. George Thompson (1804–1878), the British abolitionist whose eloquence was credited with hastening Parliament's passage of the act emancipating the slaves in the British West Indies, toured the United States in 1834–35. Although his speeches electrified antislavery audiences, Thompson encountered so much harassment and violence from proslavery mobs that he had to cut short his tour and escape Boston in an open boat. Child and her husband David helped Thompson dodge proslavery mobs. On his third visit to the United States during the Civil War, Thompson received accolades and addressed the U.S. Congress.

8. William Selby Harney (1800–1889), one of several military officers on the Indian Peace Commission whose report Child quotes in the Appeal for the Indians, won renown for his role in the Seminole War in 1840 and increased his fame by defeating the Sioux at the battle of Sand Hill.

9. See An Appeal for the Indians, note 2.

10. Black Kettle (?–1868) was the Southern Cheyenne chief whose village on Sand Creek, Colorado, was wiped out by Colonel John Chivington in 1864. He was killed in the massacre on the Washita in 1868, led by Colonel George Custer.

11. See *An Appeal for the Indians*, note 10, and the headnote to "Willie Wharton."

12. See *An Appeal for the Indians*, note 14.

13. Indian Agricultural Fair: For details on this fair, held by Iroquois in New York, see the article "Can Indians Be Civilized?" reprinted from the *Friend's Intelligencer* in the *National Anti-Slavery Standard* of 16 January 1869, and Child's article "Indian Civilization," in the *Independent* of 11 February 1869.

14. Thomas Nast (1840–1902) was famous for his political cartoons in *Harper's Weekly* during the Civil War and Reconstruction, which strongly supported abolitionist goals. Most widely remembered are his cartoons of the Tammany Hall Tweed Ring in New York.

15. Ulysses S. Grant (1822–1885) led the Union Army to victory in the Civil War and became the eighteenth president of the United States (1868–1876). Child initially praised his "Peace Policy" toward Indians, but by 1873, she admitted to her friend Sarah Shaw that though it had "looked candid and just on paper," the results seemed to indicate that Grant had not "taken adequate care that it should be carried out" (*SL* 515).

16. Telemachus, an Asiatic monk, was stoned to death in A.D. 404, when he protested against gladiatorial contests by leaping into the arena to separate the combatants. His martyrdom led to the abolition of these contests.

ORDER FORM
■ ■ ■ ■ ■ ■ *AMERICAN WOMEN WRITERS SERIES* ■ ■ ■ ■ ■ ■

☐ Special Offer on the Complete Set!
All 18 volumes in the Series (in paperback) for only $200.00, a 25% discount off the list price of $274.00

Individual volumes in the American Women Writers Series

☐ **Alternative Alcott**, by Louisa May Alcott. Elaine Showalter, editor
1987. 462 pp. Paper, $15.00.

☐ **"The Amber Gods" and Other Stories**, by Harriet Prescott Spofford. Alfred Bendixen, editor
1989. 300 pp. Paper, $15.00

☐ **American Women Poets of the Nineteenth Century: An Anthology.** Cheryl Walker, editor
1992. 350 pp. Paper, $15.00

☐ **Clovernook Sketches and Other Stories**, by Alice Cary. Judith Fetterley, editor
1988. 314 pp. Paper, $15.00

☐ **The Essential Margaret Fuller**, by Margaret Fuller. Jeffrey Steele, editor
1992. 450 pp. Paper, $17.00

☐ **Gail Hamilton: Selected Writings**, by Gail Hamilton. Susan Coultrap-McQuin, editor
1992. 280 pp. Paper, $15.00.

☐ *The Hidden Hand*, by E.D.E.N. Southworth. Joanne Dobson, editor
1988. 450 pp. Paper, $16.00.

☐ *Hobomok* and Other Writings on Indians, by Lydia Maria Child. Carolyn L. Karcher, editor
1986. 275 pp. Paper, $15.00

☐ *Hope Leslie*, by Catharine Maria Sedgwick. Mary Kelly, editor
1987. 373 pp. Paper, $15.00

☐ **"How Celia Changed Her Mind" and Selected Stories**, by Rose Terry Cooke. Elizabeth Ammons, editor
1986. 265 pp. Paper, $15.00

☐ *The Lamplighter*, by Maria Susanna Cummins. Nina Baym, editor
1987. 437 pp. Paper, $17.00

☐ *Moods*, by Louisa May Alcott. Sarah Elbert, editor
1991. 284 pp. Paper, $15.00

☐ *A New Home—Who'll Follow?*, by Caroline Kirkland. Sandra A. Zagarell, editor
1990. 250 pp. Paper, $15.00

☐ *Oldtown Folks*, by Harriet Beecher Stowe. Dorothy Berkson, editor
1987. 519 pp. Paper, $17.00

☐ *Quicksand* and *Passing*, by Nella Larsen. Deborah E. McDowell, editor
1986. 246 pp. Paper, $10.00

☐ **Ruth Hall and Other Writings**, by Fanny Fern. Joyce W. Warren, editor
1986. 380 pp. Paper, $15.00

☐ **Stories from the Country of Lost Borders**, by Mary Austin. Marjorie Pryse, editor
1987. 310 pp. Paper, $15.00

☐ **Women Artists, Women Exiles: "Miss Grief" and Other Stories**, by Constance Fenimore Woolson. Joan Myers Weimer, editor
1988. 292 pp. Paper, $15.00.

Postage: For the complete set, add $12.00. For other orders, add $3.00 postage for the first book, $1.00 for each additional book. New Jersey residents: please add 6% sales tax.

Copy or tear out this page and send to:

 Rutgers University Press
109 Church Street
New Brunswick, New Jersey 08901